NISEKOI

False Love

vol. 13: Don't Worry

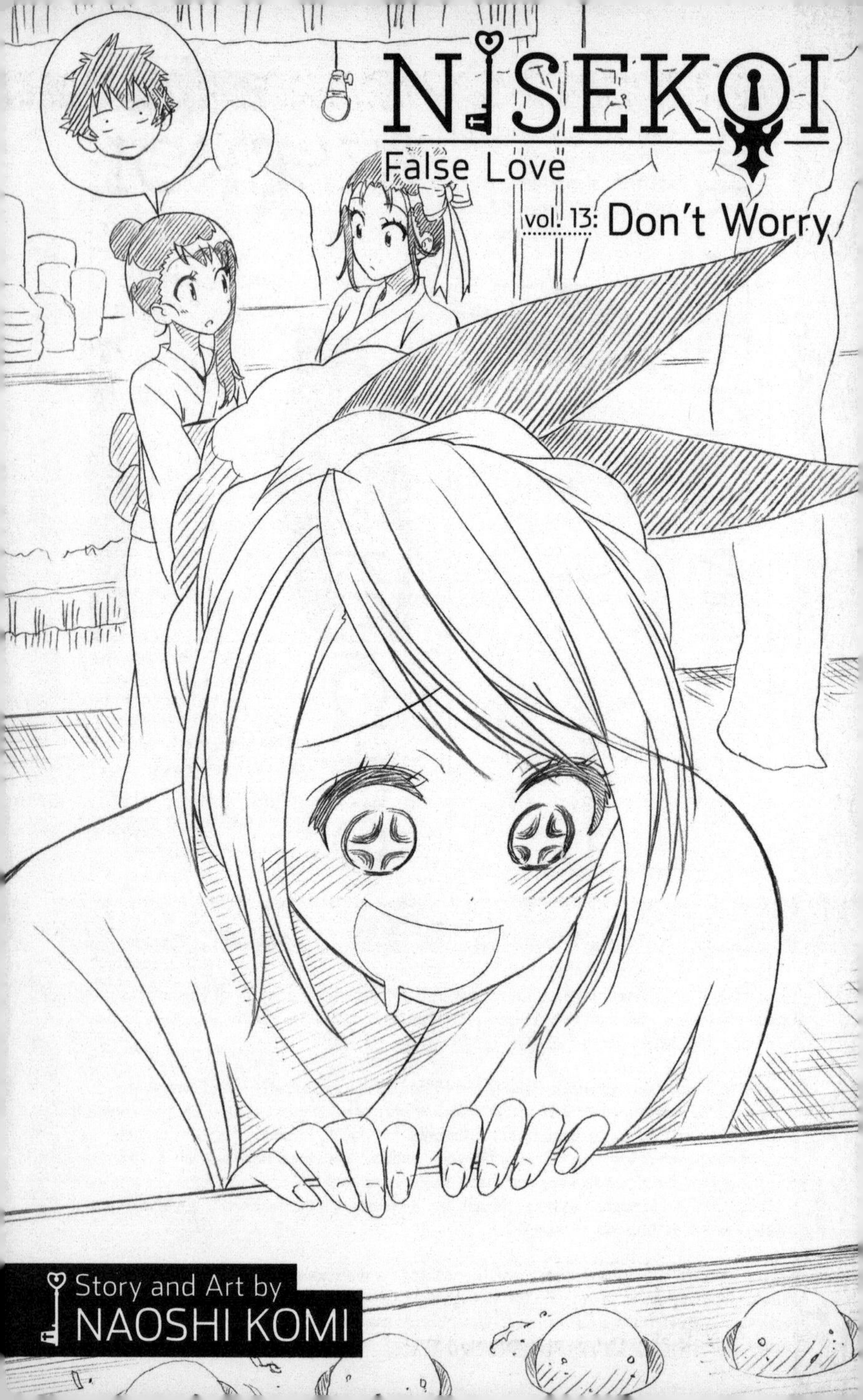

Story and Art by
NAOSHI KOMI

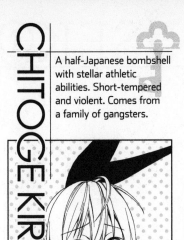

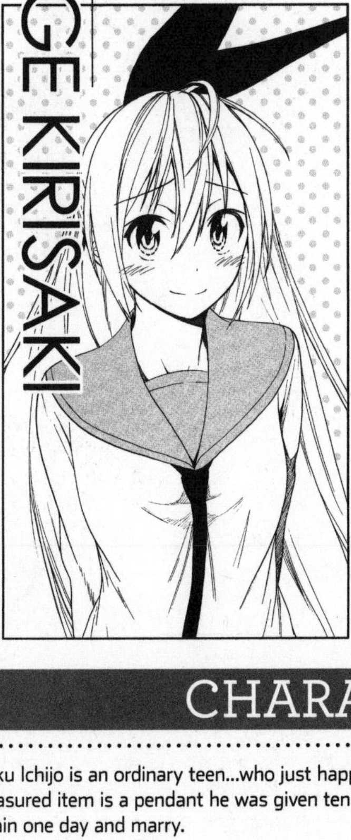

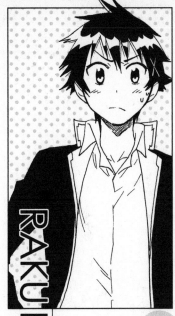

RAKU ICHIJO

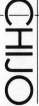

A normal teen whose family happens to be yakuza. Cherishes a pendant given to him by a girl he met ten years ago. Has a crush on Kosaki.

CHITOGE KIRISAKI

A half-Japanese bombshell with stellar athletic abilities. Short-tempered and violent. Comes from a family of gangsters.

CHARACTERS & STORY

Raku Ichijo is an ordinary teen...who just happens to come from a family of yakuza! His most treasured item is a pendant he was given ten years ago by a girl whom he promised to meet again one day and marry.

Thanks to family circumstances, Raku is forced into a false relationship with Chitoge, the daughter of a rival gangster, to keep their families from shedding blood. Despite their constant spats, Raku and Chitoge manage to fool everyone. One day, Chitoge discovers an old key, jogging memories of her own first love ten years earlier. Meanwhile, Raku's crush, Kosaki, confesses that she also has a key and made a promise with a boy ten years ago. To complicate matters, Marika Tachibana has a key as well and remembers a promise ten years ago. The mystery keeps getting more complex!

School's out for summer, and Raku and friends go to a fireworks display festival along with Kosaki's younger sister Haru, who has always disliked Raku. When Haru gets lost at the festival, she accidentally overhears a conversation between Maiko and Ruri and finds out the truth about Raku and Chitoge's relationship...

KOSAKI ONODERA

A girl Raku has a crush on. Beautiful and sweet, Kosaki has no shortage of admirers. She's a terrible cook but makes food that *looks* amazing.

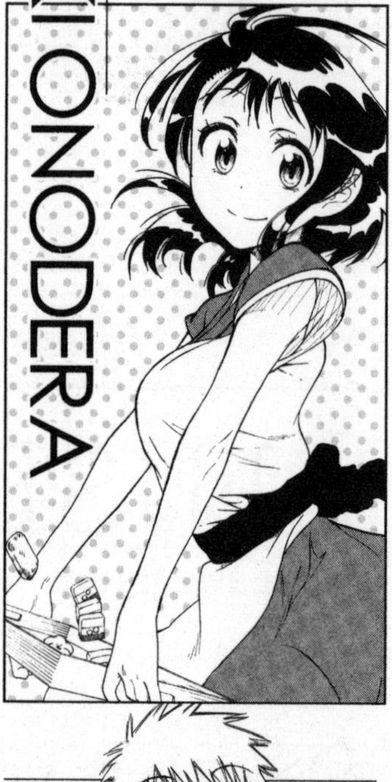

MARIKA TACHIBANA

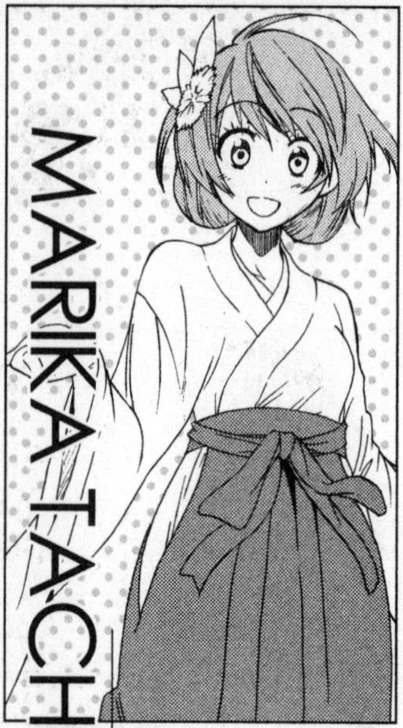

Daughter of the chief of police, Marika is Raku's fiancée, according to an agreement made by their fathers—an agreement Marika takes very seriously! Also has a key and remembers making a promise with Raku ten years ago.

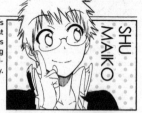

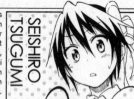

SHU MAIKO

Raku's best friend is outgoing and girl-crazy.

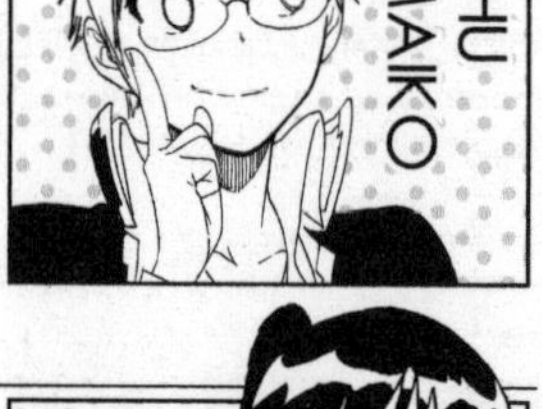

SEISHIRO TSUGUMI

Trained as an assassin in order to protect Chitoge, Tsugumi is often mistaken for a boy.

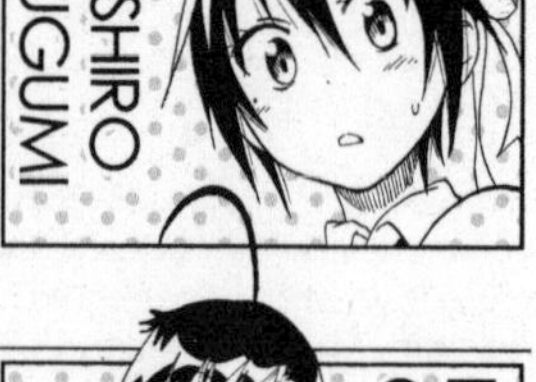

RURI MIYAMOTO

Kosaki's best gal pal. Comes off as aloof, but is actually a devoted and highly intuitive friend.

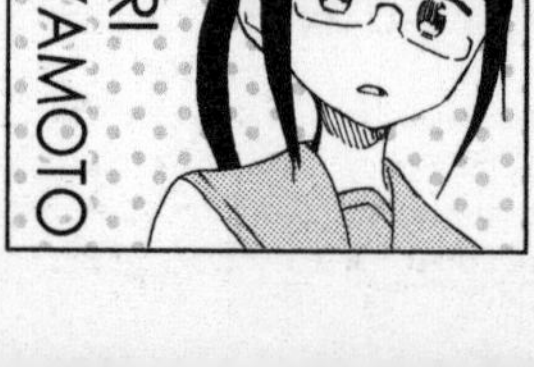

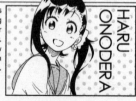

HARU ONODERA

Kosaki's adoring younger sister. Has a low opinion of Raku.

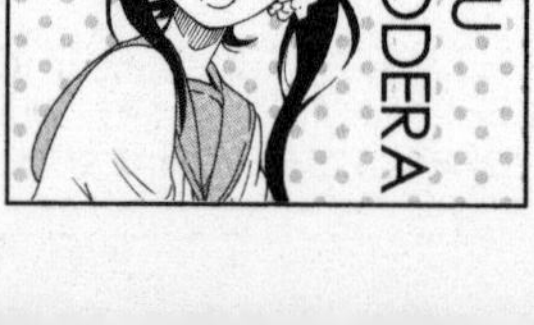

NISEKOI
False Love

vol. 13: Don't Worry

TABLE OF CONTENTS

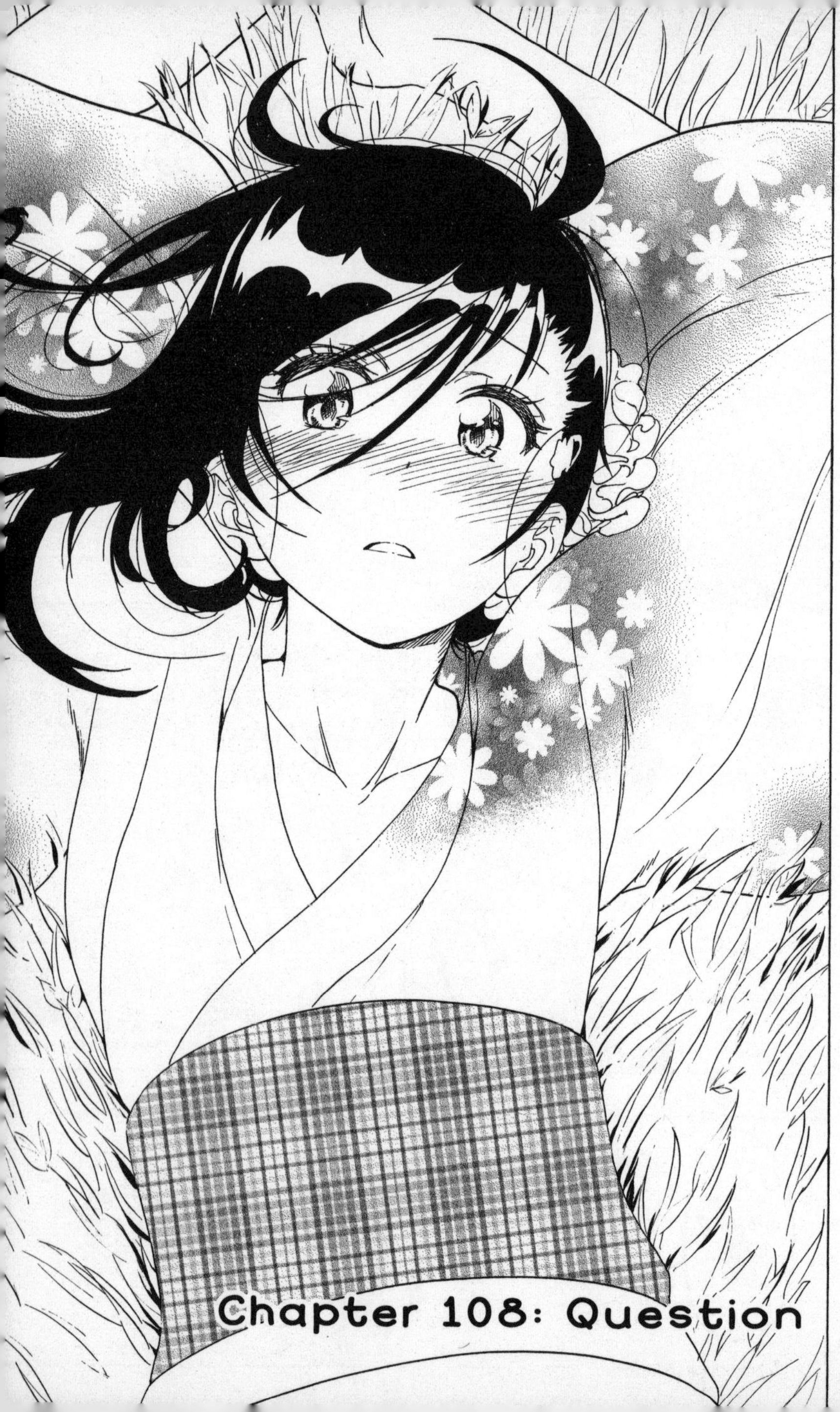

Chapter 108: Question

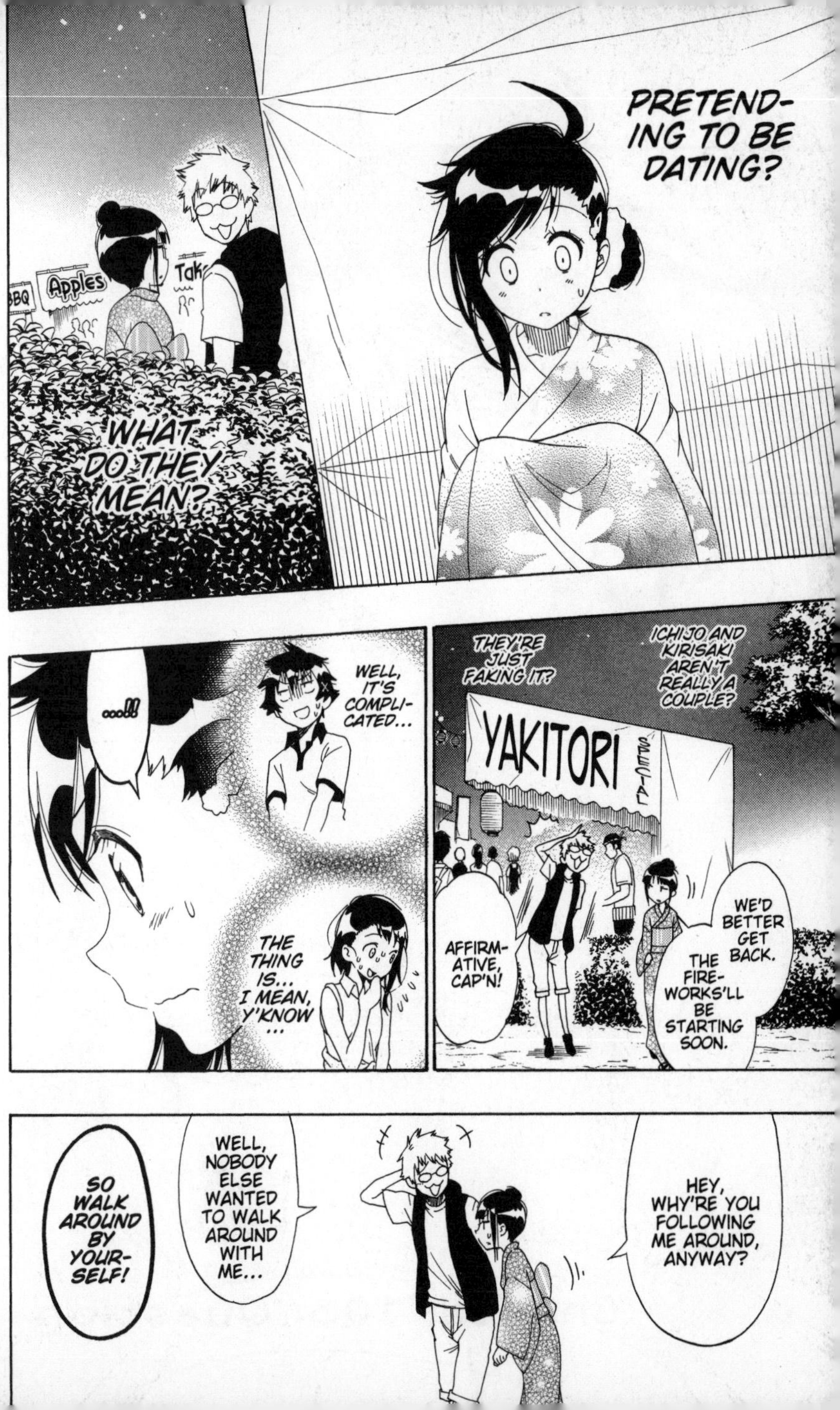
PRETEND-ING TO BE DATING?
WHAT DO THEY MEAN?
BBQ
Apples
Tak
ICHIJO AND KIRISAKI AREN'T REALLY A COUPLE?
THEY'RE JUST FAKING IT?
YAKITORI
SPECIAL
WE'D BETTER GET BACK. THE FIRE-WORKS'LL BE STARTING SOON.
AFFIRM-ATIVE, CAP'N!
WELL, IT'S COMPLI-CATED...
...!!
THE THING IS... I MEAN, Y'KNOW...
HEY, WHY'RE YOU FOLLOWING ME AROUND, ANYWAY?
WELL, NOBODY ELSE WANTED TO WALK AROUND WITH ME...
SO WALK AROUND BY YOUR-SELF!

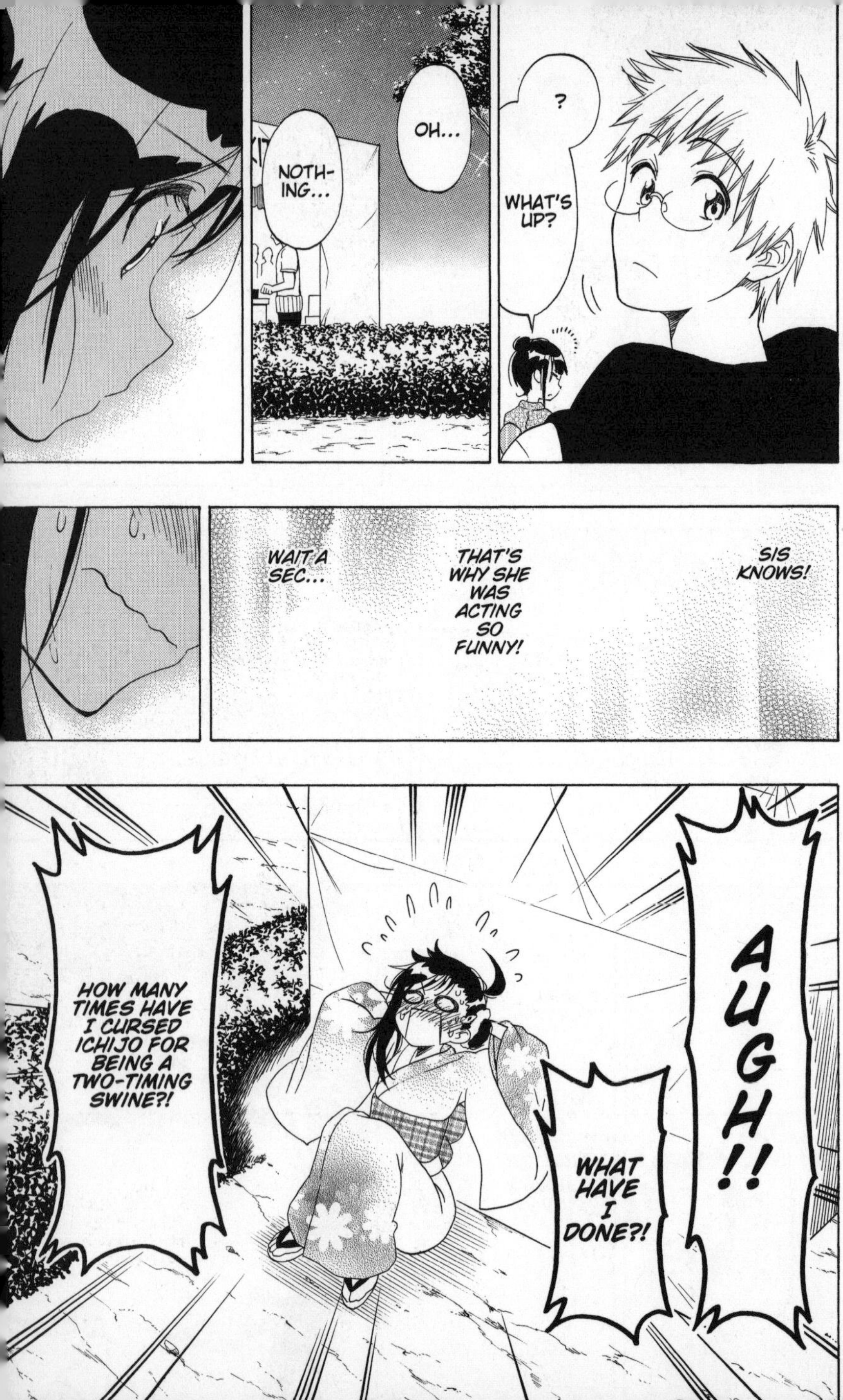
?
WHAT'S UP?
OH...
NOTH-ING...
SIS KNOWS!
THAT'S WHY SHE WAS ACTING SO FUNNY!
WAIT A SEC...
AUGH!!
WHAT HAVE I DONE?!
HOW MANY TIMES HAVE I CURSED ICHIJO FOR BEING A TWO-TIMING SWINE?!

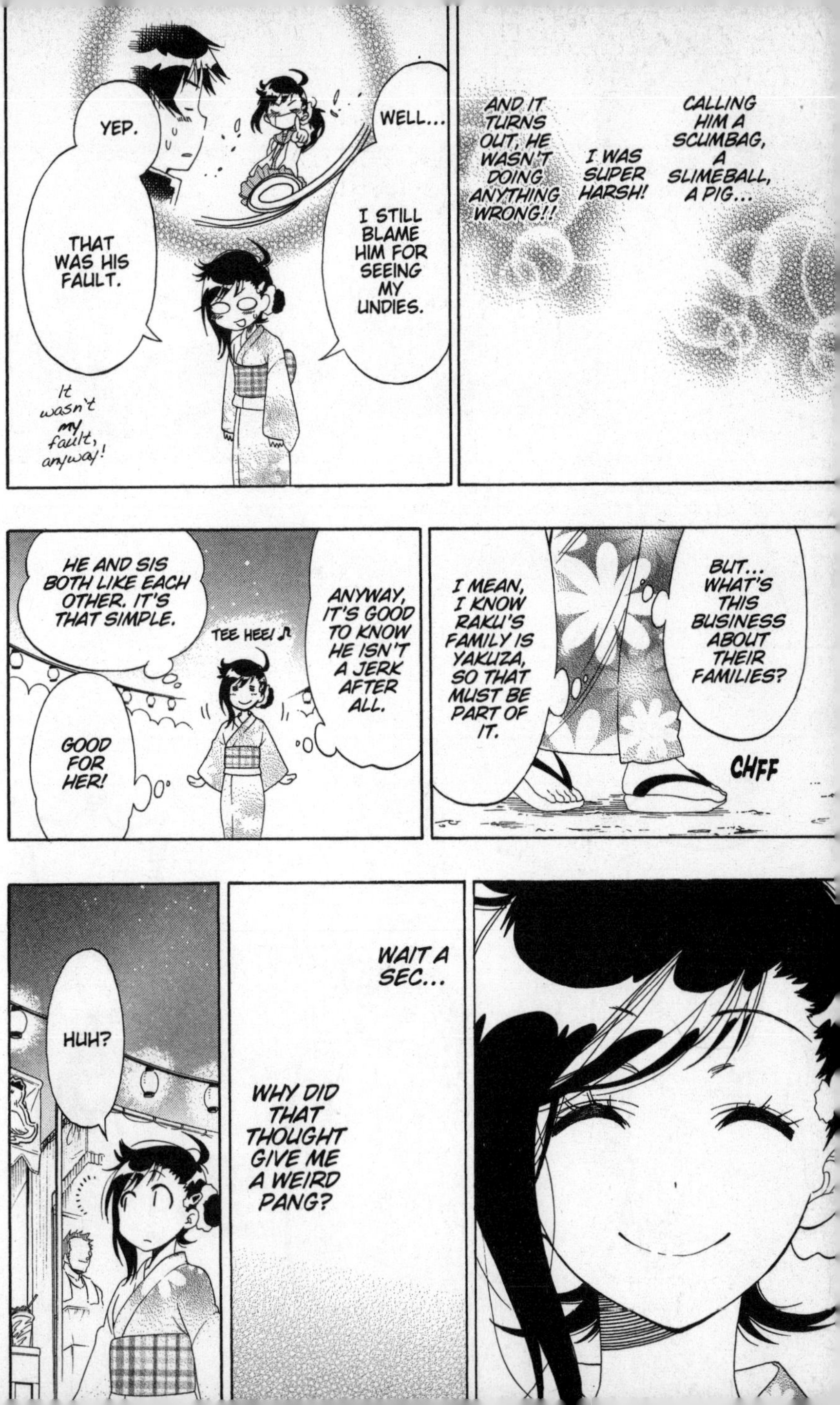
CALLING HIM A SCUMBAG, A SLIMEBALL, A PIG...
I WAS SUPER HARSH!
AND IT TURNS OUT, HE WASN'T DOING ANYTHING WRONG!!
WELL...
I STILL BLAME HIM FOR SEEING MY UNDIES.
YEP.
THAT WAS HIS FAULT.
It wasn't my fault, anyway!
BUT... WHAT'S THIS BUSINESS ABOUT THEIR FAMILIES?
I MEAN, I KNOW RAKU'S FAMILY IS YAKUZA, SO THAT MUST BE PART OF IT.
CHFF
ANYWAY, IT'S GOOD TO KNOW HE ISN'T A JERK AFTER ALL.
TEE HEE! ♪
HE AND SIS BOTH LIKE EACH OTHER. IT'S THAT SIMPLE.
GOOD FOR HER!
WAIT A SEC...
WHY DID THAT THOUGHT GIVE ME A WEIRD PANG?
HUH?

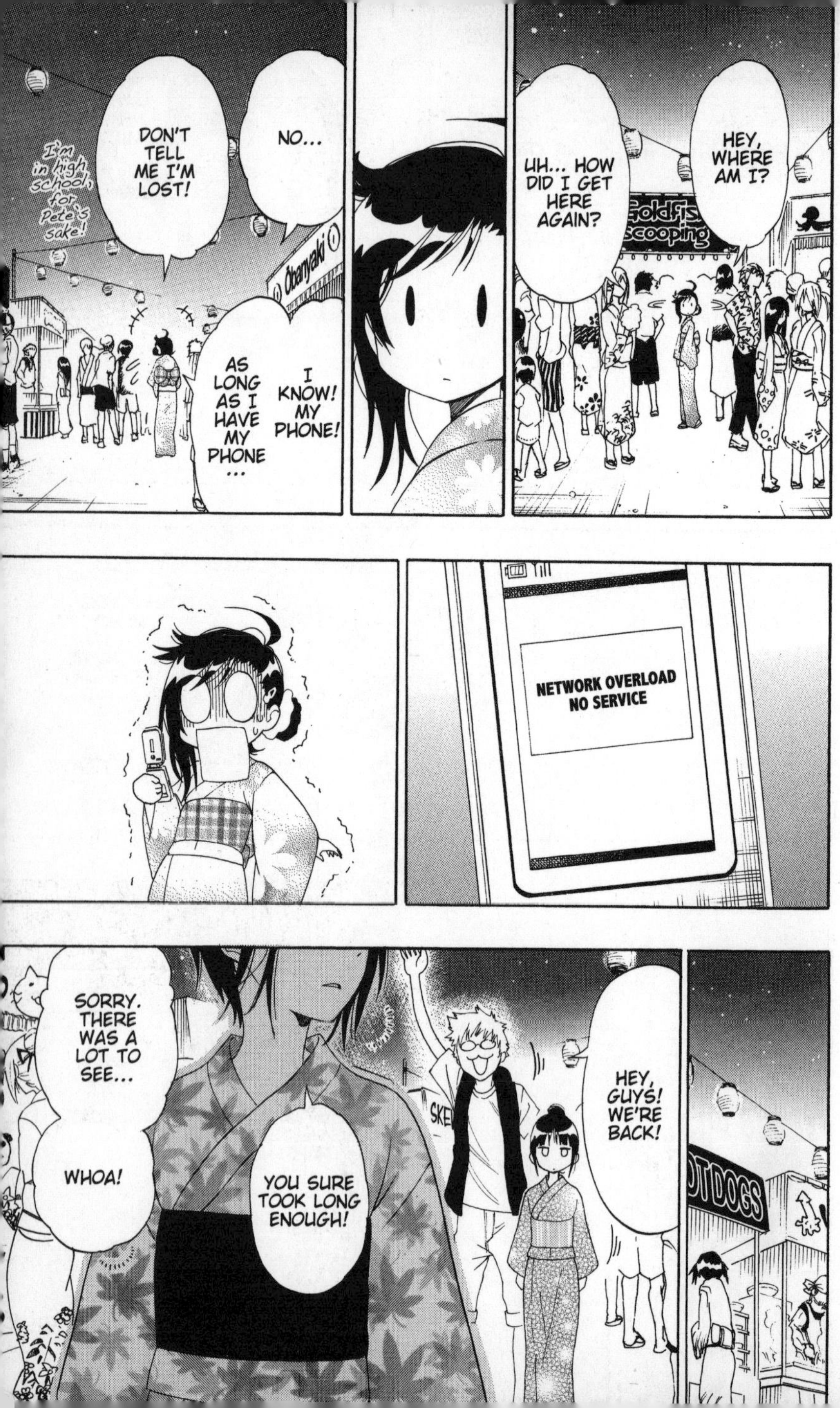
HEY, WHERE AM I?
UH... HOW DID I GET HERE AGAIN?
Goldfis scooping
NO...
DON'T TELL ME I'M LOST!
I'm in high school, for Pete's sake!
Ōbanyaki
I KNOW! MY PHONE!
AS LONG AS I HAVE MY PHONE...
NETWORK OVERLOAD
NO SERVICE
OTDOGS
HEY, GUYS! WE'RE BACK!
YOU SURE TOOK LONG ENOUGH!
SORRY. THERE WAS A LOT TO SEE...
WHOA!

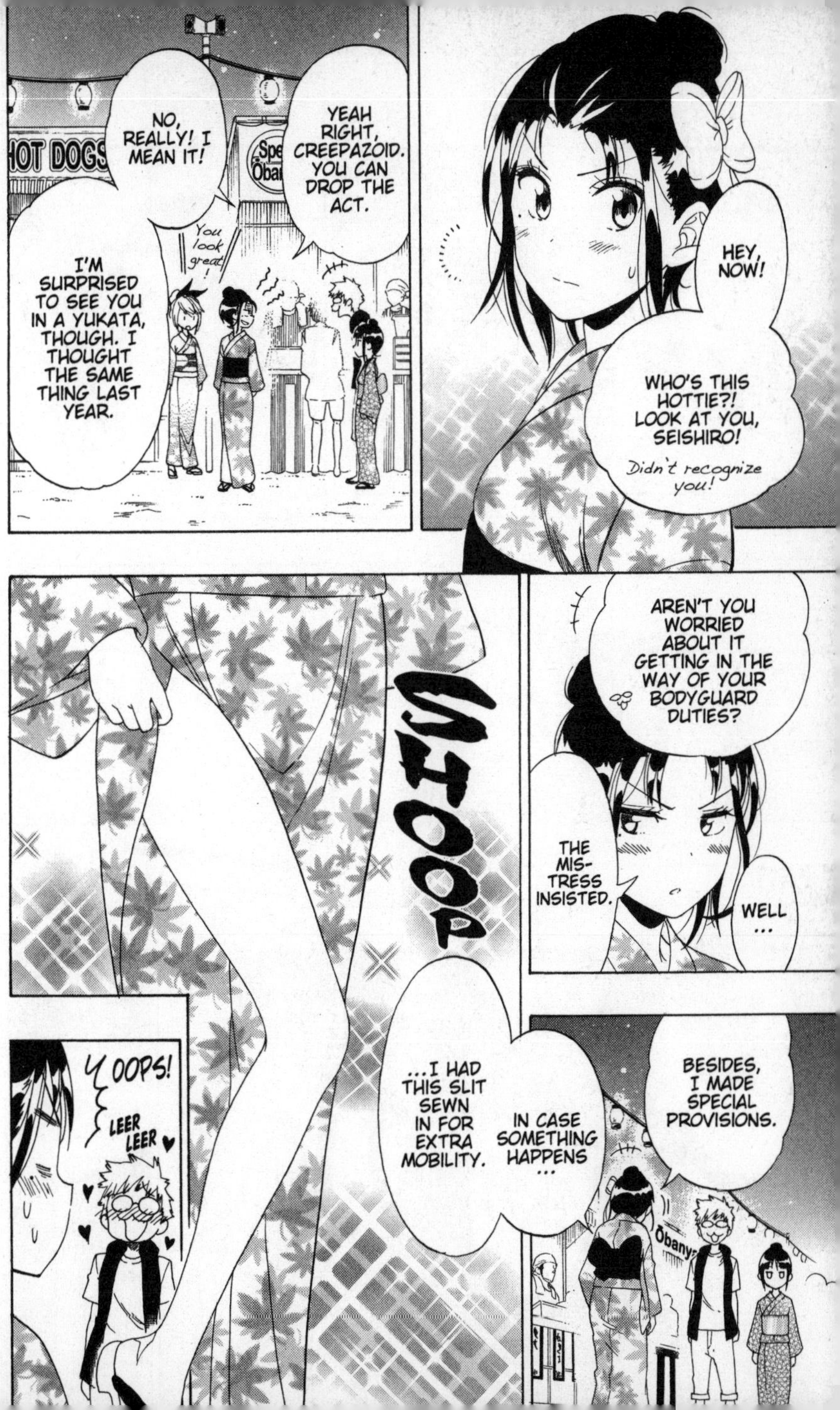
HEY, NOW!
WHO'S THIS HOTTIE?! LOOK AT YOU, SEISHIRO!
Didn't recognize you!
YEAH RIGHT, CREEPAZOID. YOU CAN DROP THE ACT.
NO, REALLY! I MEAN IT!
You look great!
HOT DOGS
I'M SURPRISED TO SEE YOU IN A YUKATA, THOUGH. I THOUGHT THE SAME THING LAST YEAR.
AREN'T YOU WORRIED ABOUT IT GETTING IN THE WAY OF YOUR BODYGUARD DUTIES?
WELL...
THE MIS-TRESS INSISTED.
BESIDES, I MADE SPECIAL PROVISIONS.
IN CASE SOMETHING HAPPENS...
...I HAD THIS SLIT SEWN IN FOR EXTRA MOBILITY.
SHOOP
OOPS!
LEER LEER

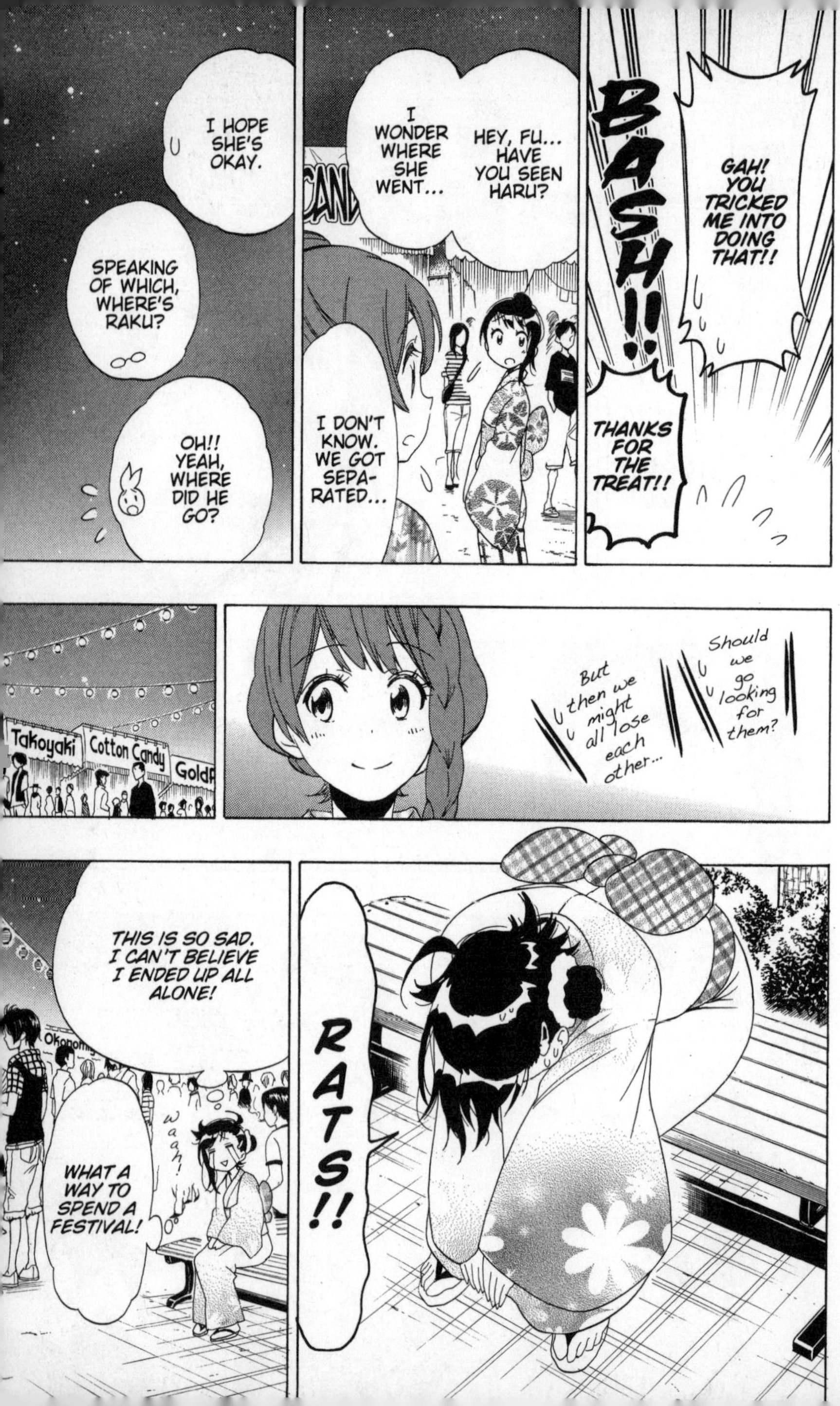
GAH! YOU TRICKED ME INTO DOING THAT!!
BASH!!
THANKS FOR THE TREAT!!
HEY, FU... HAVE YOU SEEN HARU?
I WONDER WHERE SHE WENT...
I DON'T KNOW. WE GOT SEPARATED...
I HOPE SHE'S OKAY.
SPEAKING OF WHICH, WHERE'S RAKU?
OH!! YEAH, WHERE DID HE GO?
Should we go looking for them?
But then we might all lose each other...
Takoyaki
Cotton Candy
RATS!!
THIS IS SO SAD. I CAN'T BELIEVE I ENDED UP ALL ALONE!
Waah!
WHAT A WAY TO SPEND A FESTIVAL!

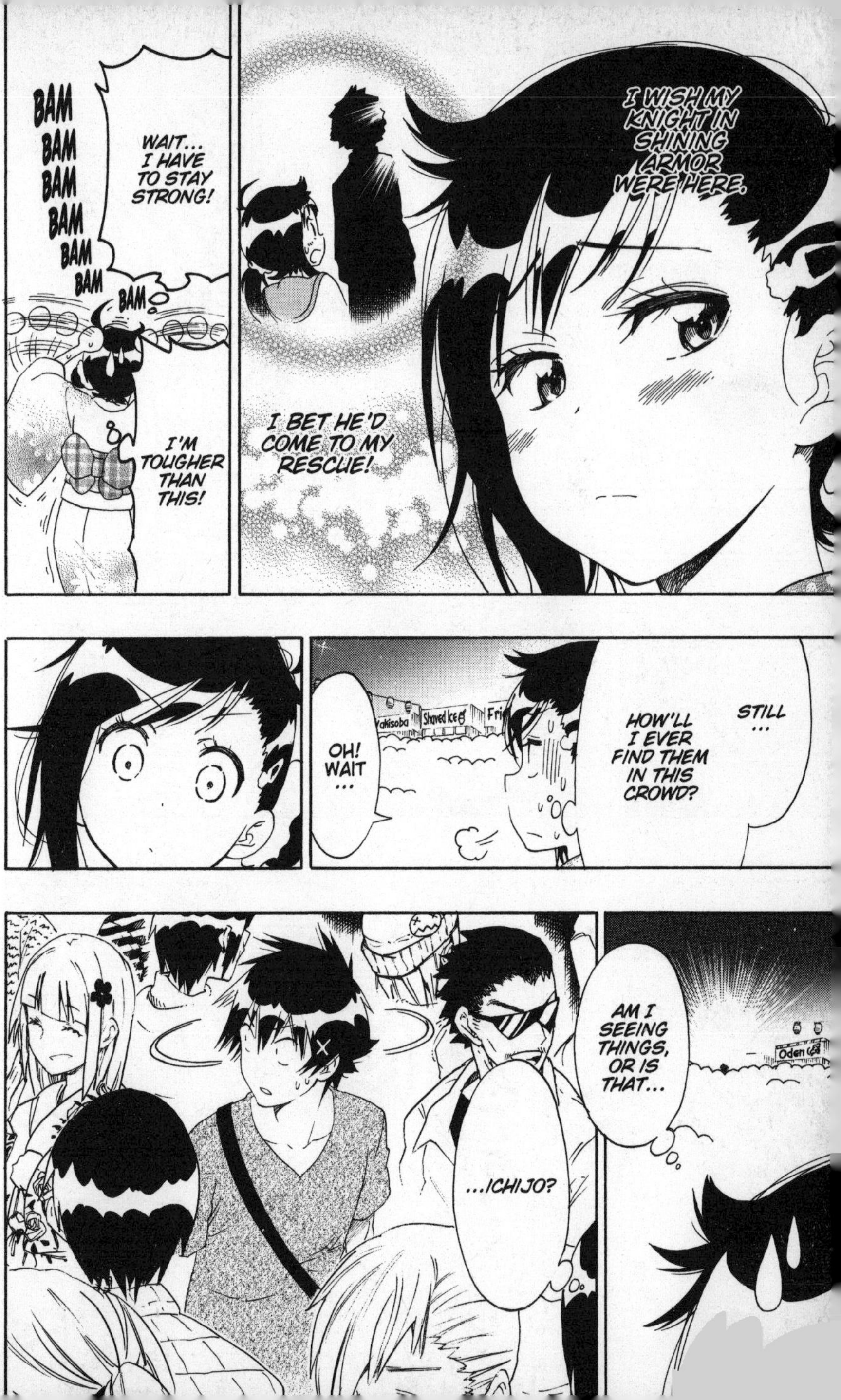
I WISH MY KNIGHT IN SHINING ARMOR WERE HERE.
I BET HE'D COME TO MY RESCUE!
WAIT... I HAVE TO STAY STRONG!
BAM BAM BAM BAM BAM BAM BAM
I'M TOUGHER THAN THIS!
STILL...
HOW'LL I EVER FIND THEM IN THIS CROWD?
OH! WAIT...
Yakisoba
Shaved Ice
AM I SEEING THINGS, OR IS THAT...
...ICHIJO?
Oden

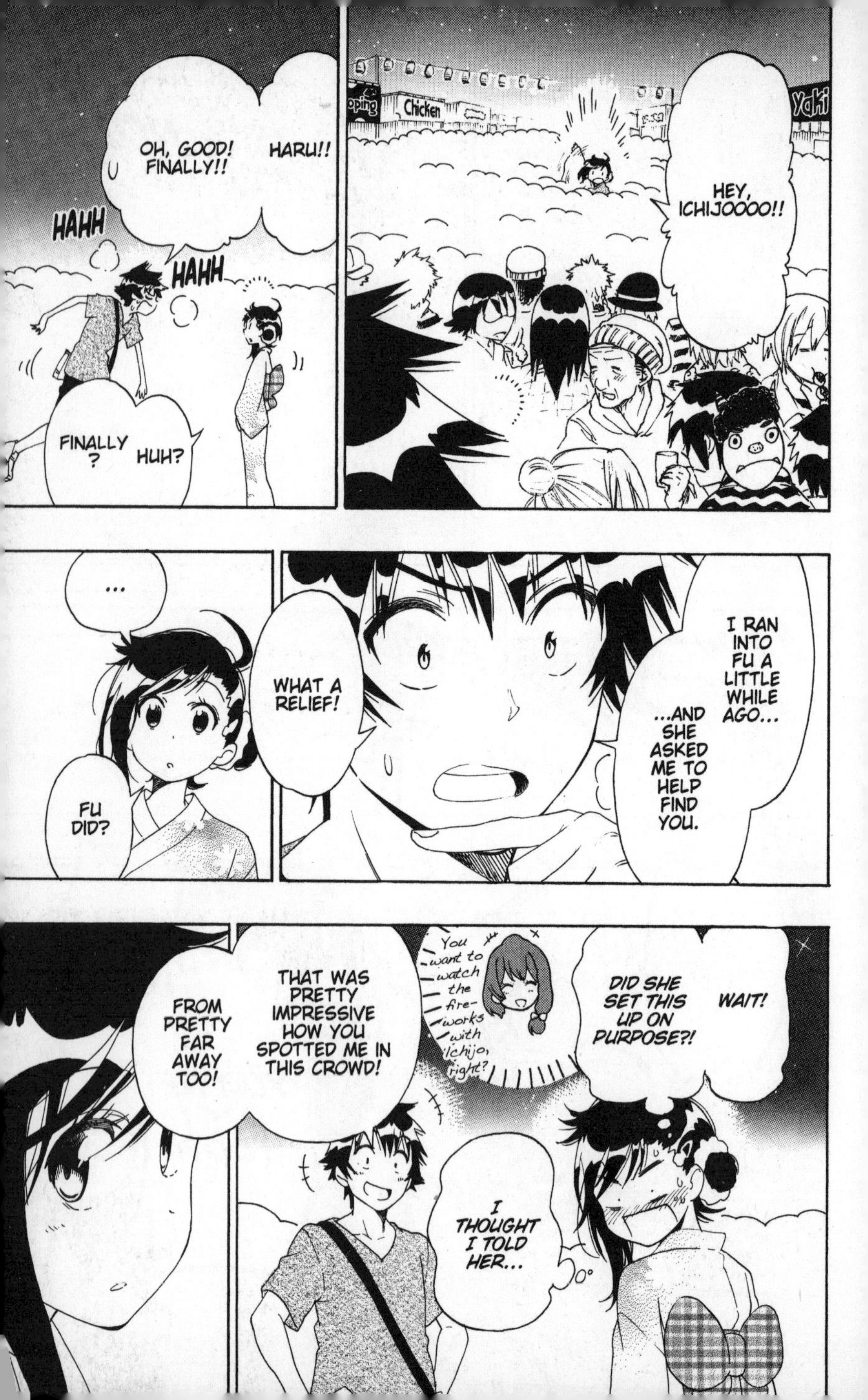
Yaki
Chicken
oping
HEY, ICHIJOOOO!!
HARU!!
OH, GOOD! FINALLY!!
HAHH
HAHH
FINALLY?
HUH?
I RAN INTO FU A LITTLE WHILE AGO...
...AND SHE ASKED ME TO HELP FIND YOU.
WHAT A RELIEF!
...
FU DID?
WAIT!
DID SHE SET THIS UP ON PURPOSE?!
You want to watch the fire-works with Ichijo, right?
THAT WAS PRETTY IMPRESSIVE HOW YOU SPOTTED ME IN THIS CROWD!
FROM PRETTY FAR AWAY TOO!
I THOUGHT I TOLD HER...

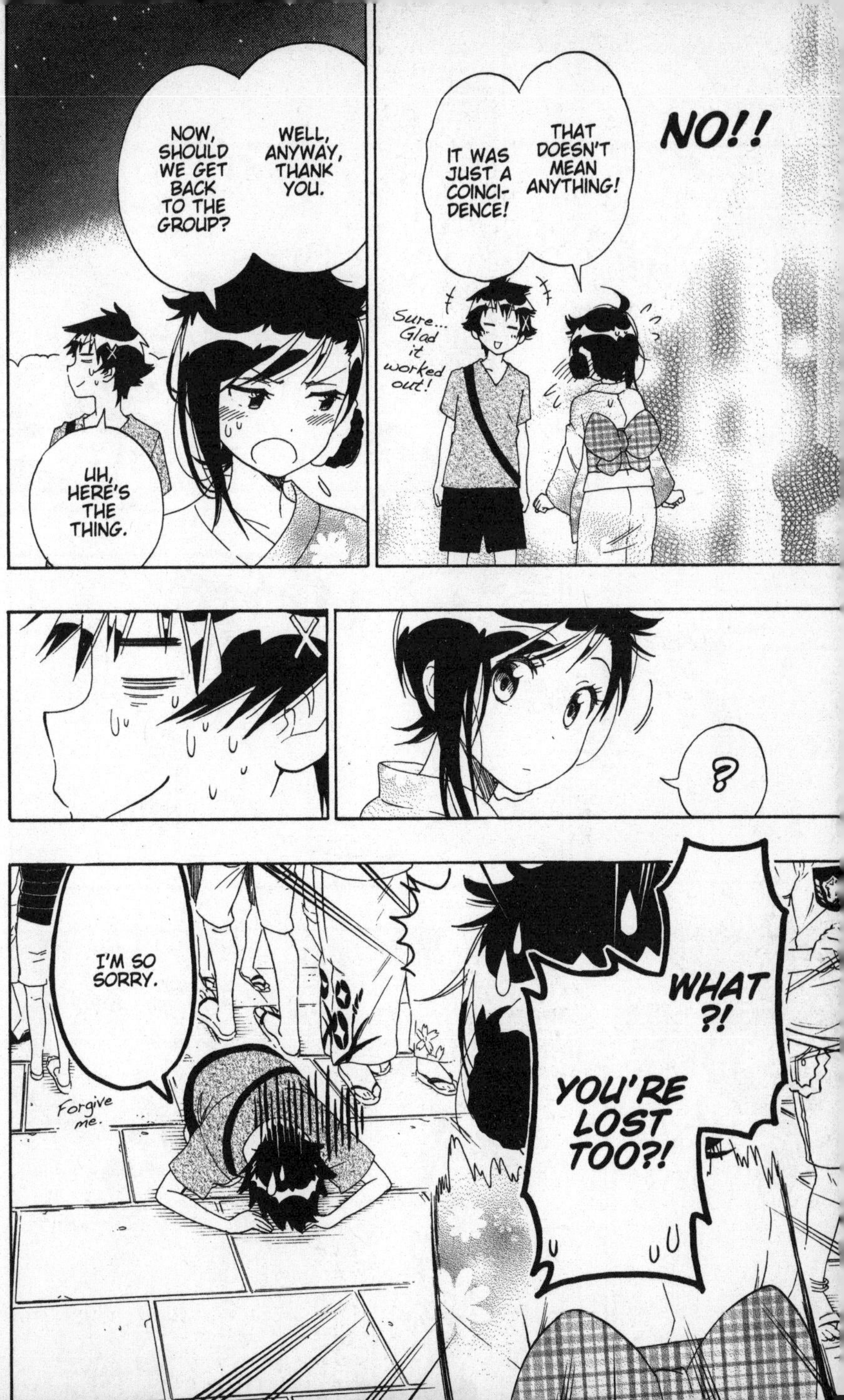
NO!!
THAT DOESN'T MEAN ANYTHING!
IT WAS JUST A COINCIDENCE!
Sure... Glad it worked out!
WELL, ANYWAY, THANK YOU.
NOW, SHOULD WE GET BACK TO THE GROUP?
UH, HERE'S THE THING.
?
I'M SO SORRY.
Forgive me.
WHAT?!
YOU'RE LOST TOO?!

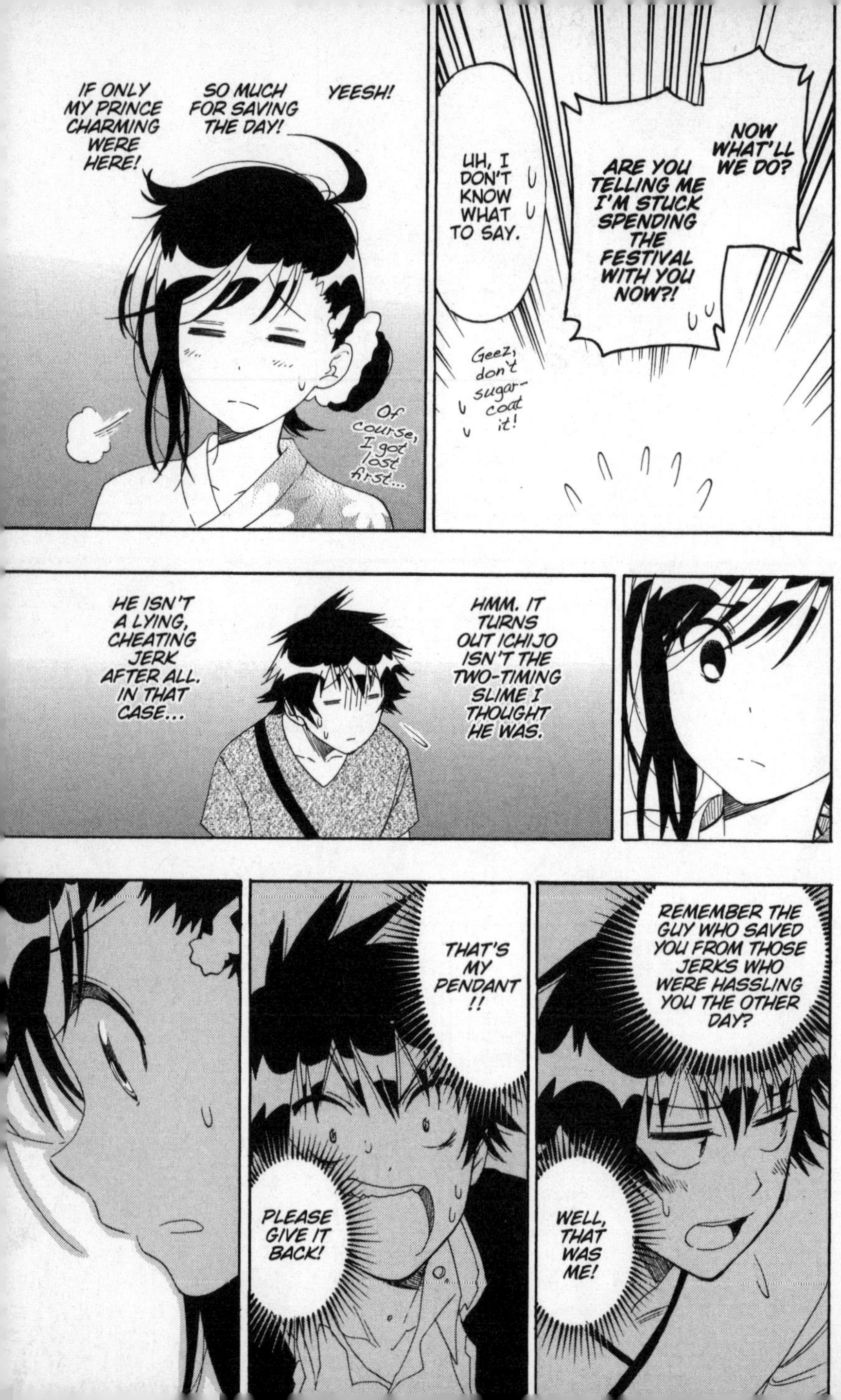
NOW WHAT'LL WE DO?
ARE YOU TELLING ME I'M STUCK SPENDING THE FESTIVAL WITH YOU NOW?!
UH, I DON'T KNOW WHAT TO SAY.
Geez, don't sugar-coat it!
YEESH!
SO MUCH FOR SAVING THE DAY!
IF ONLY MY PRINCE CHARMING WERE HERE!
Of course, I got lost first...
HMM. IT TURNS OUT ICHIJO ISN'T THE TWO-TIMING SLIME I THOUGHT HE WAS.
HE ISN'T A LYING, CHEATING JERK AFTER ALL. IN THAT CASE...
REMEMBER THE GUY WHO SAVED YOU FROM THOSE JERKS WHO WERE HASSLING YOU THE OTHER DAY?
WELL, THAT WAS ME!
THAT'S MY PENDANT!!
PLEASE GIVE IT BACK!

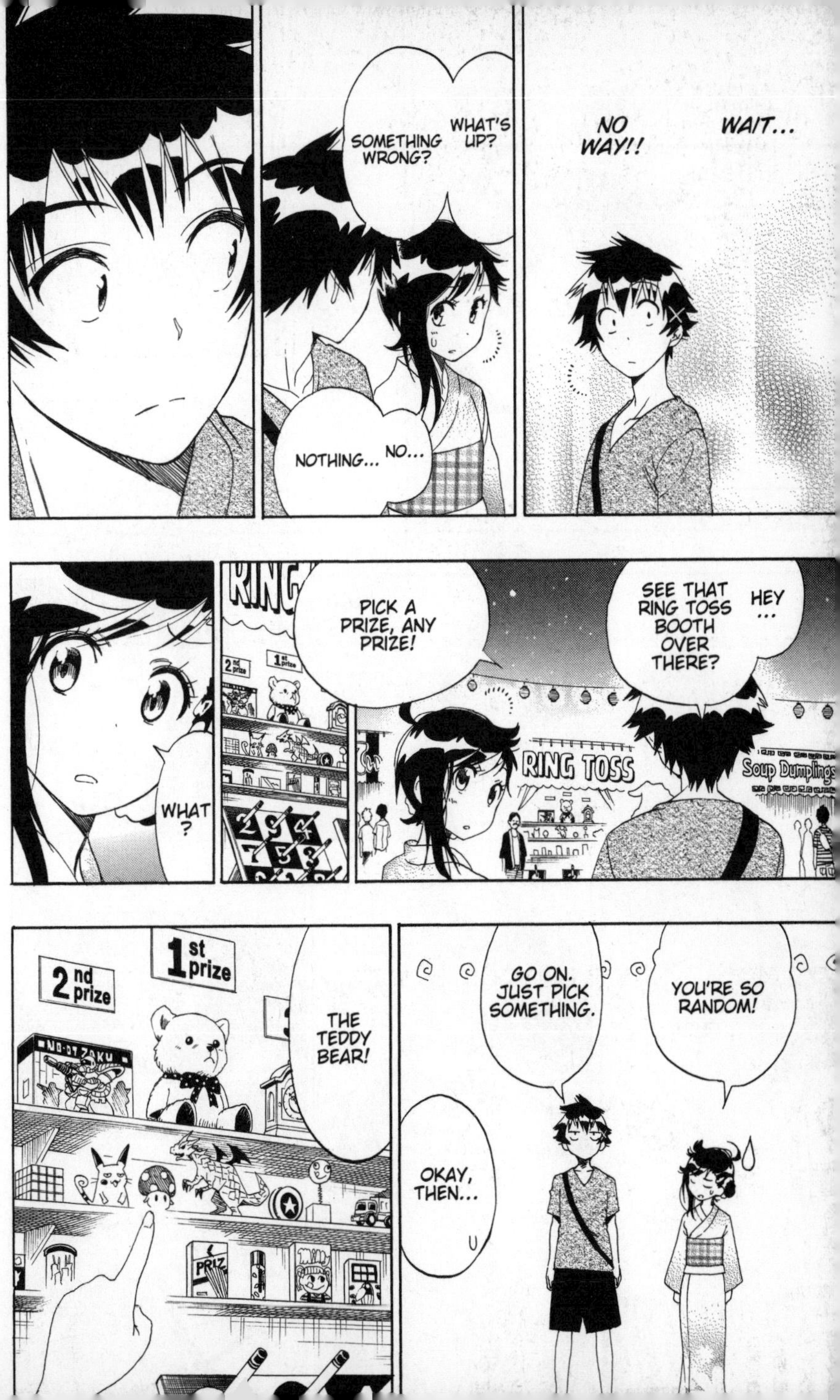
WAIT...
NO WAY!!
WHAT'S UP?
SOMETHING WRONG?
NO...
NOTHING...
HEY ...
SEE THAT RING TOSS BOOTH OVER THERE?
PICK A PRIZE, ANY PRIZE!
RING TOSS
Soup Dumplings
WHAT ?
YOU'RE SO RANDOM!
GO ON. JUST PICK SOMETHING.
OKAY, THEN...
1st prize
2nd prize
THE TEDDY BEAR!

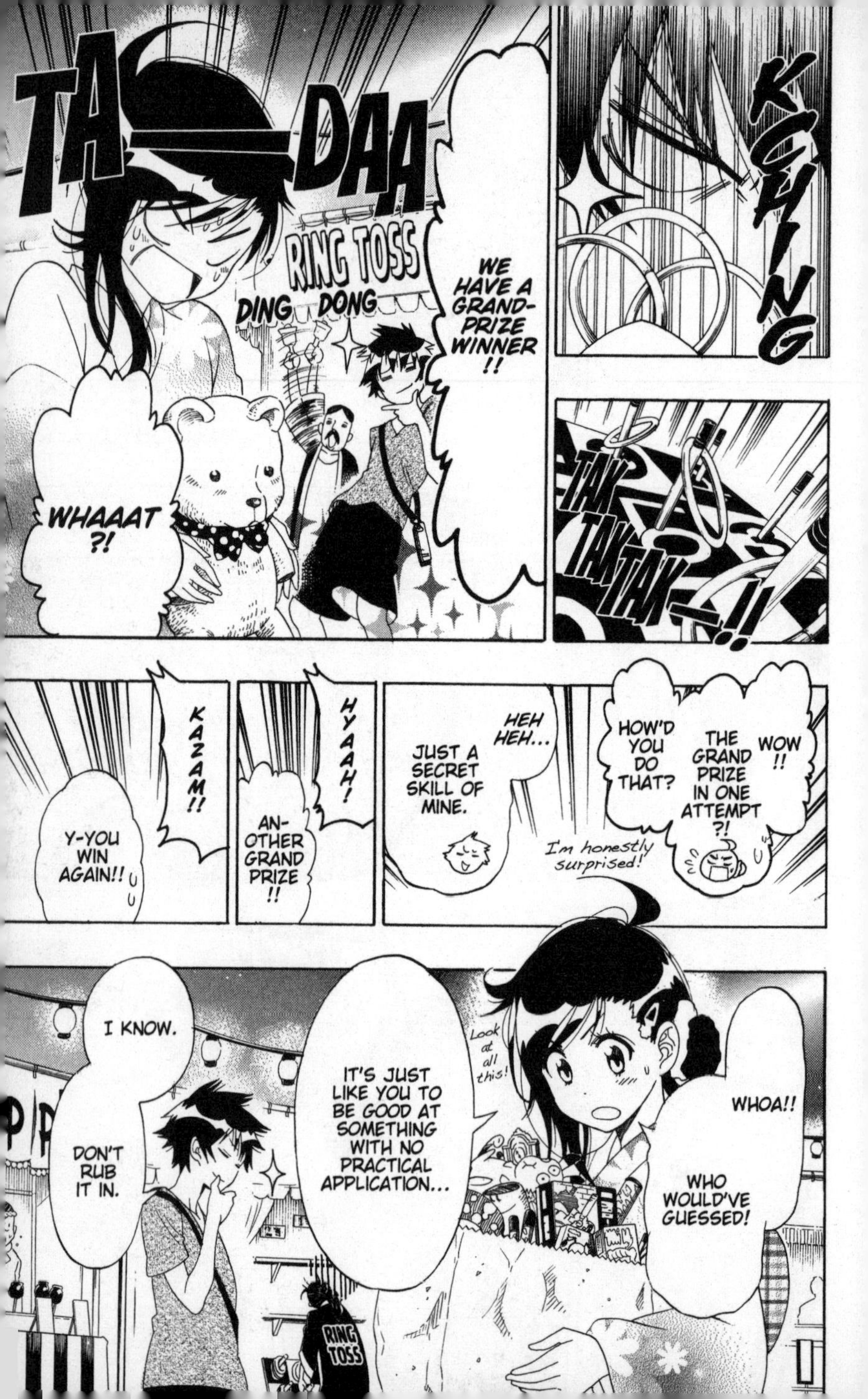
KCHING
TAK TAK TAK TAK—!!
TA-DAA
RING TOSS
DING DONG
WE HAVE A GRAND-PRIZE WINNER!!
WHAAAT?!
WOW!!
THE GRAND PRIZE IN ONE ATTEMPT?!
HOW'D YOU DO THAT?
I'm honestly surprised!
HEH HEH...
JUST A SECRET SKILL OF MINE.
HYAAAH!
AN-OTHER GRAND PRIZE!!
KAZAM!!
Y-YOU WIN AGAIN!!
WHOA!!
WHO WOULD'VE GUESSED!
Look at all this!
IT'S JUST LIKE YOU TO BE GOOD AT SOMETHING WITH NO PRACTICAL APPLICATION...
I KNOW.
DON'T RUB IT IN.
RING TOSS

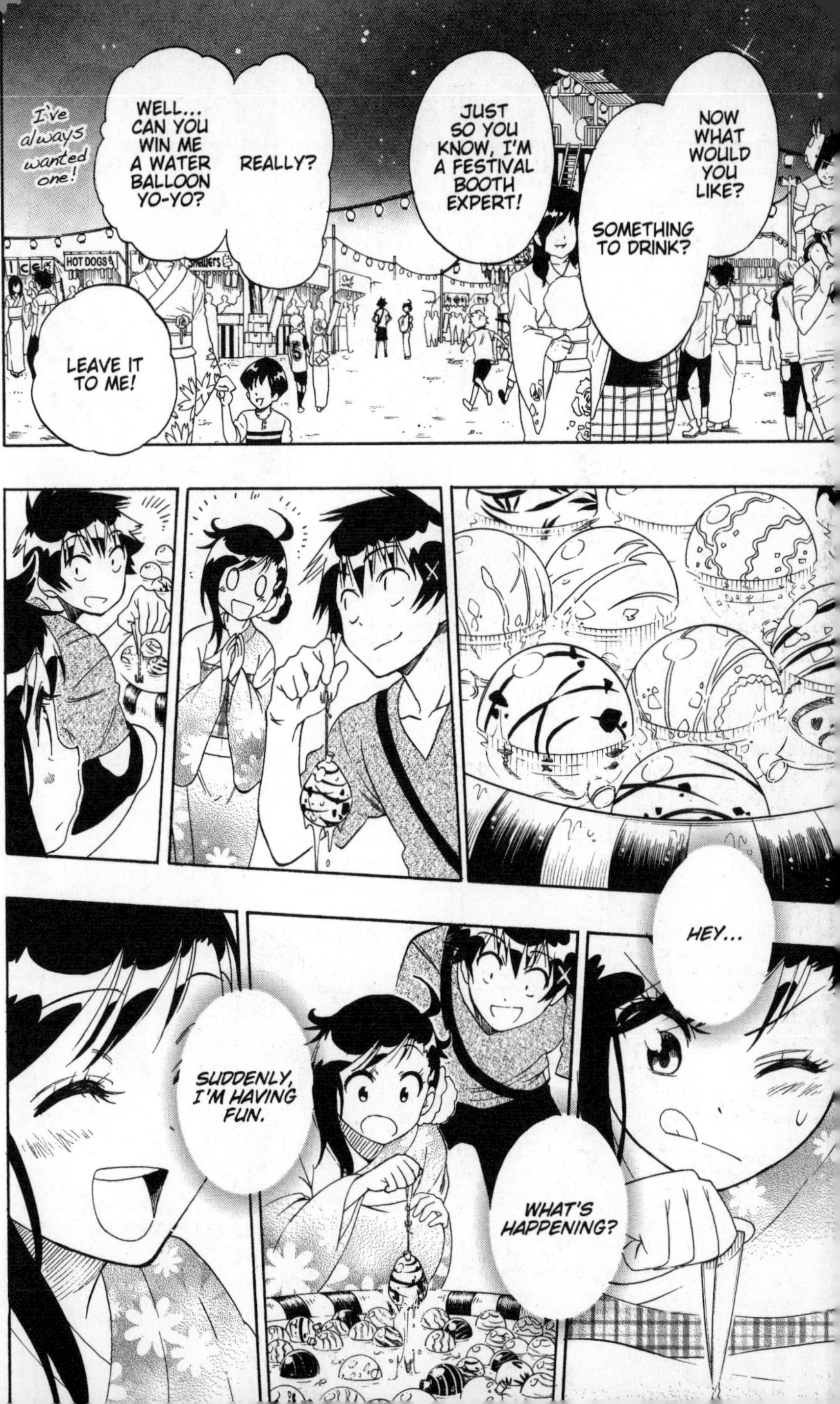
NOW WHAT WOULD YOU LIKE?
SOMETHING TO DRINK?
JUST SO YOU KNOW, I'M A FESTIVAL BOOTH EXPERT!
REALLY?
WELL... CAN YOU WIN ME A WATER BALLOON YO-YO?
I've always wanted one!
HOT DOGS
LEAVE IT TO ME!
HEY...
WHAT'S HAPPENING?
SUDDENLY, I'M HAVING FUN.

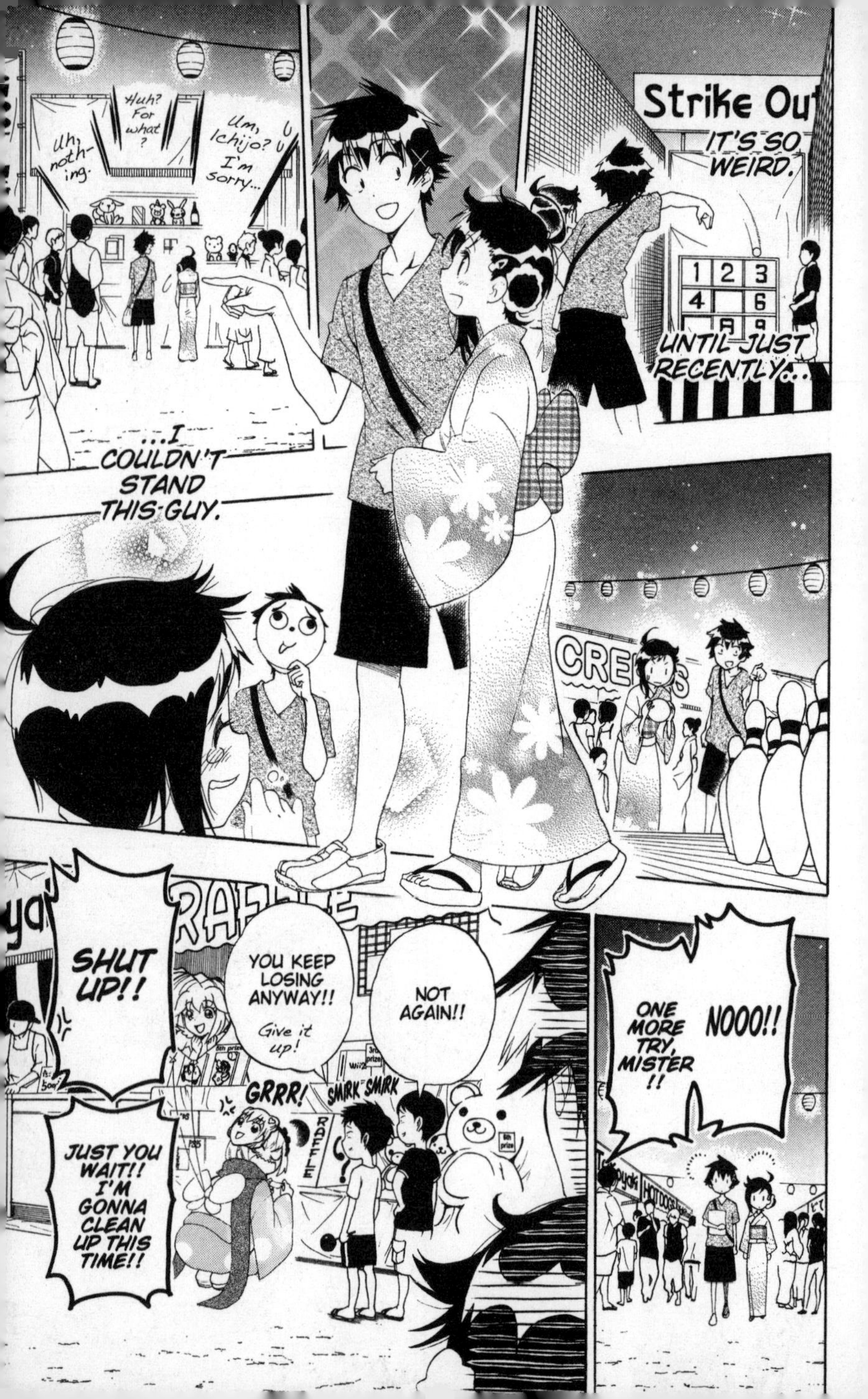
Strike Out
IT'S SO WEIRD.
UNTIL JUST RECENTLY...
Um, Ichijo? I'm sorry...
Huh? For what?
Uh, nothing.
...I COULDN'T STAND THIS GUY.
NOOO!!
ONE MORE TRY, MISTER!!
NOT AGAIN!!
YOU KEEP LOSING ANYWAY!!
Give it up!
SHUT UP!!
RAFFLE
SMIRK SMIRK
GRRR!
JUST YOU WAIT!! I'M GONNA CLEAN UP THIS TIME!!

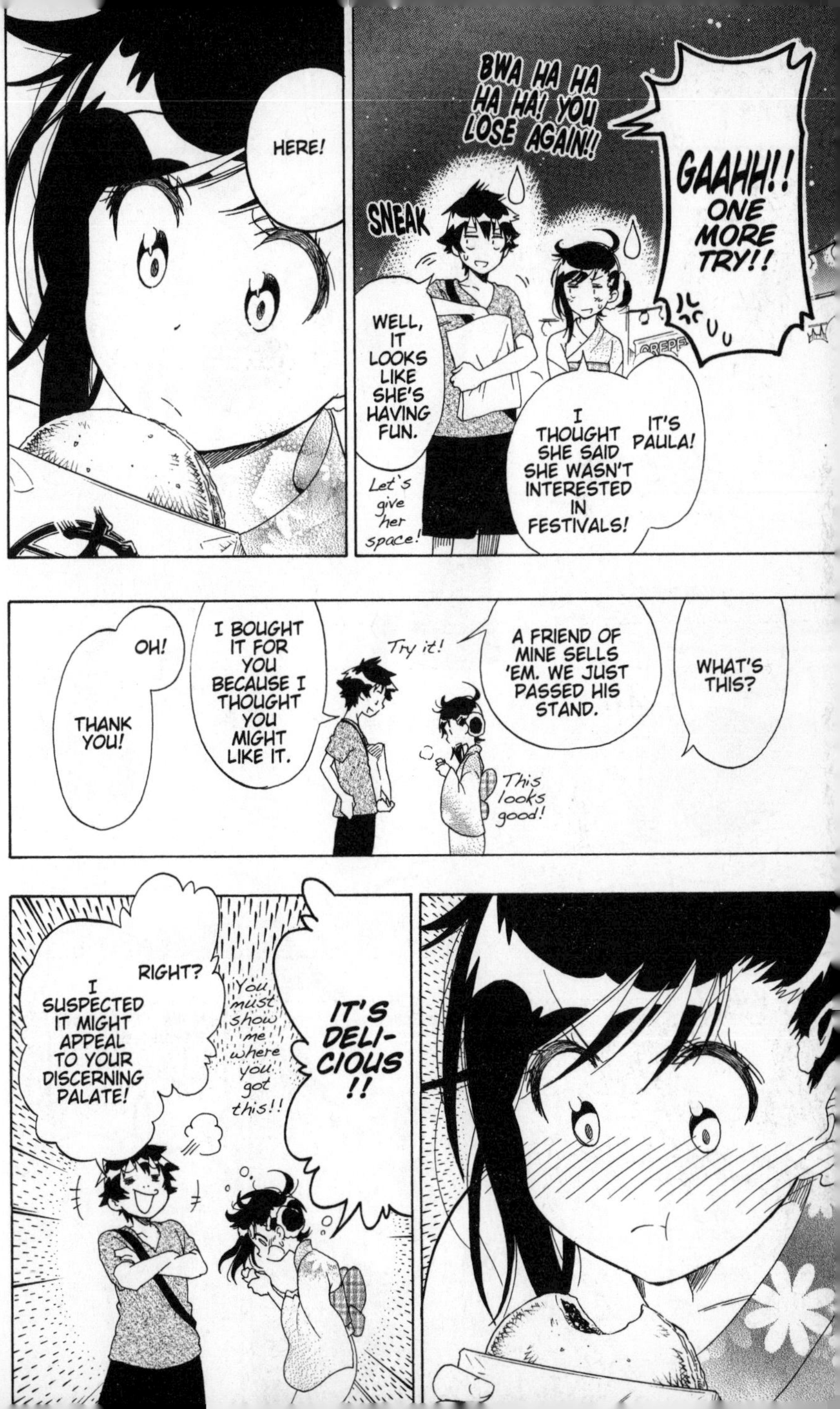
GAAHH!! ONE MORE TRY!!
BWA HA HA HA HA! YOU LOSE AGAIN!!
SNEAK
IT'S PAULA!
I THOUGHT SHE SAID SHE WASN'T INTERESTED IN FESTIVALS!
WELL, IT LOOKS LIKE SHE'S HAVING FUN.
Let's give her space!
HERE!
WHAT'S THIS?
A FRIEND OF MINE SELLS 'EM. WE JUST PASSED HIS STAND.
This looks good!
Try it!
I BOUGHT IT FOR YOU BECAUSE I THOUGHT YOU MIGHT LIKE IT.
OH! THANK YOU!
IT'S DELICIOUS!!
You must show me where you got this!!
RIGHT? I SUSPECTED IT MIGHT APPEAL TO YOUR DISCERNING PALATE!

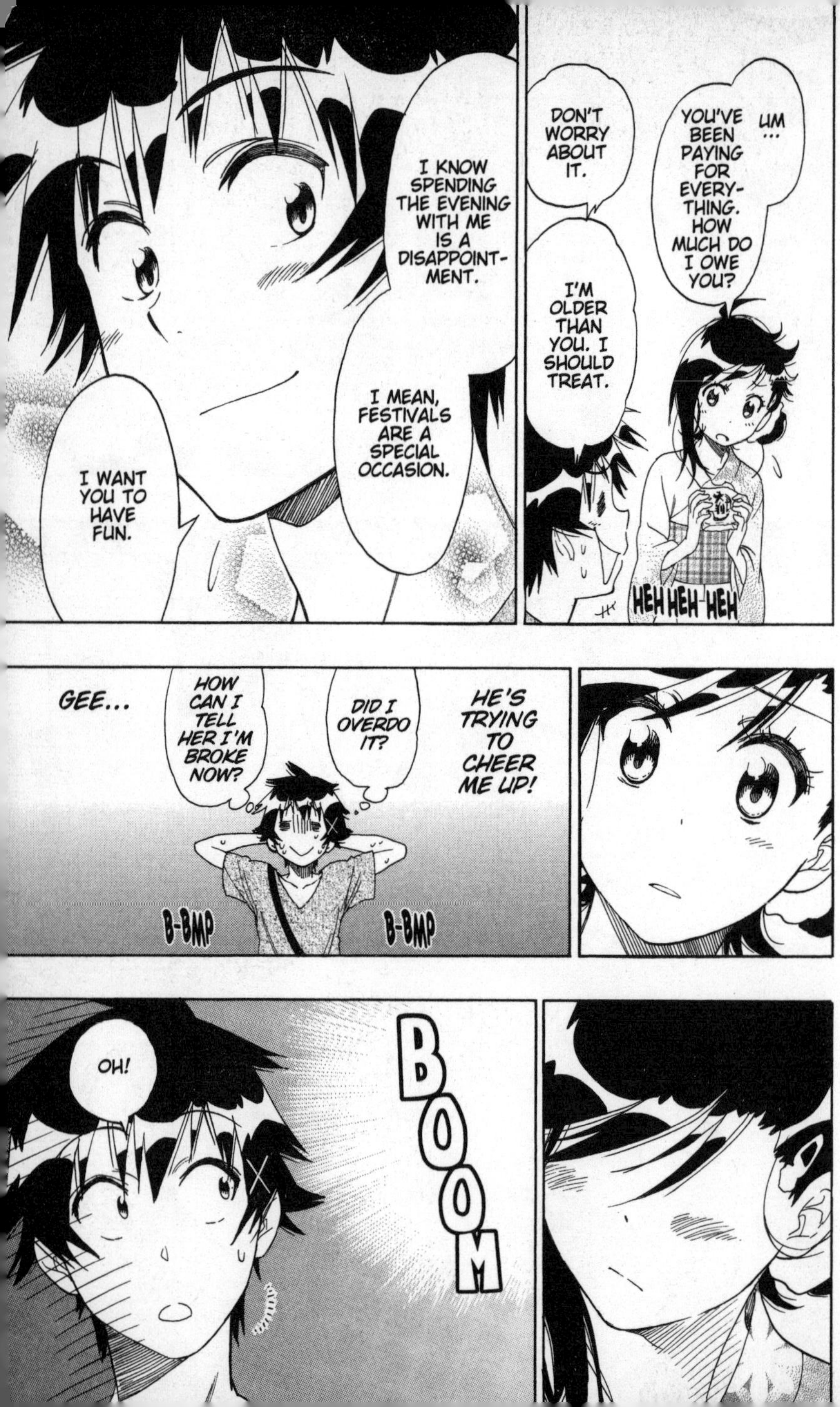
UM ...
YOU'VE BEEN PAYING FOR EVERY-THING. HOW MUCH DO I OWE YOU?
DON'T WORRY ABOUT IT.
I'M OLDER THAN YOU. I SHOULD TREAT.
HEH HEH HEH
I KNOW SPENDING THE EVENING WITH ME IS A DISAPPOINT-MENT.
I MEAN, FESTIVALS ARE A SPECIAL OCCASION.
I WANT YOU TO HAVE FUN.
HE'S TRYING TO CHEER ME UP!
DID I OVERDO IT?
HOW CAN I TELL HER I'M BROKE NOW?
GEE...
B-BMP
B-BMP
BOOM
OH!

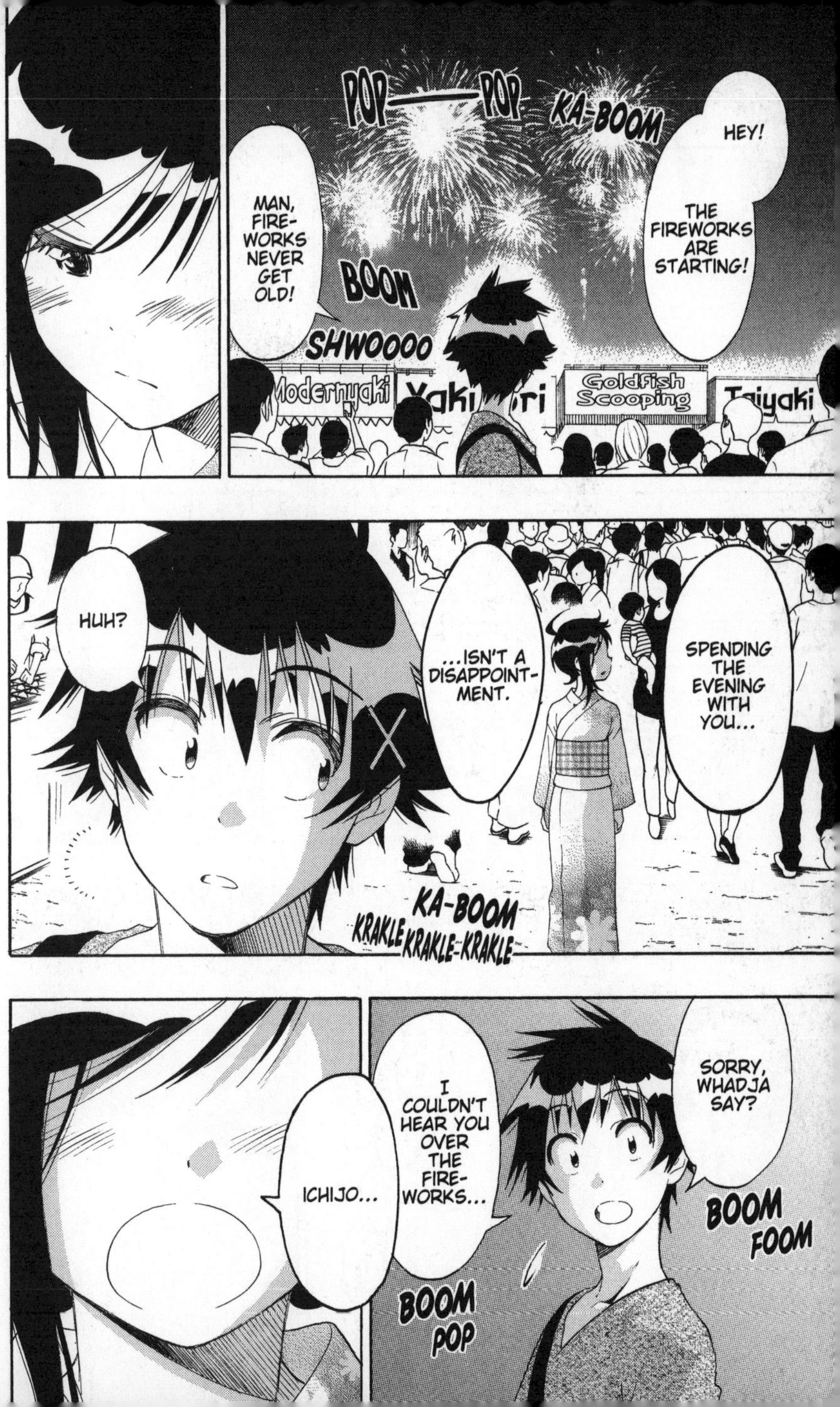
HEY!
THE FIREWORKS ARE STARTING!
KA-BOOM
POP——POP
MAN, FIRE-WORKS NEVER GET OLD!
BOOM
SHWOOOO
Taiyaki
Goldfish Scooping
Modernyaki
SPENDING THE EVENING WITH YOU...
...ISN'T A DISAPPOINT-MENT.
HUH?
KA-BOOM
KRAKLE KRAKLE-KRAKLE
SORRY, WHADJA SAY?
I COULDN'T HEAR YOU OVER THE FIRE-WORKS...
BOOM FOOM
BOOM POP
ICHIJO...

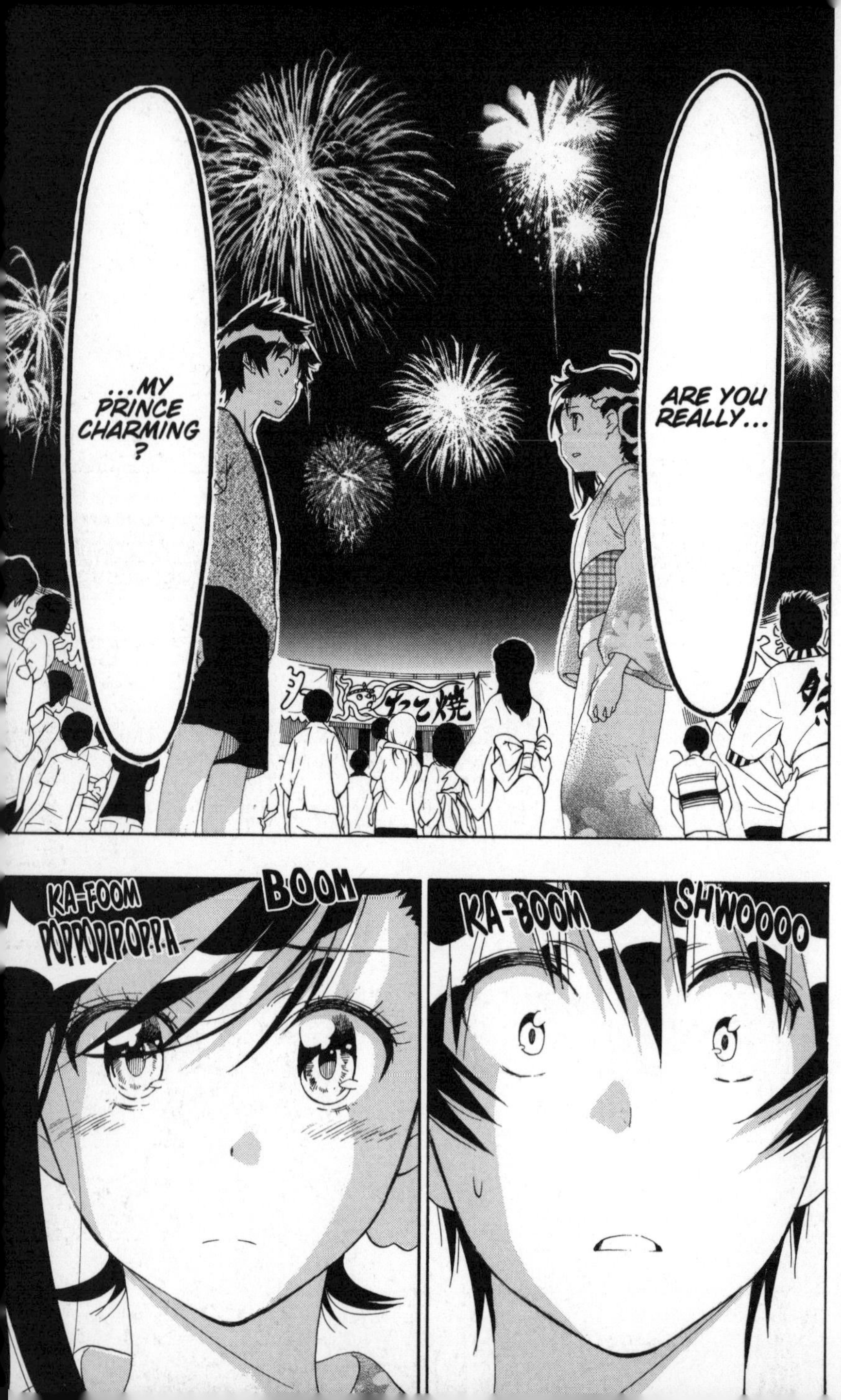
ARE YOU REALLY...
...MY PRINCE CHARMING ?
SHWOOOO
KA-BOOM
BOOM
KA-FOOM
POPPOPPOPPA

Good
luck,
Haru!

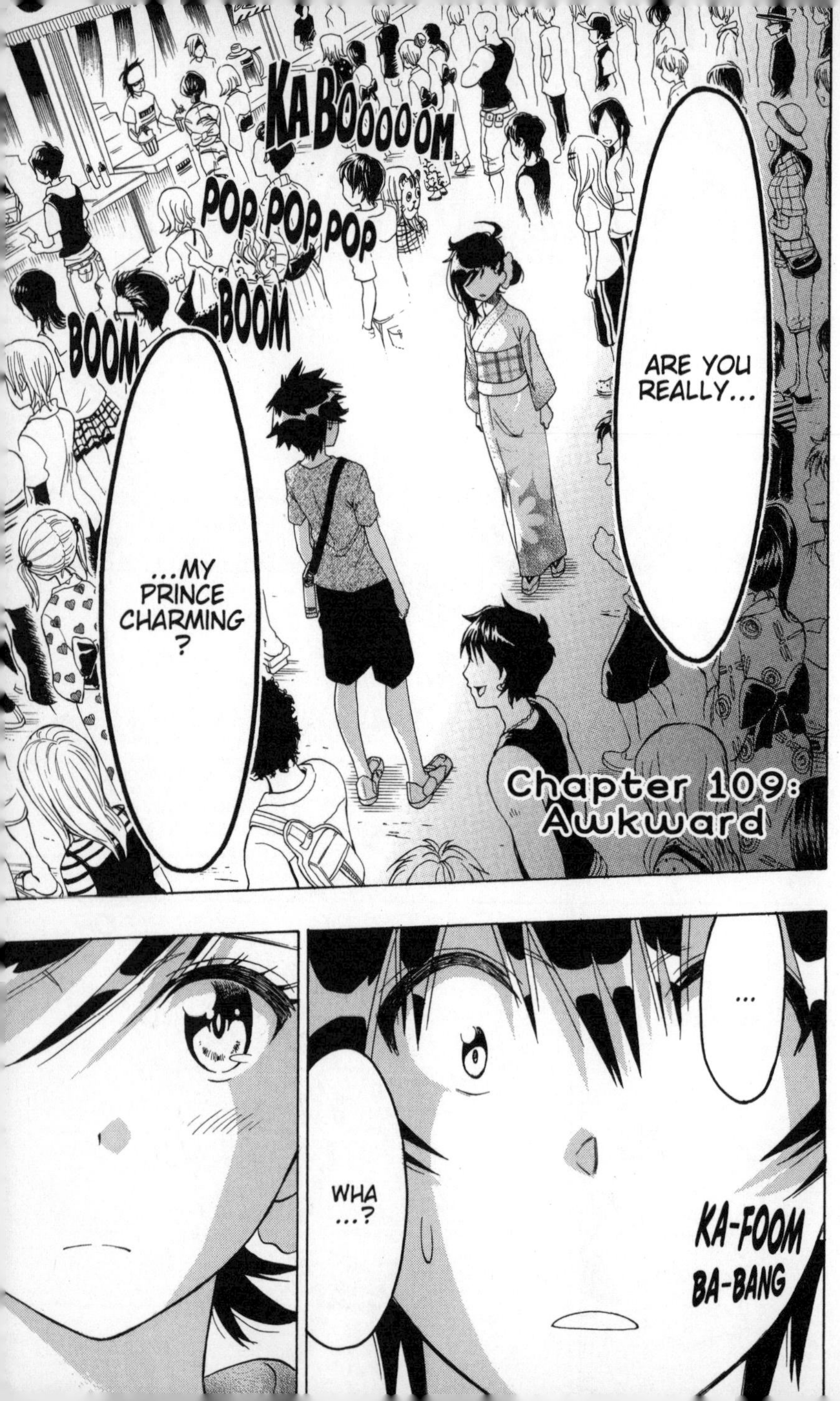
KABOOOOOM
ARE YOU REALLY...
POP POP POP
BOOM
BOOM
...MY PRINCE CHARMING?
Chapter 109: Awkward
...
KA-FOOM
BA-BANG
WHA...?

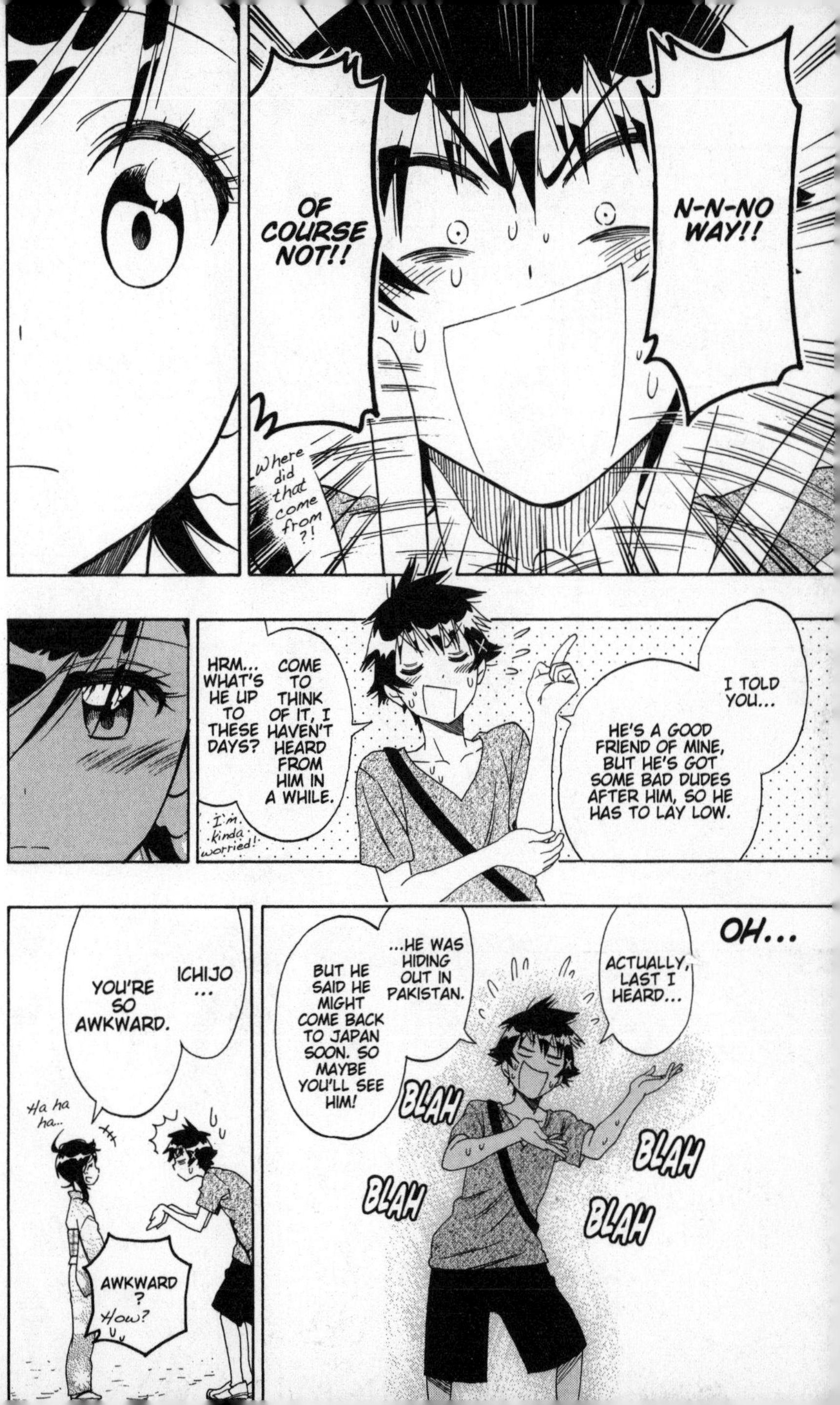
N-N-NO WAY!!
OF COURSE NOT!!
Where did that come from?!
I TOLD YOU...
HE'S A GOOD FRIEND OF MINE, BUT HE'S GOT SOME BAD DUDES AFTER HIM, SO HE HAS TO LAY LOW.
COME TO THINK OF IT, I HAVEN'T HEARD FROM HIM IN A WHILE.
HRM... WHAT'S HE UP TO THESE DAYS?
I'm kinda worried!
OH...
ACTUALLY, LAST I HEARD...
...HE WAS HIDING OUT IN PAKISTAN.
BUT HE SAID HE MIGHT COME BACK TO JAPAN SOON. SO MAYBE YOU'LL SEE HIM!
BLAH
BLAH
BLAH
BLAH
ICHIJO...
YOU'RE SO AWKWARD.
Ha ha ha...
AWKWARD? How?

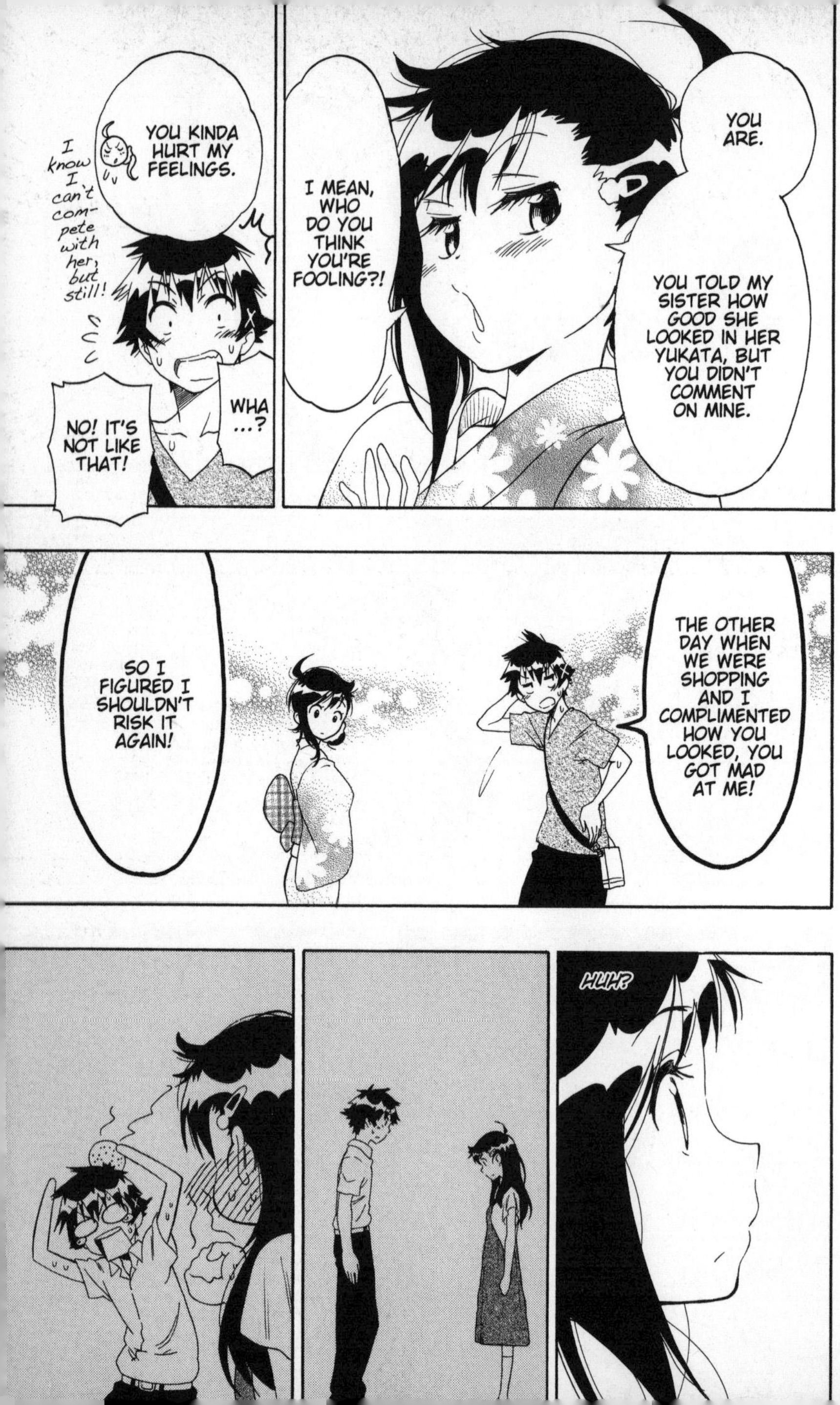
YOU ARE.
YOU TOLD MY SISTER HOW GOOD SHE LOOKED IN HER YUKATA, BUT YOU DIDN'T COMMENT ON MINE.
I MEAN, WHO DO YOU THINK YOU'RE FOOLING?!
YOU KINDA HURT MY FEELINGS.
I know I can't compete with her, but still!
WHA ...?
NO! IT'S NOT LIKE THAT!
THE OTHER DAY WHEN WE WERE SHOPPING AND I COMPLIMENTED HOW YOU LOOKED, YOU GOT MAD AT ME!
SO I FIGURED I SHOULDN'T RISK IT AGAIN!
HUH?

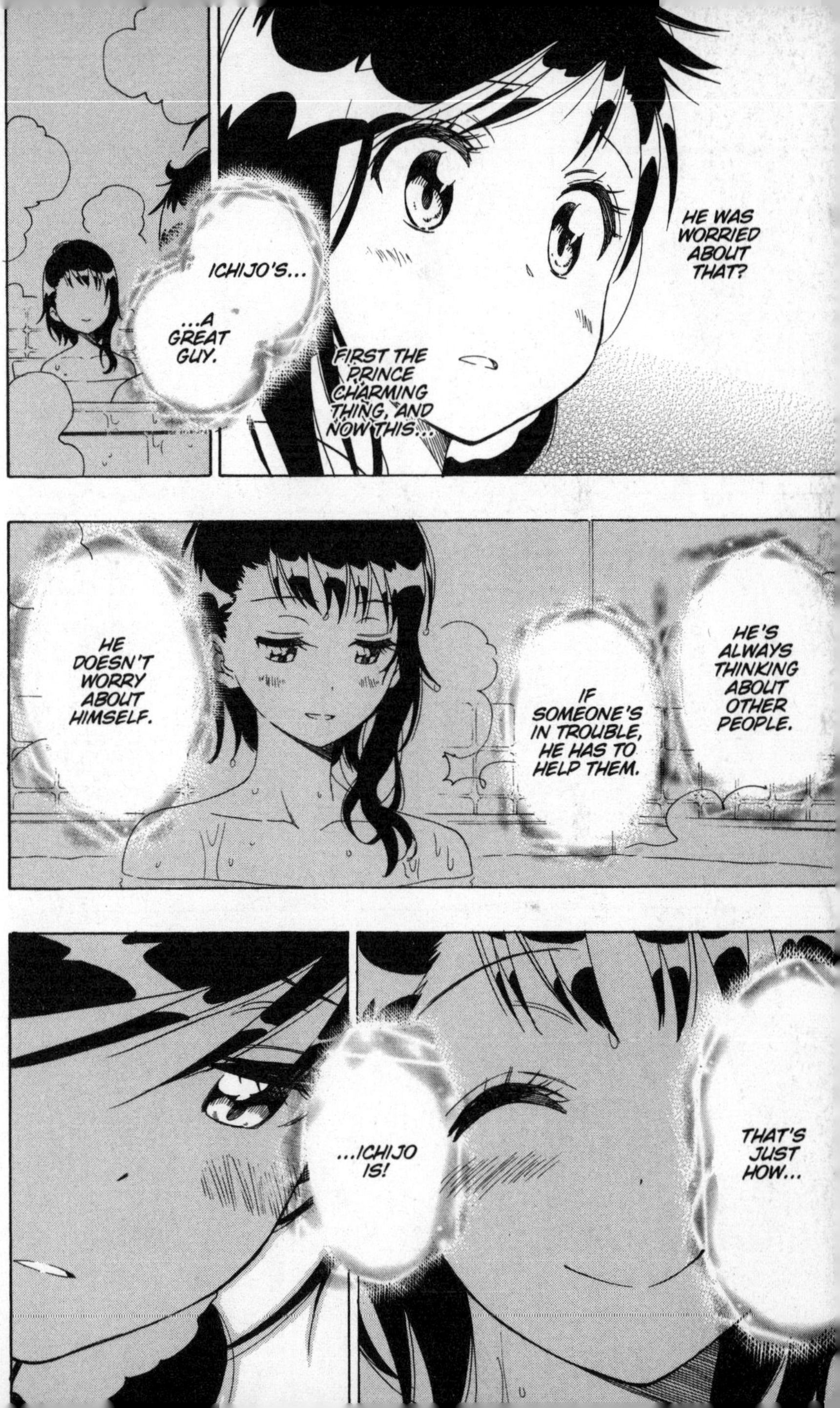
HE WAS WORRIED ABOUT THAT?
FIRST THE PRINCE CHARMING THING, AND NOW THIS...
ICHIJO'S...
...A GREAT GUY.
HE'S ALWAYS THINKING ABOUT OTHER PEOPLE.
IF SOMEONE'S IN TROUBLE, HE HAS TO HELP THEM.
HE DOESN'T WORRY ABOUT HIMSELF.
THAT'S JUST HOW...
...ICHIJO IS!

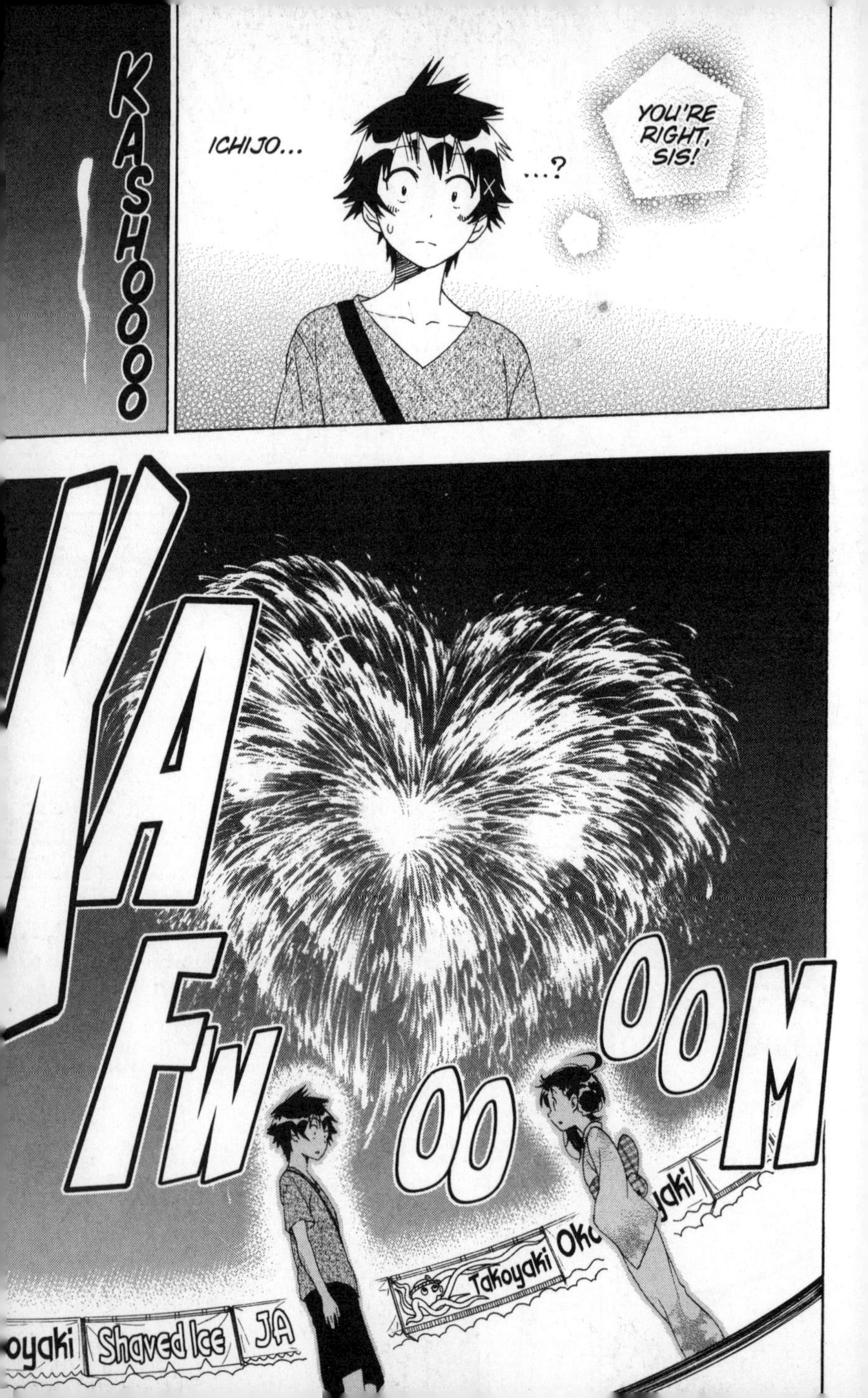
YOU'RE RIGHT, SIS!
...?
ICHIJO...
KASHOOOOO
KA
FWOOOOOM
yaki
Oko
Takoyaki
JA
Shaved Ice
oyaki

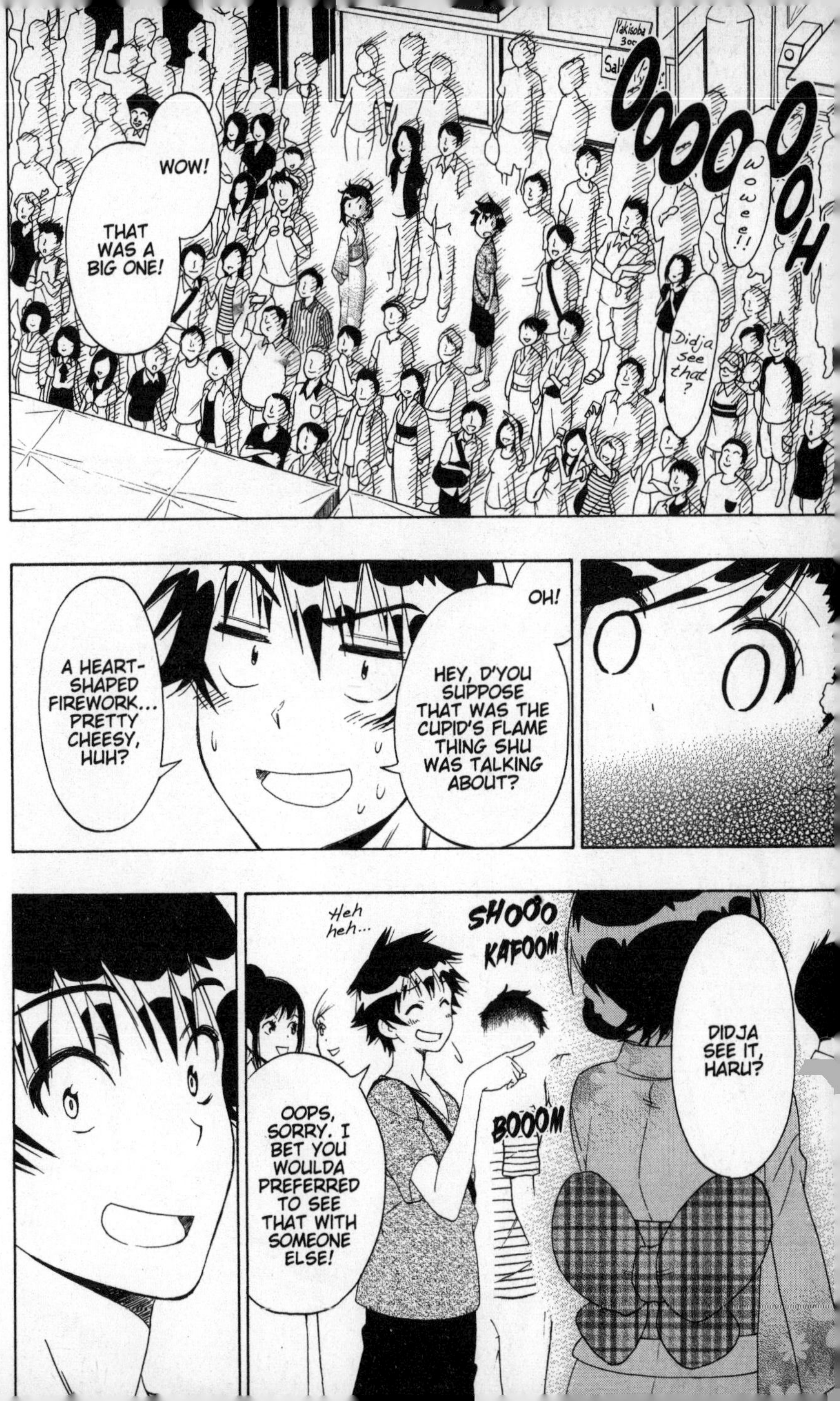
OOOOOOOH
woweee!!
Didja see that?
WOW!
THAT WAS A BIG ONE!
OH!
HEY, D'YOU SUPPOSE THAT WAS THE CUPID'S FLAME THING SHU WAS TALKING ABOUT?
A HEART-SHAPED FIREWORK... PRETTY CHEESY, HUH?
DIDJA SEE IT, HARU?
SHOOO
KAFOOM
BOOOM
Heh heh...
OOPS, SORRY. I BET YOU WOULDA PREFERRED TO SEE THAT WITH SOMEONE ELSE!

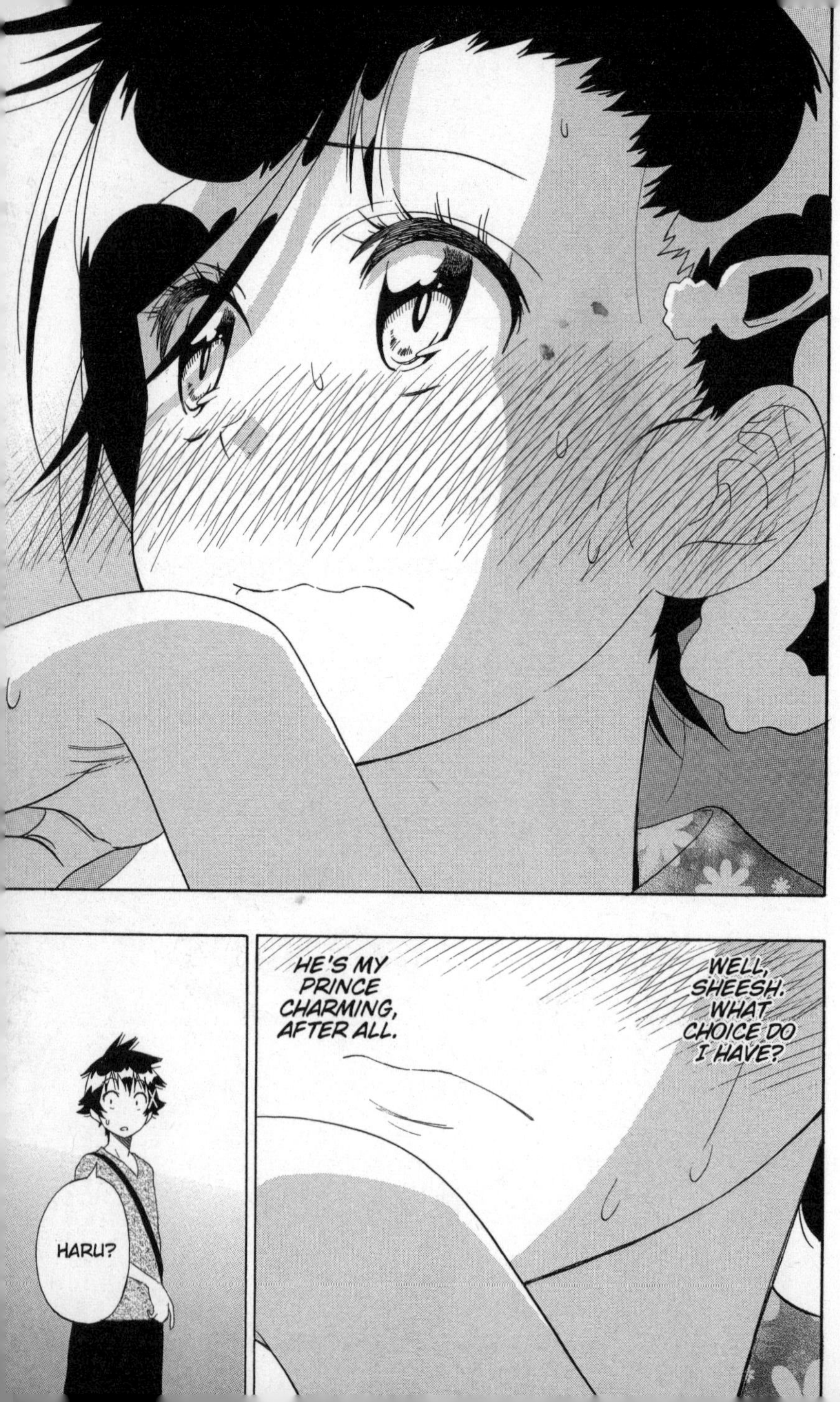
WELL, SHEESH. WHAT CHOICE DO I HAVE?
HE'S MY PRINCE CHARMING, AFTER ALL.
HARU?

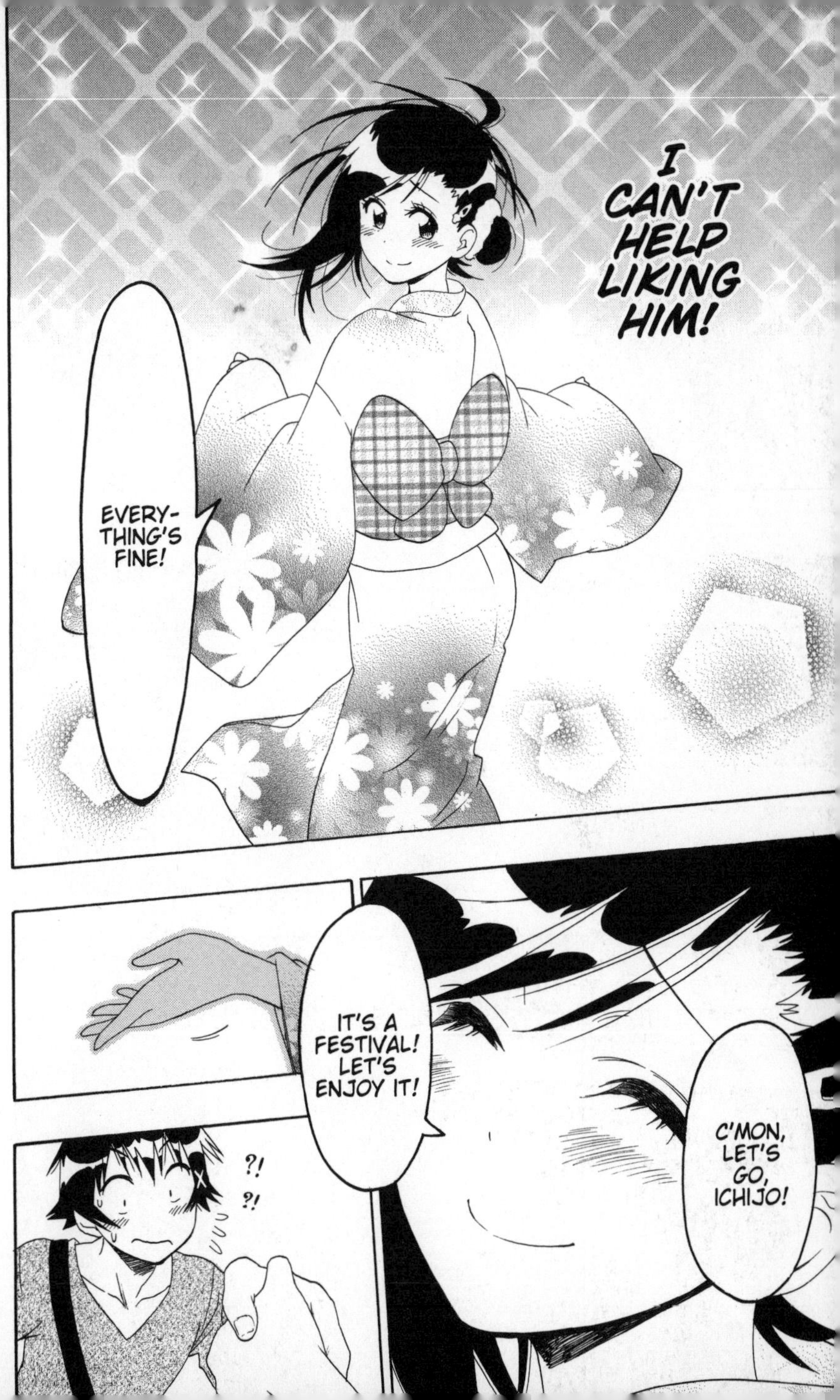
I CAN'T HELP LIKING HIM!
EVERY-THING'S FINE!
IT'S A FESTIVAL! LET'S ENJOY IT!
C'MON, LET'S GO, ICHIJO!
?!
?!

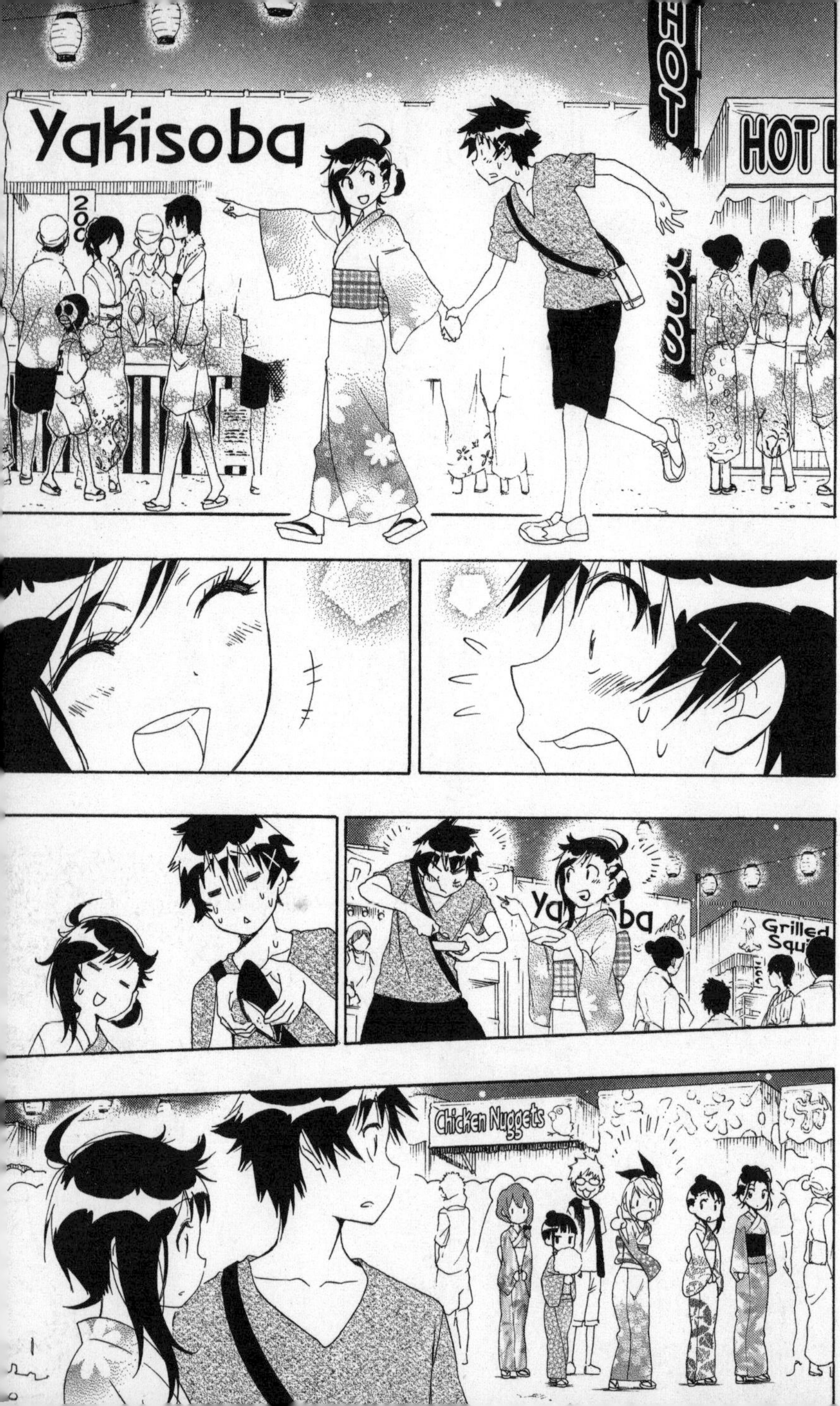
HOT
Yakisoba
Grilled
Chicken Nuggets

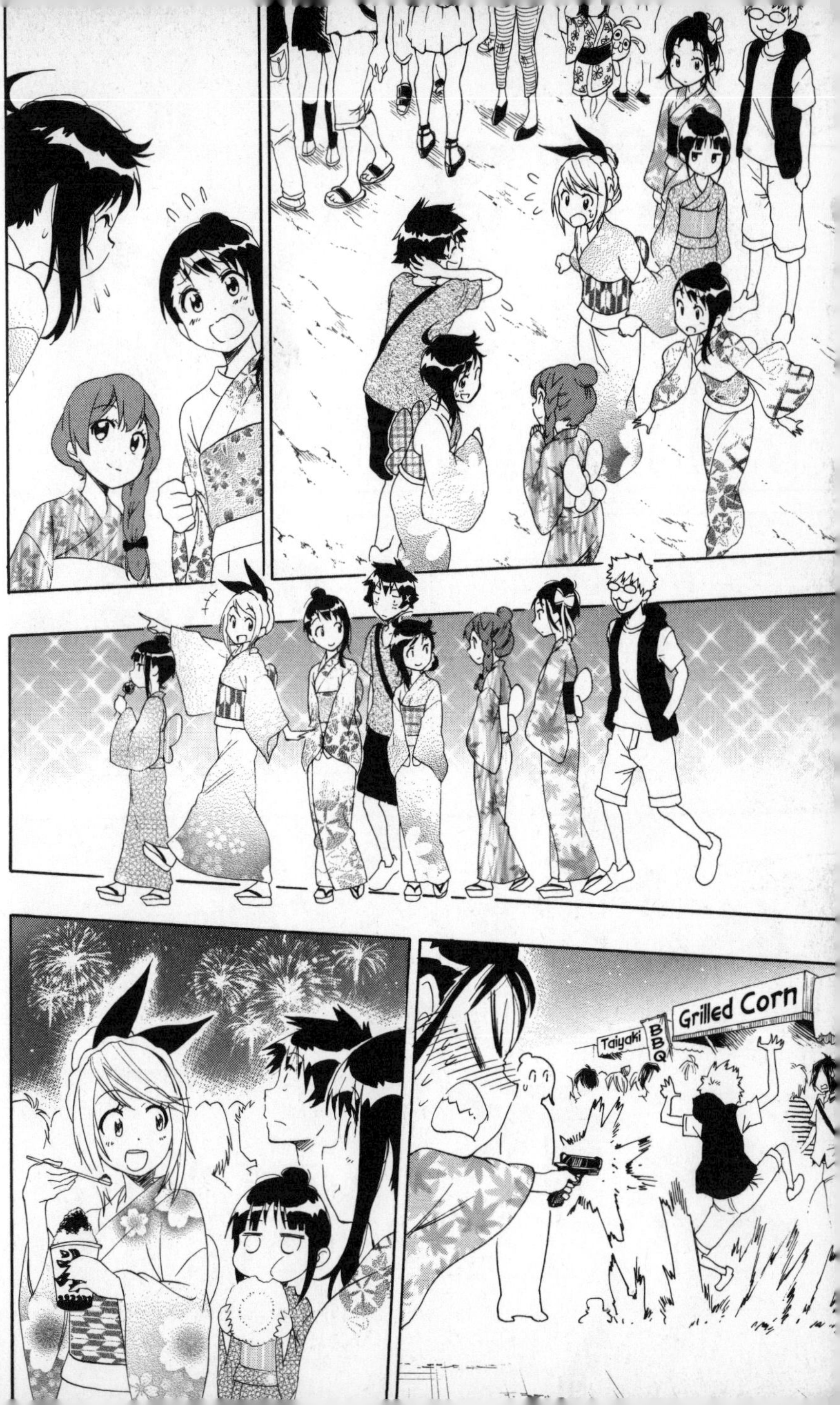
Grilled Corn
Taiyaki
BBQ

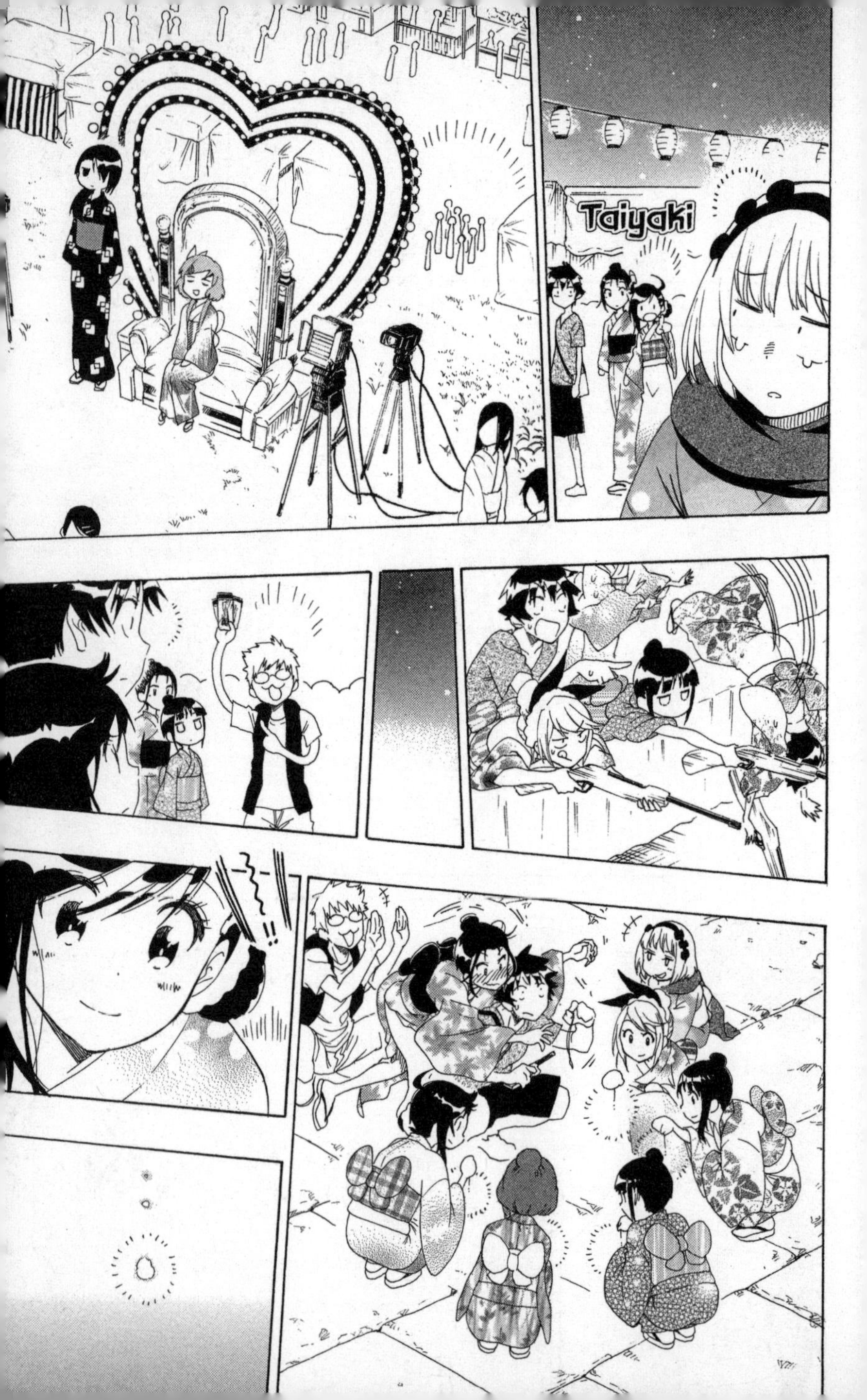
Taiyaki
!!

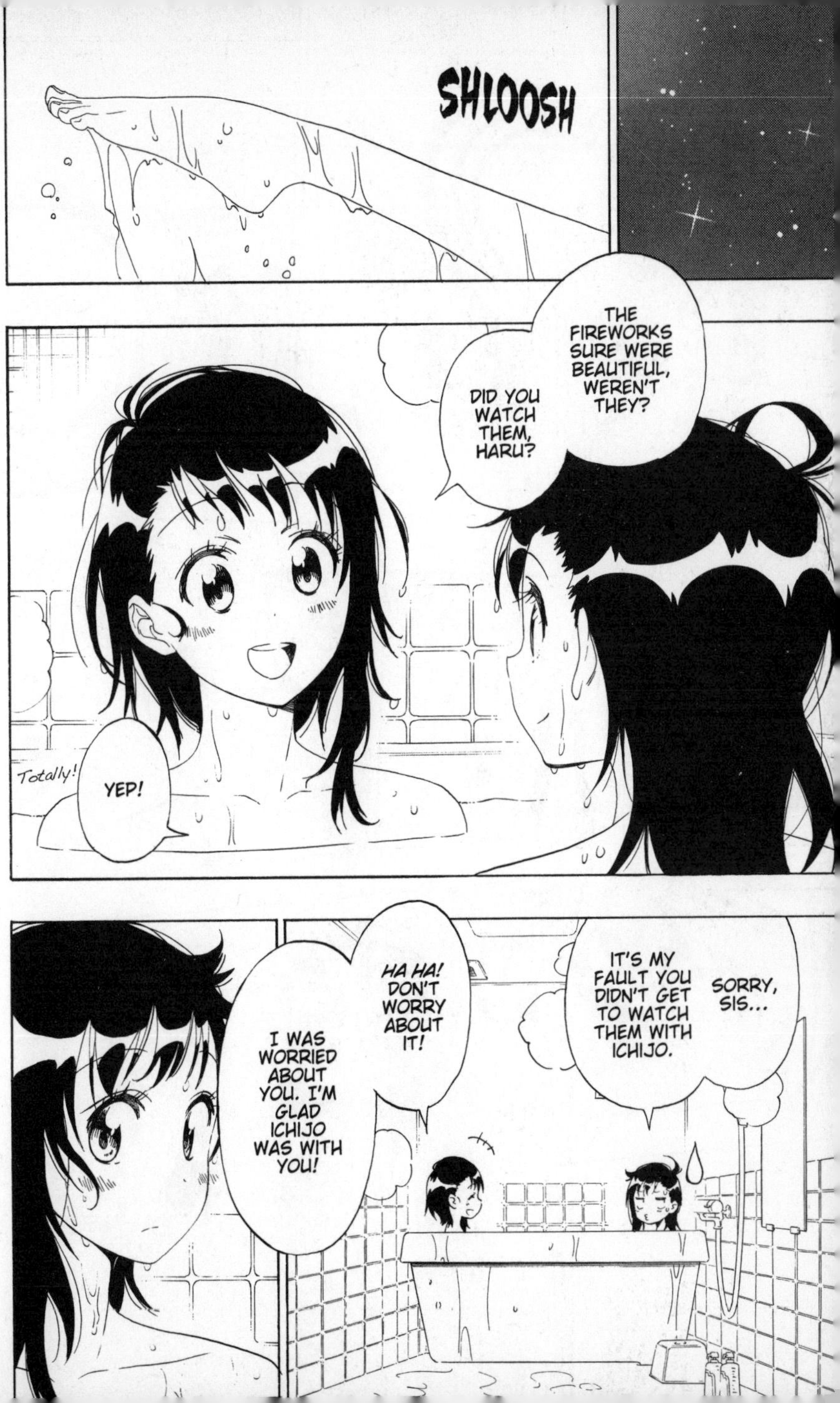
SHLOOSH
THE FIREWORKS SURE WERE BEAUTIFUL, WEREN'T THEY?
DID YOU WATCH THEM, HARU?
YEP!
Totally!
SORRY, SIS...
IT'S MY FAULT YOU DIDN'T GET TO WATCH THEM WITH ICHIJO.
HA HA! DON'T WORRY ABOUT IT!
I WAS WORRIED ABOUT YOU. I'M GLAD ICHIJO WAS WITH YOU!

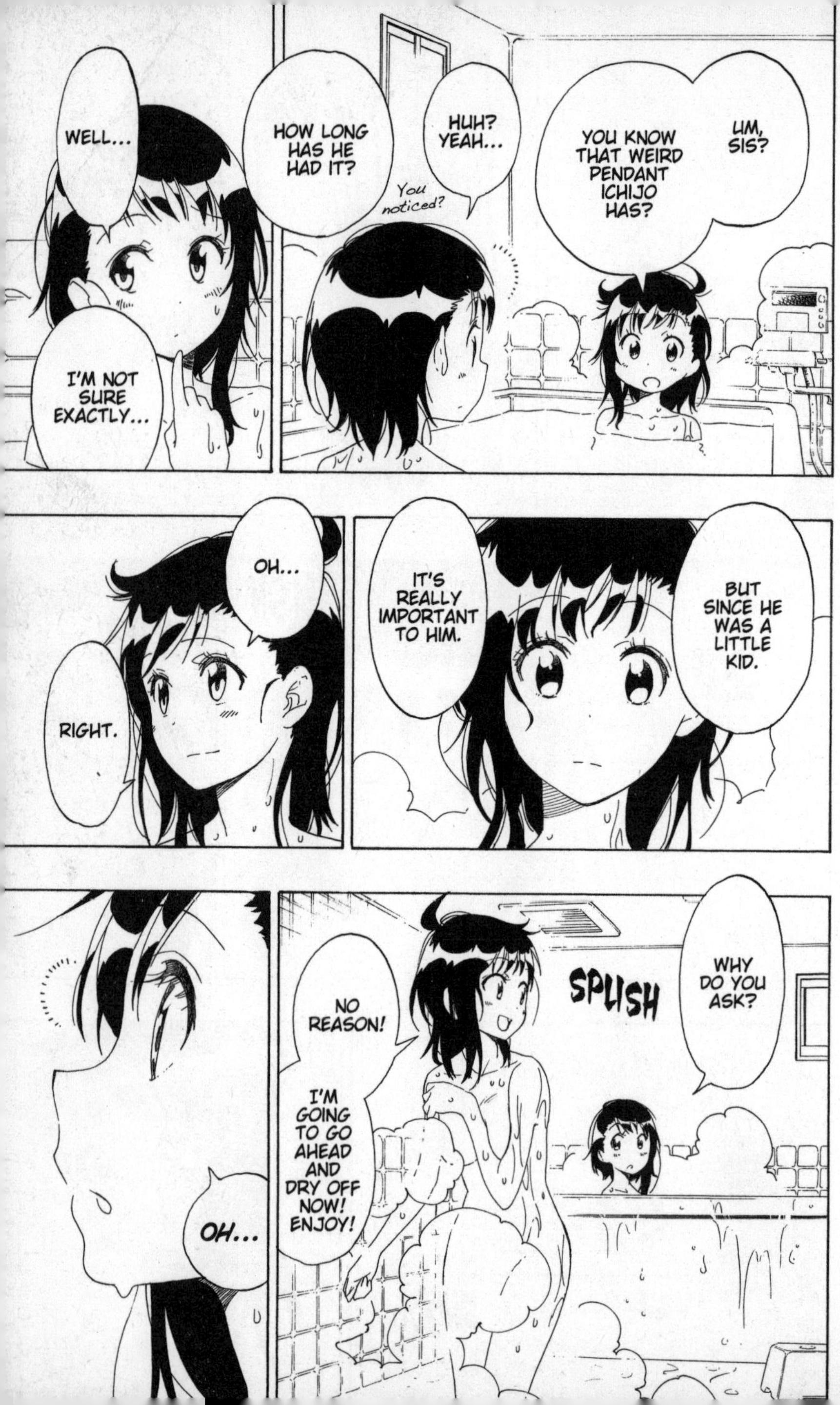
UM, SIS?
YOU KNOW THAT WEIRD PENDANT ICHIJO HAS?
HUH? YEAH...
You noticed?
HOW LONG HAS HE HAD IT?
WELL...
I'M NOT SURE EXACTLY...
BUT SINCE HE WAS A LITTLE KID.
IT'S REALLY IMPORTANT TO HIM.
OH...
RIGHT.
WHY DO YOU ASK?
SPLISH
NO REASON!
I'M GOING TO GO AHEAD AND DRY OFF NOW! ENJOY!
OH...

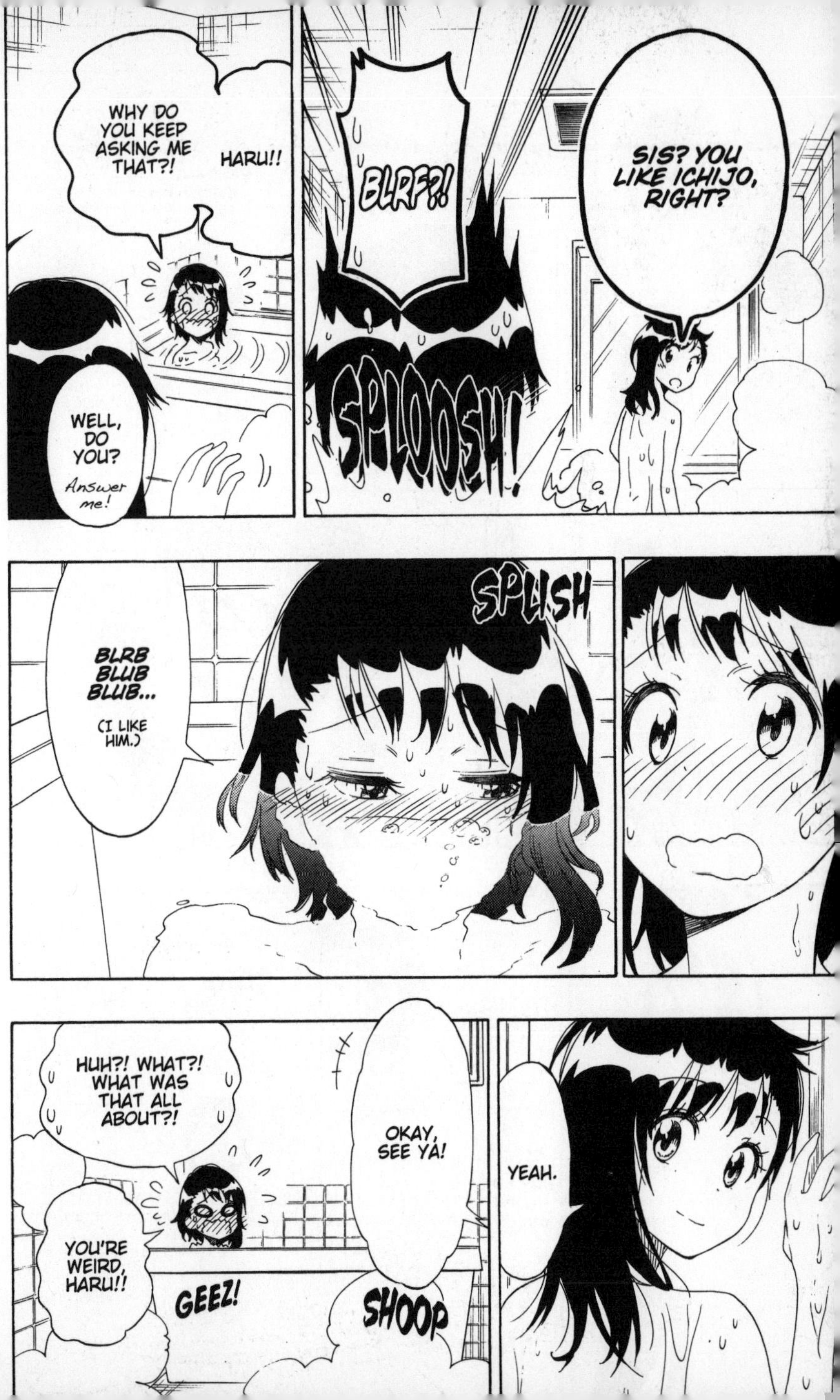
SIS? YOU LIKE ICHIJO, RIGHT?
BLRF?!
SPLOOSH!
WHY DO YOU KEEP ASKING ME THAT?! HARU!!
WELL, DO YOU?
Answer me!
SPLISH
BLRB BLUB BLUB...
(I LIKE HIM.)
YEAH.
OKAY, SEE YA!
SHOOP
HUH?! WHAT?! WHAT WAS THAT ALL ABOUT?!
GEEZ!
YOU'RE WEIRD, HARU!!

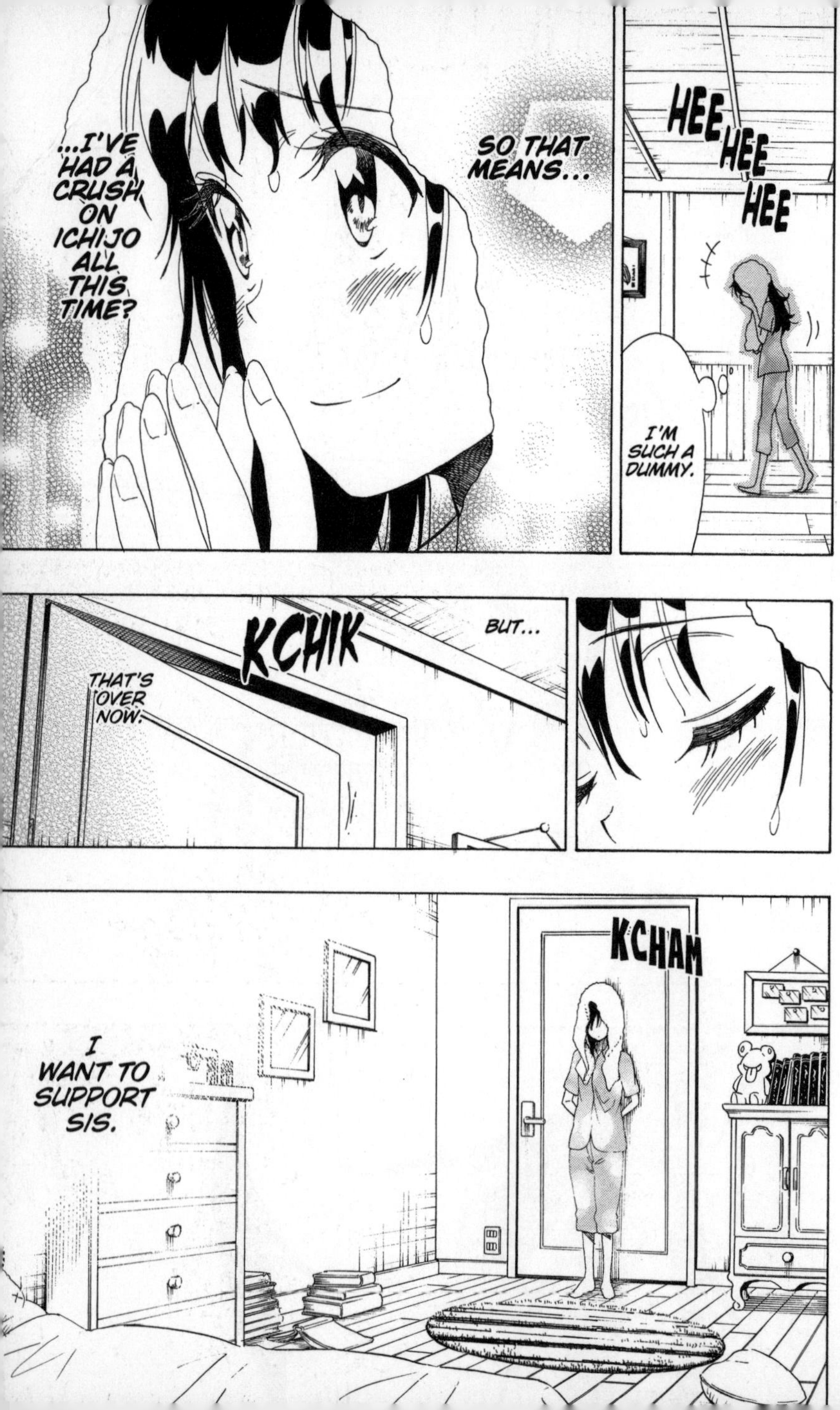
HEE HEE HEE
I'M SUCH A DUMMY.
SO THAT MEANS...
...I'VE HAD A CRUSH ON ICHIJO ALL THIS TIME?
BUT...
KCHIK
THAT'S OVER NOW.
KCHAM
I WANT TO SUPPORT SIS.

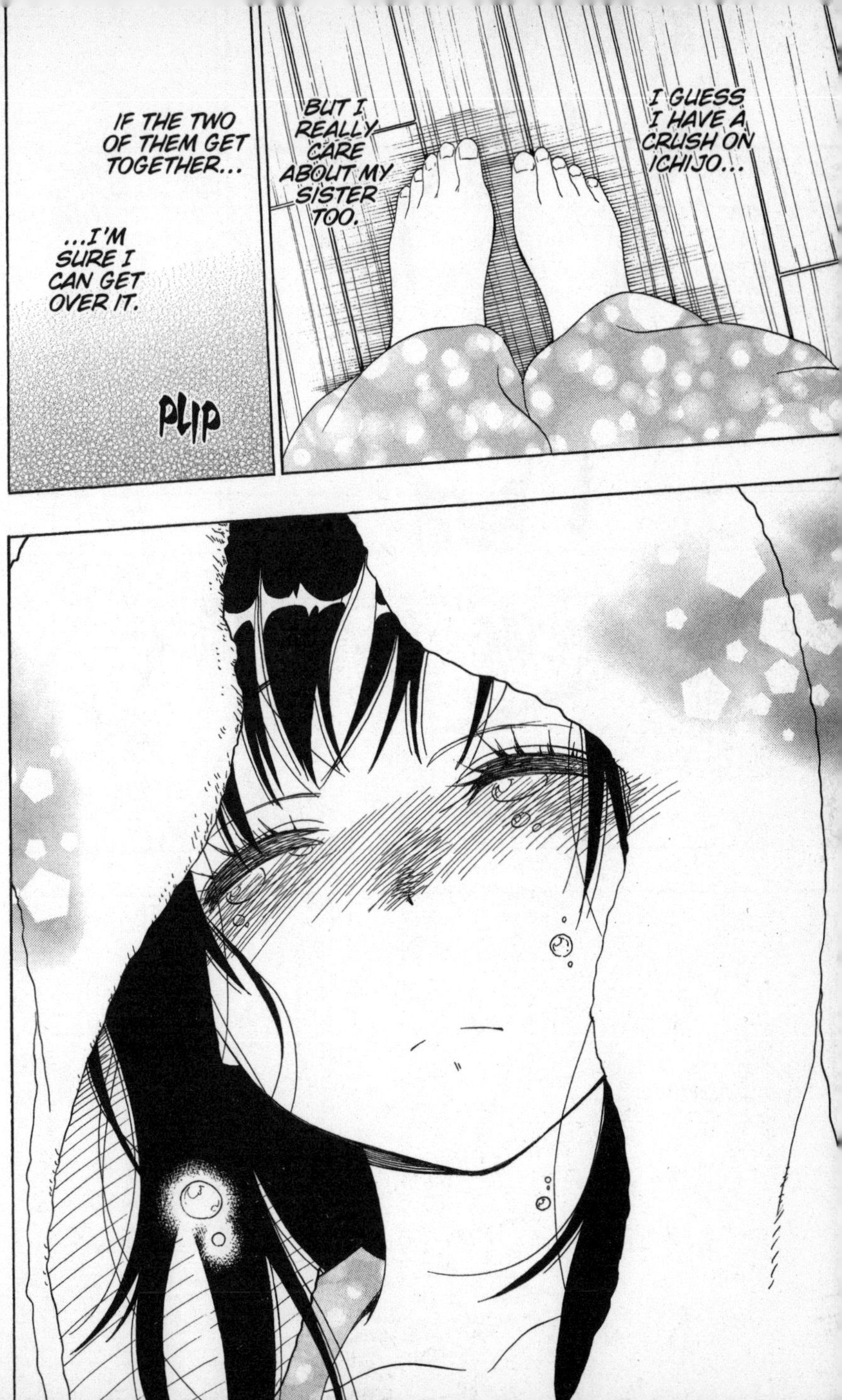
I GUESS I HAVE A CRUSH ON ICHIJO...
BUT I REALLY CARE ABOUT MY SISTER TOO.
IF THE TWO OF THEM GET TOGETHER...
...I'M SURE I CAN GET OVER IT.
PLIP

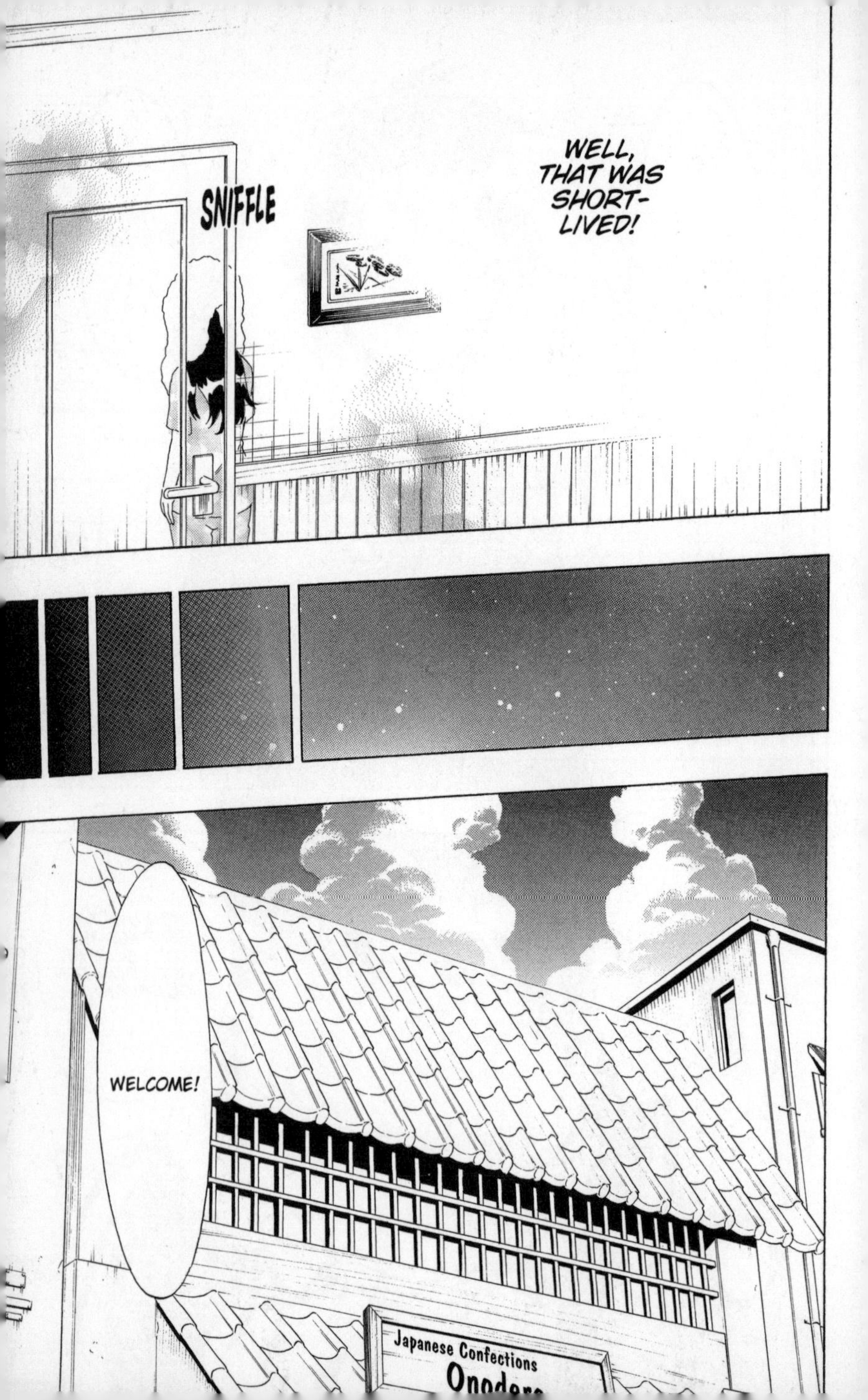
WELL, THAT WAS SHORT-LIVED!
SNIFFLE
WELCOME!
Japanese Confections
Onodera

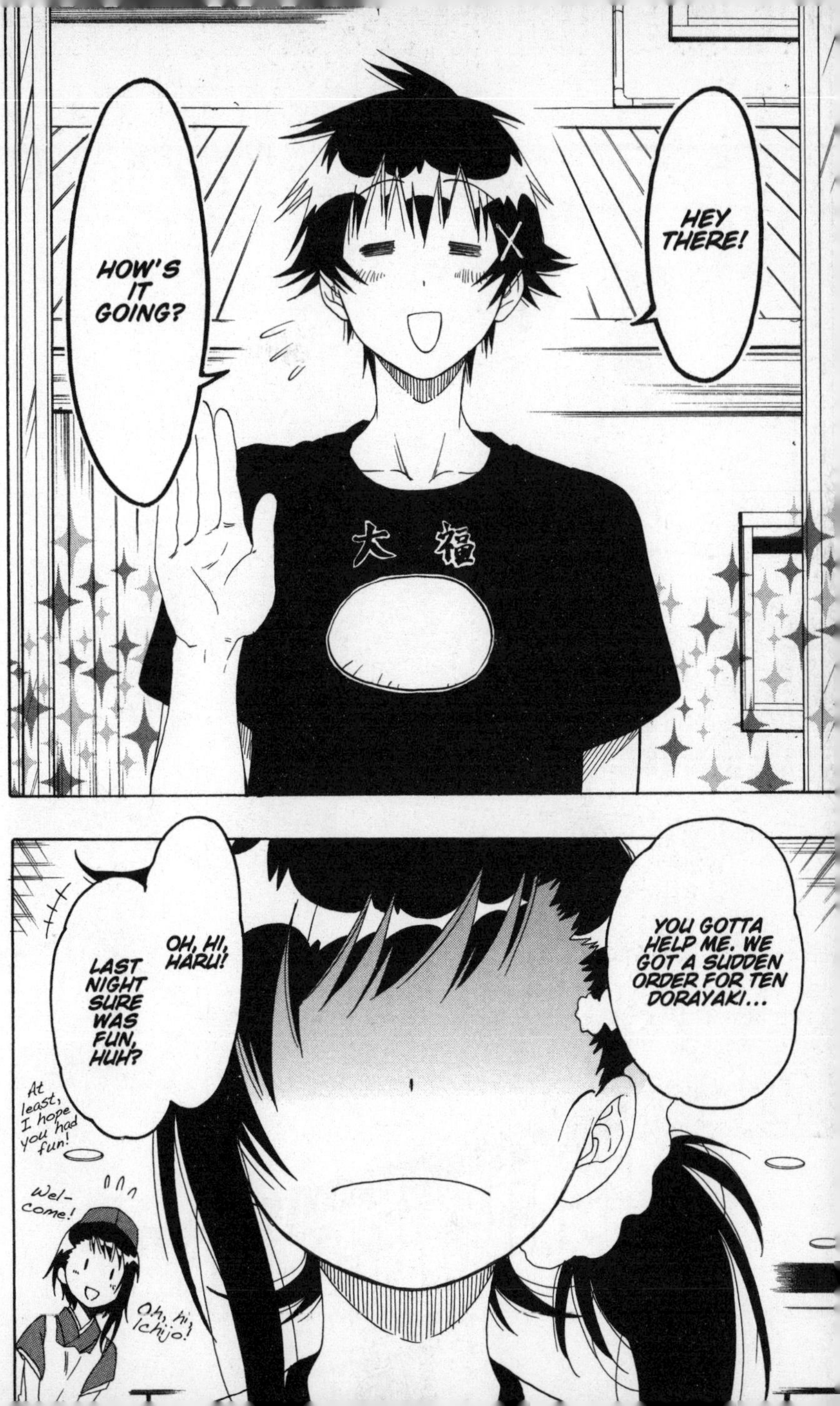
HEY THERE!
HOW'S IT GOING?
大福
YOU GOTTA HELP ME. WE GOT A SUDDEN ORDER FOR TEN DORAYAKI...
OH, HI, HARU!
LAST NIGHT SURE WAS FUN, HUH?
At least, I hope you had fun!
Wel-come!
Oh, hi, Ichijo!

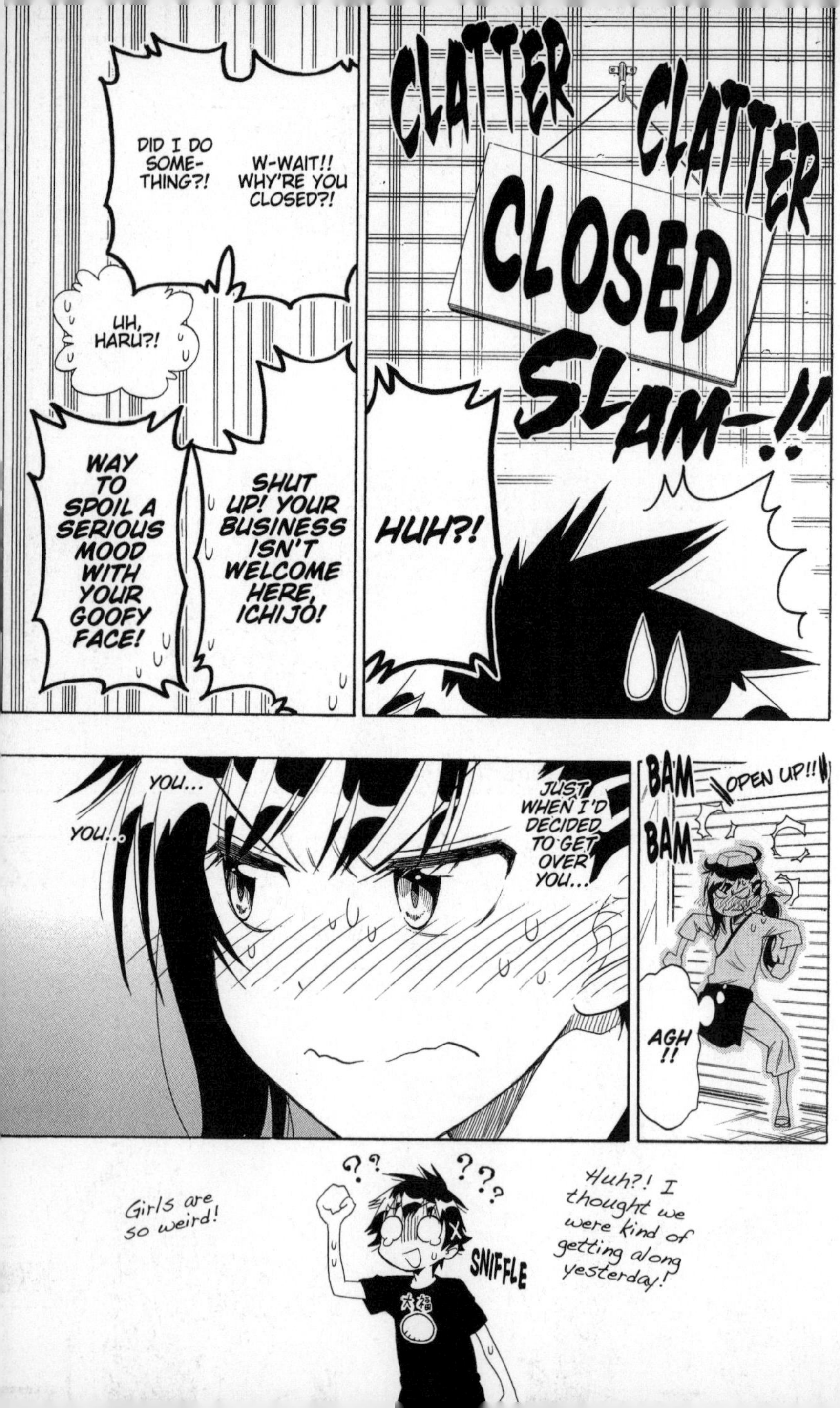
CLATTER
CLATTER
CLOSED
SLAM-!!
HUH?!
W-WAIT!! WHY'RE YOU CLOSED?!
DID I DO SOME-THING?!
UH, HARU?!
SHUT UP! YOUR BUSINESS ISN'T WELCOME HERE, ICHIJO!
WAY TO SPOIL A SERIOUS MOOD WITH YOUR GOOFY FACE!
OPEN UP!!
BAM
BAM
AGH !!
JUST WHEN I'D DECIDED TO GET OVER YOU...
YOU...
YOU...
Huh?! I thought we were kind of getting along yesterday!
SNIFFLE
Girls are so weird!

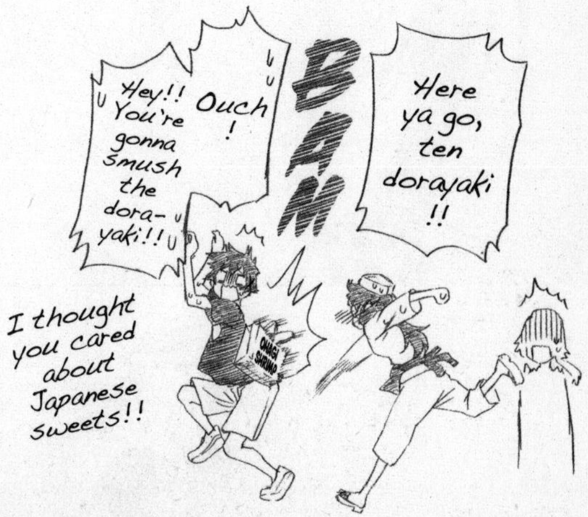
Here ya go, ten dorayaki!!
BAM
Ouch!
Hey!! You're gonna smush the dora-yaki!!
I thought you cared about Japanese sweets!!

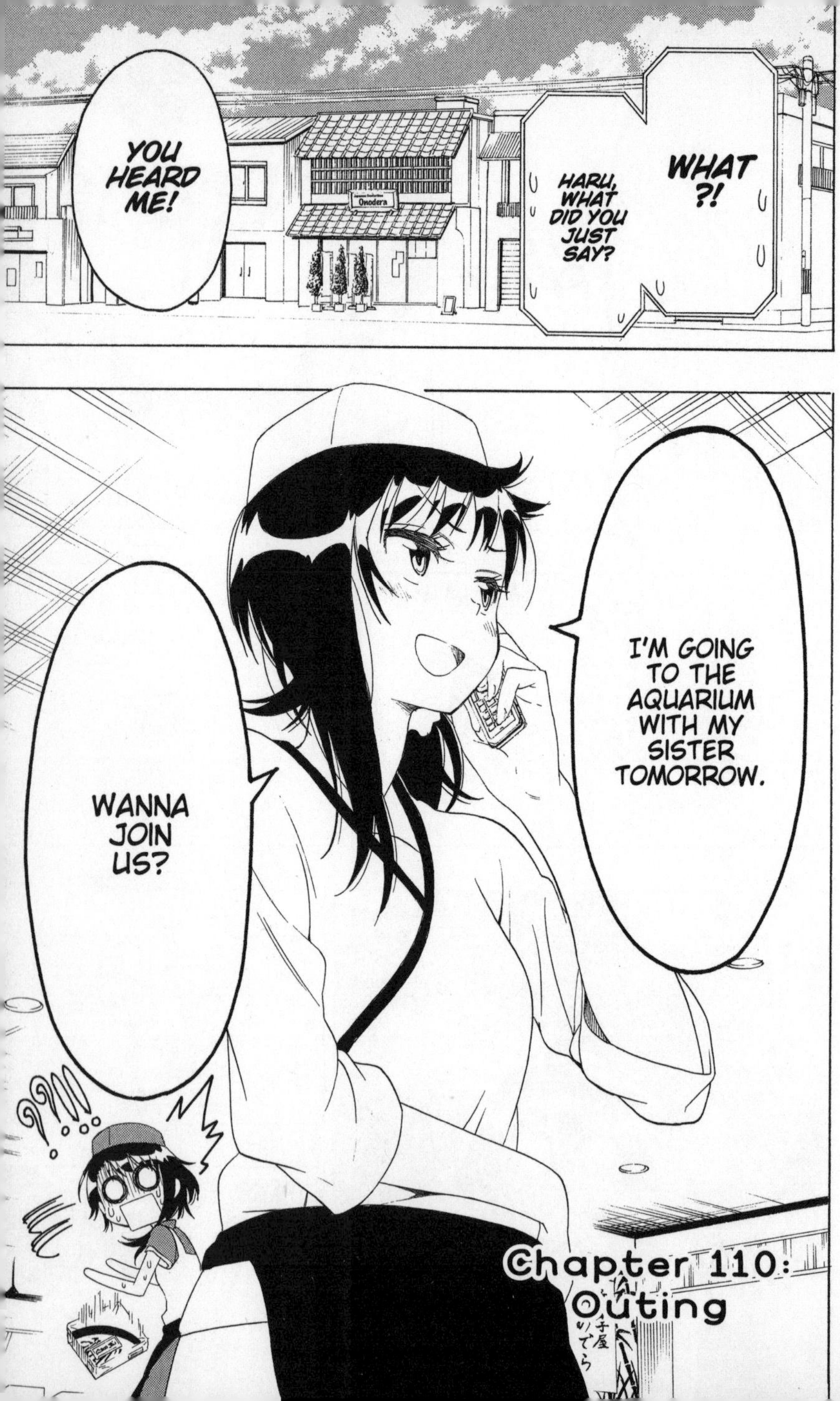
Onodera
WHAT?!
HARU, WHAT DID YOU JUST SAY?
YOU HEARD ME!
I'M GOING TO THE AQUARIUM WITH MY SISTER TOMORROW.
WANNA JOIN US?
??!!

Chapter 110: Outing

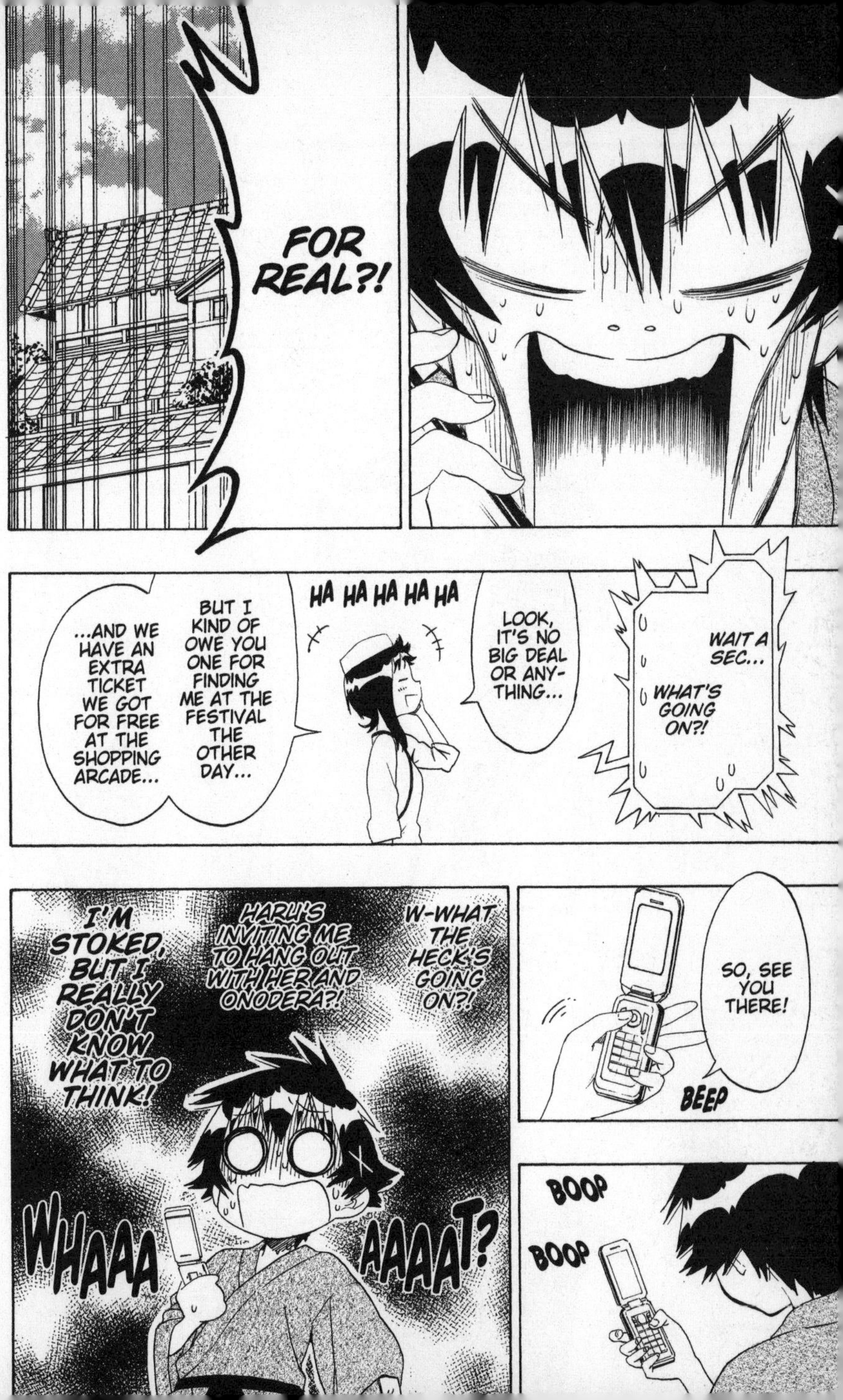
FOR REAL?!
WAIT A SEC... WHAT'S GOING ON?!
LOOK, IT'S NO BIG DEAL OR ANYTHING...
HA HA HA HA HA
BUT I KIND OF OWE YOU ONE FOR FINDING ME AT THE FESTIVAL THE OTHER DAY...
...AND WE HAVE AN EXTRA TICKET WE GOT FOR FREE AT THE SHOPPING ARCADE...
SO, SEE YOU THERE!
BEEP
BOOP
BOOP
W-WHAT THE HECK'S GOING ON?!
HARU'S INVITING ME TO HANG OUT WITH HER AND ONODERA?!
I'M STOKED, BUT I REALLY DON'T KNOW WHAT TO THINK!
WHAAAA
AAAAT?

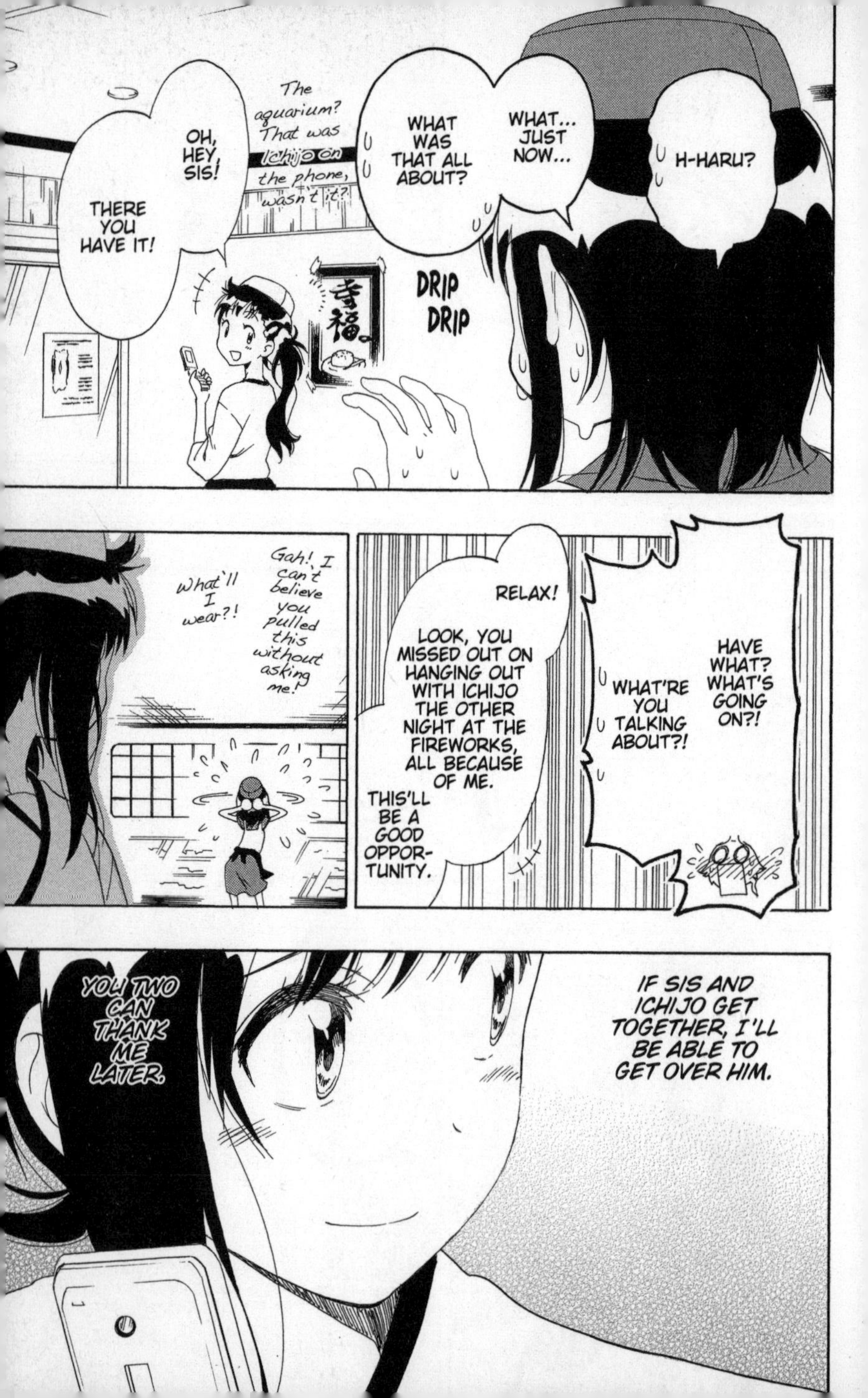
H-HARU?
WHAT... JUST NOW...
WHAT WAS THAT ALL ABOUT?
DRIP DRIP
The aquarium? That was Ichijo on the phone, wasn't it?
OH, HEY, SIS!
THERE YOU HAVE IT!
HAVE WHAT? WHAT'S GOING ON?!
WHAT'RE YOU TALKING ABOUT?!
RELAX!
LOOK, YOU MISSED OUT ON HANGING OUT WITH ICHIJO THE OTHER NIGHT AT THE FIREWORKS, ALL BECAUSE OF ME.
THIS'LL BE A GOOD OPPORTUNITY.
Gah! I can't believe you pulled this without asking me!
What'll I wear?!
IF SIS AND ICHIJO GET TOGETHER, I'LL BE ABLE TO GET OVER HIM.
YOU TWO CAN THANK ME LATER.

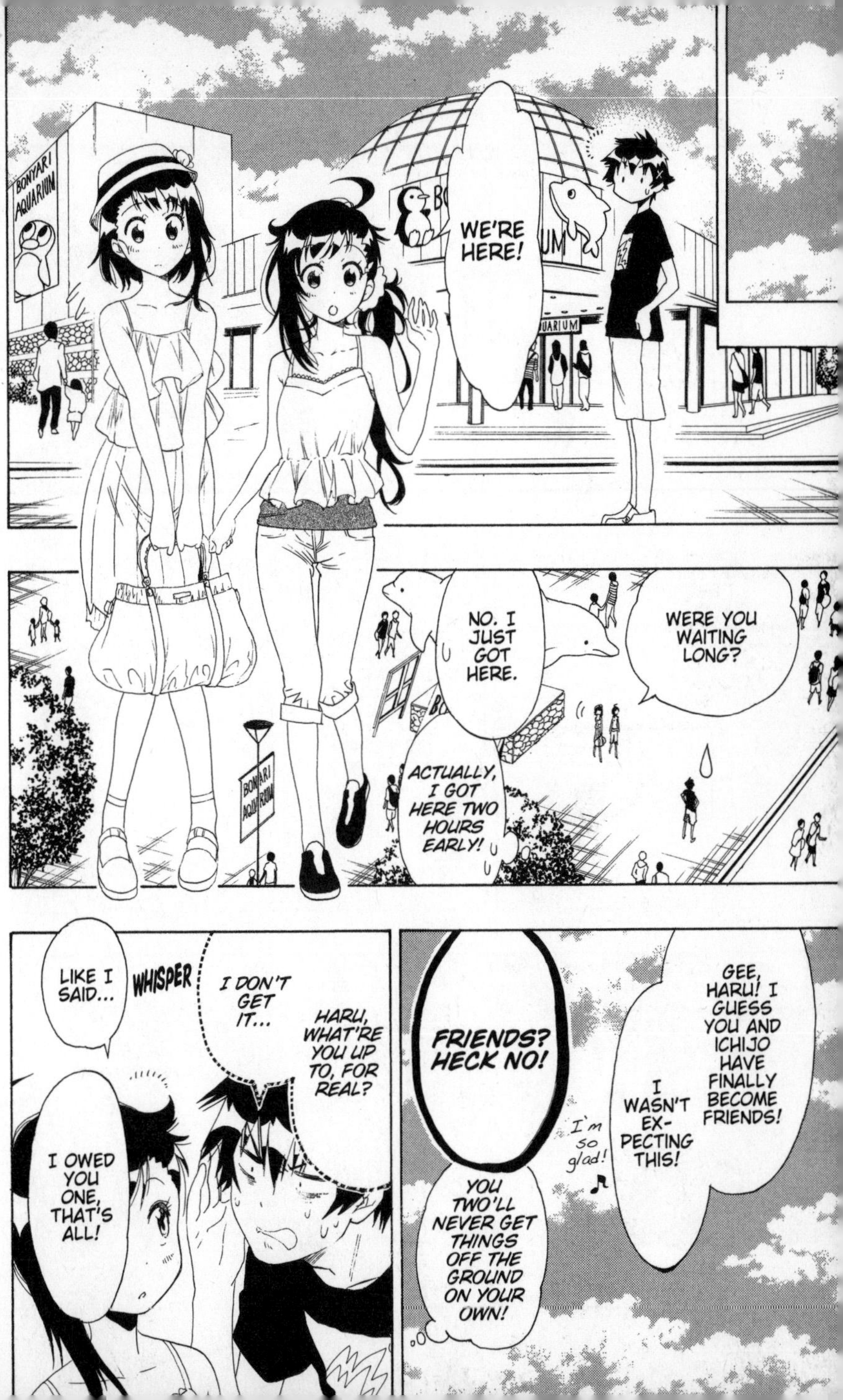
BONYARI AQUARIUM
WE'RE HERE!
WERE YOU WAITING LONG?
NO. I JUST GOT HERE.
ACTUALLY, I GOT HERE TWO HOURS EARLY!
BONYARI AQUARIUM
GEE, HARU! I GUESS YOU AND ICHIJO HAVE FINALLY BECOME FRIENDS!
I WASN'T EX-PECTING THIS!
I'm so glad!
FRIENDS? HECK NO!
YOU TWO'LL NEVER GET THINGS OFF THE GROUND ON YOUR OWN!
HARU, WHAT'RE YOU UP TO, FOR REAL?
I DON'T GET IT...
WHISPER
LIKE I SAID...
I OWED YOU ONE, THAT'S ALL!

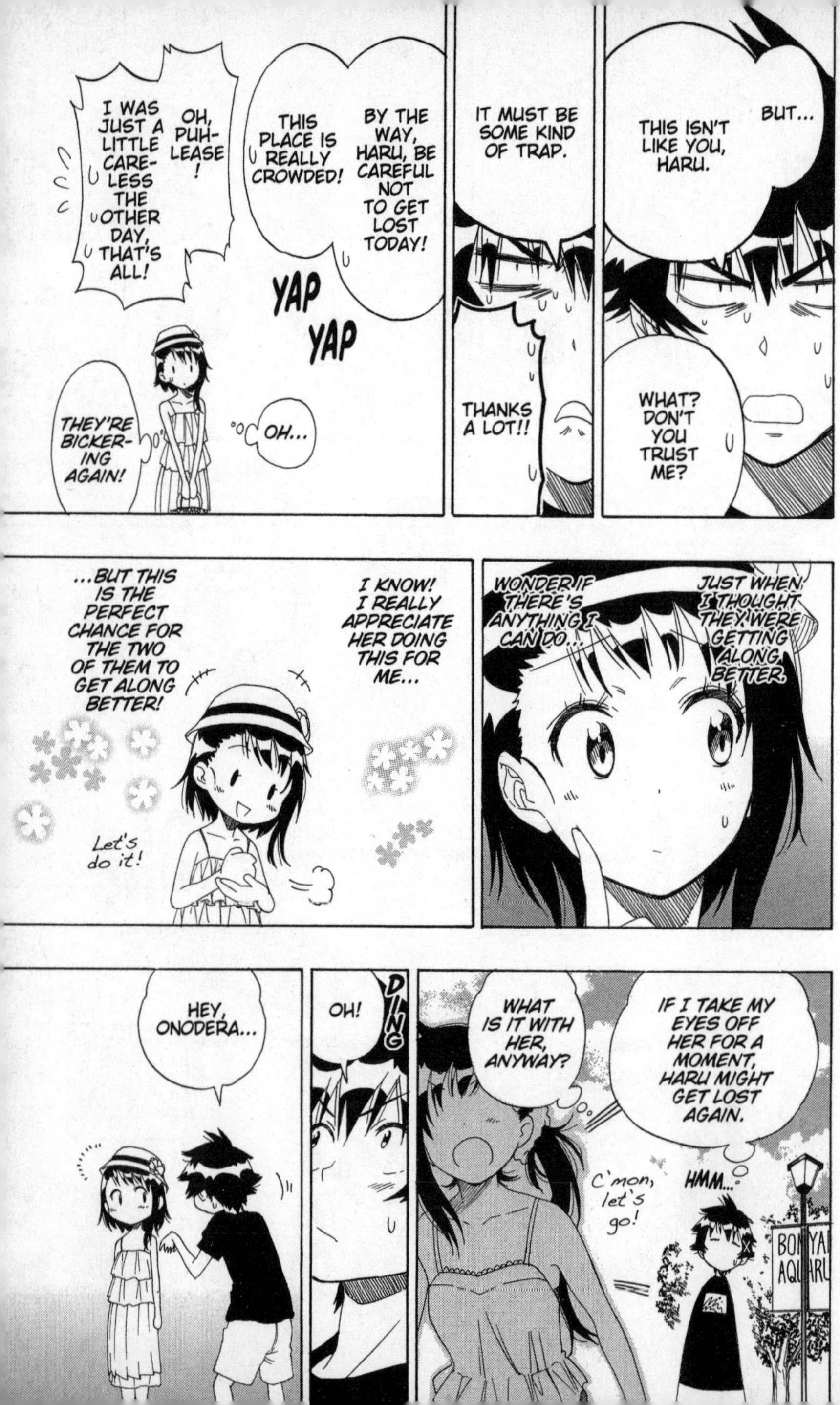
BUT...
THIS ISN'T LIKE YOU, HARU.
WHAT? DON'T YOU TRUST ME?
IT MUST BE SOME KIND OF TRAP.
THANKS A LOT!!
BY THE WAY, HARU, BE CAREFUL NOT TO GET LOST TODAY!
THIS PLACE IS REALLY CROWDED!
OH, PUH-LEASE!
I WAS JUST A LITTLE CARELESS THE OTHER DAY, THAT'S ALL!
YAP
YAP
OH...
THEY'RE BICKERING AGAIN!
JUST WHEN I THOUGHT THEY WERE GETTING ALONG BETTER.
WONDER IF THERE'S ANYTHING I CAN DO...
I KNOW! I REALLY APPRECIATE HER DOING THIS FOR ME...
...BUT THIS IS THE PERFECT CHANCE FOR THE TWO OF THEM TO GET ALONG BETTER!
Let's do it!
IF I TAKE MY EYES OFF HER FOR A MOMENT, HARU MIGHT GET LOST AGAIN.
WHAT IS IT WITH HER, ANYWAY?
HMM...
C'mon, let's go!
DING
OH!
HEY, ONODERA...

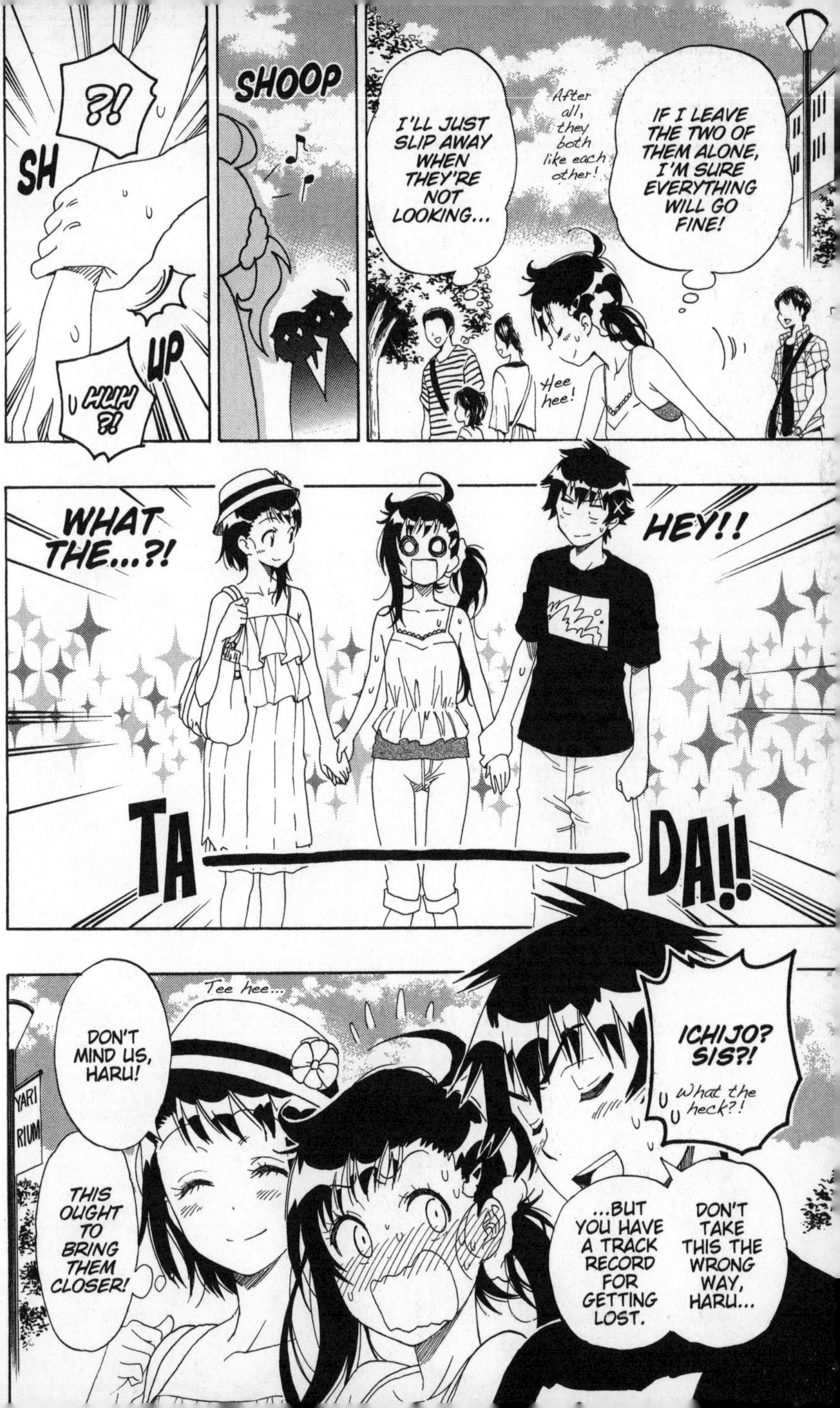
IF I LEAVE THE TWO OF THEM ALONE, I'M SURE EVERYTHING WILL GO FINE!
After all, they both like each other!
I'LL JUST SLIP AWAY WHEN THEY'RE NOT LOOKING...
Hee hee!
SHOOP
?!
SH
UP
HUH ?!
HEY!!
WHAT THE...?!
TA—DA!!
ICHIJO? SIS?!
What the heck?!
DON'T TAKE THIS THE WRONG WAY, HARU...
...BUT YOU HAVE A TRACK RECORD FOR GETTING LOST.
Tee hee...
DON'T MIND US, HARU!
THIS OUGHT TO BRING THEM CLOSER!

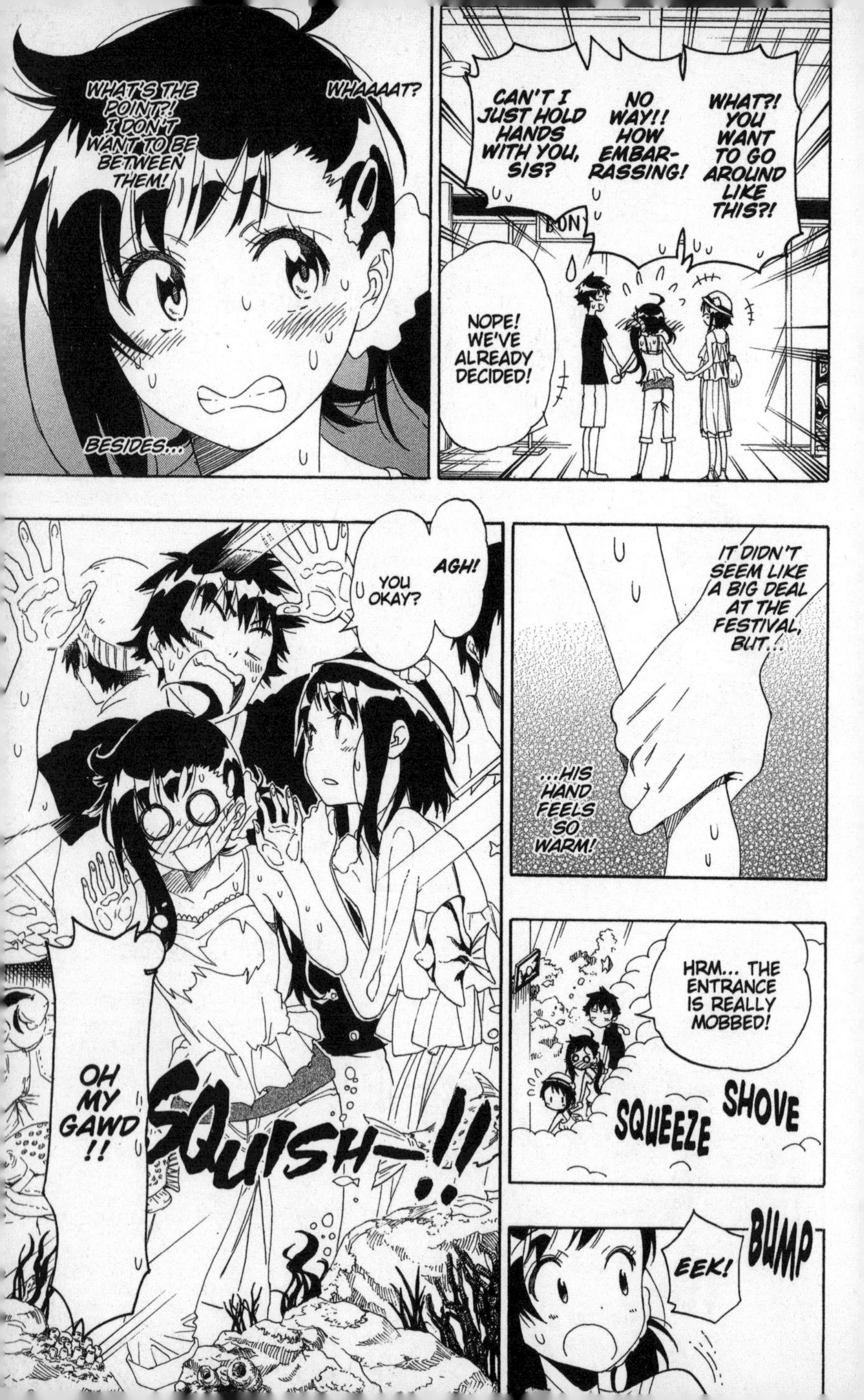
WHAT?! YOU WANT TO GO AROUND LIKE THIS?!
NO WAY!! HOW EMBARRASSING!
CAN'T I JUST HOLD HANDS WITH YOU, SIS?
NOPE! WE'VE ALREADY DECIDED!
WHAAAAT?
WHAT'S THE POINT?! I DON'T WANT TO BE BETWEEN THEM!
BESIDES...
IT DIDN'T SEEM LIKE A BIG DEAL AT THE FESTIVAL, BUT...
...HIS HAND FEELS SO WARM!
HRM... THE ENTRANCE IS REALLY MOBBED!
SHOVE
SQUEEZE
BUMP
EEK!
AGH!
YOU OKAY?
SQUISH—!!
OH MY GAWD!!

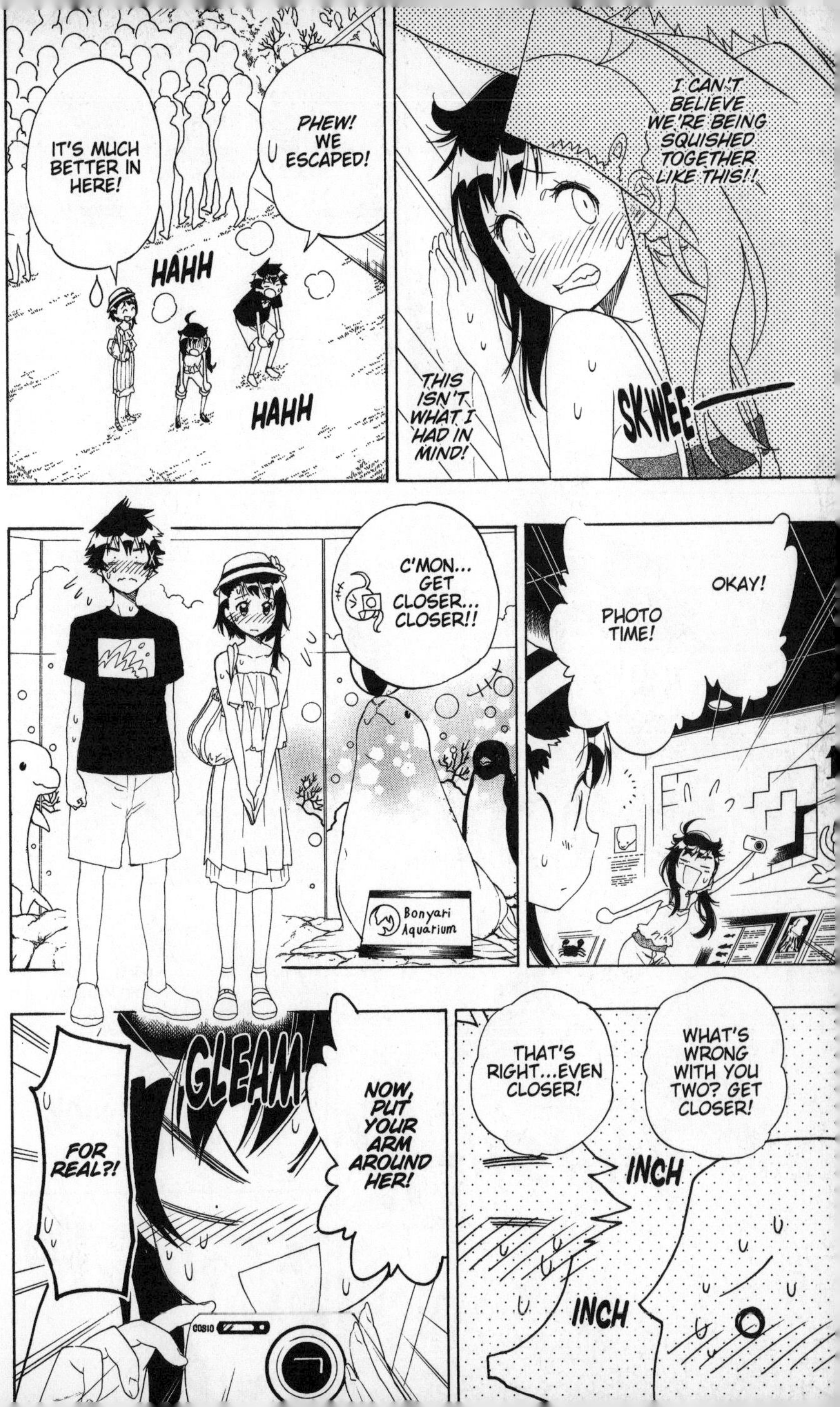
I CAN'T BELIEVE WE'RE BEING SQUISHED TOGETHER LIKE THIS!!
THIS ISN'T WHAT I HAD IN MIND!
SKWEE
PHEW! WE ESCAPED!
IT'S MUCH BETTER IN HERE!
HAHH
HAHH
OKAY!
PHOTO TIME!
C'MON... GET CLOSER... CLOSER!!
Bonyari Aquarium
WHAT'S WRONG WITH YOU TWO? GET CLOSER!
THAT'S RIGHT...EVEN CLOSER!
INCH
INCH
GLEAM
NOW, PUT YOUR ARM AROUND HER!
FOR REAL?!

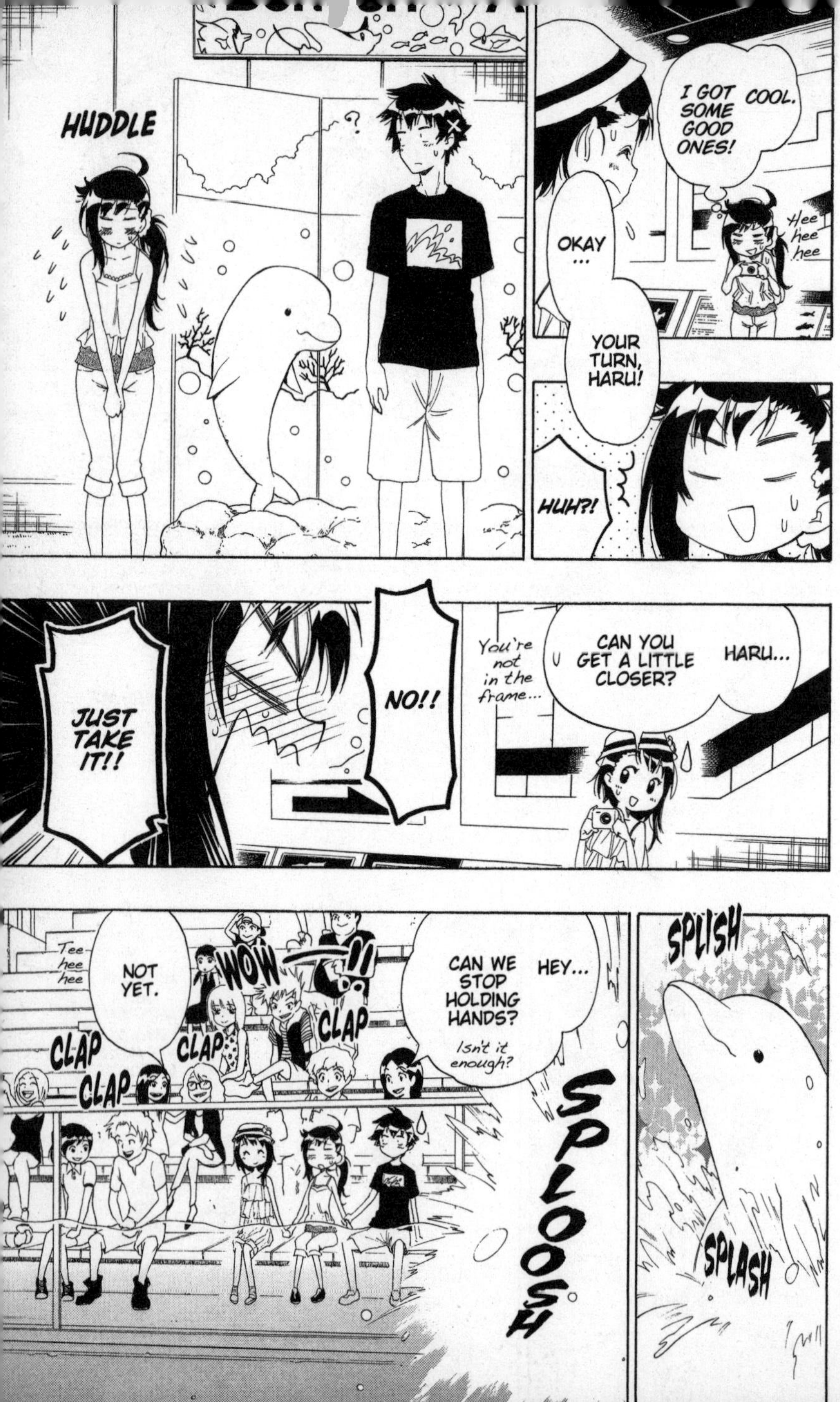
COOL.
I GOT SOME GOOD ONES!
Hee hee hee
OKAY...
YOUR TURN, HARU!
HUH?!
HUDDLE
HARU...
CAN YOU GET A LITTLE CLOSER?
You're not in the frame...
NO!!
JUST TAKE IT!!
SPLISH
SPLASH
SPLOOSH
HEY...
CAN WE STOP HOLDING HANDS?
Isn't it enough?
WOW
CLAP
CLAP
NOT YET.
Tee hee hee
CLAP
CLAP

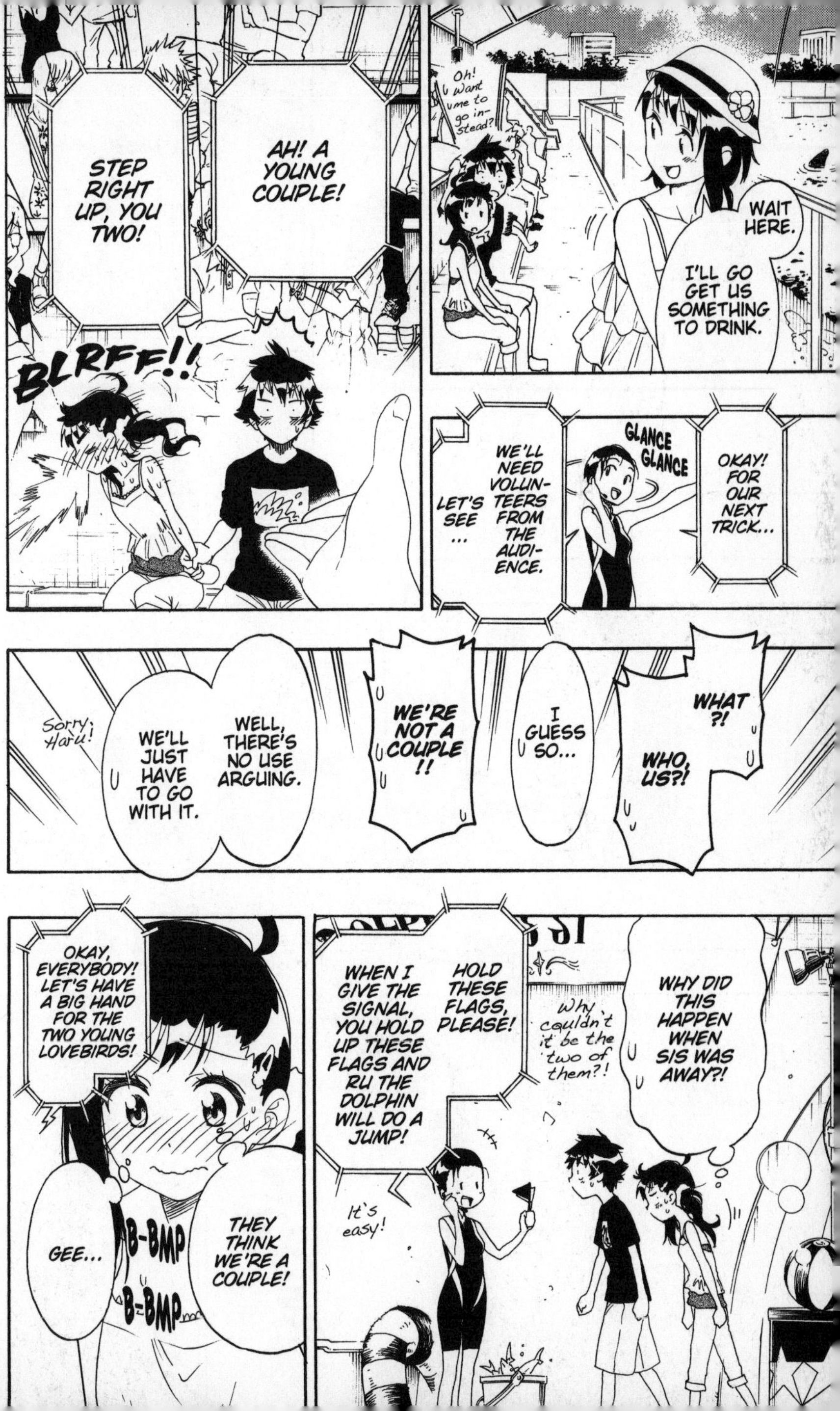
WAIT HERE.
I'LL GO GET US SOMETHING TO DRINK.
Oh! Want me to go instead?
OKAY! FOR OUR NEXT TRICK...
GLANCE GLANCE
WE'LL NEED VOLUNTEERS FROM THE AUDIENCE.
LET'S SEE...
AH! A YOUNG COUPLE!
STEP RIGHT UP, YOU TWO!
BLRFF!!
WHAT?!
WHO, US?!
I GUESS SO...
WE'RE NOT A COUPLE!!
WELL, THERE'S NO USE ARGUING.
WE'LL JUST HAVE TO GO WITH IT.
Sorry Haru!
WHY DID THIS HAPPEN WHEN SIS WAS AWAY?!
Why couldn't it be the two of them?!
HOLD THESE FLAGS, PLEASE!
WHEN I GIVE THE SIGNAL, YOU HOLD UP THESE FLAGS AND RU THE DOLPHIN WILL DO A JUMP!
It's easy!
OKAY, EVERYBODY! LET'S HAVE A BIG HAND FOR THE TWO YOUNG LOVEBIRDS!
THEY THINK WE'RE A COUPLE!
B-BMP
B-BMP
GEE...

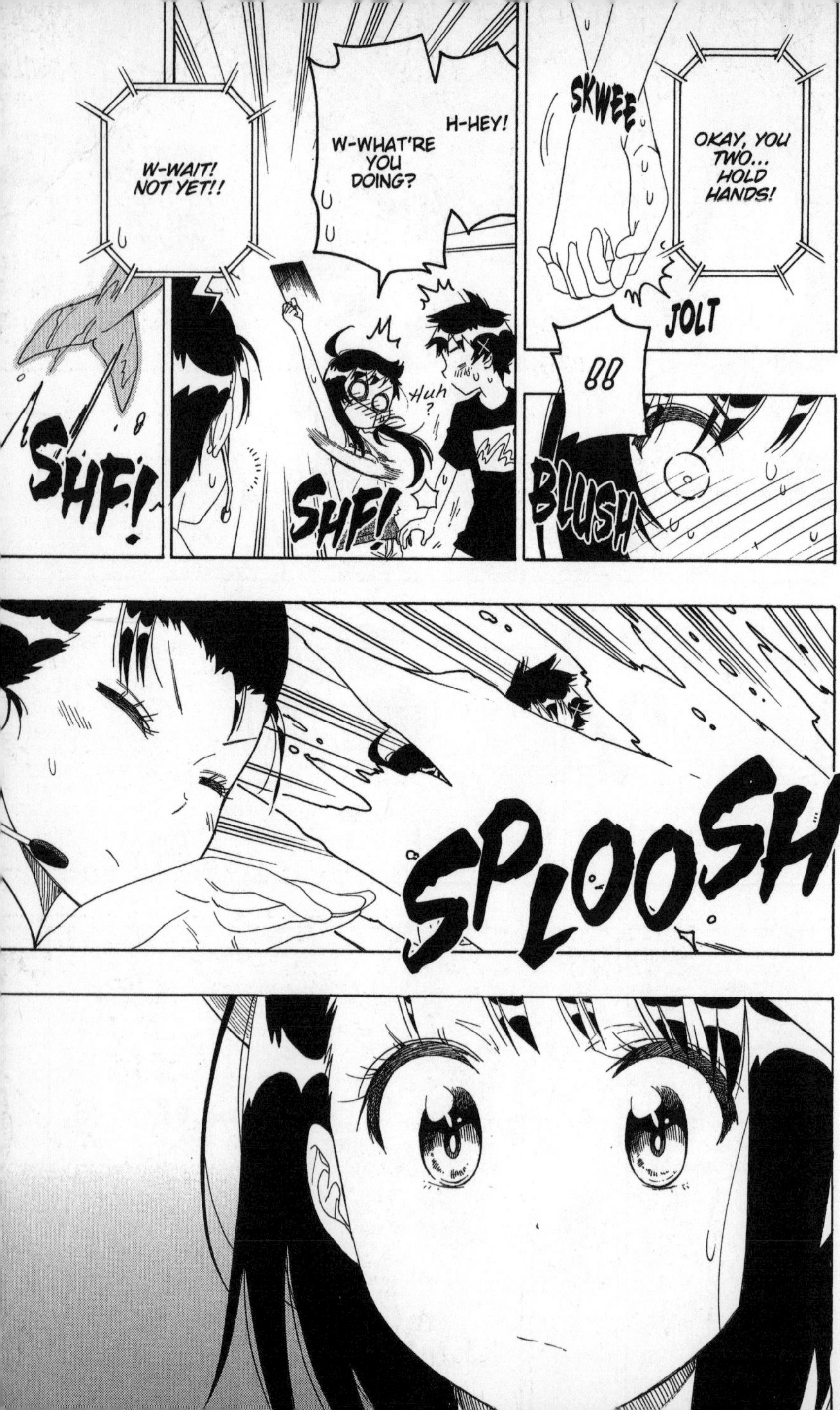

OKAY, YOU TWO... HOLD HANDS!
SKWEE
JOLT
!!
BLUSH
H-HEY!
W-WHAT'RE YOU DOING?
Huh?
SHF!
W-WAIT! NOT YET!!
SHF!
SPLOOSH

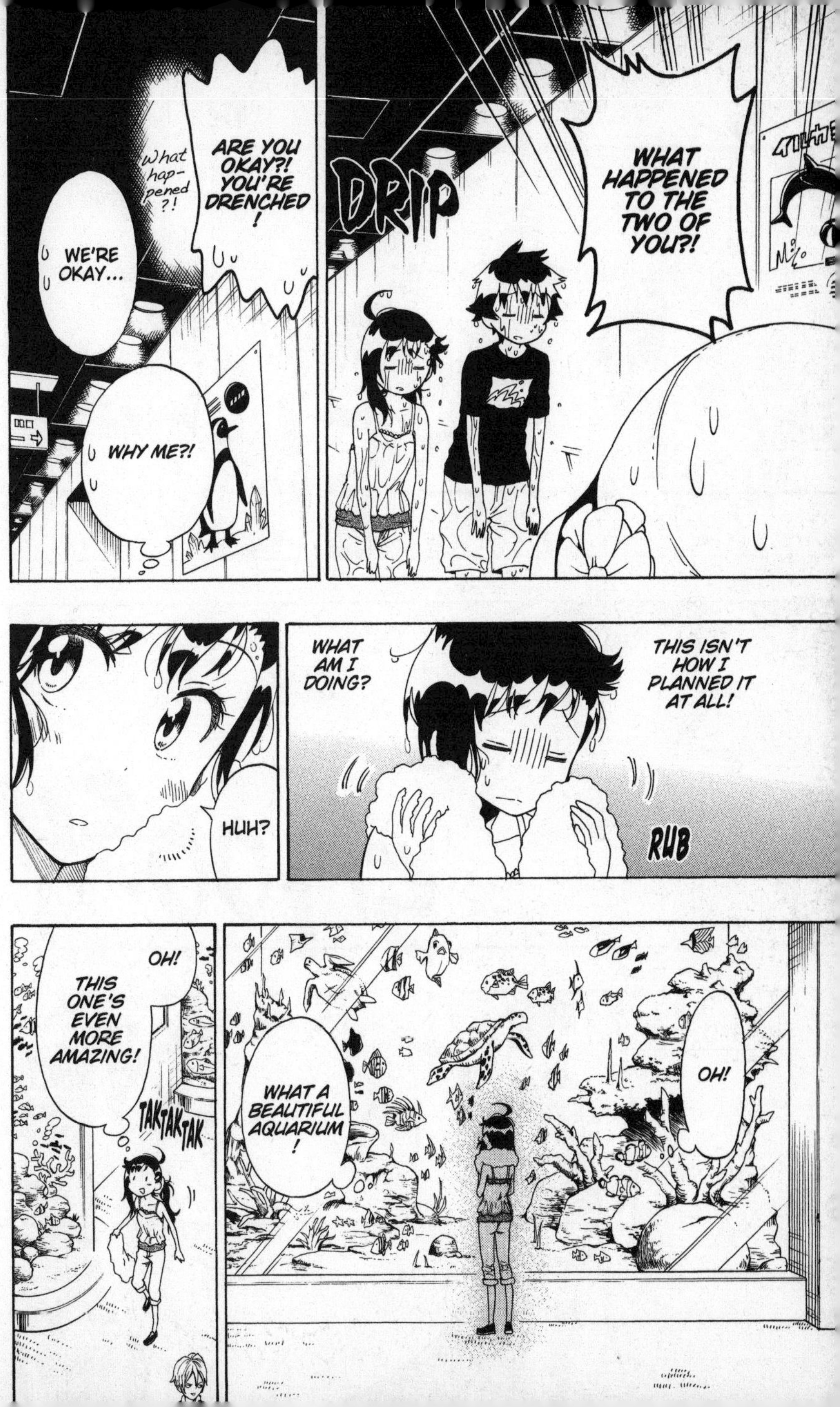
WHAT HAPPENED TO THE TWO OF YOU?!
DRIP
ARE YOU OKAY?! YOU'RE DRENCHED!
What happened?!
WE'RE OKAY...
WHY ME?!
THIS ISN'T HOW I PLANNED IT AT ALL!
WHAT AM I DOING?
RUB
HUH?
OH!
WHAT A BEAUTIFUL AQUARIUM!
OH!
THIS ONE'S EVEN MORE AMAZING!
TAKTAKTAK

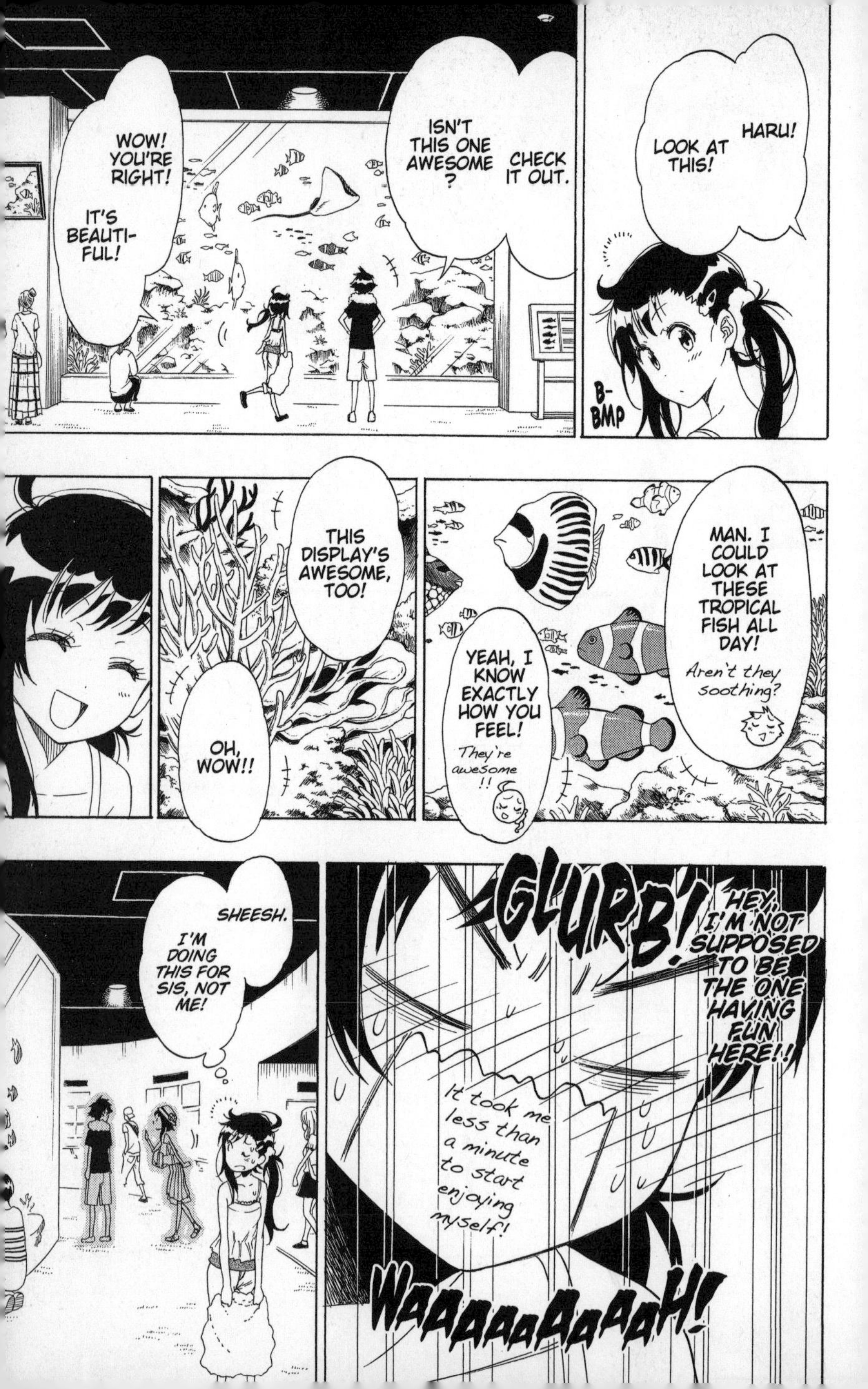
HARU!
LOOK AT THIS!
B-BMP
CHECK IT OUT.
ISN'T THIS ONE AWESOME?
WOW! YOU'RE RIGHT!
IT'S BEAUTIFUL!
MAN. I COULD LOOK AT THESE TROPICAL FISH ALL DAY!
Aren't they soothing?
YEAH, I KNOW EXACTLY HOW YOU FEEL!
They're awesome!!
THIS DISPLAY'S AWESOME, TOO!
OH, WOW!!
GLURB!
HEY, I'M NOT SUPPOSED TO BE THE ONE HAVING FUN HERE!!
It took me less than a minute to start enjoying myself!
WAAAAAAAAAAAH!
SHEESH.
I'M DOING THIS FOR SIS, NOT ME!

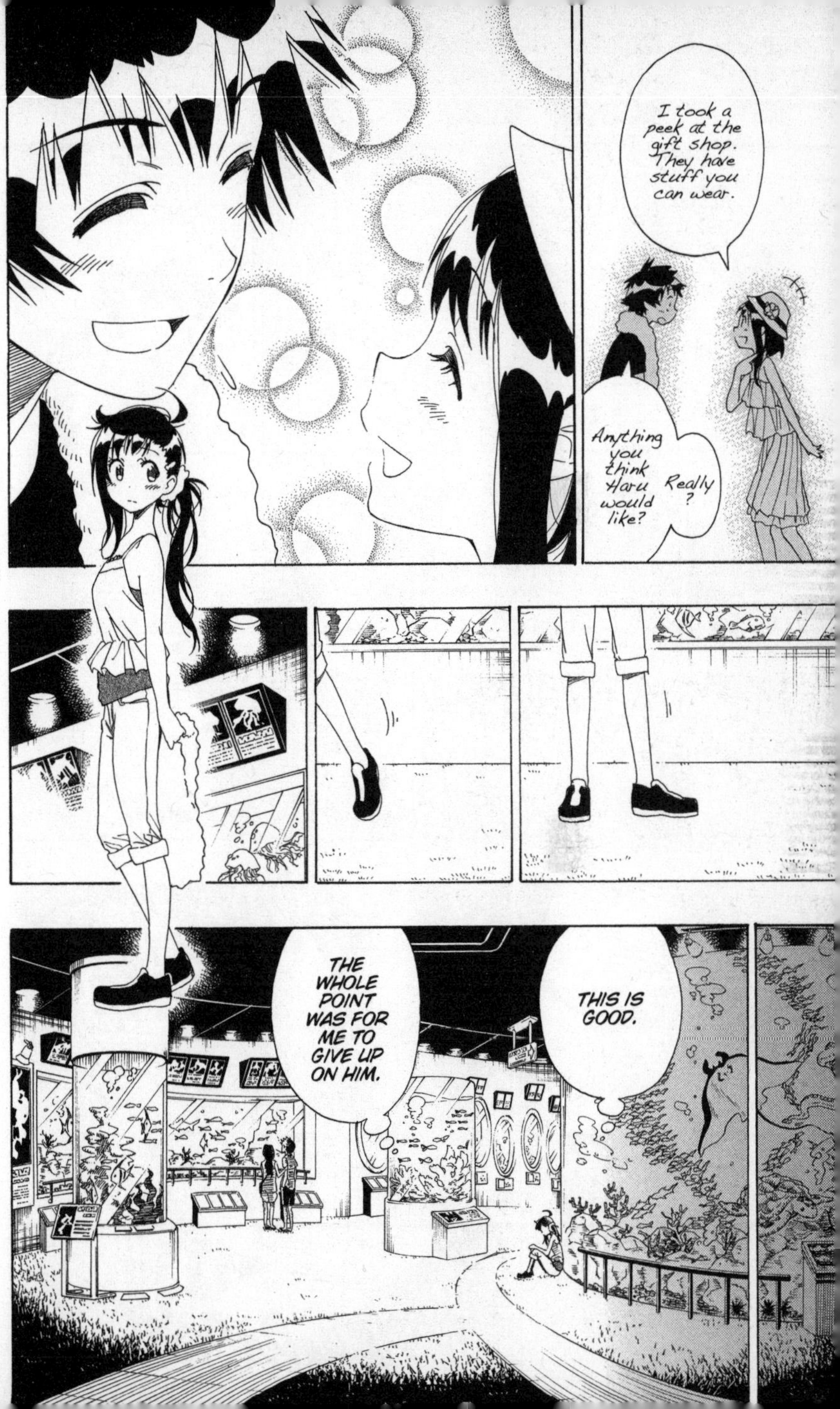
I took a peek at the gift shop. They have stuff you can wear.
Really?
Anything you think Haru would like?
THIS IS GOOD.
THE WHOLE POINT WAS FOR ME TO GIVE UP ON HIM.

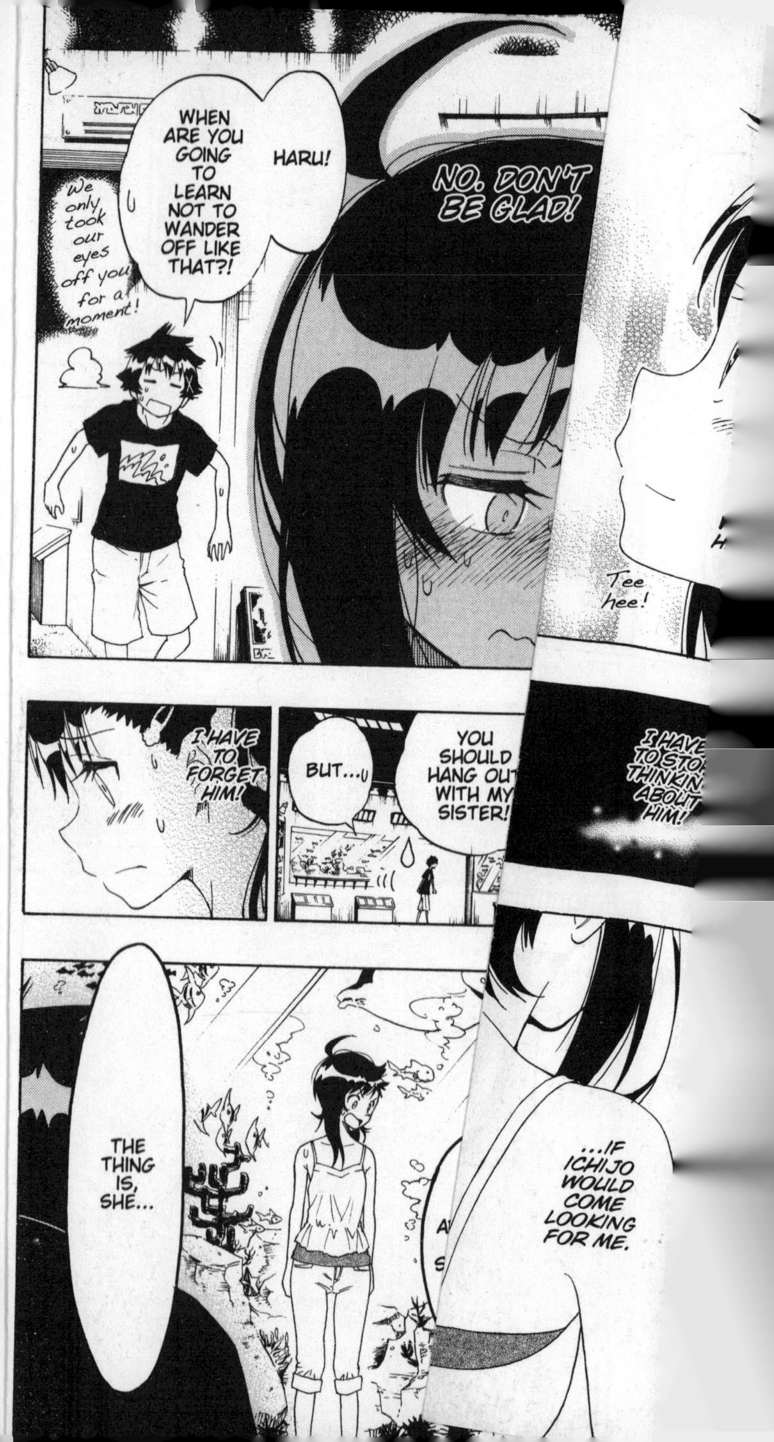
NO, DON'T BE GLAD!
HARU!
WHEN ARE YOU GOING TO LEARN NOT TO WANDER OFF LIKE THAT?!
We only took our eyes off you for a moment!
Tee hee!
YOU SHOULD HANG OUT WITH MY SISTER!
BUT...
I HAVE TO FORGET HIM!
...IF ICHIJO WOULD COME LOOKING FOR ME.
THE THING IS, SHE...
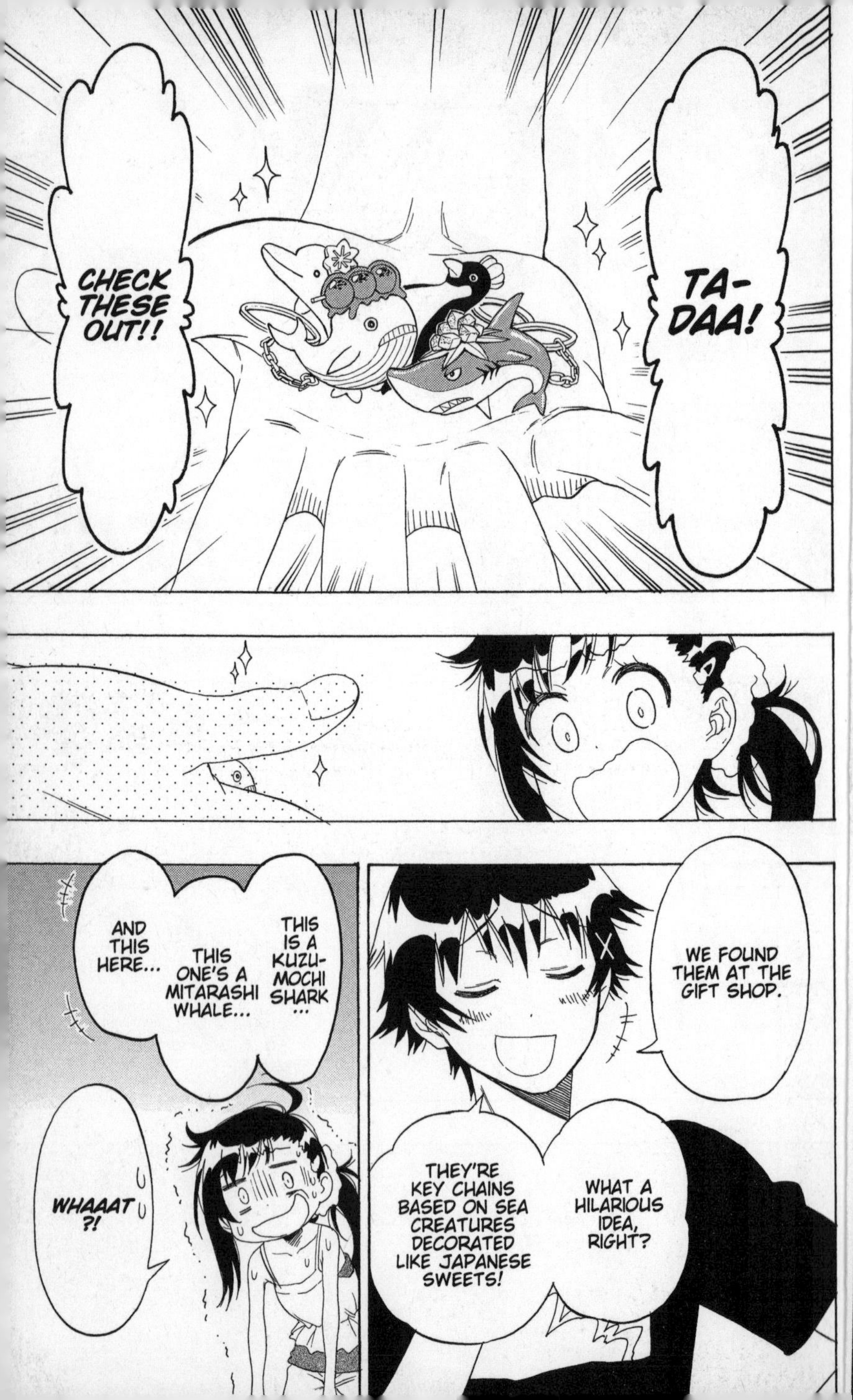
TA-DAA!
CHECK THESE OUT!!
WE FOUND THEM AT THE GIFT SHOP.
WHAT A HILARIOUS IDEA, RIGHT?
THEY'RE KEY CHAINS BASED ON SEA CREATURES DECORATED LIKE JAPANESE SWEETS!
THIS IS A KUZU-MOCHI SHARK...
THIS ONE'S A MITARASHI WHALE...
AND THIS HERE...
WHAAAT?!

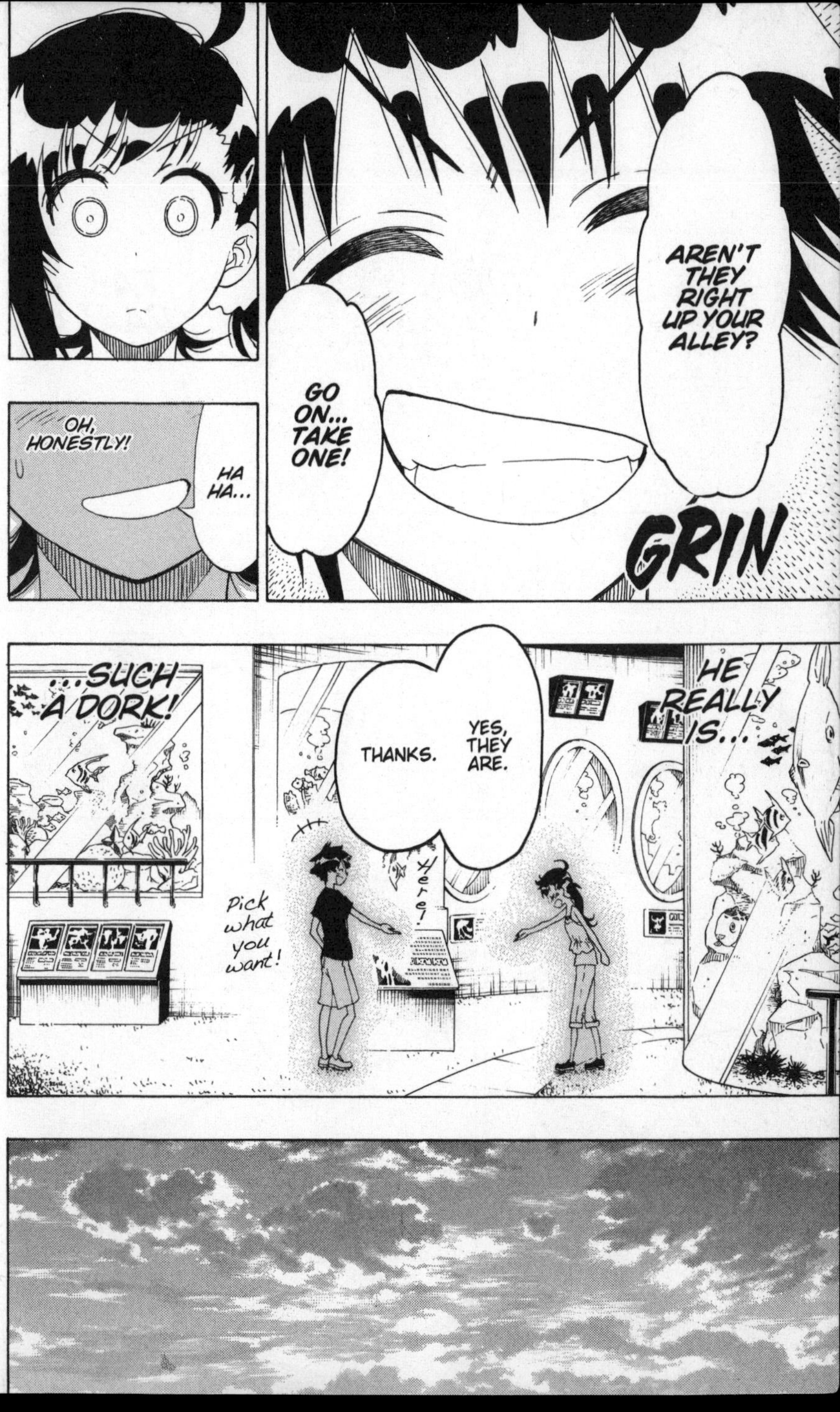
AREN'T THEY RIGHT UP YOUR ALLEY?
GO ON... TAKE ONE!
GRIN
HA HA...
OH, HONESTLY!
HE REALLY IS...
YES, THEY ARE.
THANKS.
Here!
Pick what you want!
...SUCH A DORK!

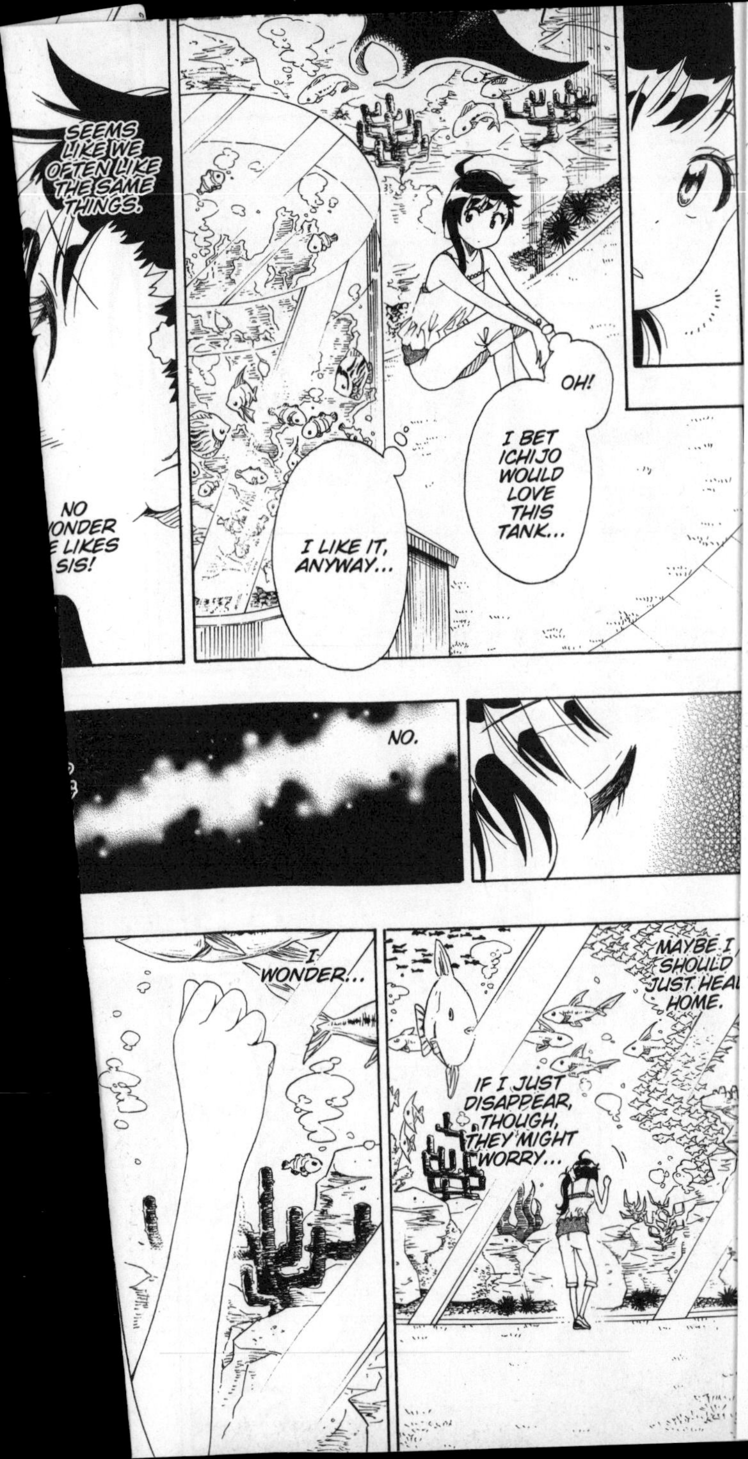
OH!
I BET ICHIJO WOULD LOVE THIS TANK...
I LIKE IT, ANYWAY...
SEEMS LIKE WE OFTEN LIKE THE SAME THINGS.
NO WONDER E LIKES SIS!
NO.
MAYBE I SHOULD JUST HEAD HOME.
IF I JUST DISAPPEAR, THOUGH, THEY MIGHT WORRY...
I WONDER...

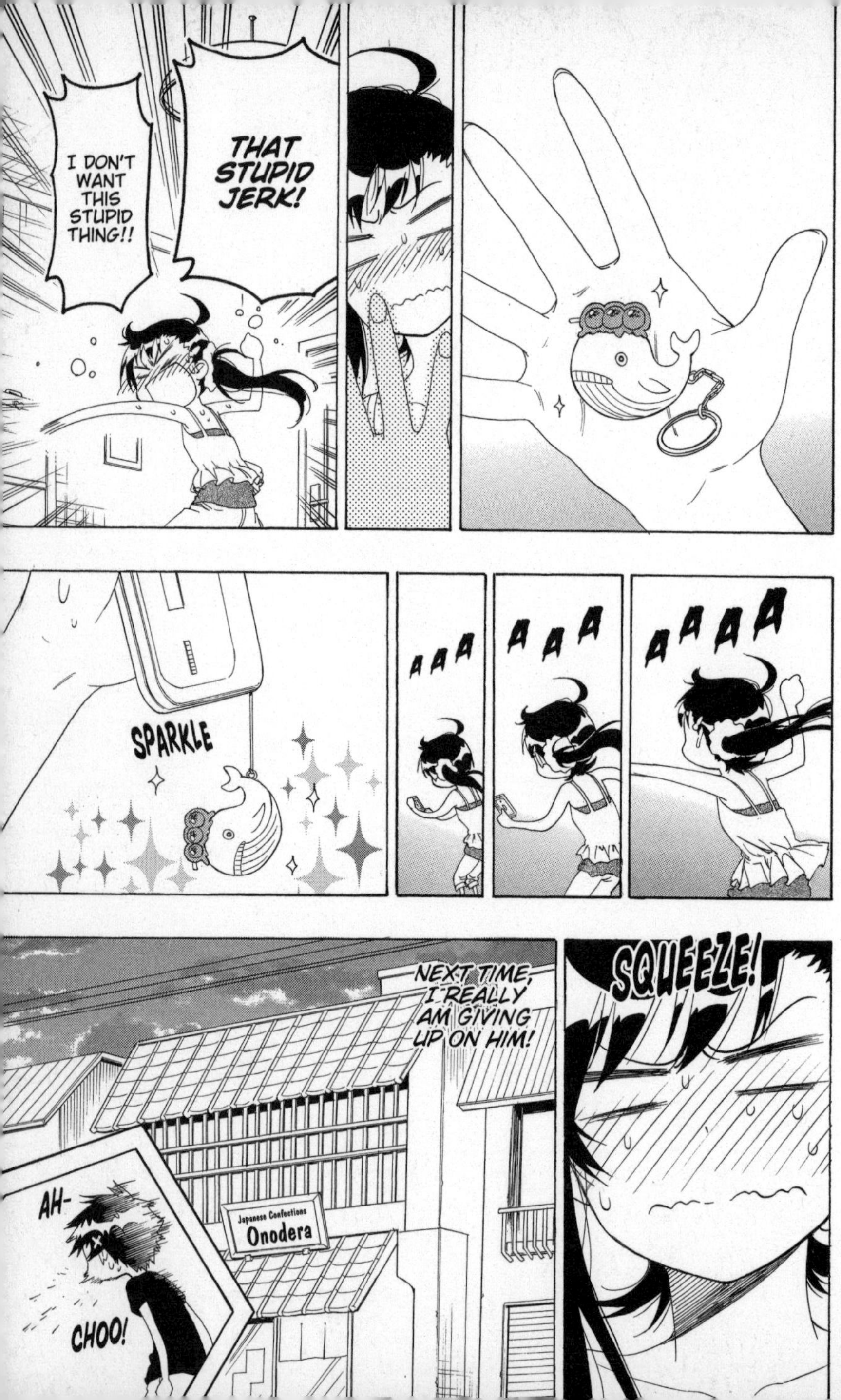
THAT STUPID JERK!
I DON'T WANT THIS STUPID THING!!
AAAA
AAA
AAA
SPARKLE
SQUEEZE!
NEXT TIME, I REALLY AM GIVING UP ON HIM!
Japanese Confections
Onodera
AH-
CHOO!

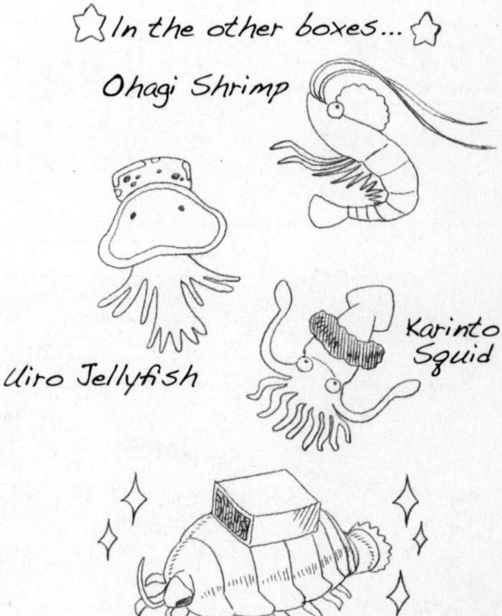

In the other boxes...
Ohagi Shrimp
Uiro Jellyfish
Karinto Squid
Secret Kintsuba Giant Isopod

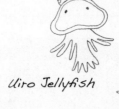

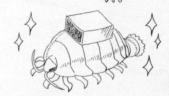

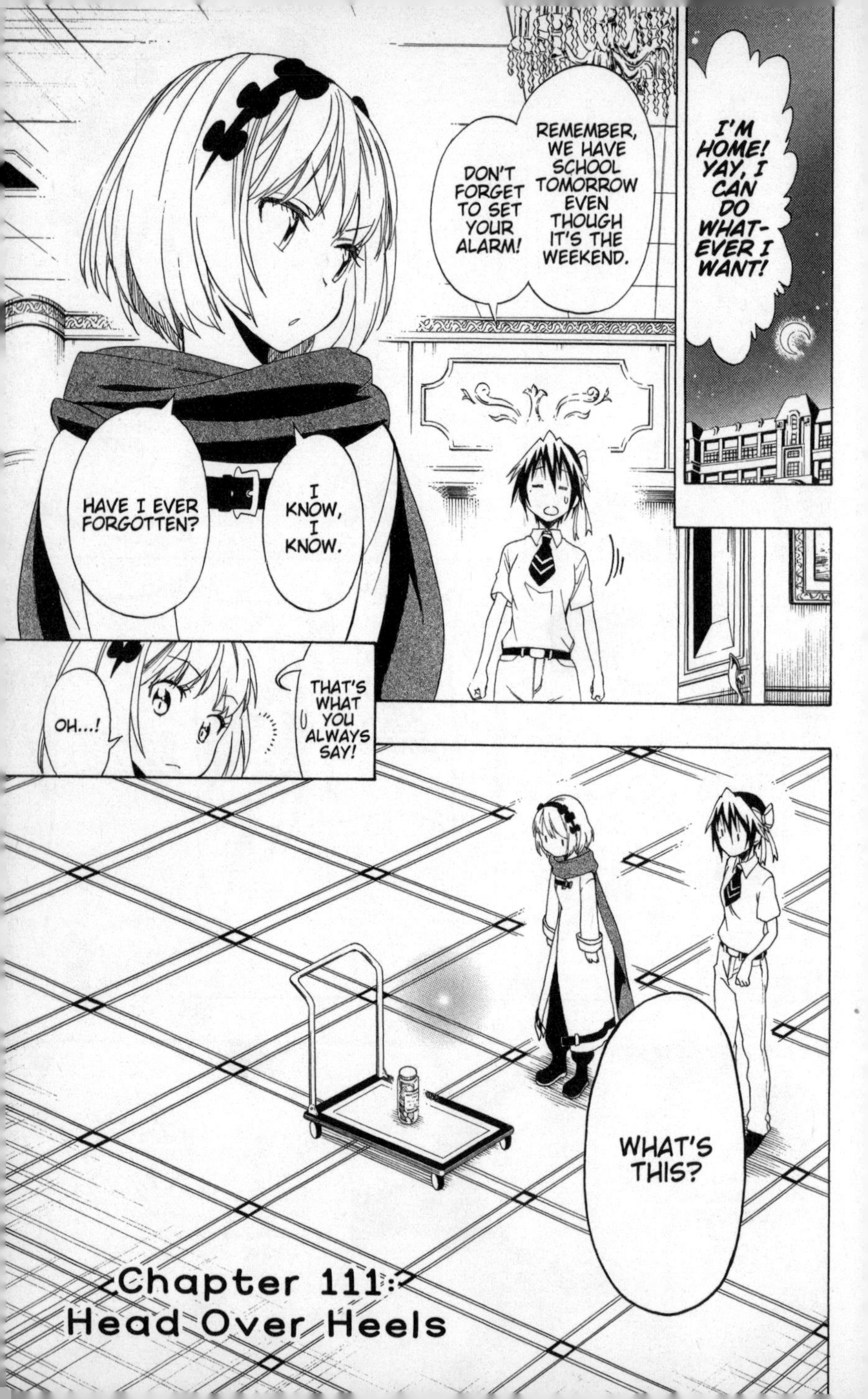
I'M HOME! YAY, I CAN DO WHAT-EVER I WANT!
REMEMBER, WE HAVE SCHOOL TOMORROW EVEN THOUGH IT'S THE WEEKEND.
DON'T FORGET TO SET YOUR ALARM!
I KNOW, I KNOW.
HAVE I EVER FORGOTTEN?
THAT'S WHAT YOU ALWAYS SAY!
OH...!
WHAT'S THIS?
Chapter 111: Head Over Heels

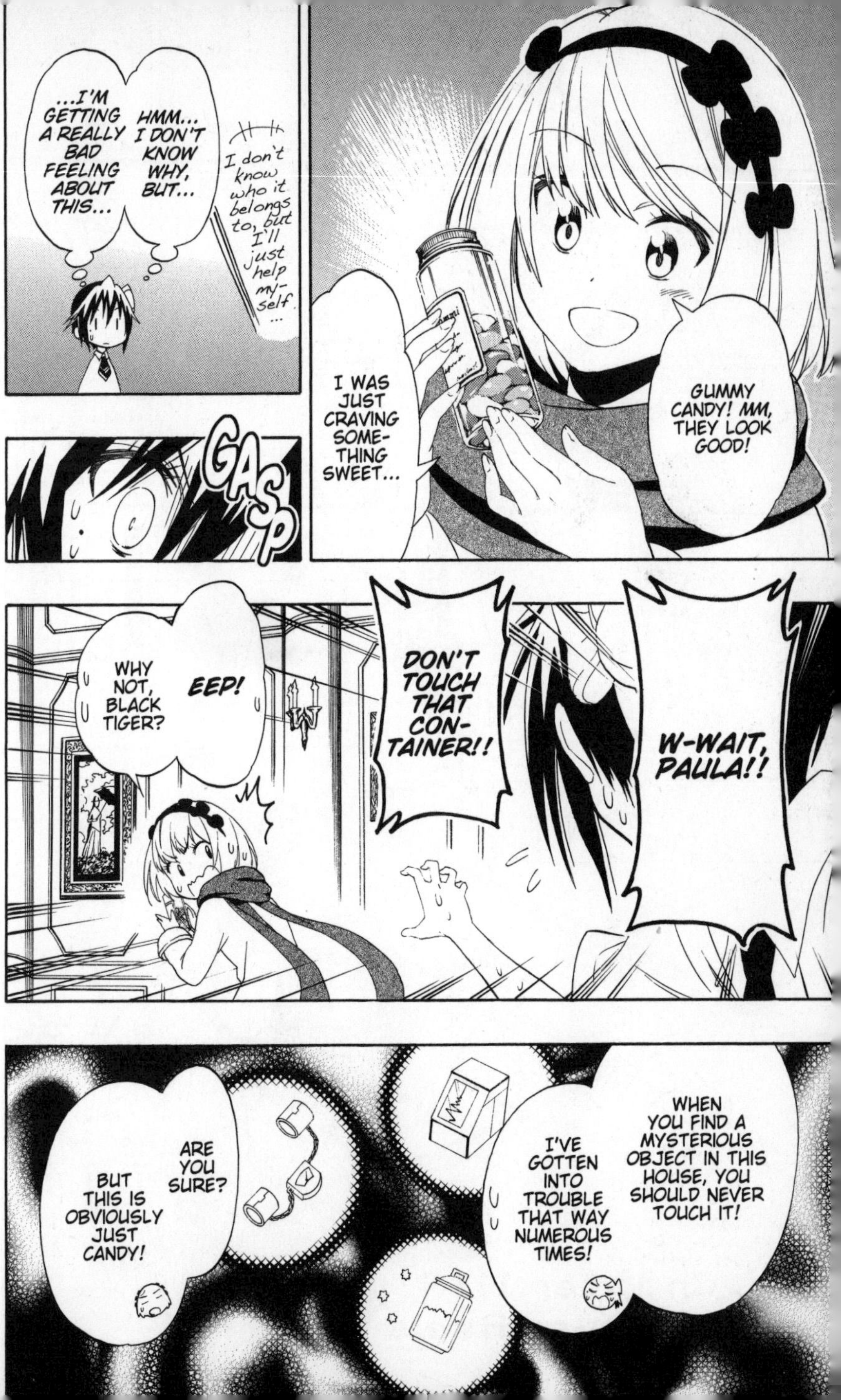
GUMMY CANDY! MM, THEY LOOK GOOD!
I WAS JUST CRAVING SOMETHING SWEET...
I don't know who it belongs to, but I'll just help myself...
HMM... I DON'T KNOW WHY, BUT...
...I'M GETTING A REALLY BAD FEELING ABOUT THIS...
GASP
W-WAIT, PAULA!!
DON'T TOUCH THAT CONTAINER!!
EEP!
WHY NOT, BLACK TIGER?
WHEN YOU FIND A MYSTERIOUS OBJECT IN THIS HOUSE, YOU SHOULD NEVER TOUCH IT!
I'VE GOTTEN INTO TROUBLE THAT WAY NUMEROUS TIMES!
ARE YOU SURE?
BUT THIS IS OBVIOUSLY JUST CANDY!

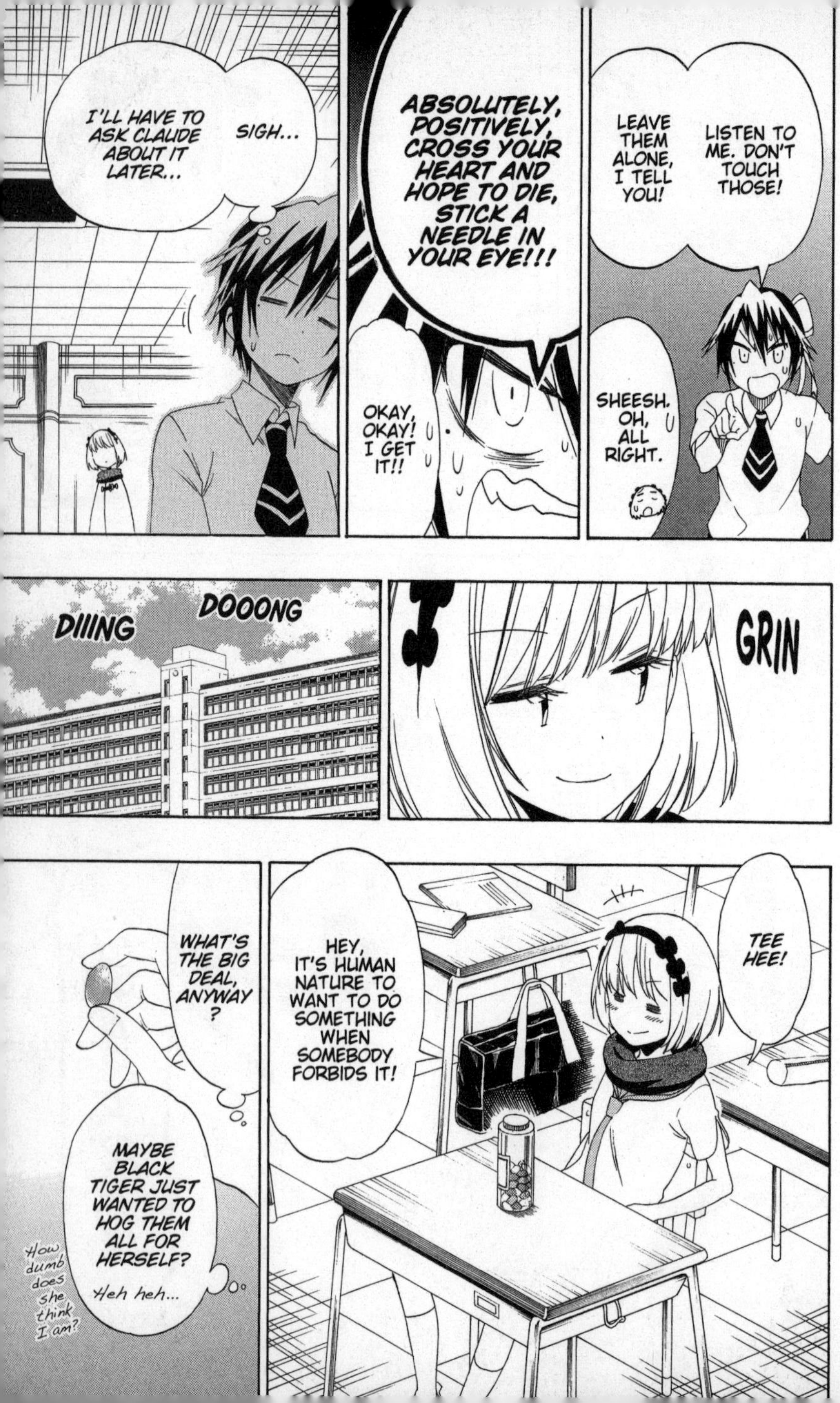
LISTEN TO ME. DON'T TOUCH THOSE!
LEAVE THEM ALONE, I TELL YOU!
SHEESH. OH, ALL RIGHT.
ABSOLUTELY, POSITIVELY, CROSS YOUR HEART AND HOPE TO DIE, STICK A NEEDLE IN YOUR EYE!!!
OKAY, OKAY! I GET IT!!
SIGH...
I'LL HAVE TO ASK CLAUDE ABOUT IT LATER...
GRIN
DOOONG
DIIING
TEE HEE!
HEY, IT'S HUMAN NATURE TO WANT TO DO SOMETHING WHEN SOMEBODY FORBIDS IT!
WHAT'S THE BIG DEAL, ANYWAY?
MAYBE BLACK TIGER JUST WANTED TO HOG THEM ALL FOR HERSELF?
Heh heh...
How dumb does she think I am?

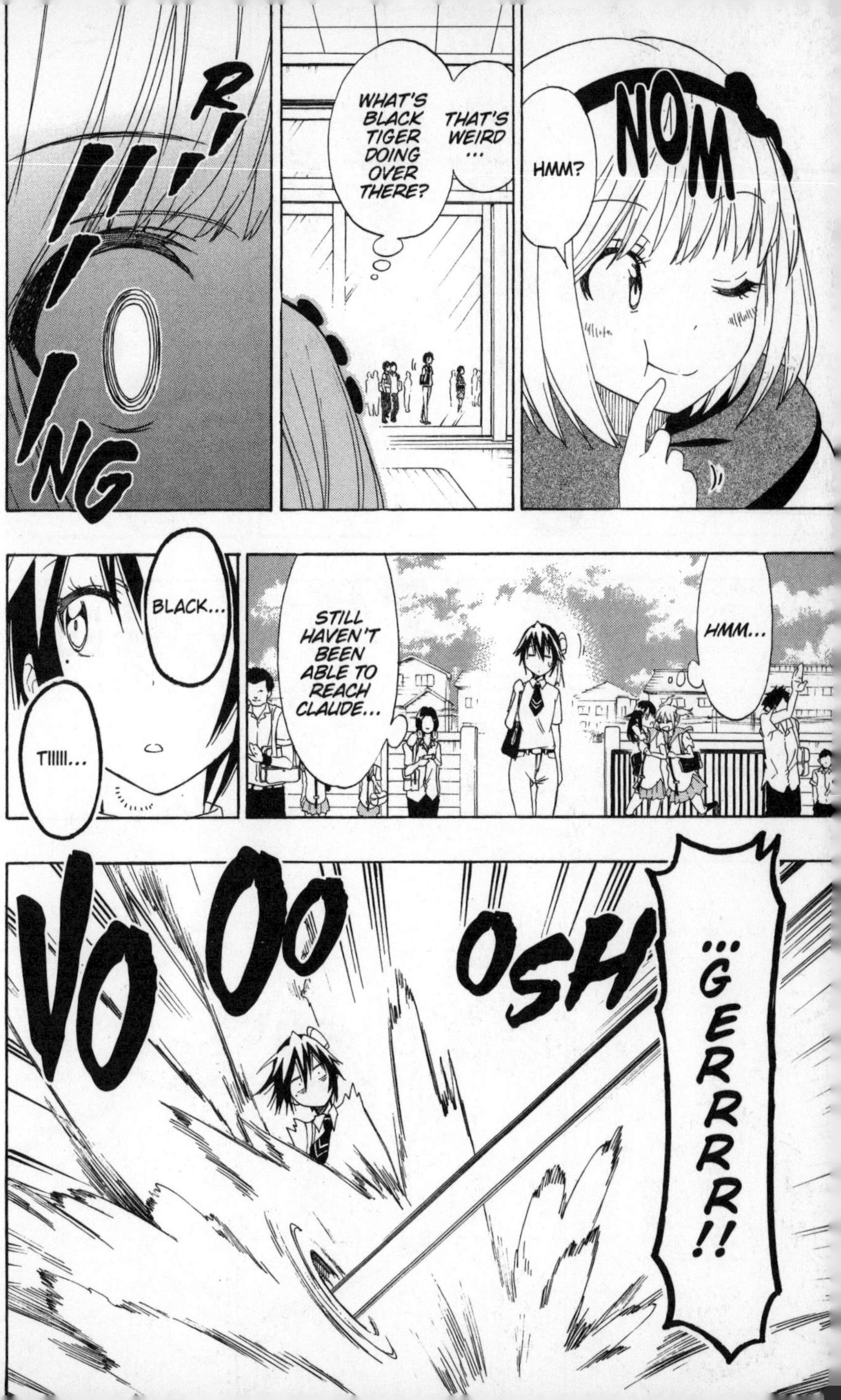
NOM
HMM?
THAT'S WEIRD...
WHAT'S BLACK TIGER DOING OVER THERE?
RIIIING
HMM...
STILL HAVEN'T BEEN ABLE TO REACH CLAUDE...
BLACK...
TIIIII...
...GERRRR!!
VOOOOOSH

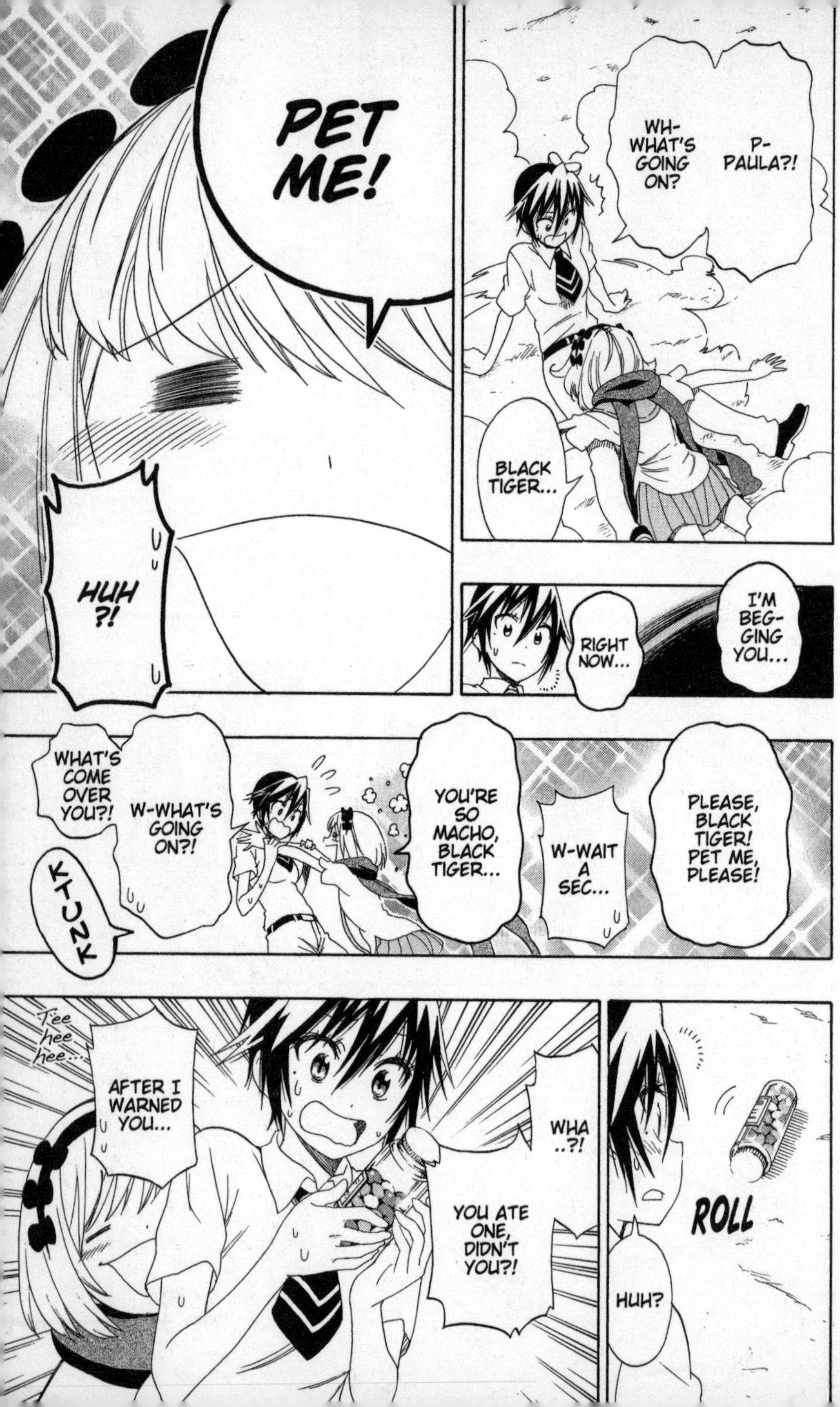
WH- WHAT'S GOING ON? P- PAULA?!
BLACK TIGER...
I'M BEG-GING YOU...
RIGHT NOW...
PET ME!
HUH ?!
PLEASE, BLACK TIGER! PET ME, PLEASE!
W-WAIT A SEC...
YOU'RE SO MACHO, BLACK TIGER...
W-WHAT'S GOING ON?!
WHAT'S COME OVER YOU?!
KTUNK
ROLL
HUH?
WHA ..?!
YOU ATE ONE, DIDN'T YOU?!
AFTER I WARNED YOU...
Tee hee hee...

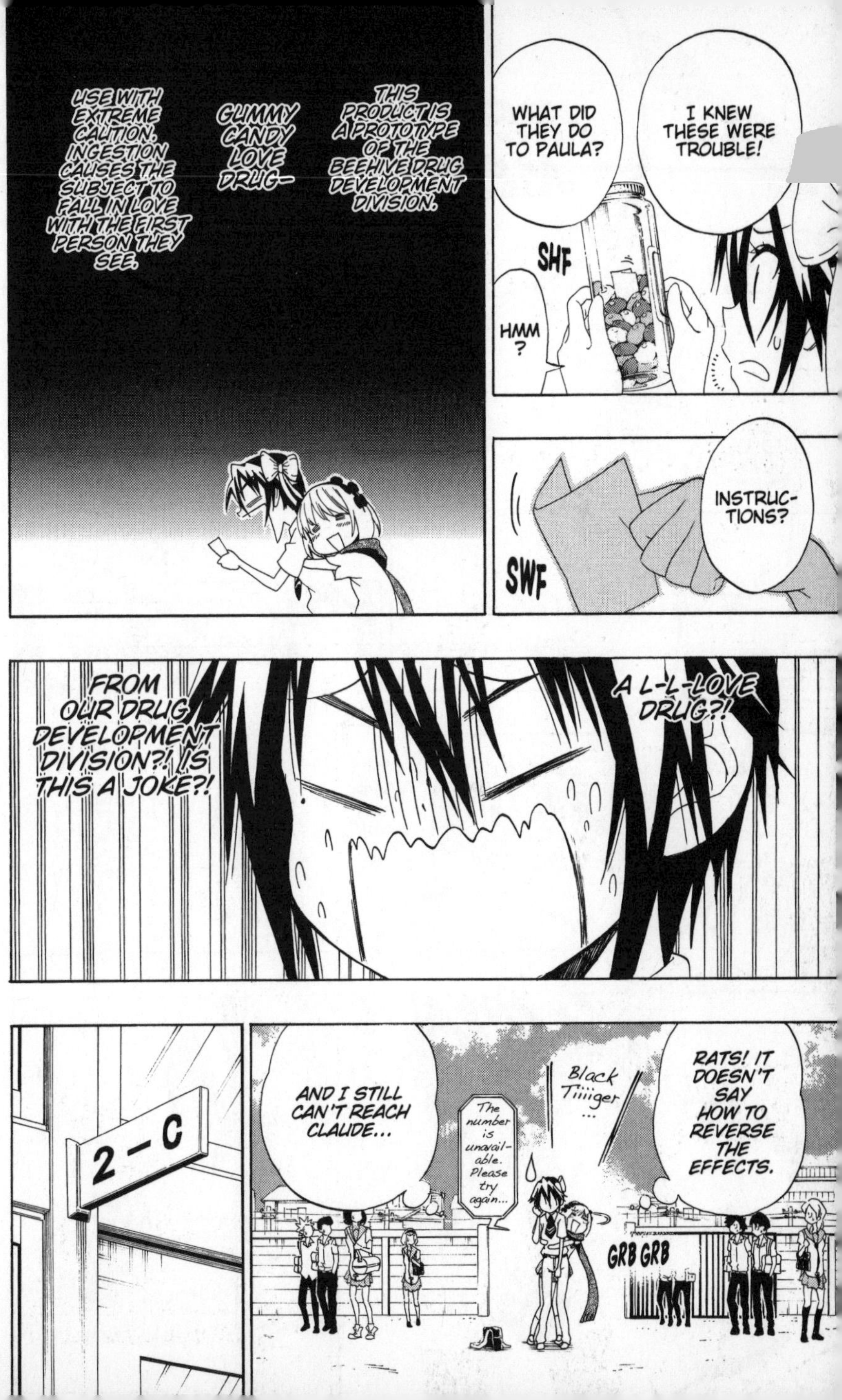
I KNEW THESE WERE TROUBLE!
WHAT DID THEY DO TO PAULA?
SHF
HMM ?
INSTRUCTIONS?
SWF
THIS PRODUCT IS A PROTOTYPE OF THE BEEHIVE DRUG DEVELOPMENT DIVISION.
GUMMY CANDY LOVE DRUG—
USE WITH EXTREME CAUTION. INGESTION CAUSES THE SUBJECT TO FALL IN LOVE WITH THE FIRST PERSON THEY SEE.
A L-L-LOVE DRUG?!
FROM OUR DRUG DEVELOPMENT DIVISION?! IS THIS A JOKE?!
RATS! IT DOESN'T SAY HOW TO REVERSE THE EFFECTS.
Black Tiiiiger...
The number is unavailable. Please try again...
AND I STILL CAN'T REACH CLAUDE...
GRB GRB
2 – C

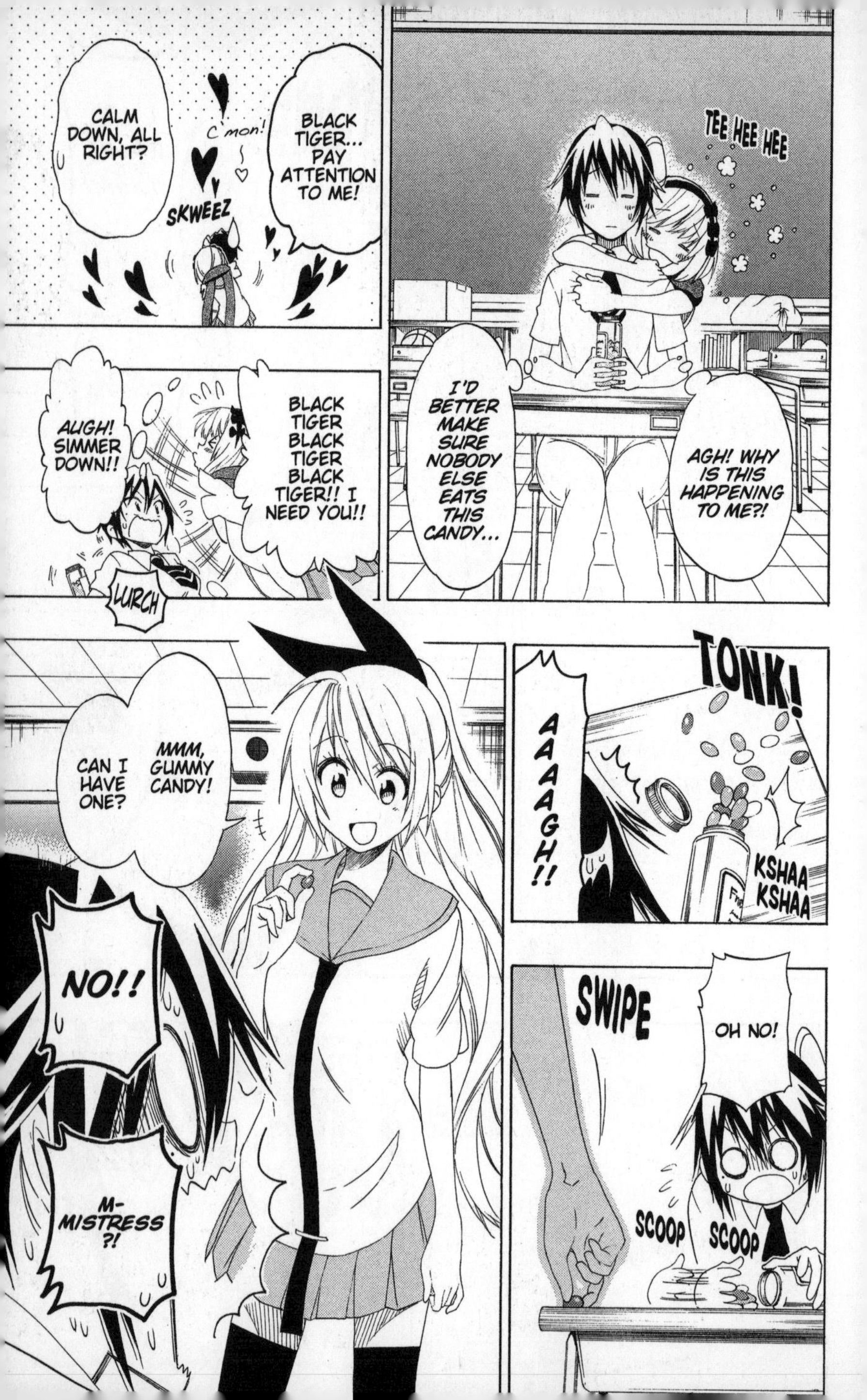
TEE HEE HEE
AGH! WHY IS THIS HAPPENING TO ME?!
I'D BETTER MAKE SURE NOBODY ELSE EATS THIS CANDY...
BLACK TIGER... PAY ATTENTION TO ME!
C'mon!
SKWEEZ
CALM DOWN, ALL RIGHT?
BLACK TIGER BLACK TIGER BLACK TIGER!! I NEED YOU!!
AUGH! SIMMER DOWN!!
LURCH
TONK!
AAAAAGH!!
KSHAA KSHAA
SWIPE
OH NO!
SCOOP
SCOOP
MMM, GUMMY CANDY!
CAN I HAVE ONE?
NO!!
M-MISTRESS?!

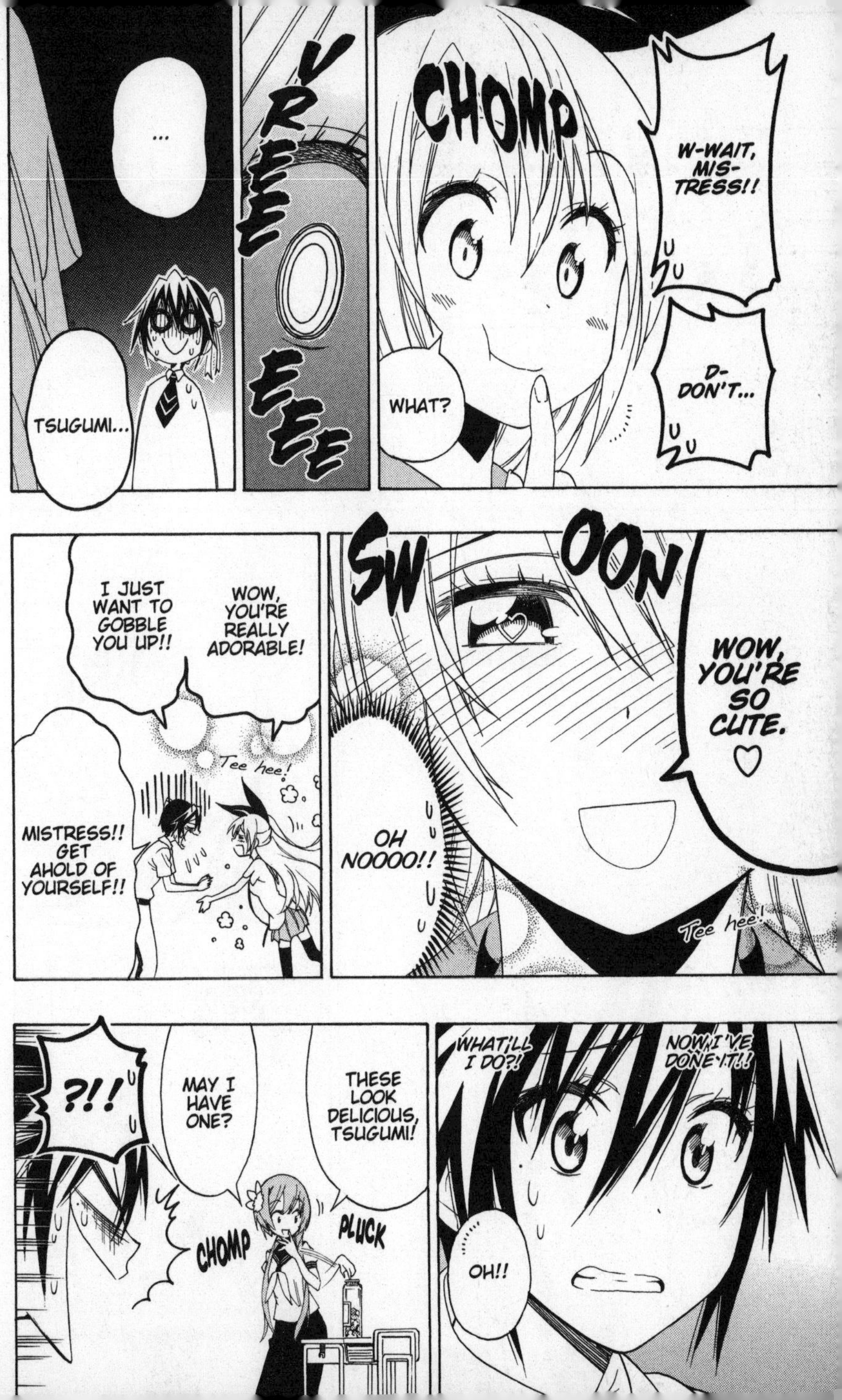
CHOMP
W-WAIT, MIS-TRESS!!
D-DON'T...
WHAT?
VREEEEE
...
TSUGUMI...
SWOON
WOW, YOU'RE SO CUTE. ♡
OH NOOOO!!
Tee hee!
WOW, YOU'RE REALLY ADORABLE!
I JUST WANT TO GOBBLE YOU UP!!
Tee hee!
MISTRESS!! GET AHOLD OF YOURSELF!!
NOW I'VE DONE IT!!
WHAT'LL I DO?!
OH!!
THESE LOOK DELICIOUS, TSUGUMI!
MAY I HAVE ONE?
PLUCK
CHOMP
?!!

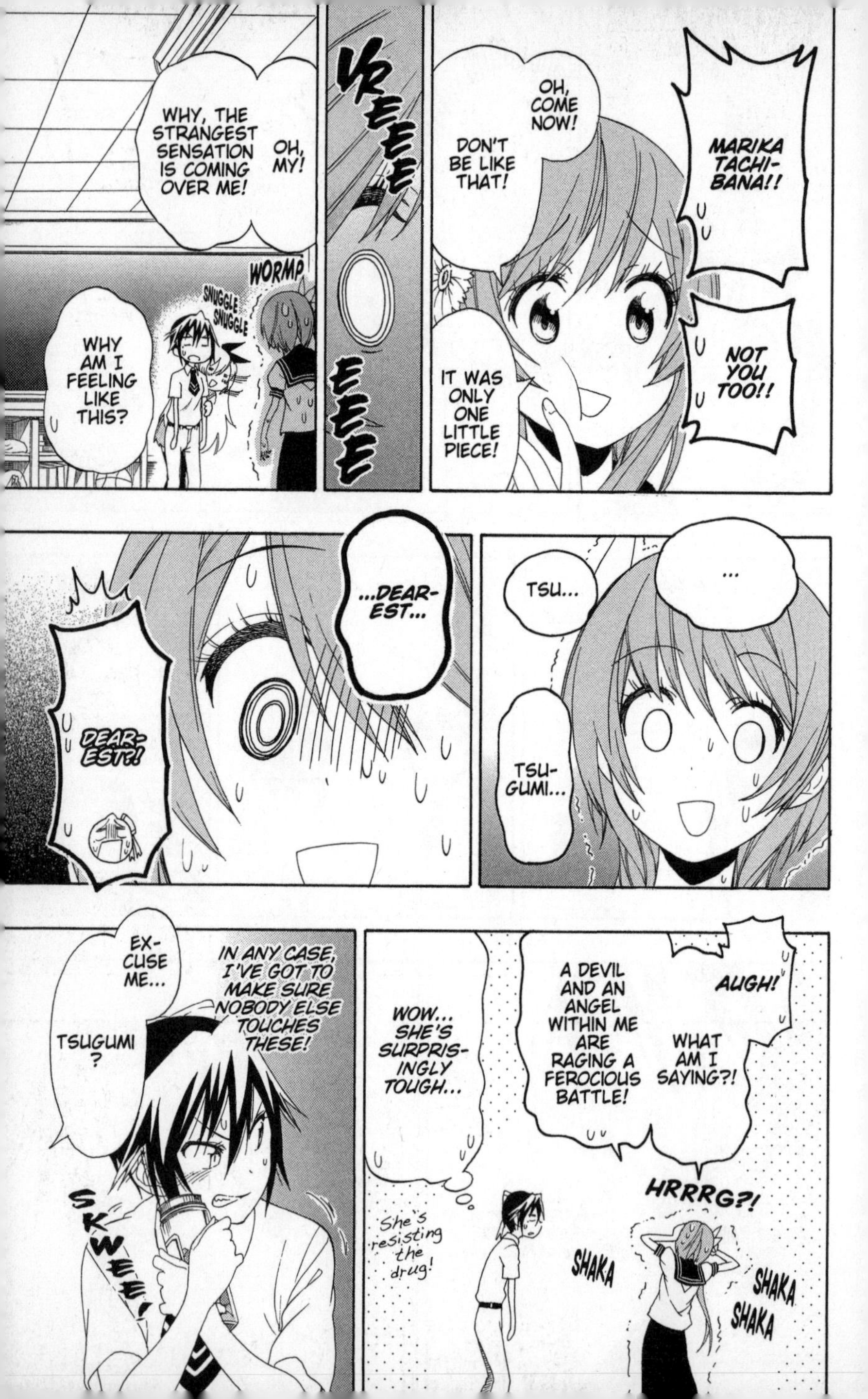
MARIKA TACHIBANA!!
NOT YOU TOO!!
OH, COME NOW!
DON'T BE LIKE THAT!
IT WAS ONLY ONE LITTLE PIECE!
VREEEE
EEEE
OH, MY!
WHY, THE STRANGEST SENSATION IS COMING OVER ME!
WORMP
SNUGGLE SNUGGLE
WHY AM I FEELING LIKE THIS?
...
TSU...
TSUGUMI...
...DEAREST...
DEAREST?!
AUGH!
WHAT AM I SAYING?!
A DEVIL AND AN ANGEL WITHIN ME ARE RAGING A FEROCIOUS BATTLE!
WOW... SHE'S SURPRISINGLY TOUGH...
She's resisting the drug!
HRRRG?!
SHAKA
SHAKA SHAKA
IN ANY CASE, I'VE GOT TO MAKE SURE NOBODY ELSE TOUCHES THESE!
EXCUSE ME...
TSUGUMI?
SKWEE!

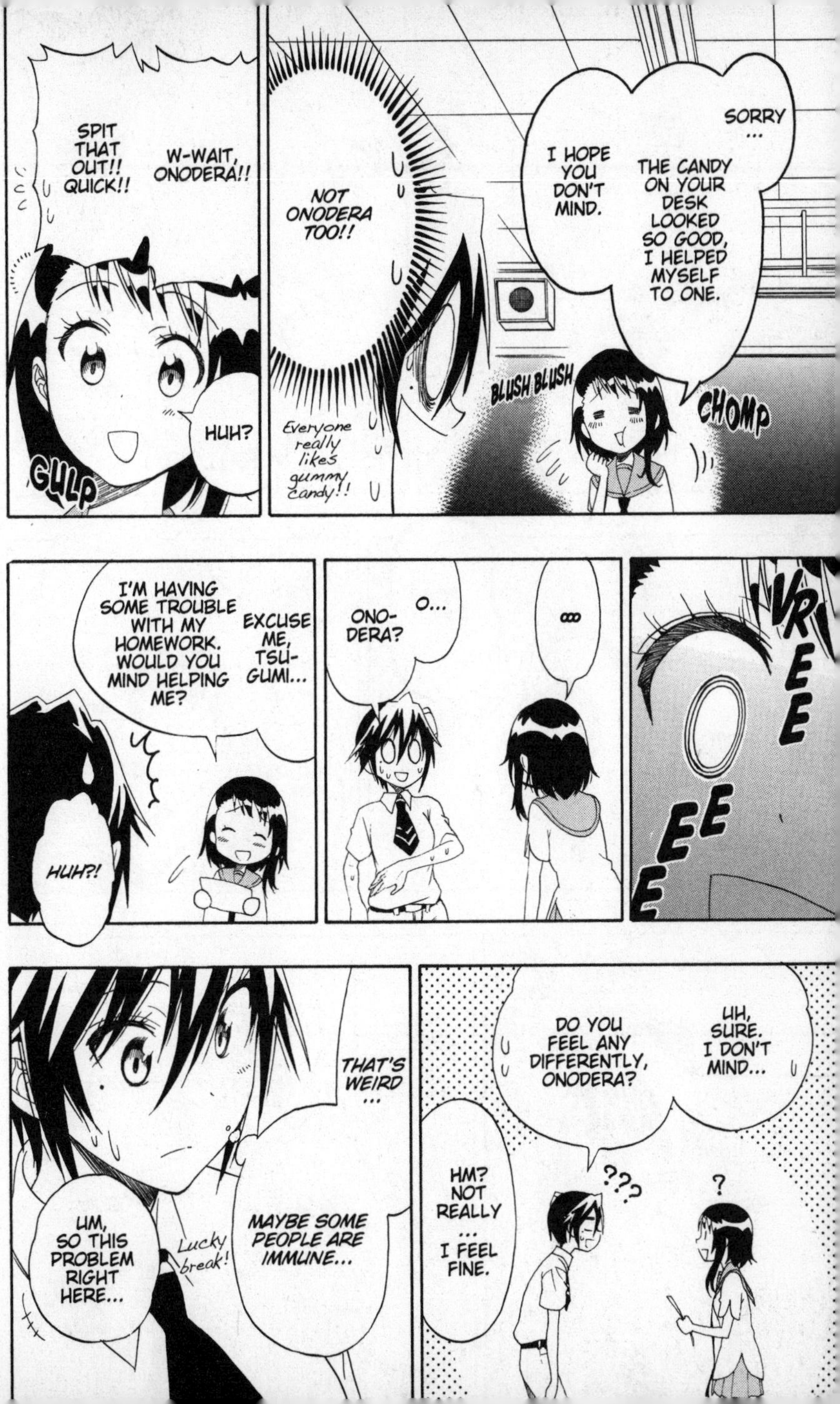
SORRY...
THE CANDY ON YOUR DESK LOOKED SO GOOD, I HELPED MYSELF TO ONE.
I HOPE YOU DON'T MIND.
BLUSH BLUSH
CHOMP
NOT ONODERA TOO!!
Everyone really likes gummy candy!!
W-WAIT, ONODERA!!
SPIT THAT OUT!! QUICK!!
HUH?
GULP
VREEEEEEE
...
O...
ONO-DERA?
EXCUSE ME, TSU-GUMI...
I'M HAVING SOME TROUBLE WITH MY HOMEWORK. WOULD YOU MIND HELPING ME?
HUH?!
UH, SURE. I DON'T MIND...
DO YOU FEEL ANY DIFFERENTLY, ONODERA?
???
?
HM? NOT REALLY... I FEEL FINE.
THAT'S WEIRD...
MAYBE SOME PEOPLE ARE IMMUNE...
Lucky break!
UM, SO THIS PROBLEM RIGHT HERE...

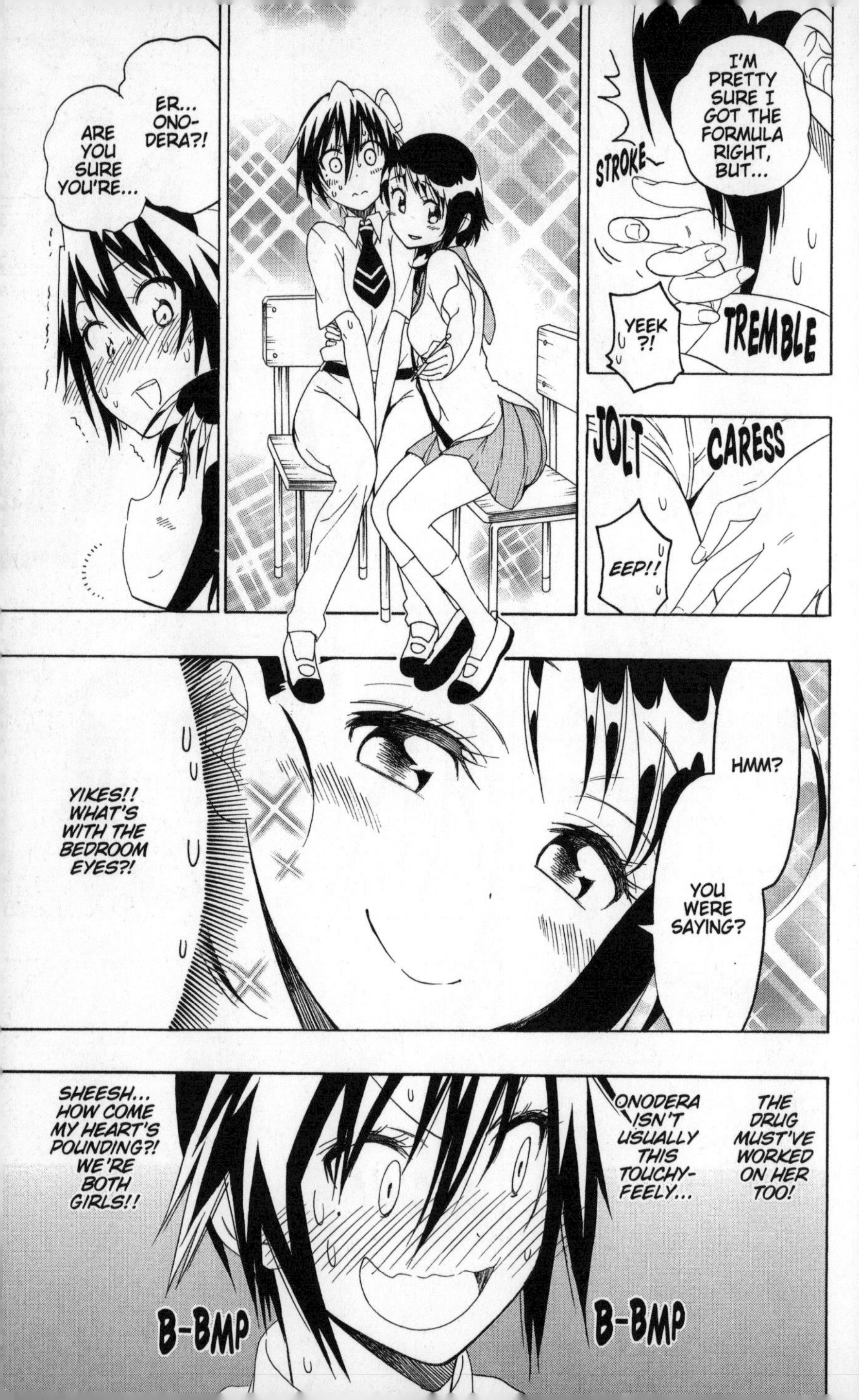

I'M PRETTY SURE I GOT THE FORMULA RIGHT, BUT...
STROKE~
YEEK ?!
TREMBLE
CARESS
JOLT
EEP!!
ER... ONO-DERA?!
ARE YOU SURE YOU'RE...
HMM?
YOU WERE SAYING?
YIKES!! WHAT'S WITH THE BEDROOM EYES?!
THE DRUG MUST'VE WORKED ON HER TOO!
ONODERA ISN'T USUALLY THIS TOUCHY-FEELY...
SHEESH... HOW COME MY HEART'S POUNDING?! WE'RE BOTH GIRLS!!
B-BMP
B-BMP

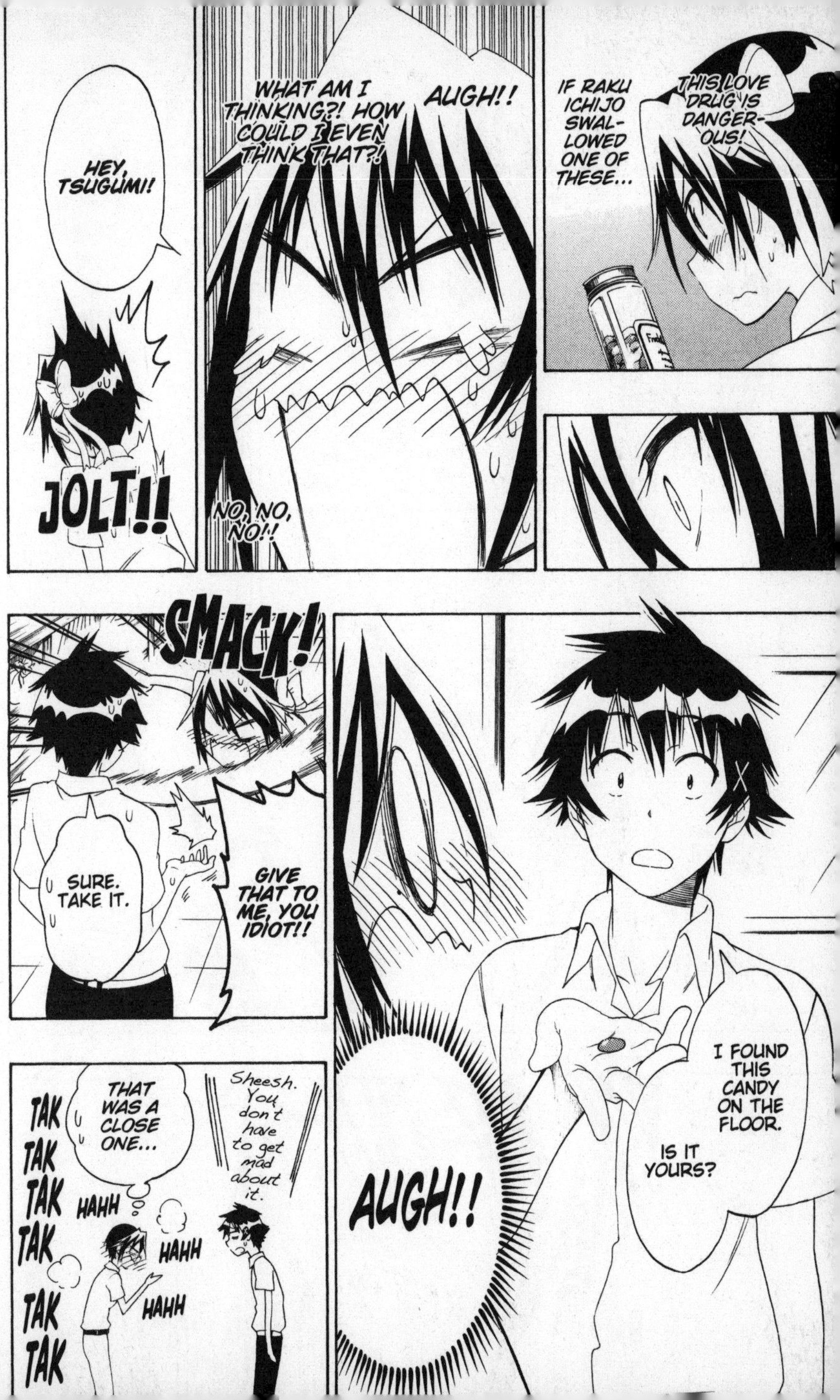
THIS LOVE DRUG IS DANGEROUS!
IF RAKU ICHIJO SWALLOWED ONE OF THESE...
AUGH!!
WHAT AM I THINKING?! HOW COULD I EVEN THINK THAT?!
NO, NO, NO!!
HEY, TSUGUMI!
JOLT!!
I FOUND THIS CANDY ON THE FLOOR.
IS IT YOURS?
AUGH!!
SMACK!
GIVE THAT TO ME, YOU IDIOT!!
SURE. TAKE IT.
Sheesh. You don't have to get mad about it.
THAT WAS A CLOSE ONE...
TAK TAK TAK TAK TAK TAK
HAHH HAHH HAHH

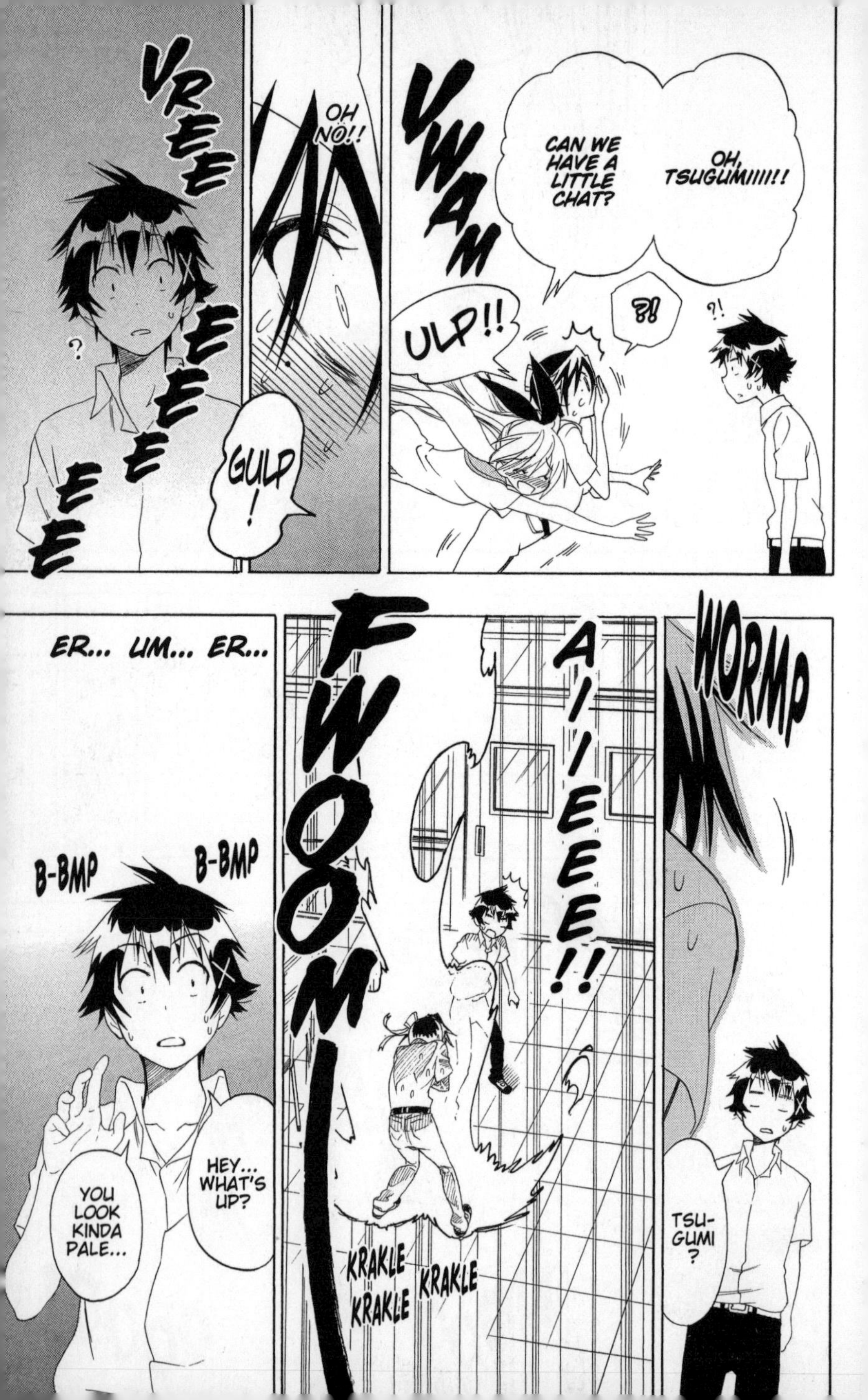
OH, TSUGUMIIIII!!
CAN WE HAVE A LITTLE CHAT?
?!
?!
ULP!!
VWAM
OH NO!!
GULP!
VREEEEEEE
?
WORMP
TSU-GUMI?
AIIEEEE!!
FWOOM!
KRAKLE KRAKLE KRAKLE
ER... UM... ER...
B-BMP
B-BMP
HEY... WHAT'S UP?
YOU LOOK KINDA PALE...

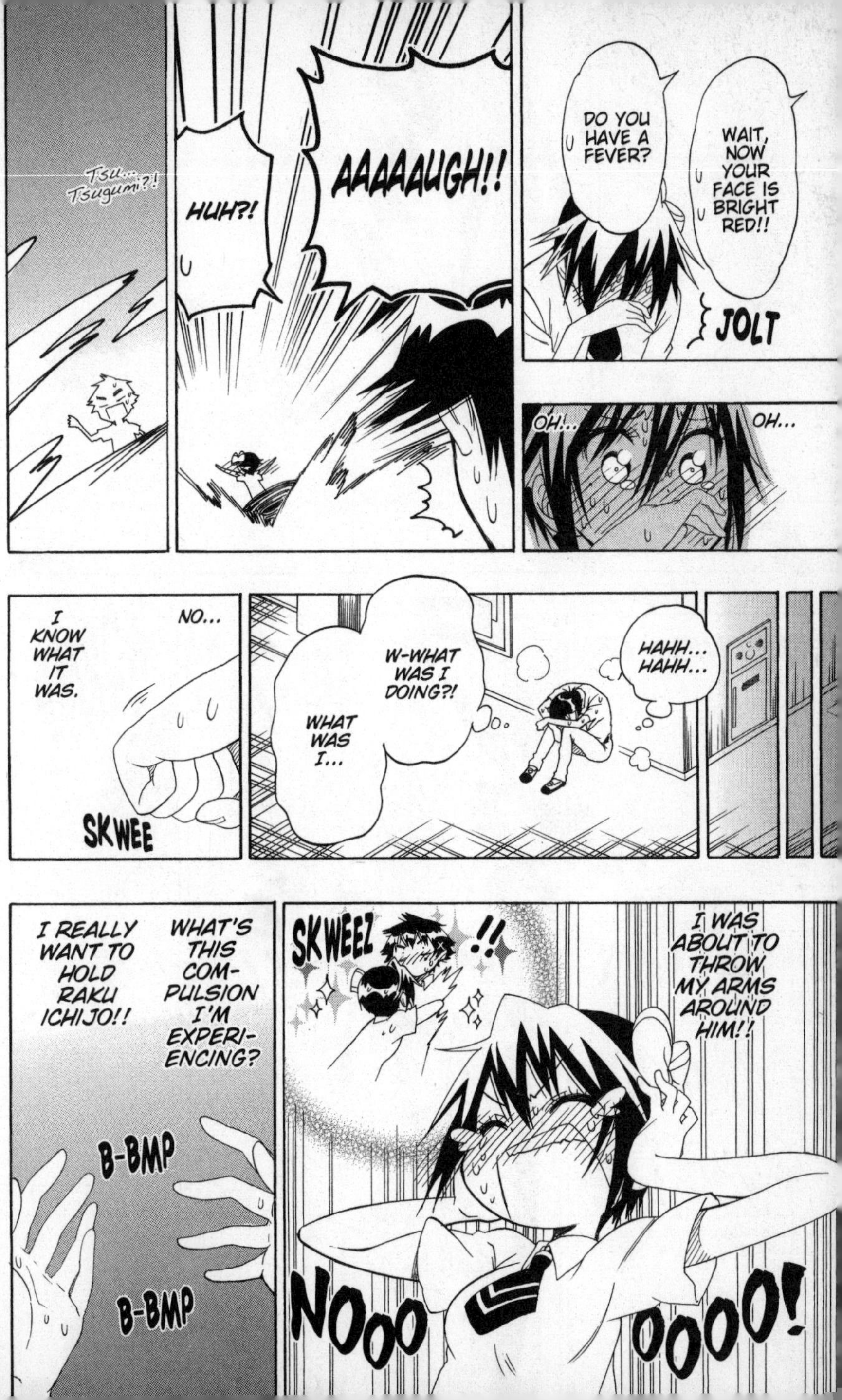
WAIT, NOW YOUR FACE IS BRIGHT RED!!
DO YOU HAVE A FEVER?
JOLT
OH...
OH...
AAAAAUGH!!
HUH?!
Tsu... Tsugumi?!
HAHH... HAHH...
W-WHAT WAS I DOING?!
WHAT WAS I...
NO...
I KNOW WHAT IT WAS.
SKWEE
I WAS ABOUT TO THROW MY ARMS AROUND HIM!!
!!
SKWEEZ
NOOO OOOO!
WHAT'S THIS COM-PULSION I'M EXPERI-ENCING?
I REALLY WANT TO HOLD RAKU ICHIJO!!
B-BMP
B-BMP

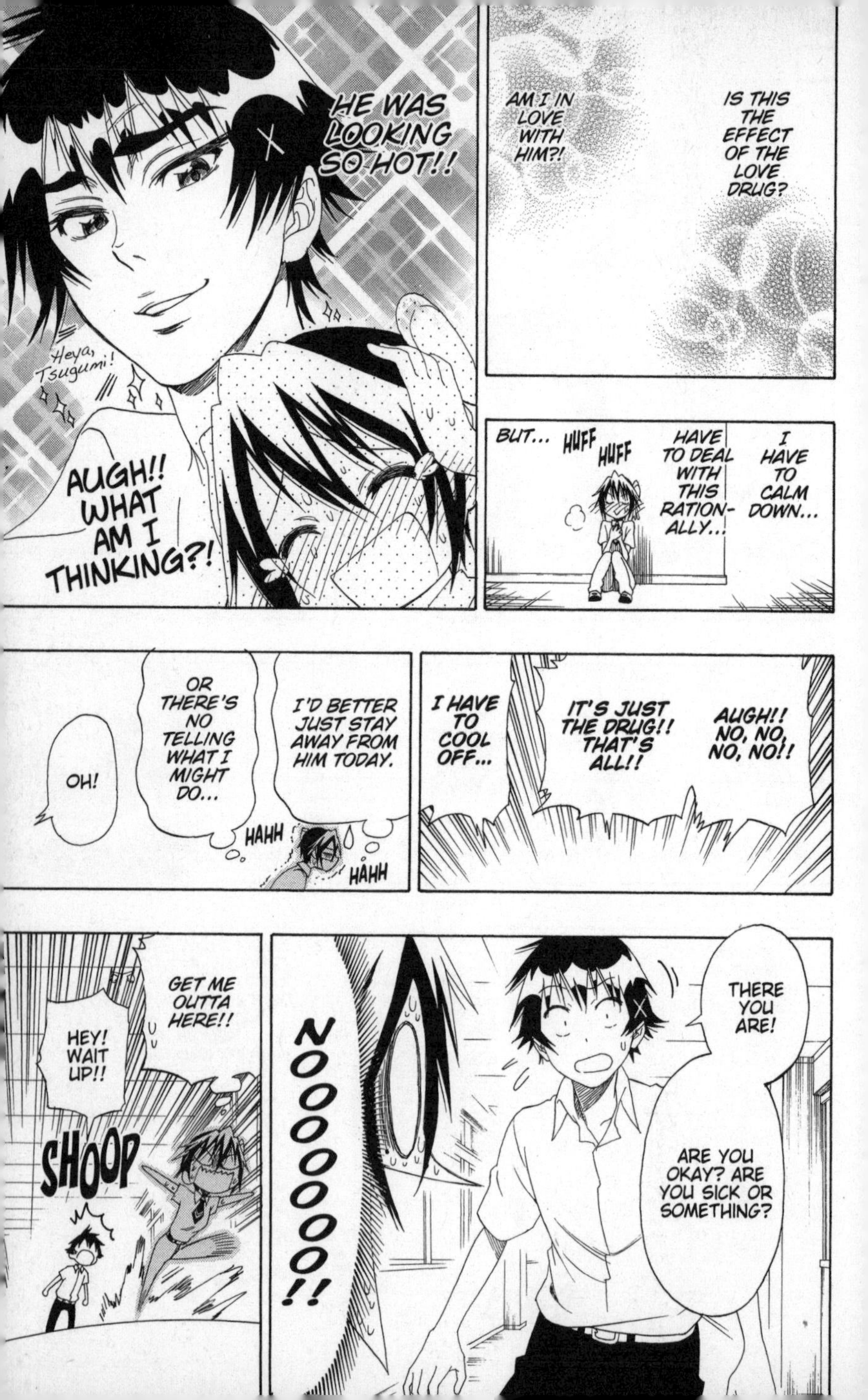

IS THIS THE EFFECT OF THE LOVE DRUG?
AM I IN LOVE WITH HIM?!
I HAVE TO CALM DOWN...
HAVE TO DEAL WITH THIS RATION-ALLY...
HUFF
HUFF
BUT...
HE WAS LOOKING SO HOT!!
Heya, Tsugumi!
AUGH!! WHAT AM I THINKING?!
AUGH!! NO, NO, NO, NO!!
IT'S JUST THE DRUG!! THAT'S ALL!!
I HAVE TO COOL OFF...
I'D BETTER JUST STAY AWAY FROM HIM TODAY.
OR THERE'S NO TELLING WHAT I MIGHT DO...
HAHH
HAHH
OH!
THERE YOU ARE!
ARE YOU OKAY? ARE YOU SICK OR SOMETHING?
NOOOOOOOOO!!
GET ME OUTTA HERE!!
HEY! WAIT UP!!
SHOOP

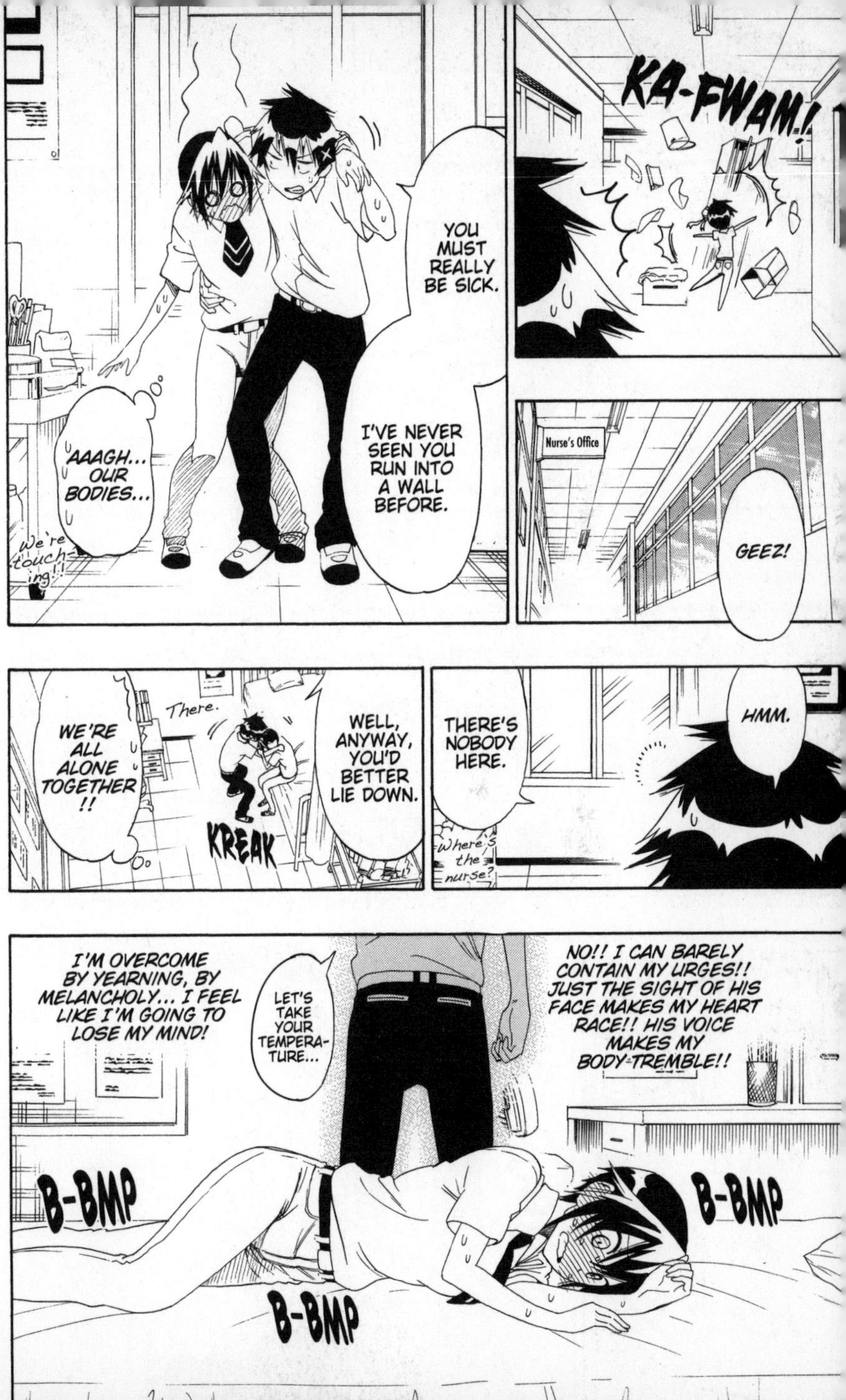
KA-FWAM!
Nurse's Office
GEEZ!
YOU MUST REALLY BE SICK.
I'VE NEVER SEEN YOU RUN INTO A WALL BEFORE.
AAAGH... OUR BODIES...
We're touching!!
HMM.
THERE'S NOBODY HERE.
Where's the nurse?
WELL, ANYWAY, YOU'D BETTER LIE DOWN.
KREAK
There.
WE'RE ALL ALONE TOGETHER!!
NO!! I CAN BARELY CONTAIN MY URGES!! JUST THE SIGHT OF HIS FACE MAKES MY HEART RACE!! HIS VOICE MAKES MY BODY TREMBLE!!
LET'S TAKE YOUR TEMPERATURE...
I'M OVERCOME BY YEARNING, BY MELANCHOLY... I FEEL LIKE I'M GOING TO LOSE MY MIND!
B-BMP
B-BMP
B-BMP

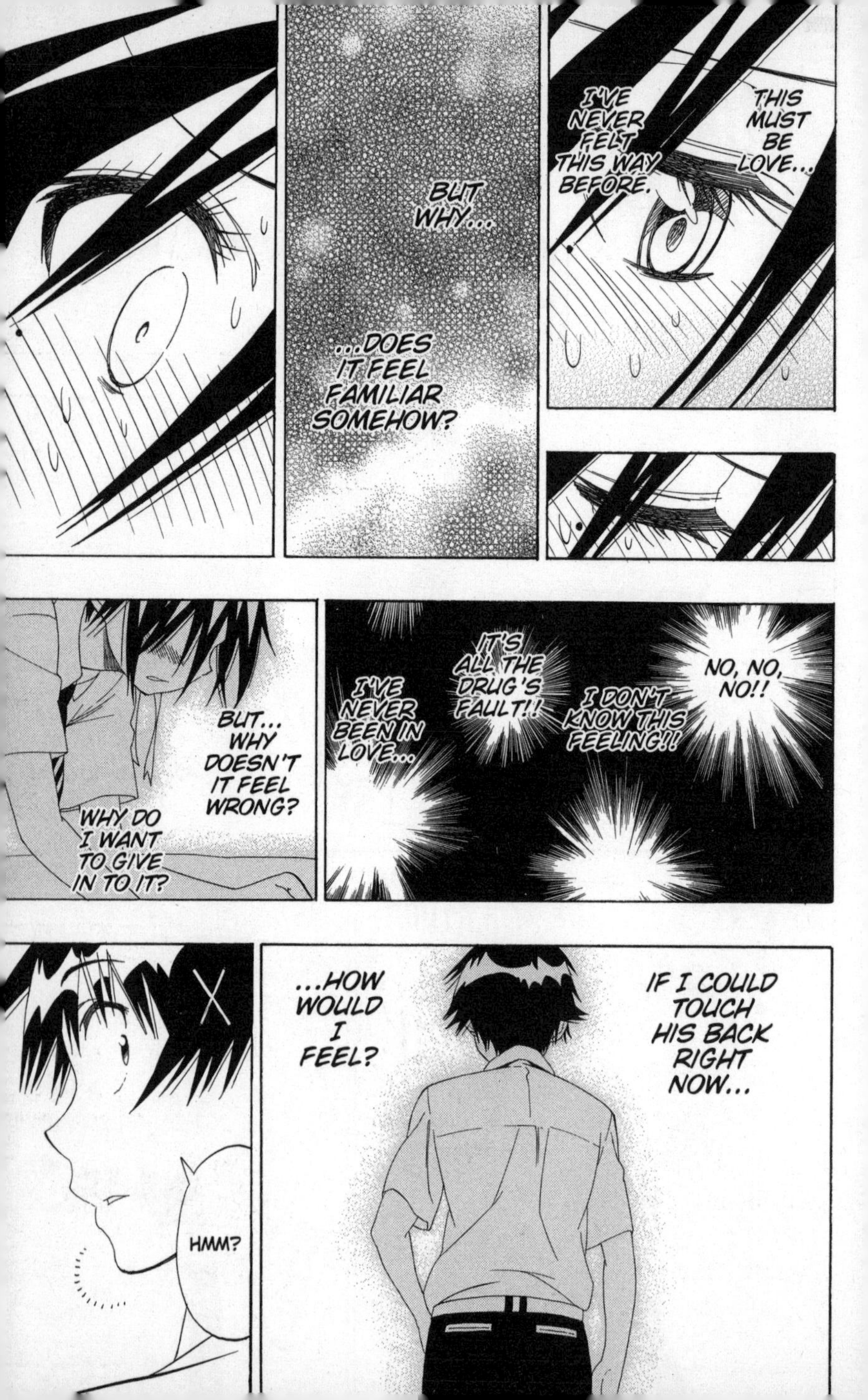
THIS MUST BE LOVE...
I'VE NEVER FELT THIS WAY BEFORE.
BUT WHY...
...DOES IT FEEL FAMILIAR SOMEHOW?
NO, NO, NO!!
I DON'T KNOW THIS FEELING!!
IT'S ALL THE DRUG'S FAULT!!
I'VE NEVER BEEN IN LOVE...
BUT... WHY DOESN'T IT FEEL WRONG?
WHY DO I WANT TO GIVE IN TO IT?
IF I COULD TOUCH HIS BACK RIGHT NOW...
...HOW WOULD I FEEL?
HMM?

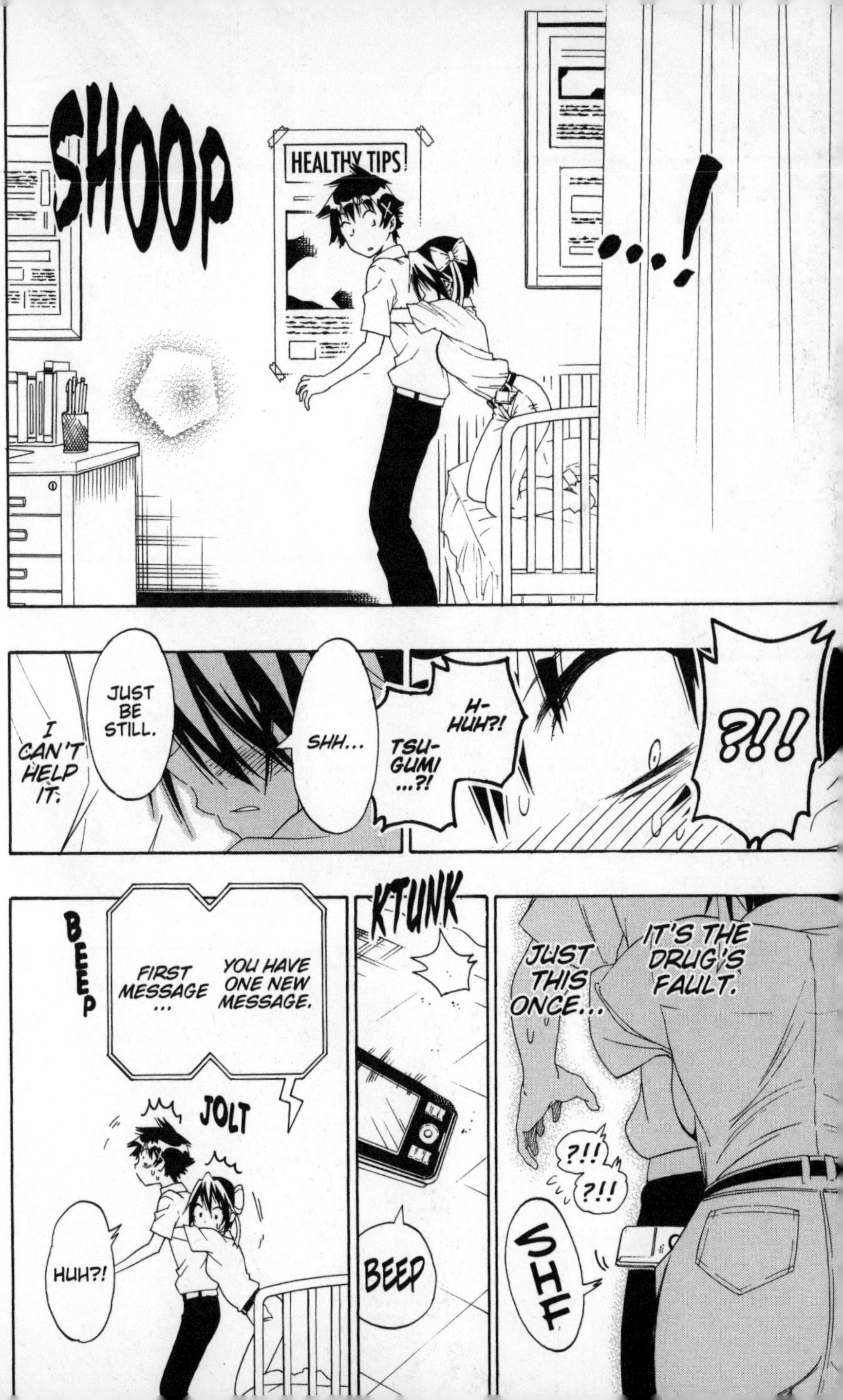
...!
HEALTHY TIPS
SHOOP
?!!
H-HUH?!
TSU-GUMI...?!
SHH...
JUST BE STILL.
I CAN'T HELP IT.
IT'S THE DRUG'S FAULT.
JUST THIS ONCE...
?!!
?!!
SHF
KTUNK
BEEP
BEEP
YOU HAVE ONE NEW MESSAGE.
FIRST MESSAGE...
JOLT
HUH?!

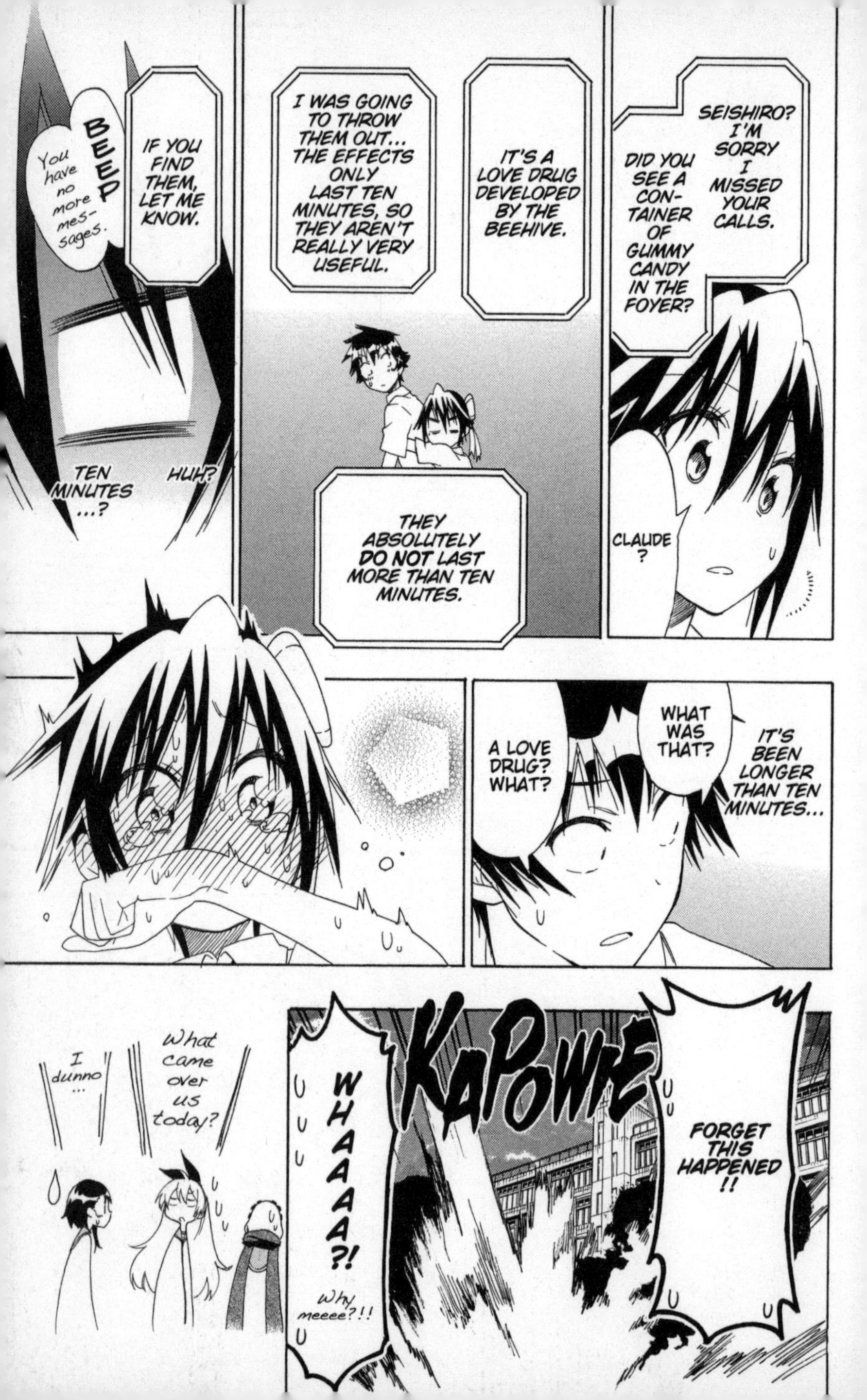
SEISHIRO? I'M SORRY I MISSED YOUR CALLS.
DID YOU SEE A CONTAINER OF GUMMY CANDY IN THE FOYER?
CLAUDE?
IT'S A LOVE DRUG DEVELOPED BY THE BEEHIVE.
I WAS GOING TO THROW THEM OUT... THE EFFECTS ONLY LAST TEN MINUTES, SO THEY AREN'T REALLY VERY USEFUL.
THEY ABSOLUTELY DO NOT LAST MORE THAN TEN MINUTES.
IF YOU FIND THEM, LET ME KNOW.
BEEP
You have no more messages.
HUH?
TEN MINUTES ...?
WHAT WAS THAT?
IT'S BEEN LONGER THAN TEN MINUTES...
A LOVE DRUG? WHAT?
KAPOWIE
FORGET THIS HAPPENED!!
WHAAAAA?!
Why meeee?!!
What came over us today?
I dunno...

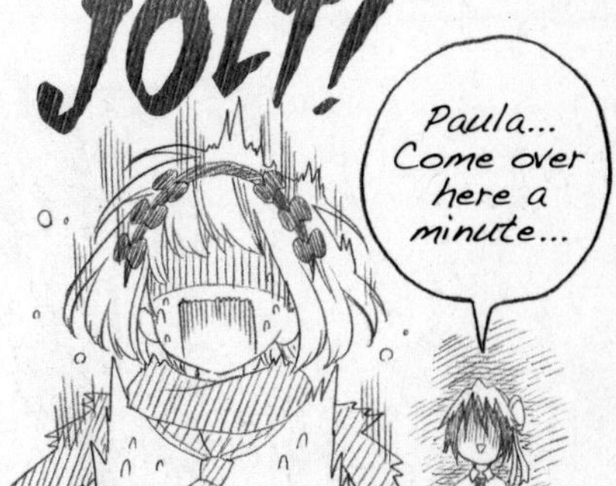
JOLT!
Paula... Come over here a minute...

Chapter 112: Steps

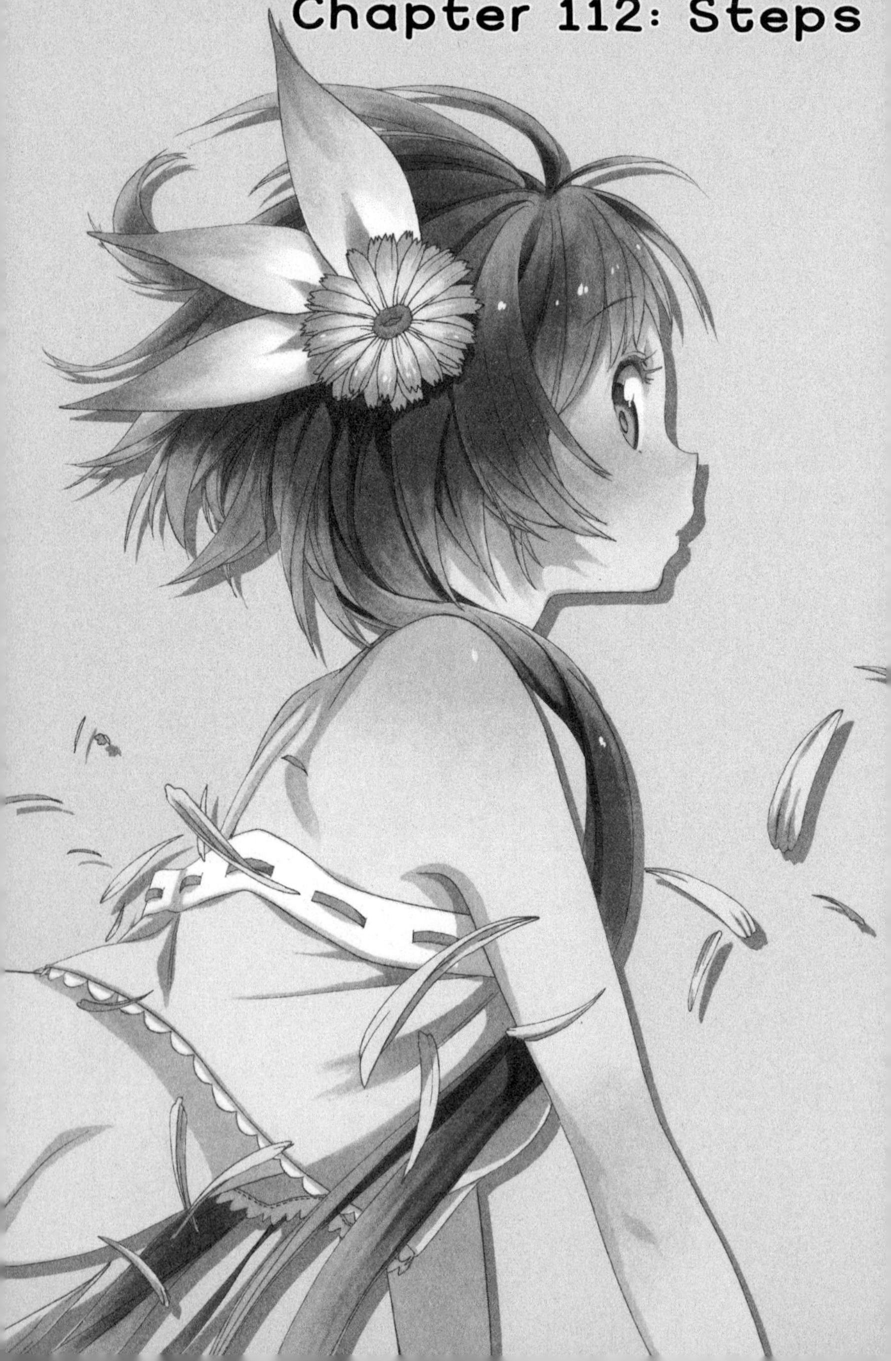

NISEKOI

False Love

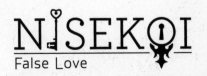

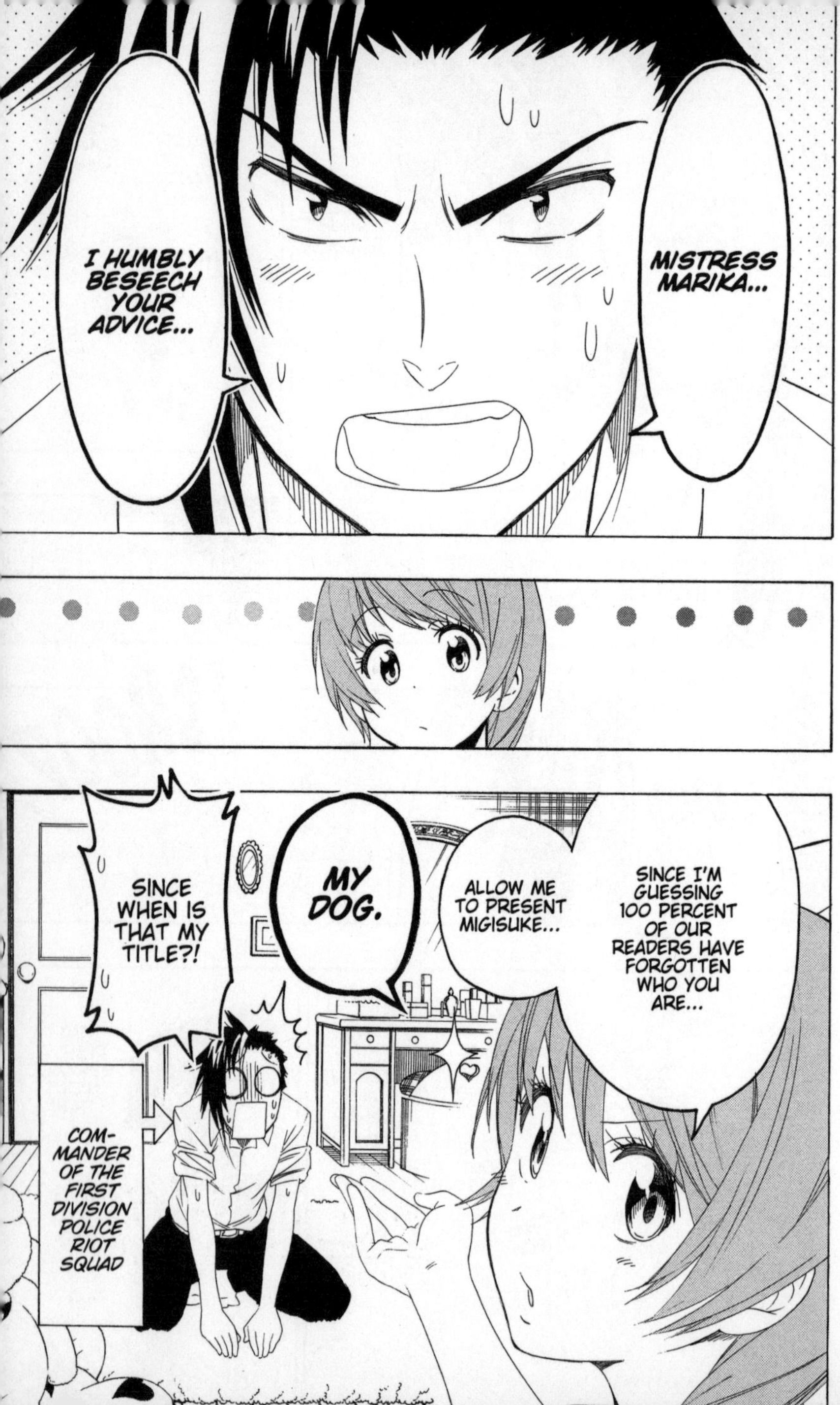
MISTRESS MARIKA...
I HUMBLY BESEECH YOUR ADVICE...
SINCE I'M GUESSING 100 PERCENT OF OUR READERS HAVE FORGOTTEN WHO YOU ARE...
ALLOW ME TO PRESENT MIGISUKE...
MY DOG.
SINCE WHEN IS THAT MY TITLE?!
COM-MANDER OF THE FIRST DIVISION POLICE RIOT SQUAD

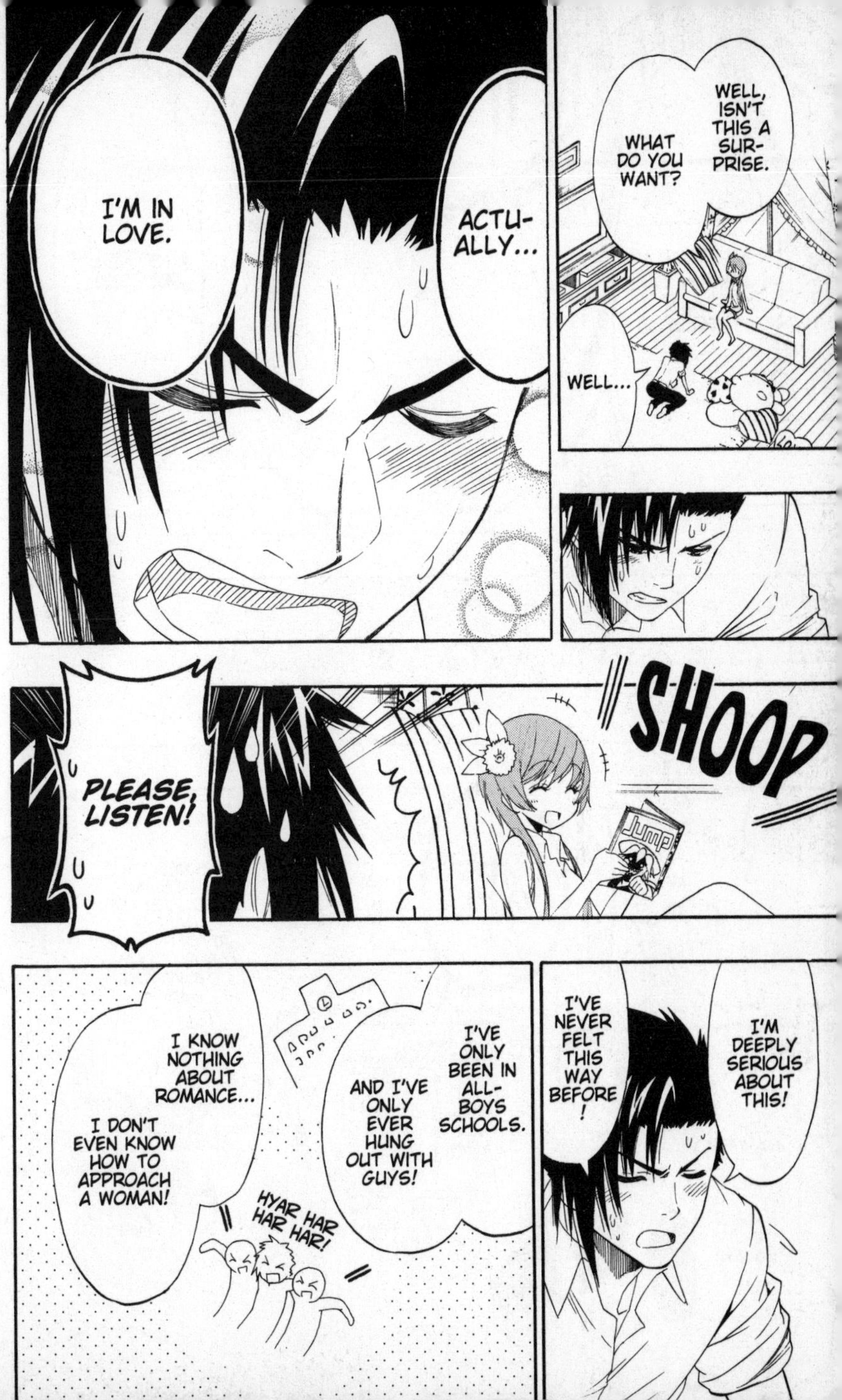
WELL, ISN'T THIS A SUR-PRISE.
WHAT DO YOU WANT?
WELL...
ACTU-ALLY...
I'M IN LOVE.
SHOOP
PLEASE, LISTEN!
I'M DEEPLY SERIOUS ABOUT THIS!
I'VE NEVER FELT THIS WAY BEFORE!
I'VE ONLY BEEN IN ALL-BOYS SCHOOLS.
AND I'VE ONLY EVER HUNG OUT WITH GUYS!
I KNOW NOTHING ABOUT ROMANCE...
I DON'T EVEN KNOW HOW TO APPROACH A WOMAN!
HYAR HAR HAR HAR!

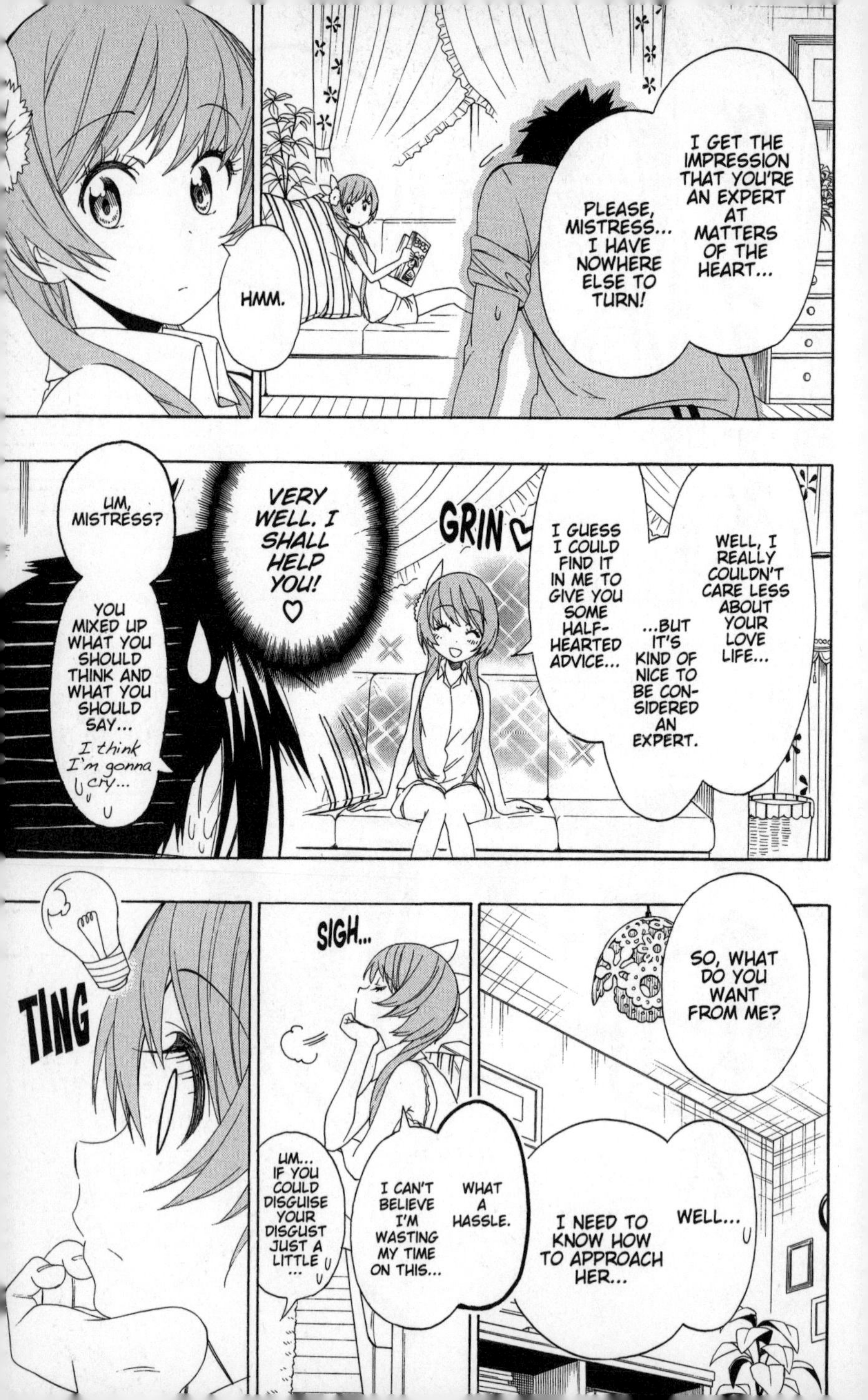

I GET THE IMPRESSION THAT YOU'RE AN EXPERT AT MATTERS OF THE HEART...
PLEASE, MISTRESS... I HAVE NOWHERE ELSE TO TURN!
HMM.
WELL, I REALLY COULDN'T CARE LESS ABOUT YOUR LOVE LIFE...
...BUT IT'S KIND OF NICE TO BE CONSIDERED AN EXPERT.
I GUESS I COULD FIND IT IN ME TO GIVE YOU SOME HALF-HEARTED ADVICE...
GRIN ♡
VERY WELL. I SHALL HELP YOU! ♡
UM, MISTRESS?
YOU MIXED UP WHAT YOU SHOULD THINK AND WHAT YOU SHOULD SAY...
I think I'm gonna cry...
SO, WHAT DO YOU WANT FROM ME?
WELL...
I NEED TO KNOW HOW TO APPROACH HER...
SIGH...
WHAT A HASSLE.
I CAN'T BELIEVE I'M WASTING MY TIME ON THIS...
UM... IF YOU COULD DISGUISE YOUR DISGUST JUST A LITTLE...
TING

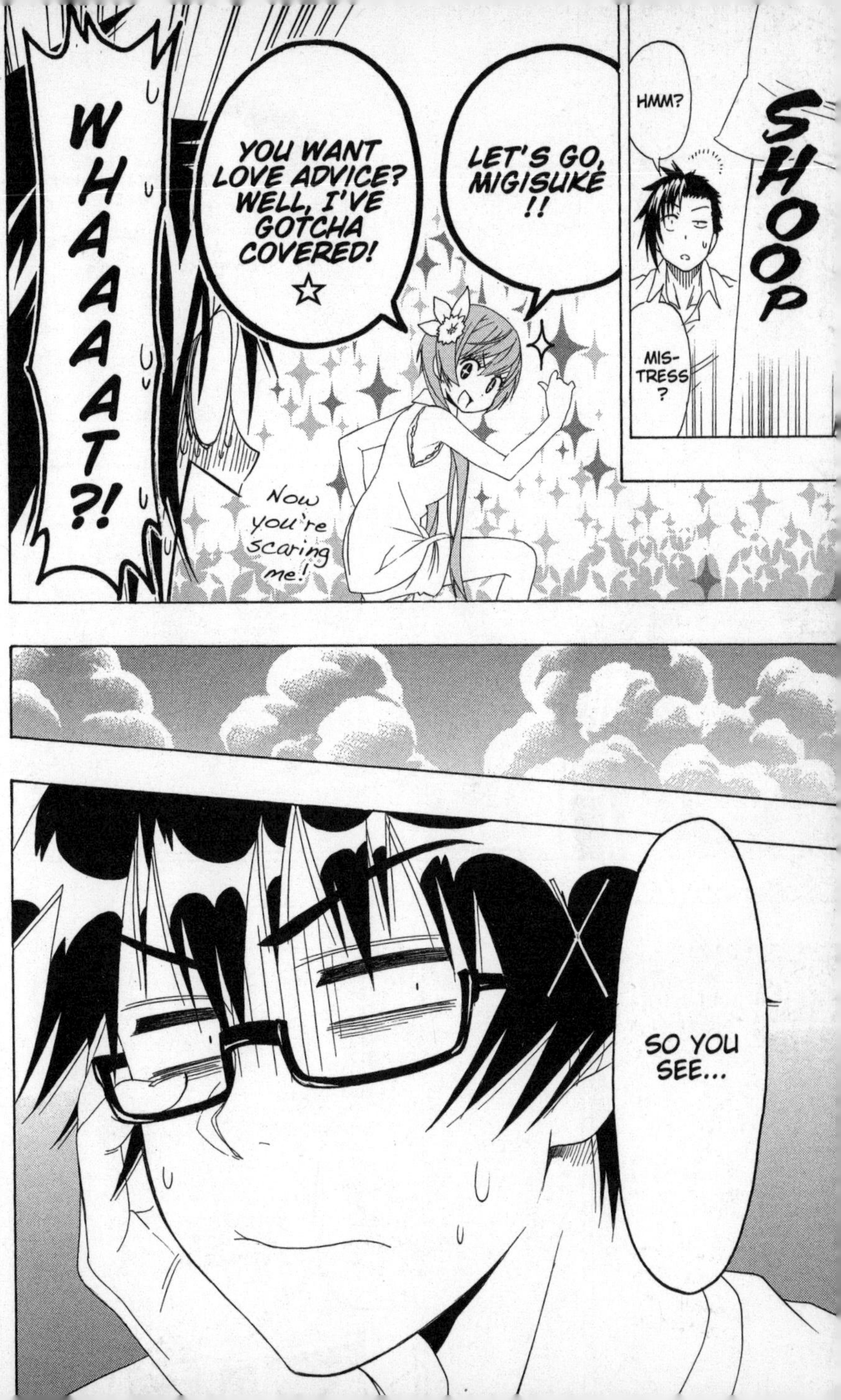
SHOOP
HMM?
MISTRESS?
LET'S GO, MIGISUKE!!
YOU WANT LOVE ADVICE? WELL, I'VE GOTCHA COVERED! ☆
WHAAAAAT?!
Now you're scaring me!
SO YOU SEE...

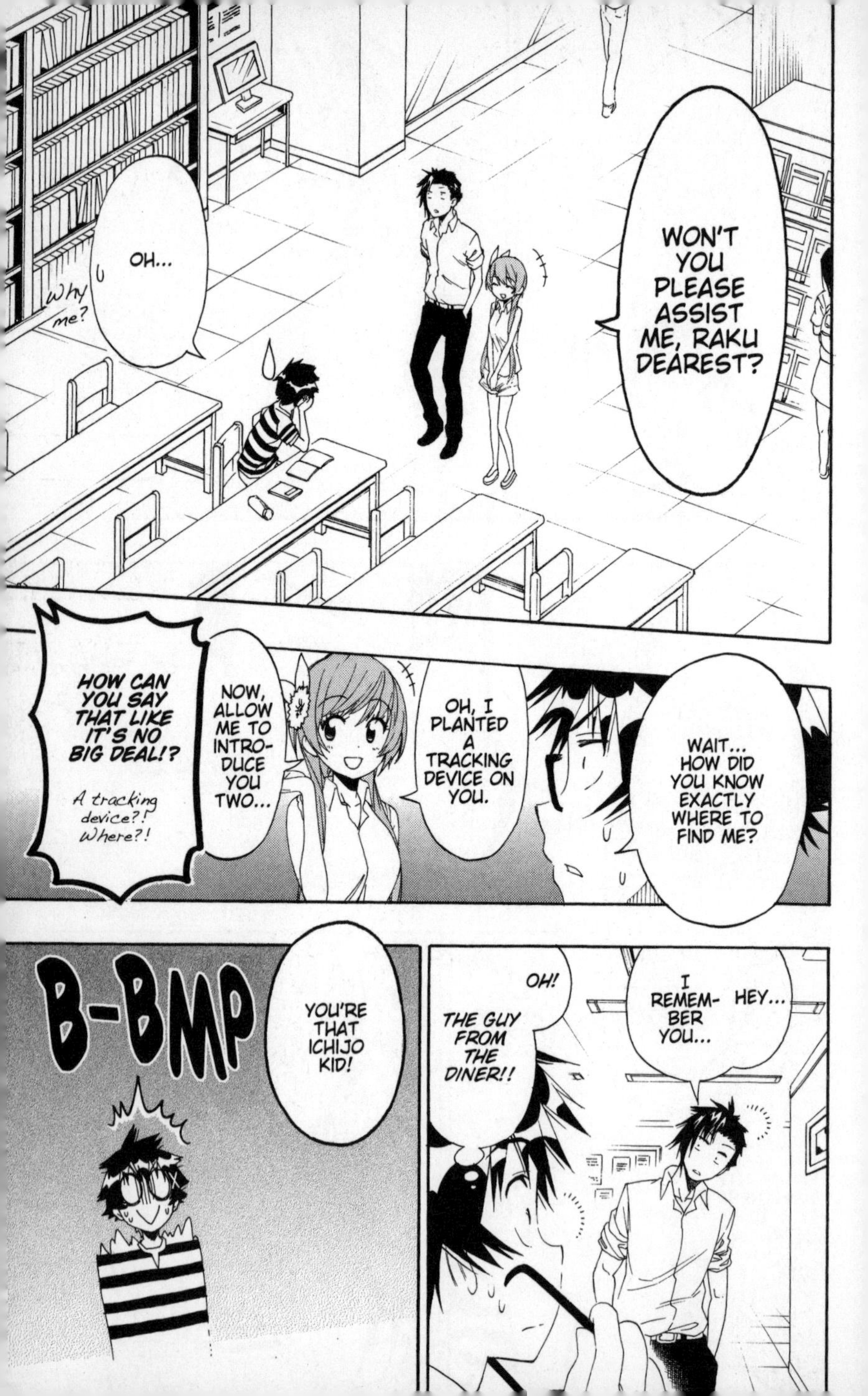
WON'T YOU PLEASE ASSIST ME, RAKU DEAREST?
OH...
Why me?
WAIT... HOW DID YOU KNOW EXACTLY WHERE TO FIND ME?
OH, I PLANTED A TRACKING DEVICE ON YOU.
NOW, ALLOW ME TO INTRO-DUCE YOU TWO...
HOW CAN YOU SAY THAT LIKE IT'S NO BIG DEAL!?
A tracking device?! Where?!
HEY...
I REMEM-BER YOU...
OH!
THE GUY FROM THE DINER!!
YOU'RE THAT ICHIJO KID!
B-BMP

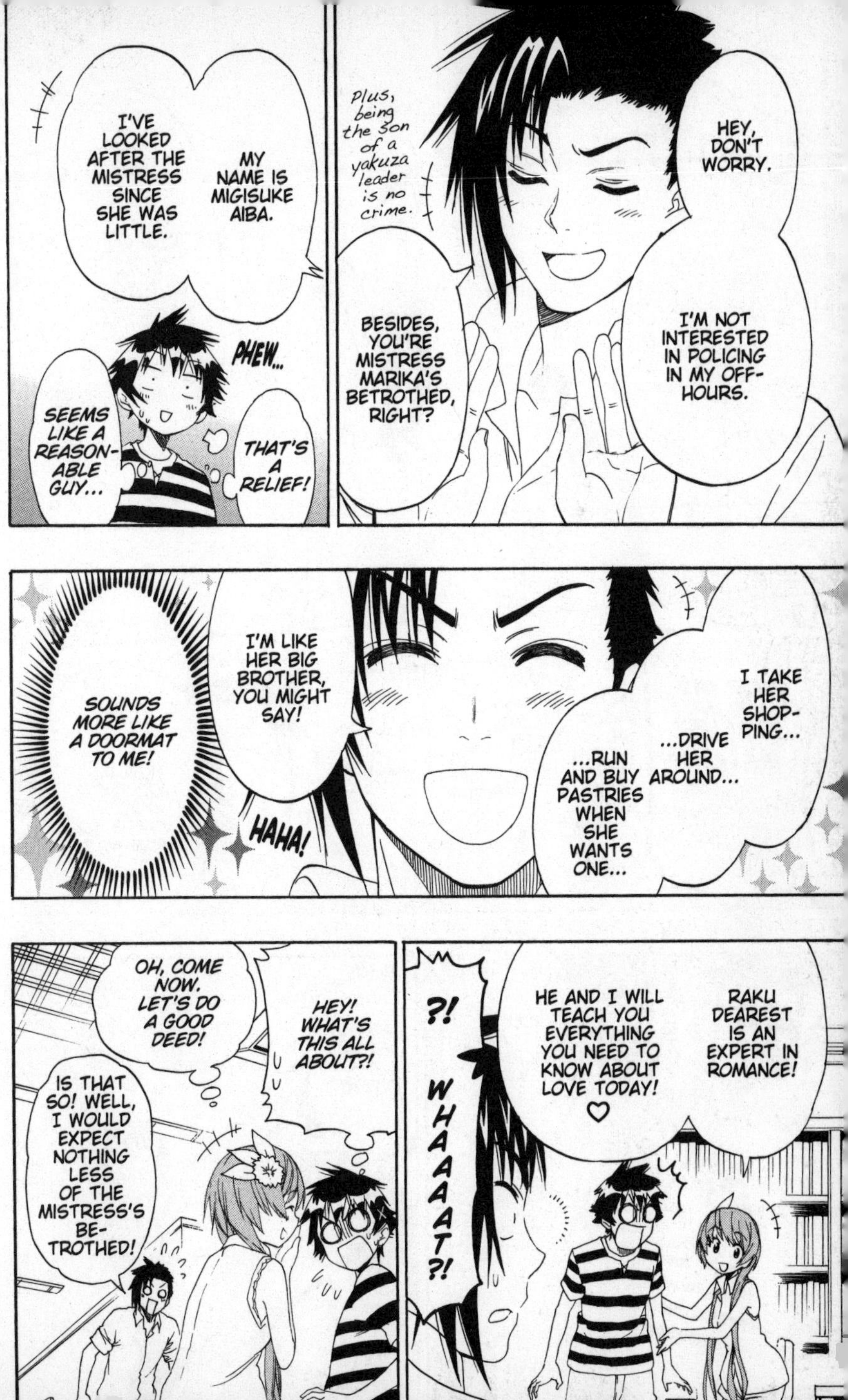
HEY, DON'T WORRY.
I'M NOT INTERESTED IN POLICING IN MY OFF-HOURS.
Plus, being the son of a yakuza leader is no crime.
BESIDES, YOU'RE MISTRESS MARIKA'S BETROTHED, RIGHT?
MY NAME IS MIGISUKE AIBA.
I'VE LOOKED AFTER THE MISTRESS SINCE SHE WAS LITTLE.
PHEW...
THAT'S A RELIEF!
SEEMS LIKE A REASON-ABLE GUY...
I TAKE HER SHOP-PING...
...DRIVE HER AROUND...
...RUN AND BUY PASTRIES WHEN SHE WANTS ONE...
I'M LIKE HER BIG BROTHER, YOU MIGHT SAY!
HAHA!
SOUNDS MORE LIKE A DOORMAT TO ME!
RAKU DEAREST IS AN EXPERT IN ROMANCE!
HE AND I WILL TEACH YOU EVERYTHING YOU NEED TO KNOW ABOUT LOVE TODAY! ♡
?!
WHAAAAAT?!
HEY! WHAT'S THIS ALL ABOUT?!
OH, COME NOW. LET'S DO A GOOD DEED!
IS THAT SO! WELL, I WOULD EXPECT NOTHING LESS OF THE MISTRESS'S BE-TROTHED!

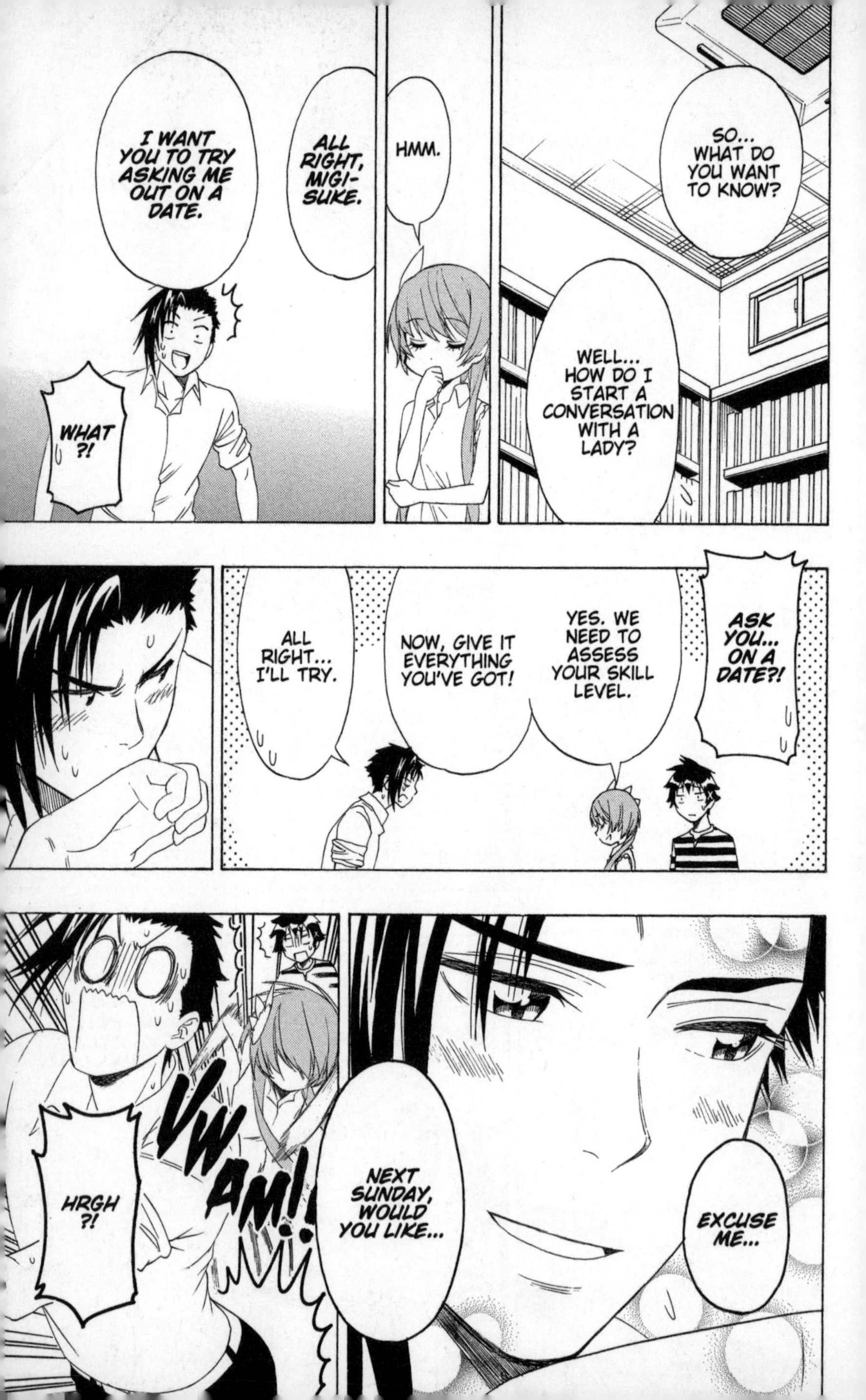

SO... WHAT DO YOU WANT TO KNOW?
WELL... HOW DO I START A CONVERSATION WITH A LADY?
HMM.
ALL RIGHT, MIGI-SUKE.
I WANT YOU TO TRY ASKING ME OUT ON A DATE.
WHAT?!
ASK YOU... ON A DATE?!
YES. WE NEED TO ASSESS YOUR SKILL LEVEL.
NOW, GIVE IT EVERYTHING YOU'VE GOT!
ALL RIGHT... I'LL TRY.
EXCUSE ME...
NEXT SUNDAY, WOULD YOU LIKE...
VWAM!!
HRGH?!

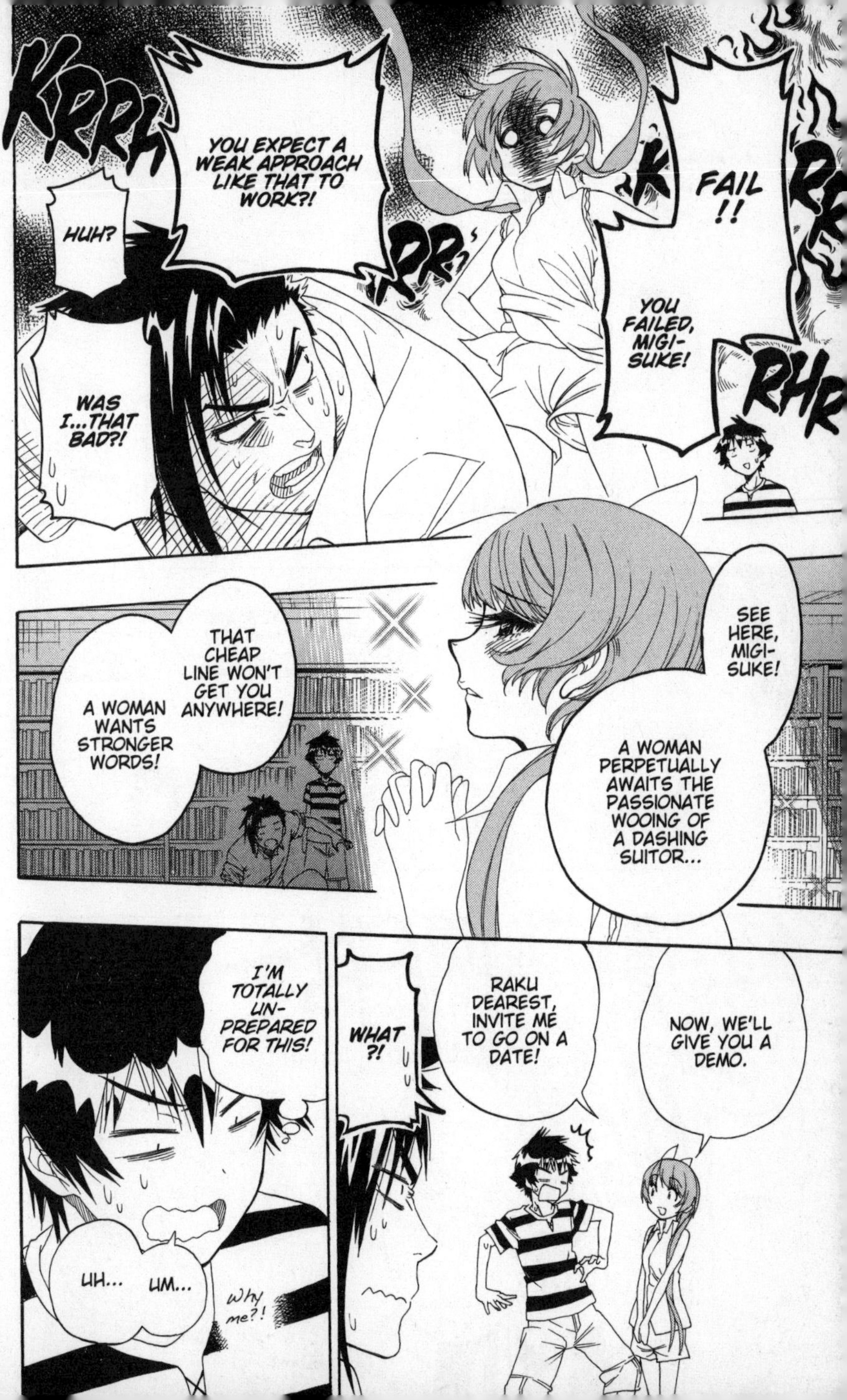
FAIL!!
YOU FAILED, MIGI-SUKE!
YOU EXPECT A WEAK APPROACH LIKE THAT TO WORK?!
KRRK
HUH?
WAS I...THAT BAD?!
SEE HERE, MIGI-SUKE!
A WOMAN PERPETUALLY AWAITS THE PASSIONATE WOOING OF A DASHING SUITOR...
THAT CHEAP LINE WON'T GET YOU ANYWHERE!
A WOMAN WANTS STRONGER WORDS!
NOW, WE'LL GIVE YOU A DEMO.
RAKU DEAREST, INVITE ME TO GO ON A DATE!
WHAT?!
I'M TOTALLY UN-PREPARED FOR THIS!
UH... UM...
Why me?!

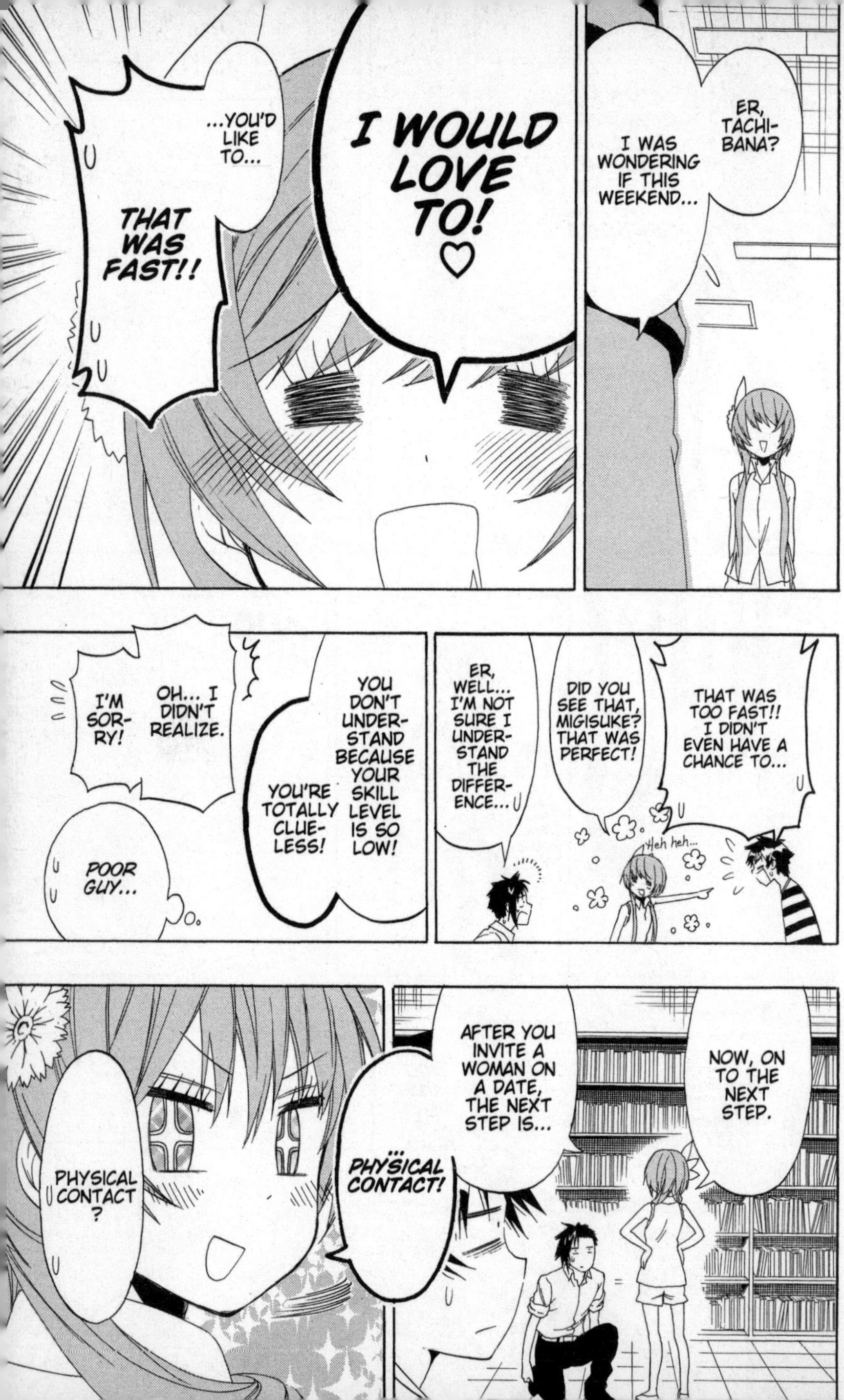
ER, TACHIBANA?
I WAS WONDERING IF THIS WEEKEND...
I WOULD LOVE TO! ♡
...YOU'D LIKE TO...
THAT WAS FAST!!
THAT WAS TOO FAST!! I DIDN'T EVEN HAVE A CHANCE TO...
DID YOU SEE THAT, MIGISUKE? THAT WAS PERFECT!
Heh heh...
ER, WELL... I'M NOT SURE I UNDERSTAND THE DIFFERENCE...
YOU DON'T UNDERSTAND BECAUSE YOUR SKILL LEVEL IS SO LOW!
YOU'RE TOTALLY CLUELESS!
OH... I DIDN'T REALIZE.
I'M SORRY!
POOR GUY...
NOW, ON TO THE NEXT STEP.
AFTER YOU INVITE A WOMAN ON A DATE, THE NEXT STEP IS...
...PHYSICAL CONTACT!
PHYSICAL CONTACT?

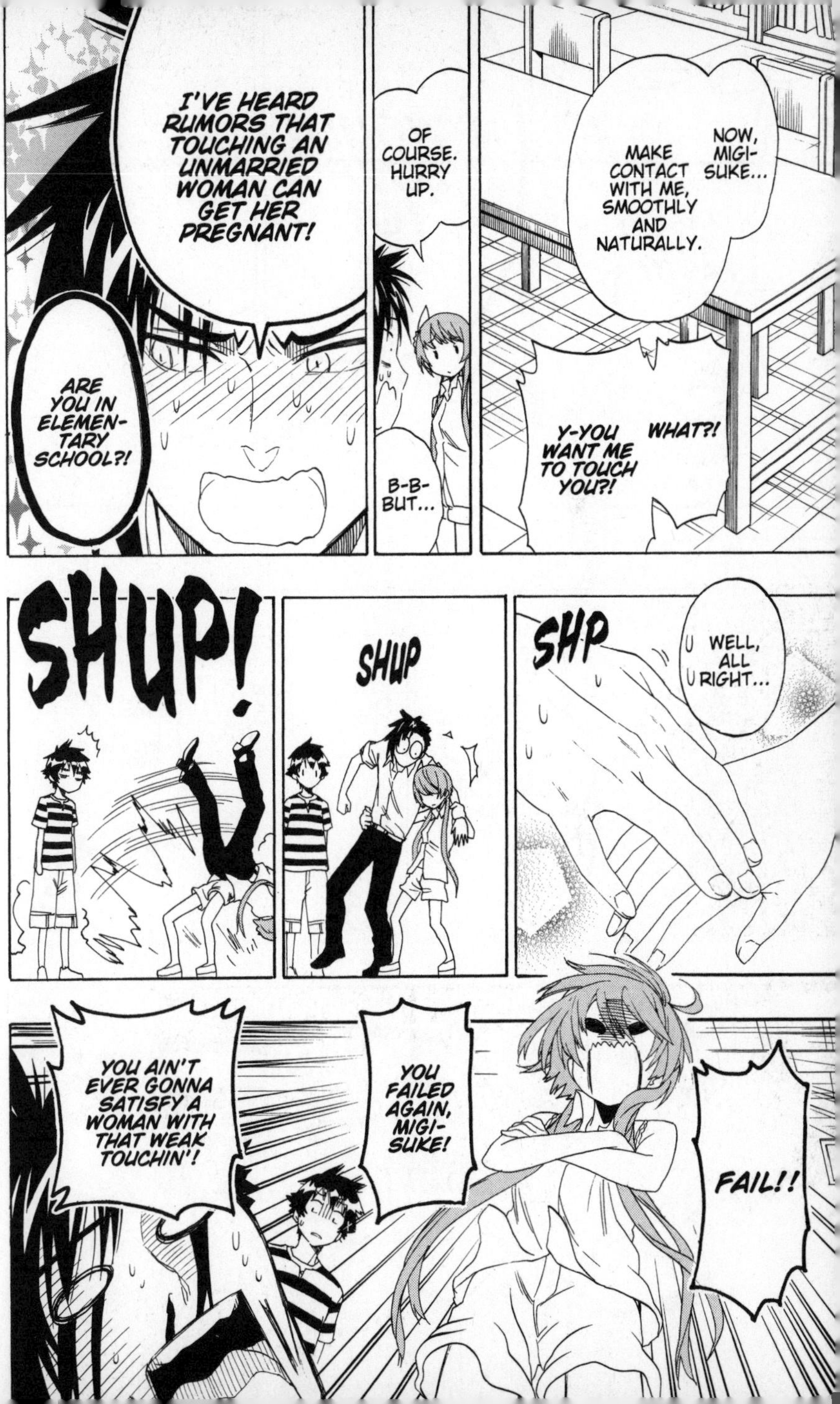
NOW, MIGI-SUKE...
MAKE CONTACT WITH ME, SMOOTHLY AND NATURALLY.
WHAT?!
Y-YOU WANT ME TO TOUCH YOU?!
OF COURSE. HURRY UP.
B-B-BUT...
I'VE HEARD RUMORS THAT TOUCHING AN UNMARRIED WOMAN CAN GET HER PREGNANT!
ARE YOU IN ELEMENTARY SCHOOL?!
WELL, ALL RIGHT...
SHP
SHUP
SHUP!
FAIL!!
YOU FAILED AGAIN, MIGI-SUKE!
YOU AIN'T EVER GONNA SATISFY A WOMAN WITH THAT WEAK TOUCHIN'!

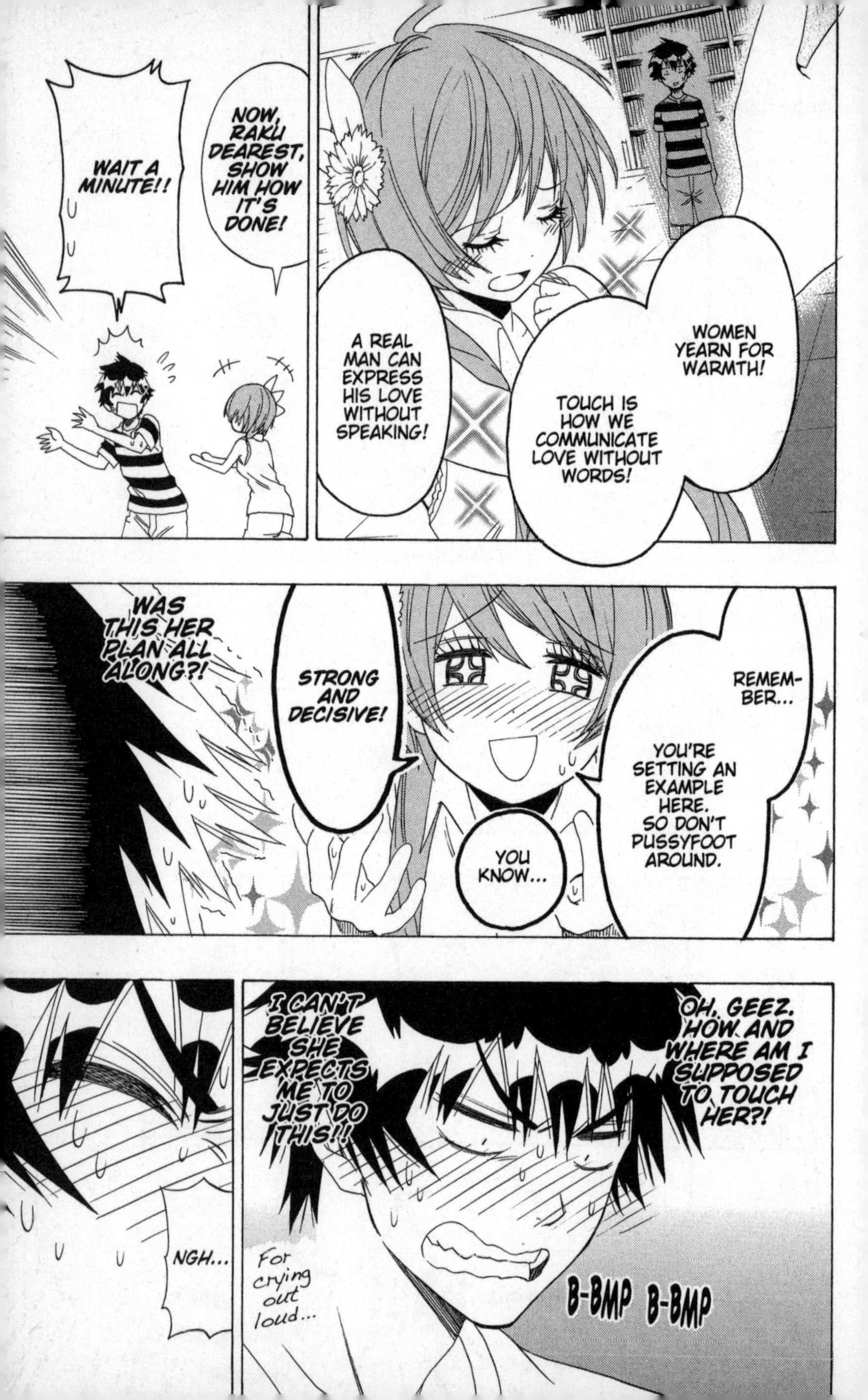
WOMEN YEARN FOR WARMTH!
TOUCH IS HOW WE COMMUNICATE LOVE WITHOUT WORDS!
A REAL MAN CAN EXPRESS HIS LOVE WITHOUT SPEAKING!
NOW, RAKU DEAREST, SHOW HIM HOW IT'S DONE!
WAIT A MINUTE!!
REMEM-BER...
YOU'RE SETTING AN EXAMPLE HERE. SO DON'T PUSSYFOOT AROUND.
YOU KNOW...
STRONG AND DECISIVE!
WAS THIS HER PLAN ALL ALONG?!
OH, GEEZ. HOW AND WHERE AM I SUPPOSED TO TOUCH HER?!
I CAN'T BELIEVE SHE EXPECTS ME TO JUST DO THIS!!
B-BMP B-BMP
For crying out loud...
NGH...

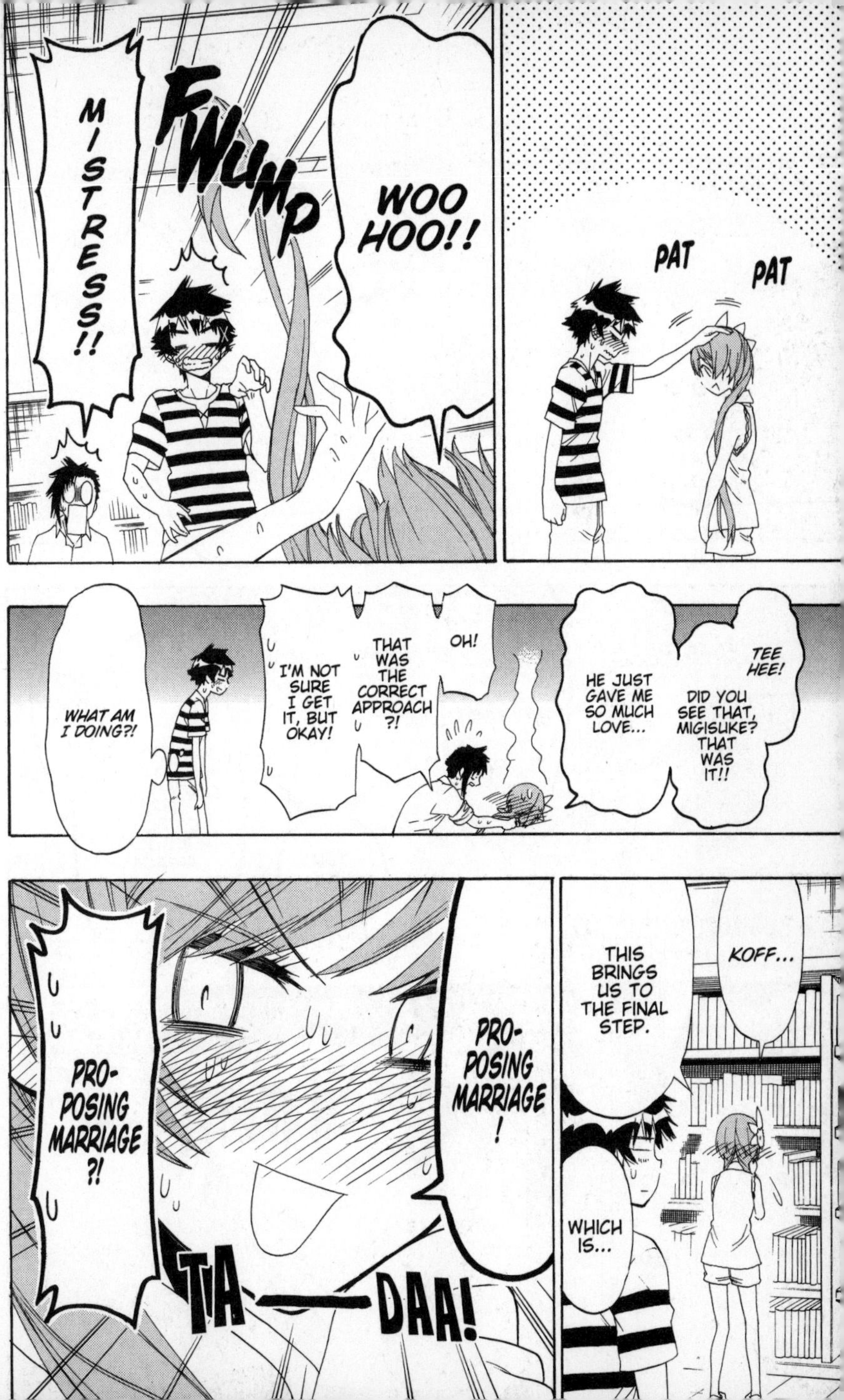
PAT
PAT
WOO HOO!!
FWUMP
MISTRESS!!
TEE HEE!
DID YOU SEE THAT, MIGISUKE? THAT WAS IT!!
HE JUST GAVE ME SO MUCH LOVE...
OH!
THAT WAS THE CORRECT APPROACH?!
I'M NOT SURE I GET IT, BUT OKAY!
WHAT AM I DOING?!
KOFF...
THIS BRINGS US TO THE FINAL STEP.
WHICH IS...
PRO-POSING MARRIAGE!
TA-—DAA!
PRO-POSING MARRIAGE?!

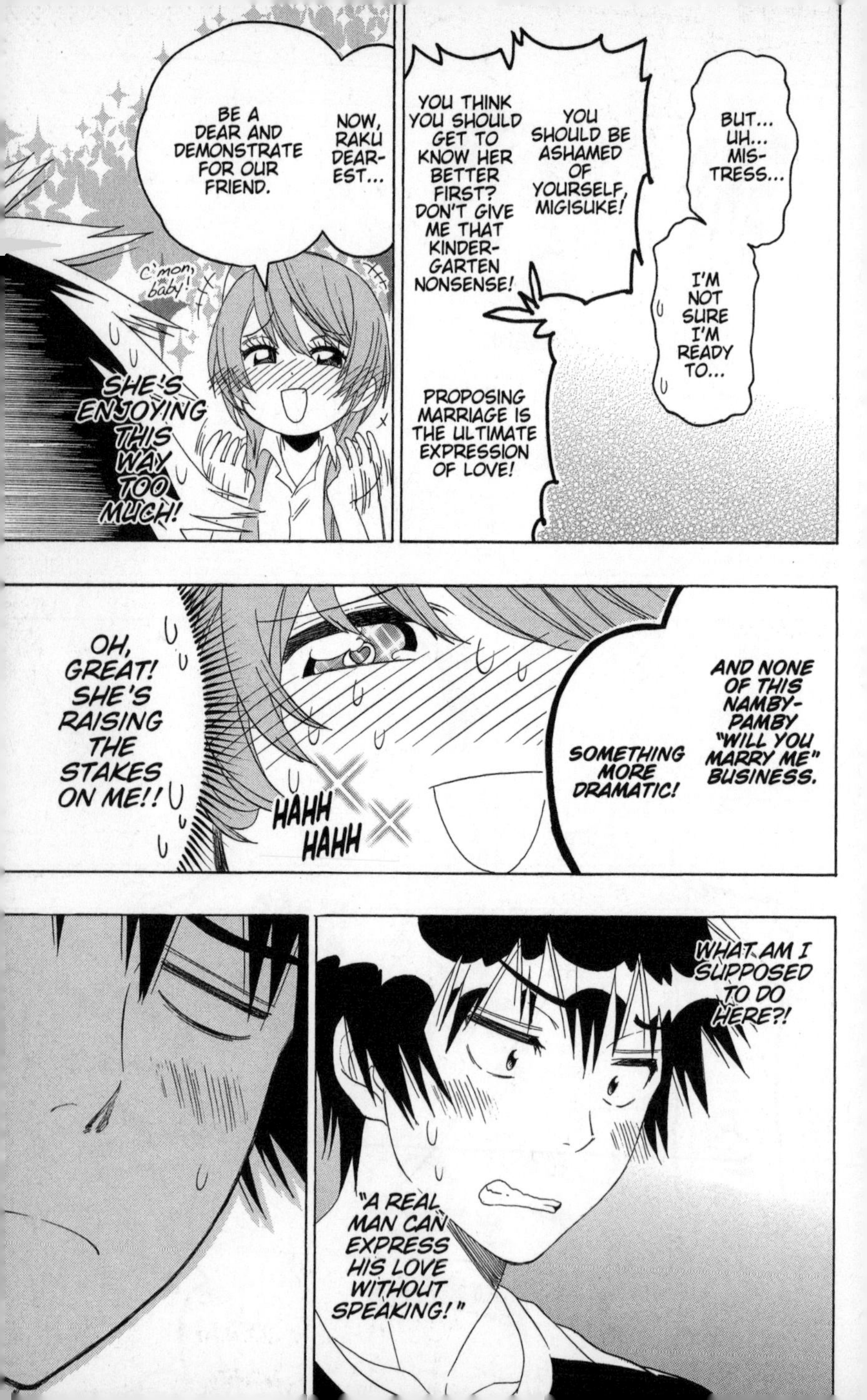
BUT... UH... MIS-TRESS...
I'M NOT SURE I'M READY TO...
YOU SHOULD BE ASHAMED OF YOURSELF, MIGISUKE!
YOU THINK YOU SHOULD GET TO KNOW HER BETTER FIRST? DON'T GIVE ME THAT KINDER-GARTEN NONSENSE!
PROPOSING MARRIAGE IS THE ULTIMATE EXPRESSION OF LOVE!
NOW, RAKU DEAR-EST...
BE A DEAR AND DEMONSTRATE FOR OUR FRIEND.
C'mon, baby!
SHE'S ENJOYING THIS WAY TOO MUCH!
AND NONE OF THIS NAMBY-PAMBY "WILL YOU MARRY ME" BUSINESS.
SOMETHING MORE DRAMATIC!
HAHH HAHH
OH, GREAT! SHE'S RAISING THE STAKES ON ME!!
WHAT AM I SUPPOSED TO DO HERE?!
"A REAL MAN CAN EXPRESS HIS LOVE WITHOUT SPEAKING!"

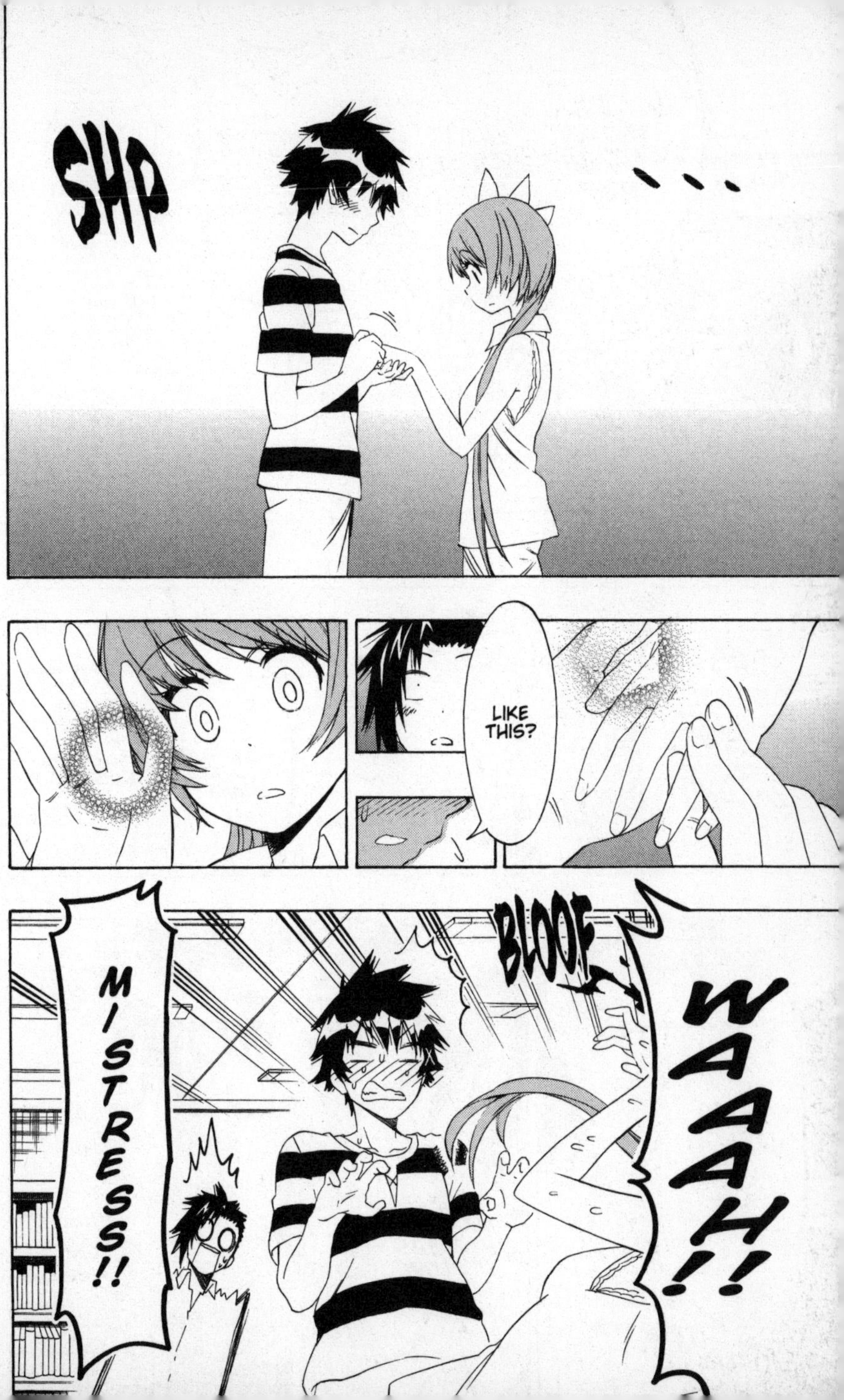

...
SHP
LIKE THIS?
WAAAH!!
BLOOF
MISTRESS!!

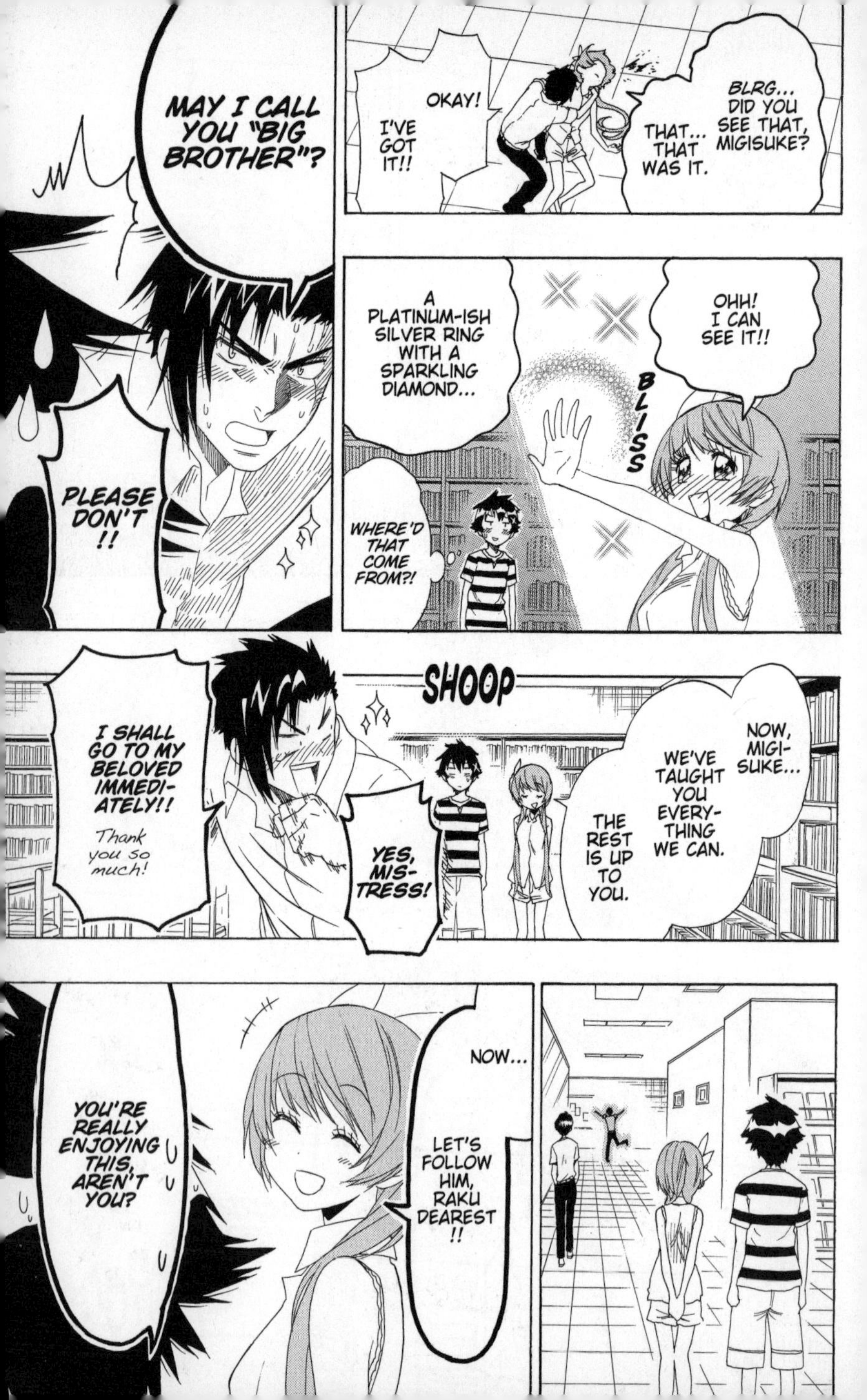
BLRG... DID YOU SEE THAT, MIGISUKE?
THAT... THAT WAS IT.
OKAY!
I'VE GOT IT!!
OHH! I CAN SEE IT!!
BLISS
A PLATINUM-ISH SILVER RING WITH A SPARKLING DIAMOND...
WHERE'D THAT COME FROM?!
MAY I CALL YOU "BIG BROTHER"?
PLEASE DON'T!!
NOW, MIGISUKE...
WE'VE TAUGHT YOU EVERYTHING WE CAN.
THE REST IS UP TO YOU.
SHOOP
YES, MISTRESS!
I SHALL GO TO MY BELOVED IMMEDIATELY!!
Thank you so much!
NOW...
LET'S FOLLOW HIM, RAKU DEAREST!!
YOU'RE REALLY ENJOYING THIS, AREN'T YOU?

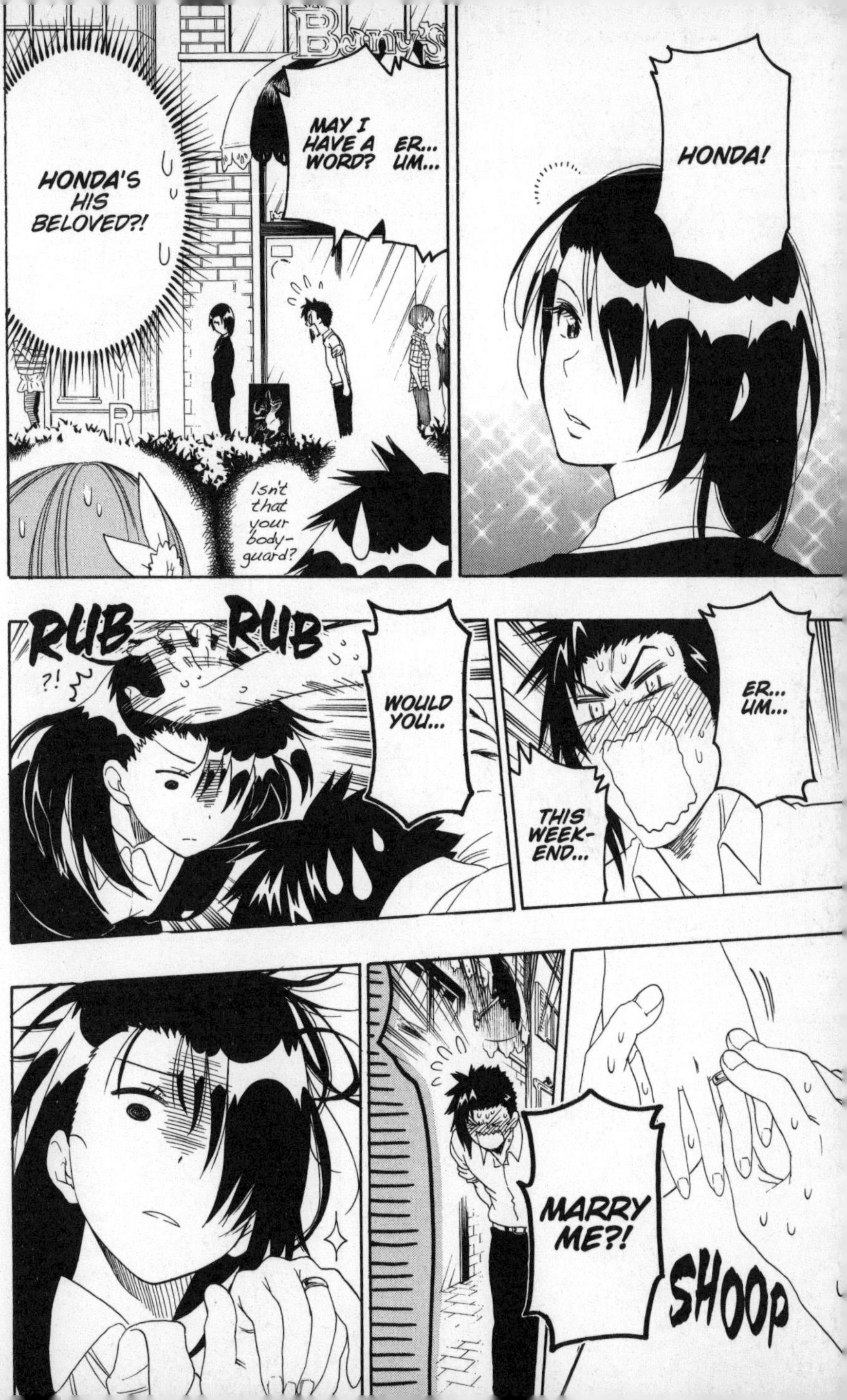
HONDA!
ER... UM...
MAY I HAVE A WORD?
HONDA'S HIS BELOVED?!
Isn't that your bodyguard?
ER... UM...
THIS WEEKEND...
WOULD YOU...
RUB RUB
?!
MARRY ME?!
SHOOP

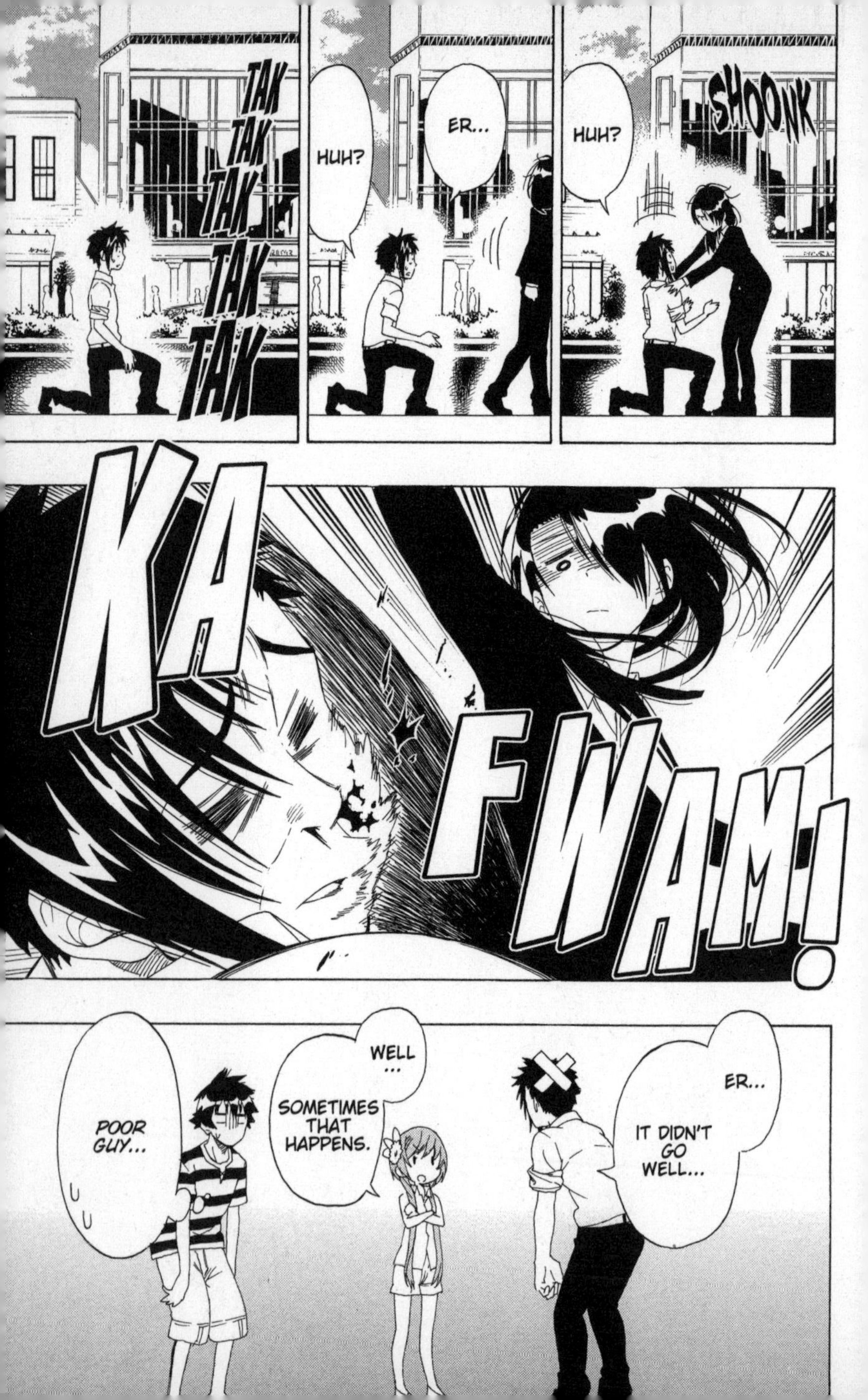
SHOONK
HUH?
ER...
HUH?
TAK TAK TAK TAK TAK TAK
KA
FWAM!
ER...
IT DIDN'T GO WELL...
WELL...
SOMETIMES THAT HAPPENS.
POOR GUY...

Chapter 113: Great-Grandpa

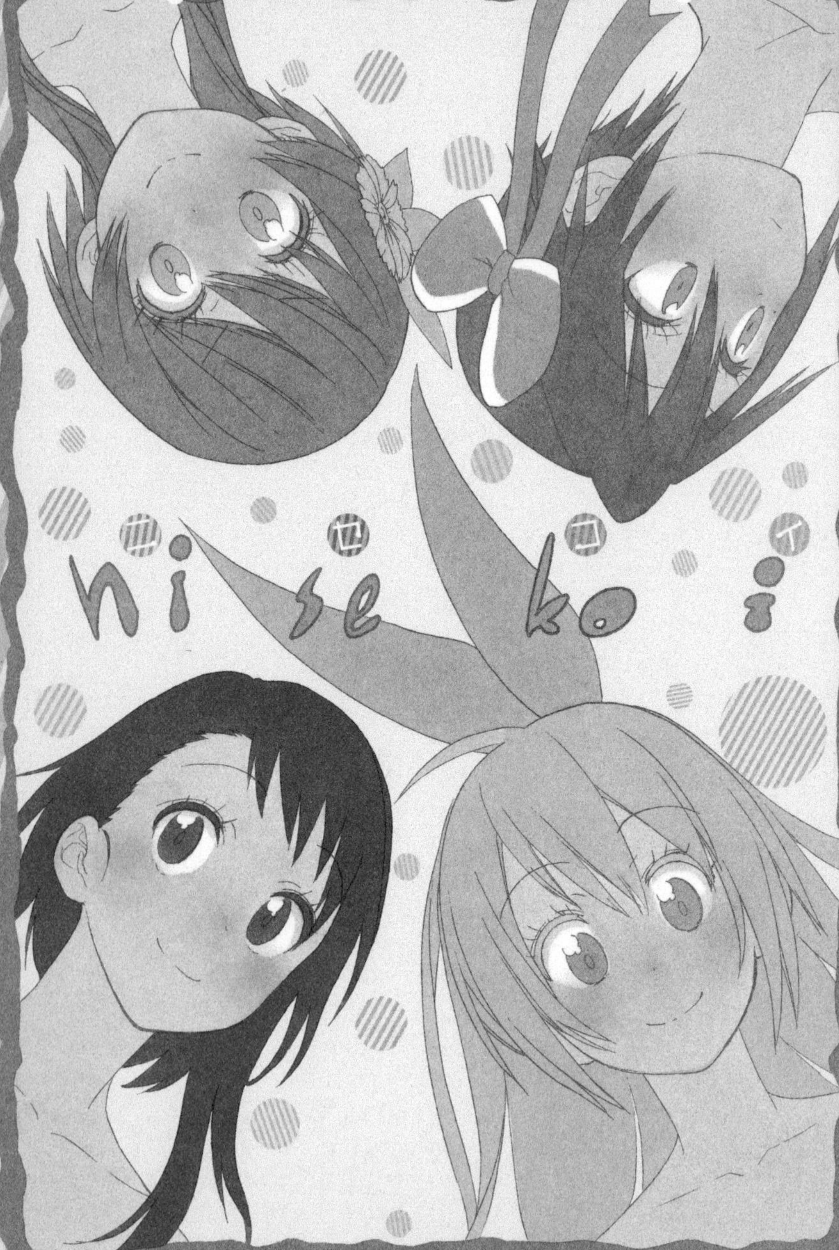
ni se ko i

NISEKOI
False Love

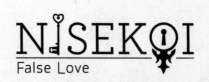

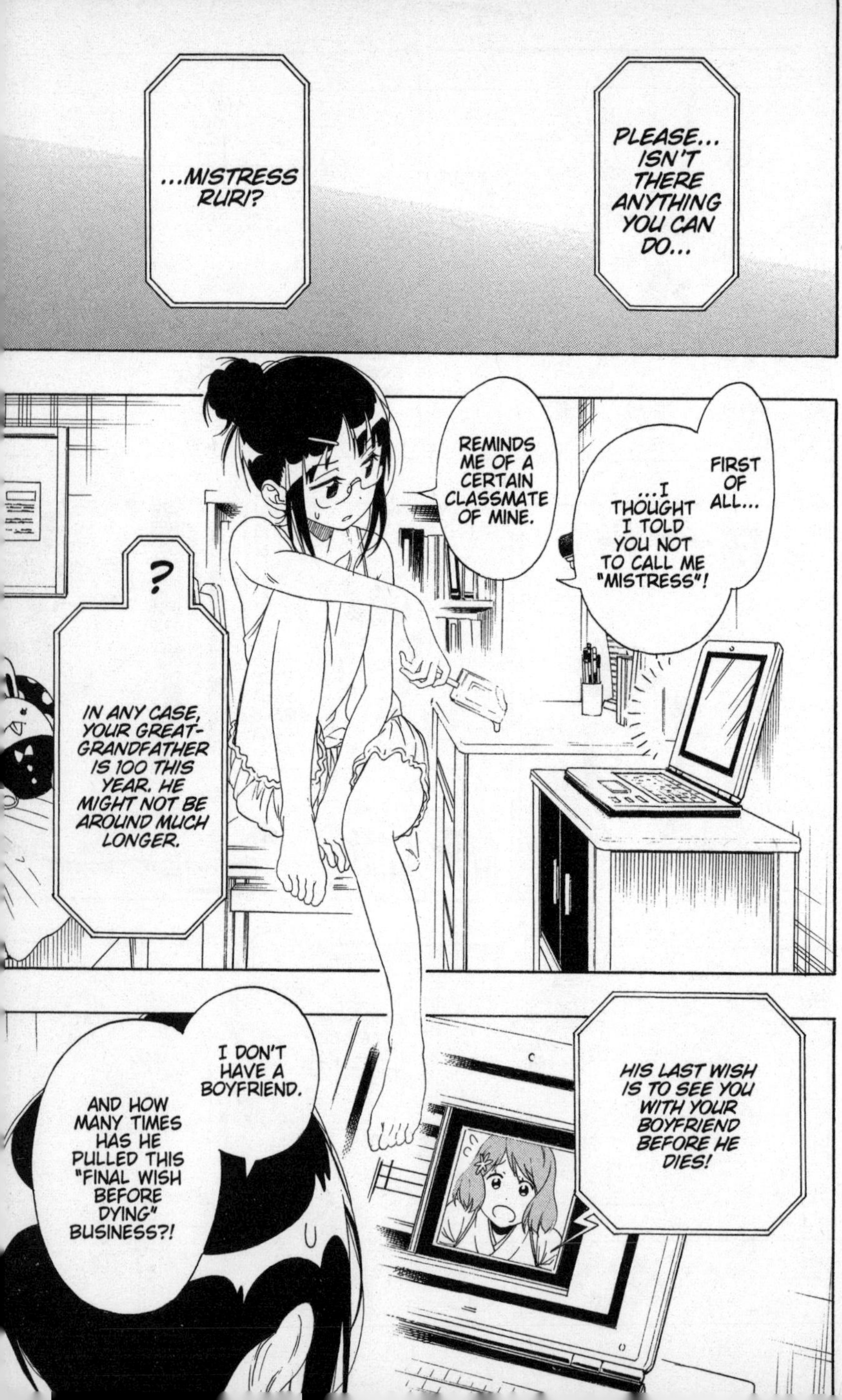
PLEASE... ISN'T THERE ANYTHING YOU CAN DO...
...MISTRESS RURI?
FIRST OF ALL...
...I THOUGHT I TOLD YOU NOT TO CALL ME "MISTRESS"!
REMINDS ME OF A CERTAIN CLASSMATE OF MINE.
?
IN ANY CASE, YOUR GREAT-GRANDFATHER IS 100 THIS YEAR. HE MIGHT NOT BE AROUND MUCH LONGER.
HIS LAST WISH IS TO SEE YOU WITH YOUR BOYFRIEND BEFORE HE DIES!
I DON'T HAVE A BOYFRIEND.
AND HOW MANY TIMES HAS HE PULLED THIS "FINAL WISH BEFORE DYING" BUSINESS?!

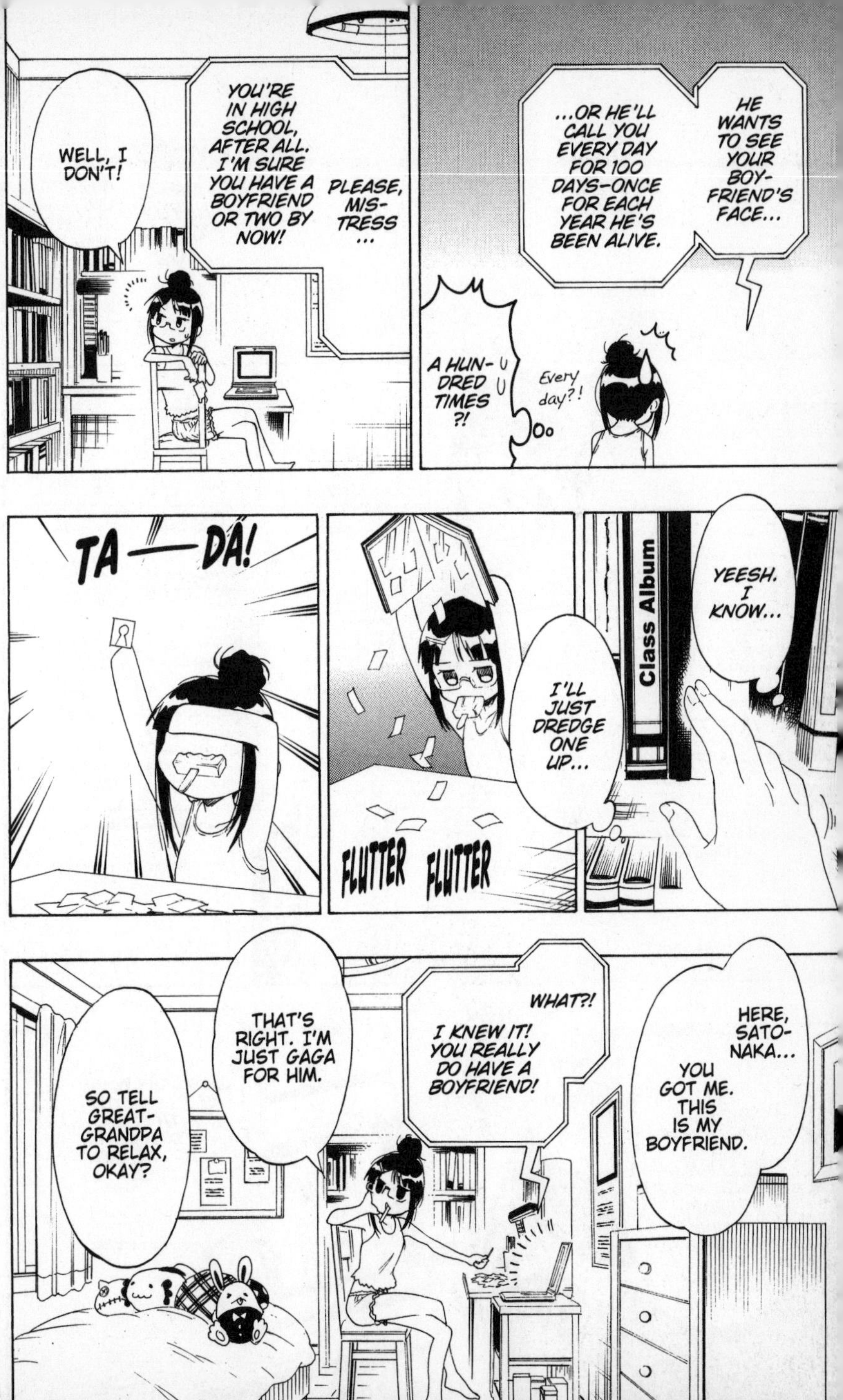
HE WANTS TO SEE YOUR BOYFRIEND'S FACE...
...OR HE'LL CALL YOU EVERY DAY FOR 100 DAYS—ONCE FOR EACH YEAR HE'S BEEN ALIVE.
A HUNDRED TIMES?!
Every day?!
PLEASE, MISTRESS...
YOU'RE IN HIGH SCHOOL, AFTER ALL. I'M SURE YOU HAVE A BOYFRIEND OR TWO BY NOW!
WELL, I DON'T!
YEESH. I KNOW...
Class Album
I'LL JUST DREDGE ONE UP...
FLUTTER FLUTTER
TA—DA!
HERE, SATONAKA...
YOU GOT ME. THIS IS MY BOYFRIEND.
WHAT?!
I KNEW IT! YOU REALLY DO HAVE A BOYFRIEND!
THAT'S RIGHT. I'M JUST GAGA FOR HIM.
SO TELL GREAT-GRANDPA TO RELAX, OKAY?

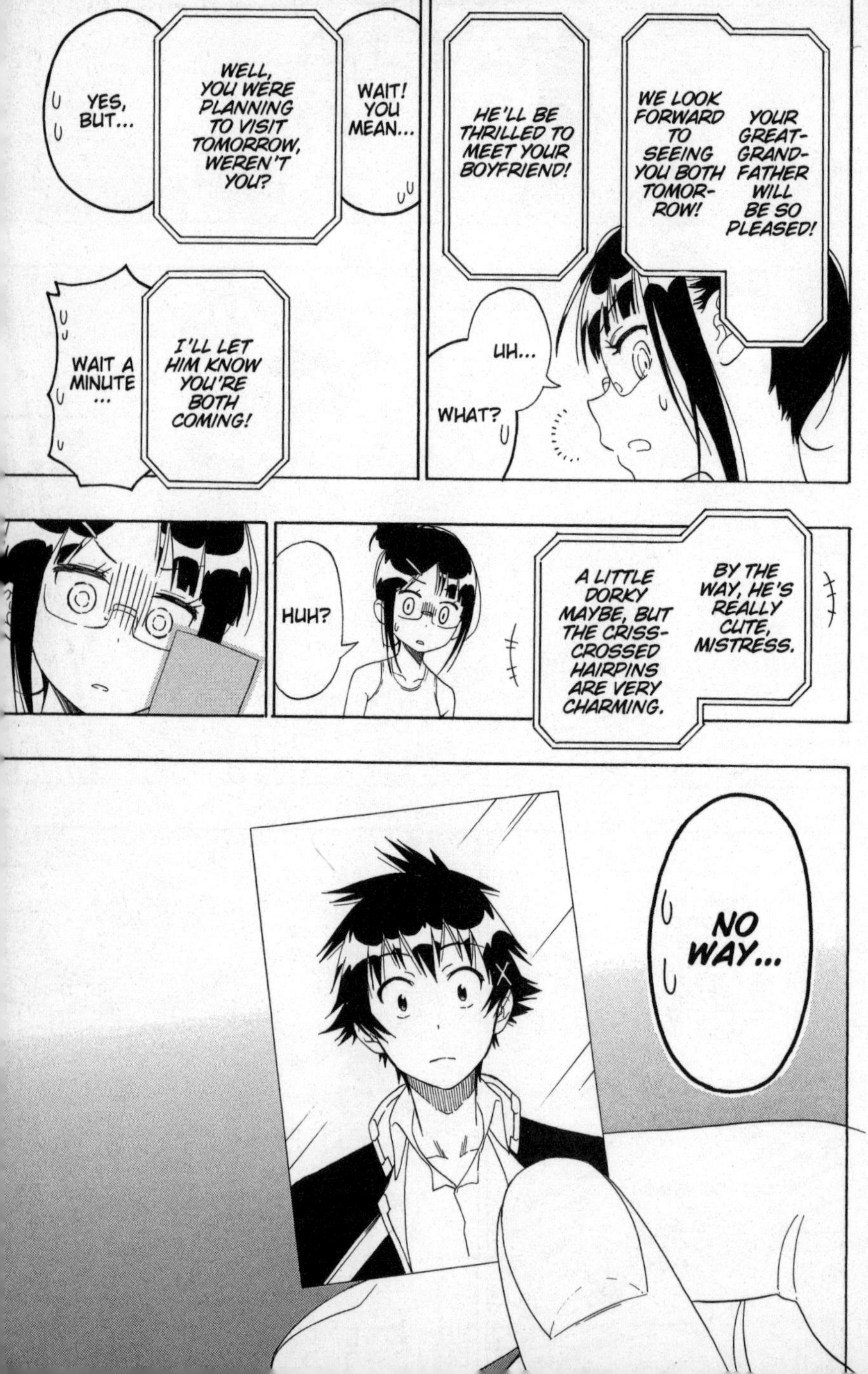
YOUR GREAT-GRANDFATHER WILL BE SO PLEASED!
WE LOOK FORWARD TO SEEING YOU BOTH TOMORROW!
HE'LL BE THRILLED TO MEET YOUR BOYFRIEND!
UH...
WHAT?
WAIT! YOU MEAN...
WELL, YOU WERE PLANNING TO VISIT TOMORROW, WEREN'T YOU?
YES, BUT...
I'LL LET HIM KNOW YOU'RE BOTH COMING!
WAIT A MINUTE...
BY THE WAY, HE'S REALLY CUTE, MISTRESS.
A LITTLE DORKY MAYBE, BUT THE CRISS-CROSSED HAIRPINS ARE VERY CHARMING.
HUH?
NO WAY...

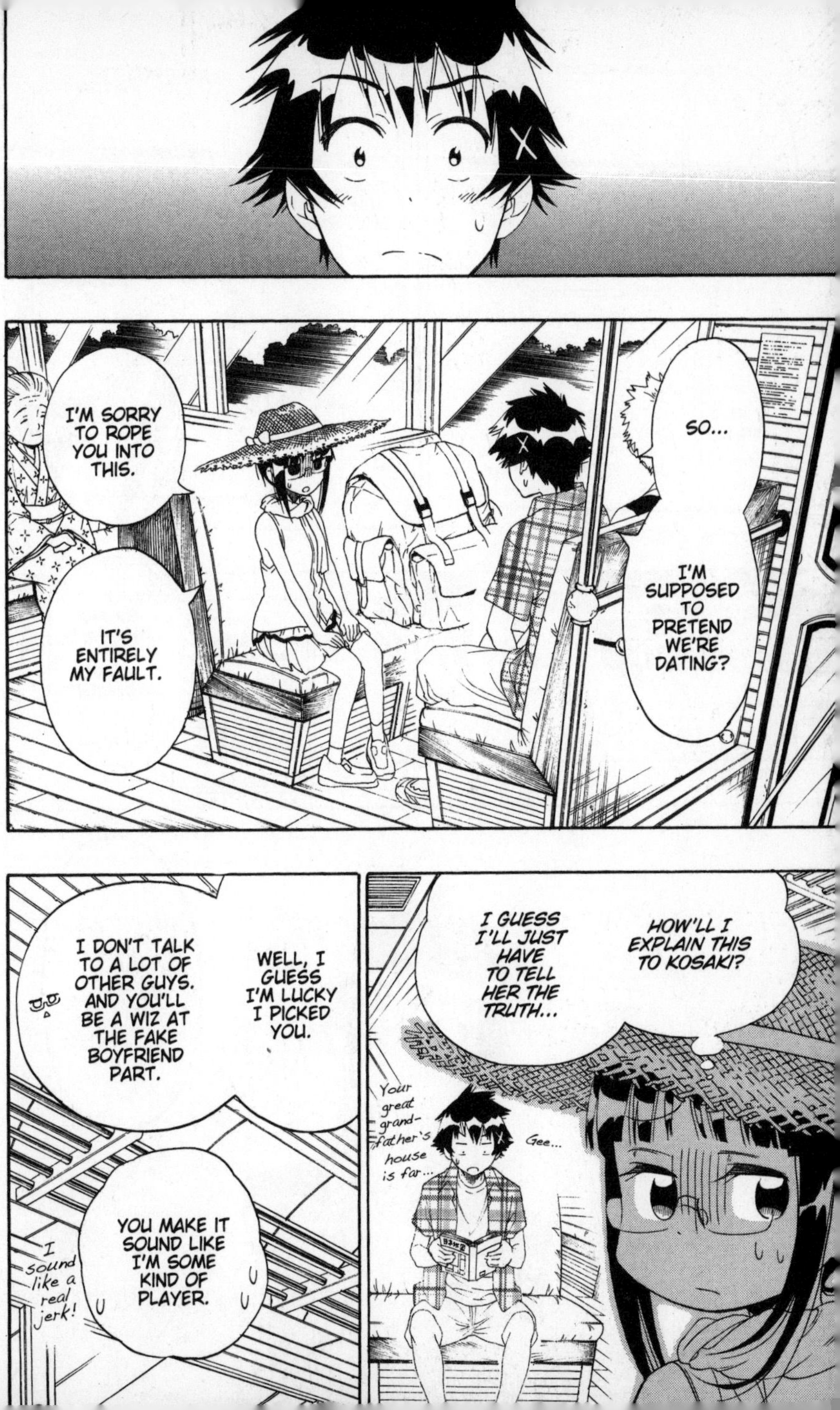
SO... I'M SUPPOSED TO PRETEND WE'RE DATING?
I'M SORRY TO ROPE YOU INTO THIS.
IT'S ENTIRELY MY FAULT.
HOW'LL I EXPLAIN THIS TO KOSAKI?
I GUESS I'LL JUST HAVE TO TELL HER THE TRUTH...
Gee...
Your great grand-father's house is far...
WELL, I GUESS I'M LUCKY I PICKED YOU.
I DON'T TALK TO A LOT OF OTHER GUYS. AND YOU'LL BE A WIZ AT THE FAKE BOYFRIEND PART.
YOU MAKE IT SOUND LIKE I'M SOME KIND OF PLAYER.
I sound like a real jerk!

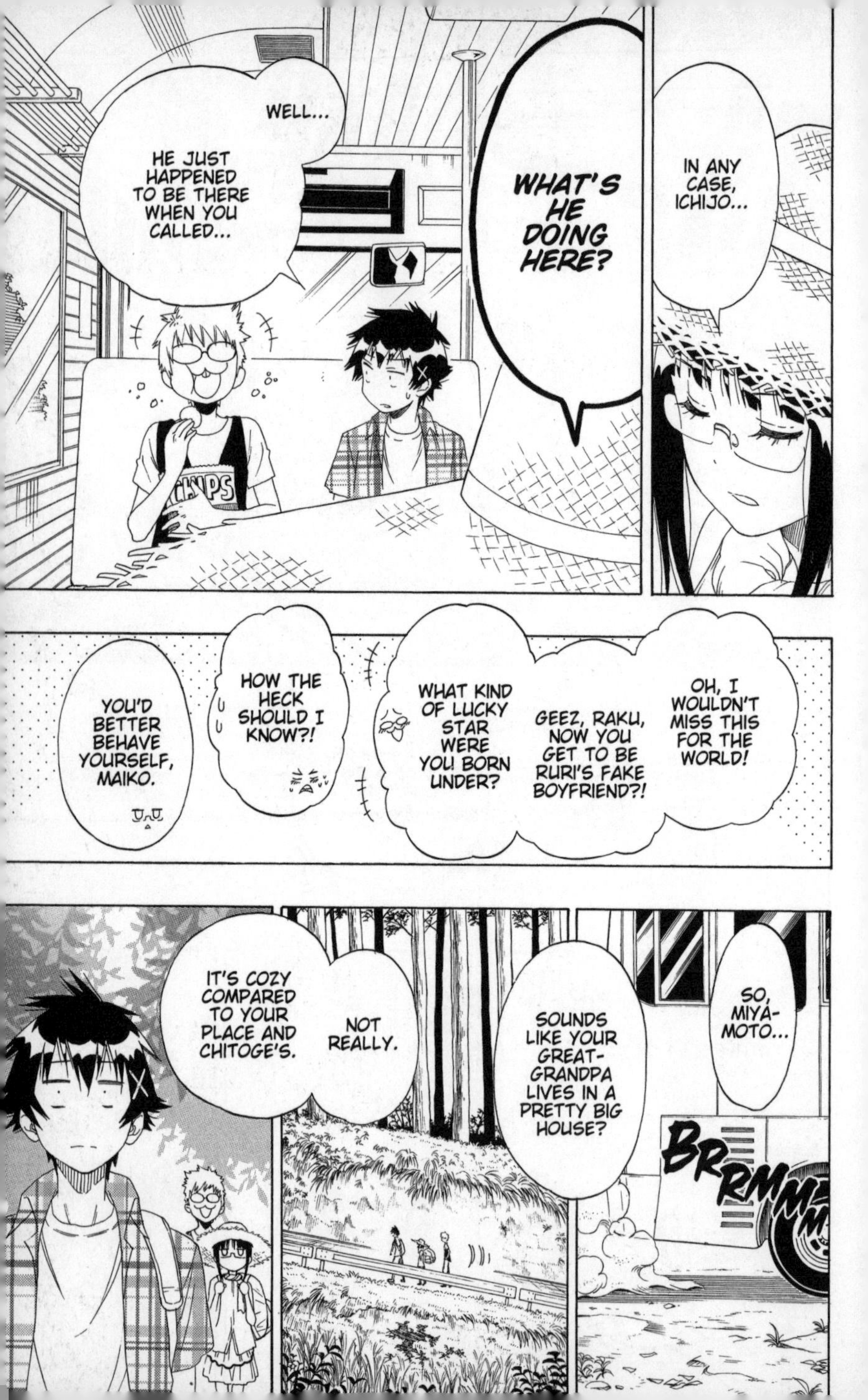
IN ANY CASE, ICHIJO...
WHAT'S HE DOING HERE?
WELL...
HE JUST HAPPENED TO BE THERE WHEN YOU CALLED...
CHIPS
OH, I WOULDN'T MISS THIS FOR THE WORLD!
GEEZ, RAKU, NOW YOU GET TO BE RURI'S FAKE BOYFRIEND?!
WHAT KIND OF LUCKY STAR WERE YOU BORN UNDER?
HOW THE HECK SHOULD I KNOW?!
YOU'D BETTER BEHAVE YOURSELF, MAIKO.
SO, MIYAMOTO...
BRRMMM
SOUNDS LIKE YOUR GREAT-GRANDPA LIVES IN A PRETTY BIG HOUSE?
NOT REALLY.
IT'S COZY COMPARED TO YOUR PLACE AND CHITOGE'S.

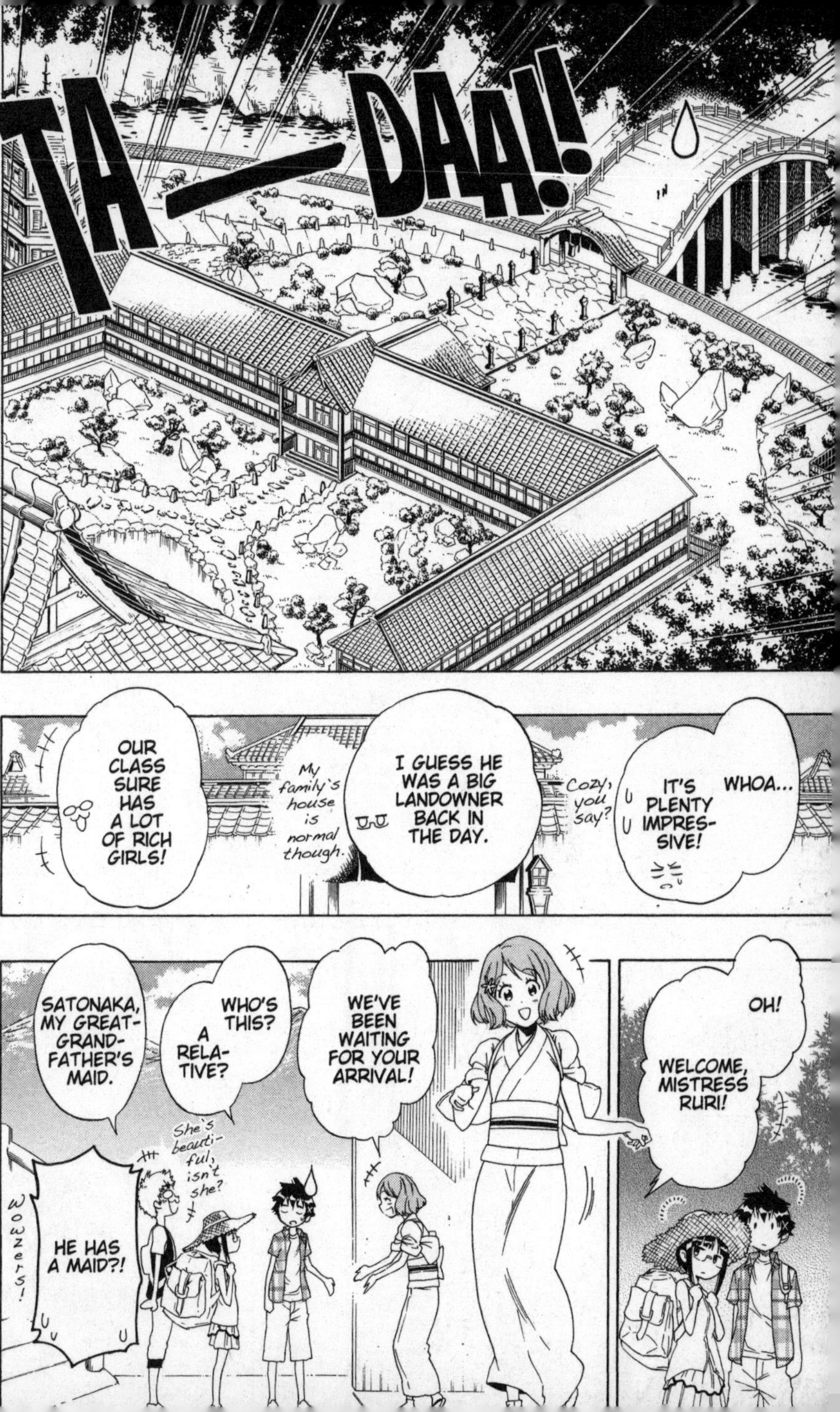
TA—DAA!
WHOA... IT'S PLENTY IMPRESSIVE!
Cozy, you say?
I GUESS HE WAS A BIG LANDOWNER BACK IN THE DAY.
My family's house is normal though.
OUR CLASS SURE HAS A LOT OF RICH GIRLS!
OH!
WELCOME, MISTRESS RURI!
WE'VE BEEN WAITING FOR YOUR ARRIVAL!
WHO'S THIS? A RELATIVE?
SATONAKA, MY GREAT-GRANDFATHER'S MAID.
She's beautiful, isn't she?
HE HAS A MAID?!
Wowzers!

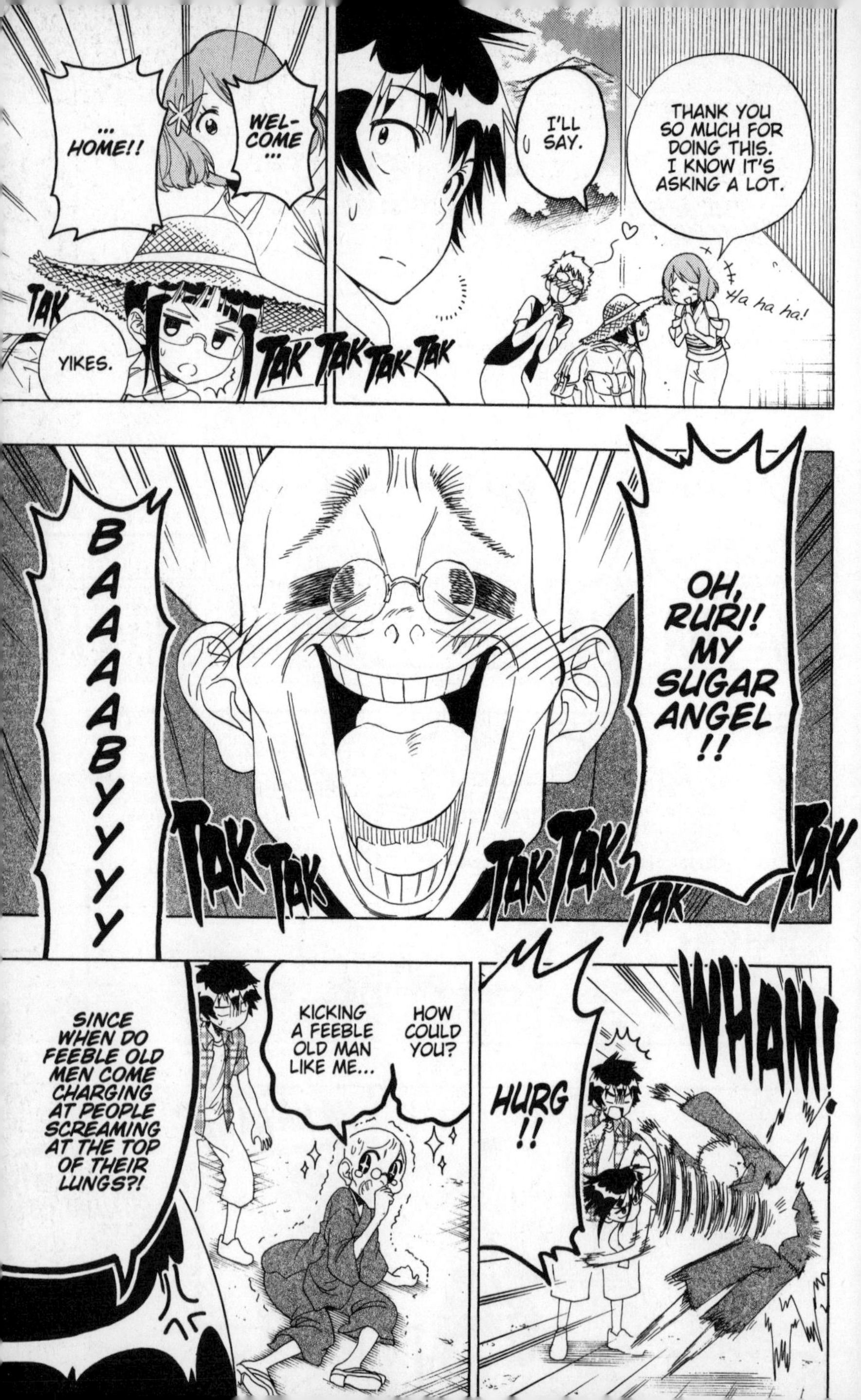
THANK YOU SO MUCH FOR DOING THIS. I KNOW IT'S ASKING A LOT.
Ha ha ha!
I'LL SAY.
TAK TAK TAK TAK
WEL-COME...
...HOME!!
TAK
YIKES.
OH, RURI! MY SUGAR ANGEL!!
TAK
TAK
TAK TAK
BAAAAABYYYY
TAK TAK
WHAM!
HURG!!
HOW COULD YOU?
KICKING A FEEBLE OLD MAN LIKE ME...
SINCE WHEN DO FEEBLE OLD MEN COME CHARGING AT PEOPLE SCREAMING AT THE TOP OF THEIR LUNGS?!

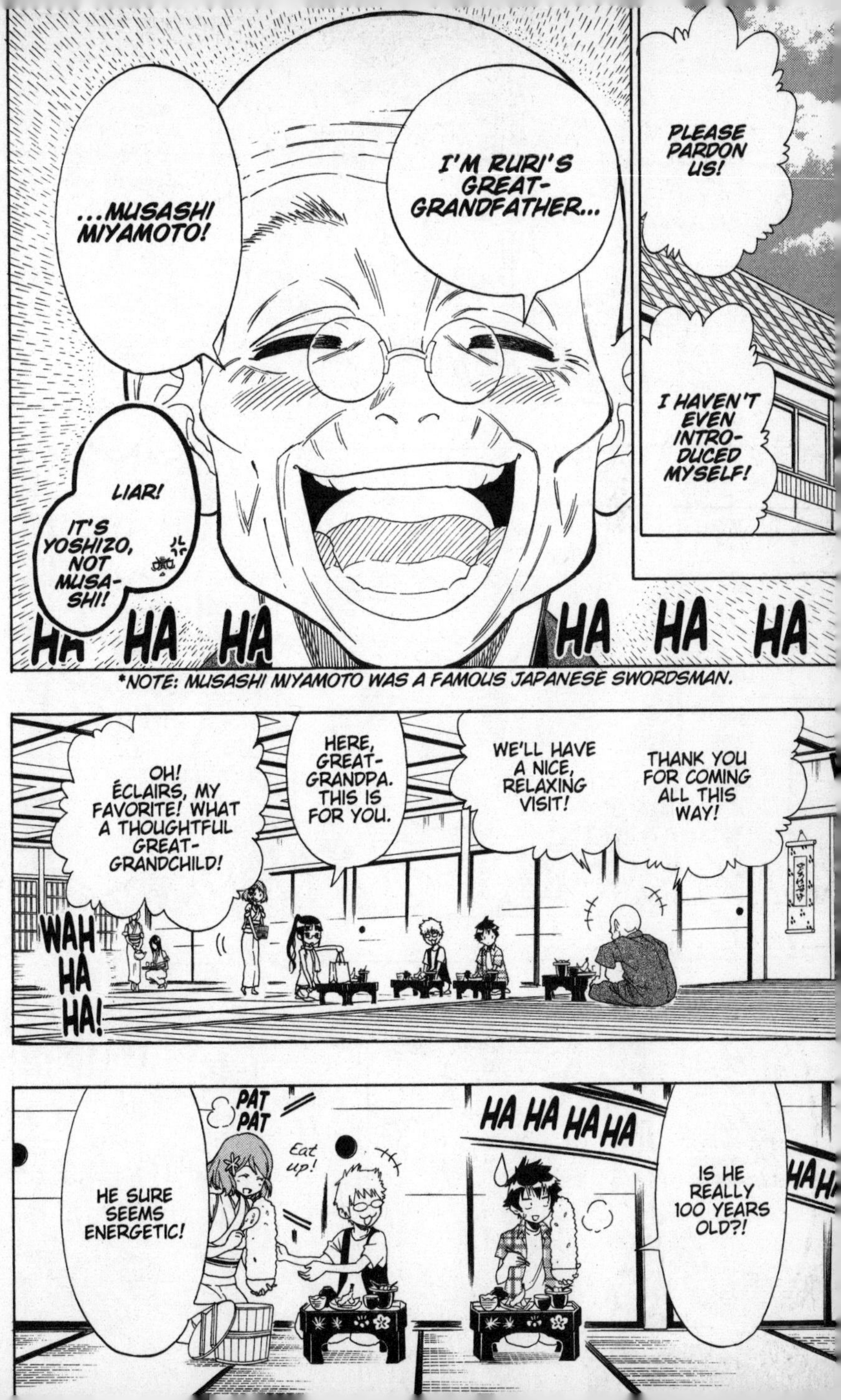
PLEASE PARDON US!
I HAVEN'T EVEN INTRODUCED MYSELF!
I'M RURI'S GREAT-GRANDFATHER...
...MUSASHI MIYAMOTO!
HA HA HA HA HA HA
LIAR! IT'S YOSHIZO, NOT MUSASHI!
*NOTE: MUSASHI MIYAMOTO WAS A FAMOUS JAPANESE SWORDSMAN.
THANK YOU FOR COMING ALL THIS WAY!
WE'LL HAVE A NICE, RELAXING VISIT!
HERE, GREAT-GRANDPA. THIS IS FOR YOU.
OH! ÉCLAIRS, MY FAVORITE! WHAT A THOUGHTFUL GREAT-GRANDCHILD!
WAH HA HA!
IS HE REALLY 100 YEARS OLD?!
HA HA HA HA
HA
Eat up!
PAT PAT
HE SURE SEEMS ENERGETIC!

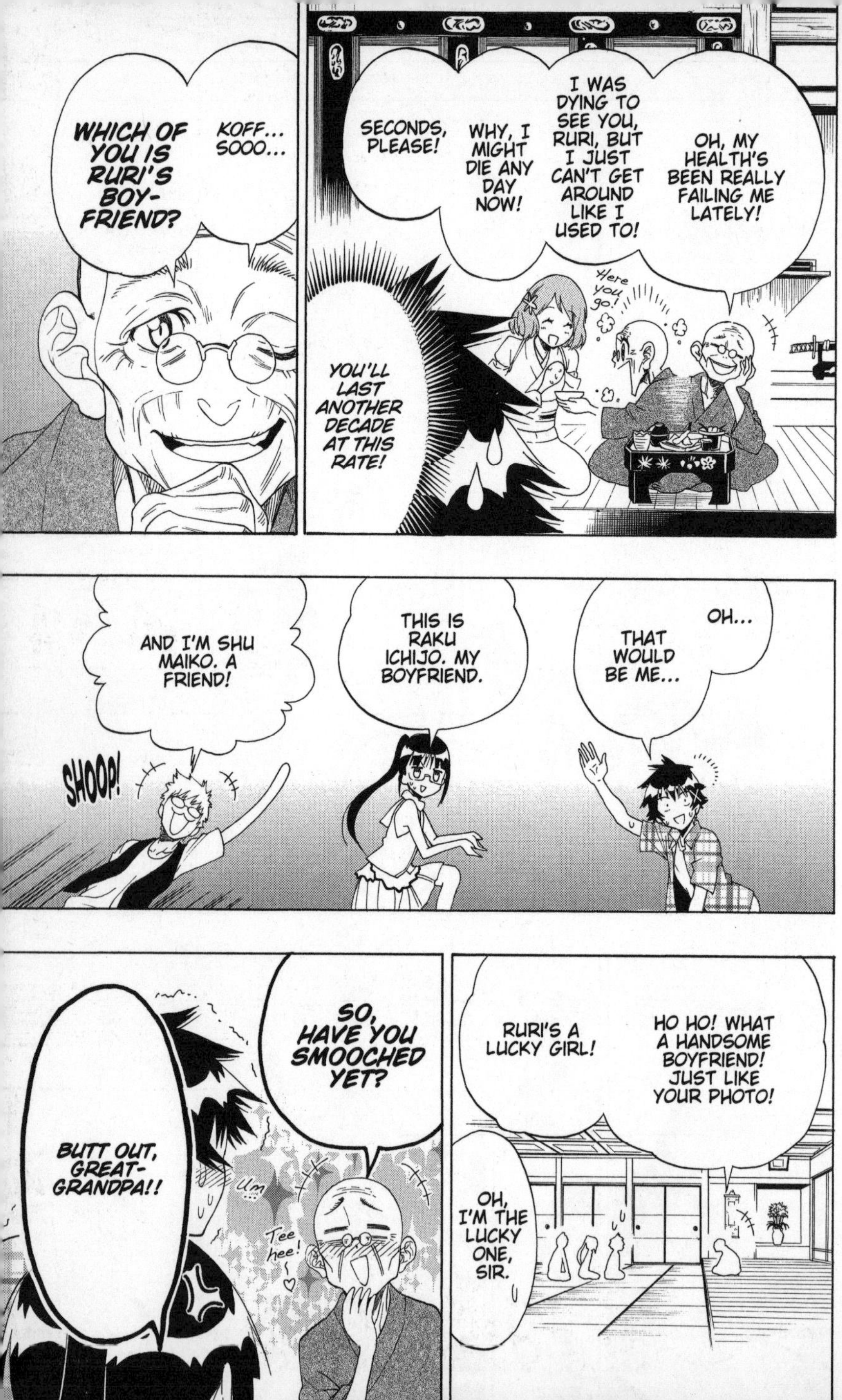
OH, MY HEALTH'S BEEN REALLY FAILING ME LATELY!
I WAS DYING TO SEE YOU, RURI, BUT I JUST CAN'T GET AROUND LIKE I USED TO!
WHY, I MIGHT DIE ANY DAY NOW!
SECONDS, PLEASE!
Here you go!
YOU'LL LAST ANOTHER DECADE AT THIS RATE!
KOFF... SOOO...
WHICH OF YOU IS RURI'S BOY-FRIEND?
OH...
THAT WOULD BE ME...
THIS IS RAKU ICHIJO. MY BOYFRIEND.
AND I'M SHU MAIKO. A FRIEND!
SHOOP!
HO HO! WHAT A HANDSOME BOYFRIEND! JUST LIKE YOUR PHOTO!
RURI'S A LUCKY GIRL!
OH, I'M THE LUCKY ONE, SIR.
SO, HAVE YOU SMOOCHED YET?
Um...
Tee hee!
BUTT OUT, GREAT-GRANDPA!!

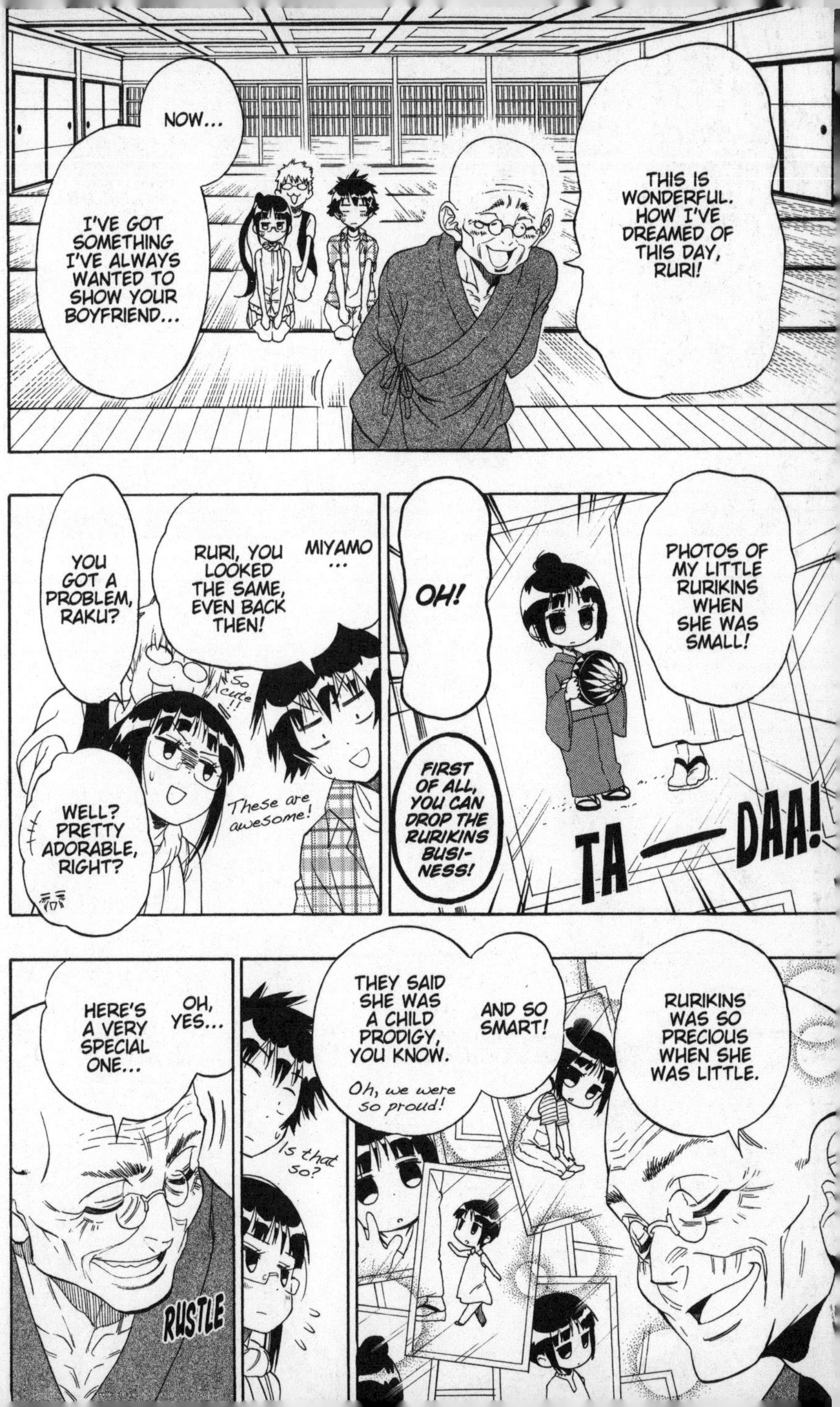
THIS IS WONDERFUL. HOW I'VE DREAMED OF THIS DAY, RURI!
NOW...
I'VE GOT SOMETHING I'VE ALWAYS WANTED TO SHOW YOUR BOYFRIEND...
PHOTOS OF MY LITTLE RURIKINS WHEN SHE WAS SMALL!
OH!
TA—DAA!
FIRST OF ALL, YOU CAN DROP THE RURIKINS BUSINESS!
MIYAMO...
RURI, YOU LOOKED THE SAME, EVEN BACK THEN!
YOU GOT A PROBLEM, RAKU?
So cute!!
These are awesome!
WELL? PRETTY ADORABLE, RIGHT?
RURIKINS WAS SO PRECIOUS WHEN SHE WAS LITTLE.
AND SO SMART!
THEY SAID SHE WAS A CHILD PRODIGY, YOU KNOW.
Oh, we were so proud!
Is that so?
OH, YES...
HERE'S A VERY SPECIAL ONE...
RUSTLE

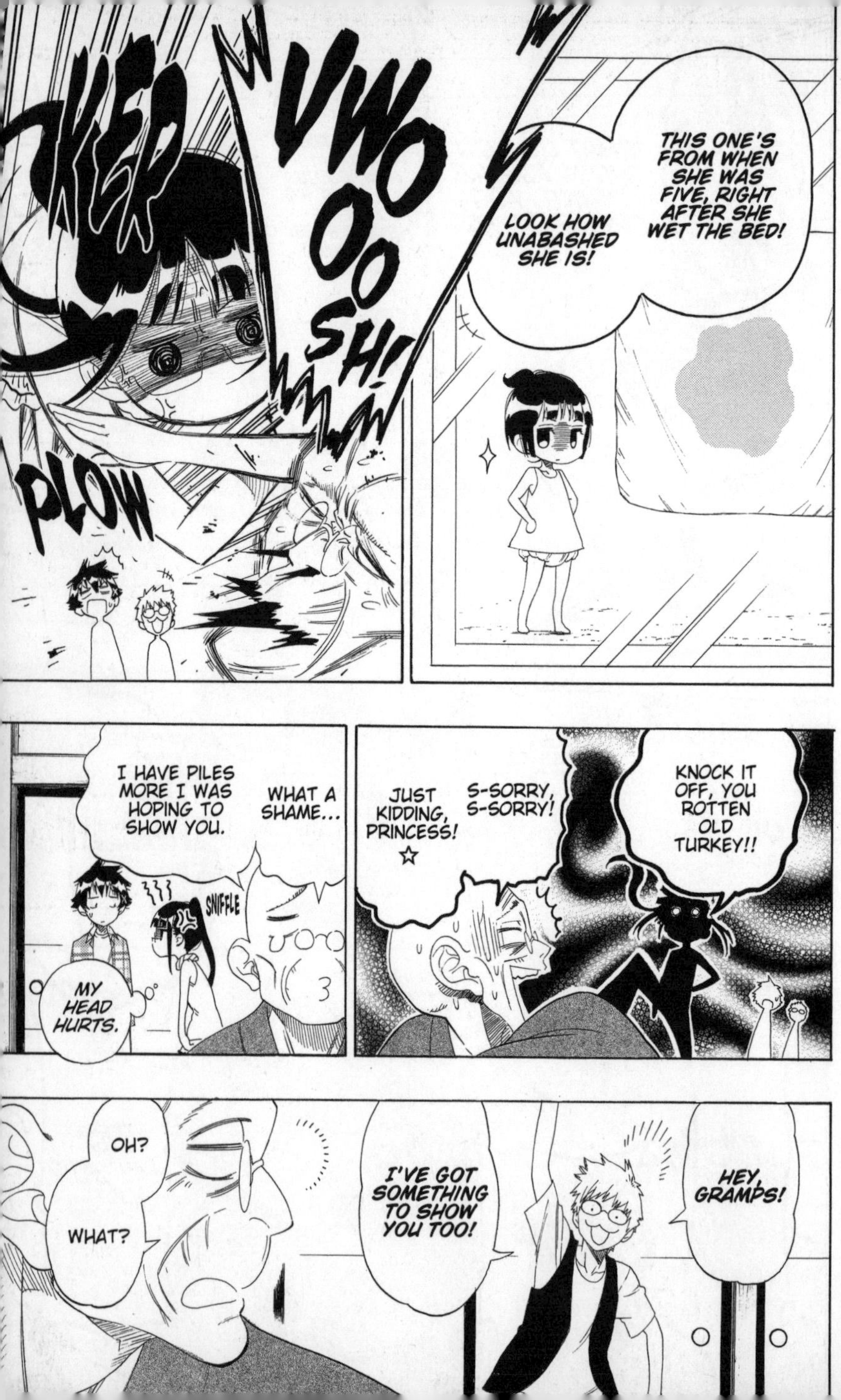

THIS ONE'S FROM WHEN SHE WAS FIVE, RIGHT AFTER SHE WET THE BED!
LOOK HOW UNABASHED SHE IS!
VWOOOOSH!
PLOW
KNOCK IT OFF, YOU ROTTEN OLD TURKEY!!
S-SORRY, S-SORRY!
JUST KIDDING, PRINCESS! ☆
WHAT A SHAME...
I HAVE PILES MORE I WAS HOPING TO SHOW YOU.
SNIFFLE
MY HEAD HURTS.
HEY, GRAMPS!
I'VE GOT SOMETHING TO SHOW YOU TOO!
OH?
WHAT?

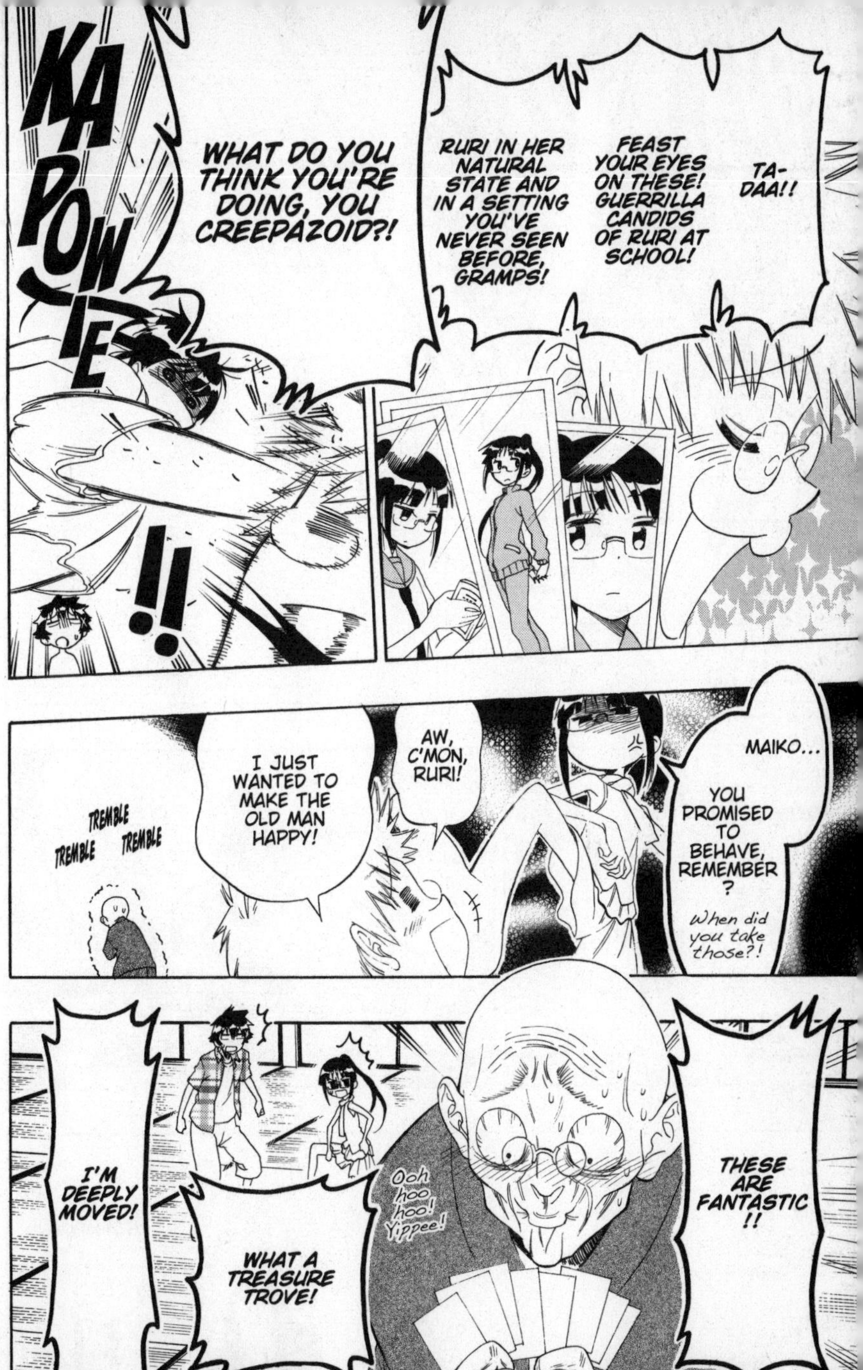
TA-DAA!!
FEAST YOUR EYES ON THESE! GUERRILLA CANDIDS OF RURI AT SCHOOL!
RURI IN HER NATURAL STATE AND IN A SETTING YOU'VE NEVER SEEN BEFORE, GRAMPS!
WHAT DO YOU THINK YOU'RE DOING, YOU CREEPAZOID?!
KAPOWIE
!!
MAIKO...
YOU PROMISED TO BEHAVE, REMEMBER?
When did you take those?!
AW, C'MON, RURI!
I JUST WANTED TO MAKE THE OLD MAN HAPPY!
TREMBLE
TREMBLE
TREMBLE
THESE ARE FANTASTIC!!
Ooh hoo hoo! Yippee!
WHAT A TREASURE TROVE!
I'M DEEPLY MOVED!

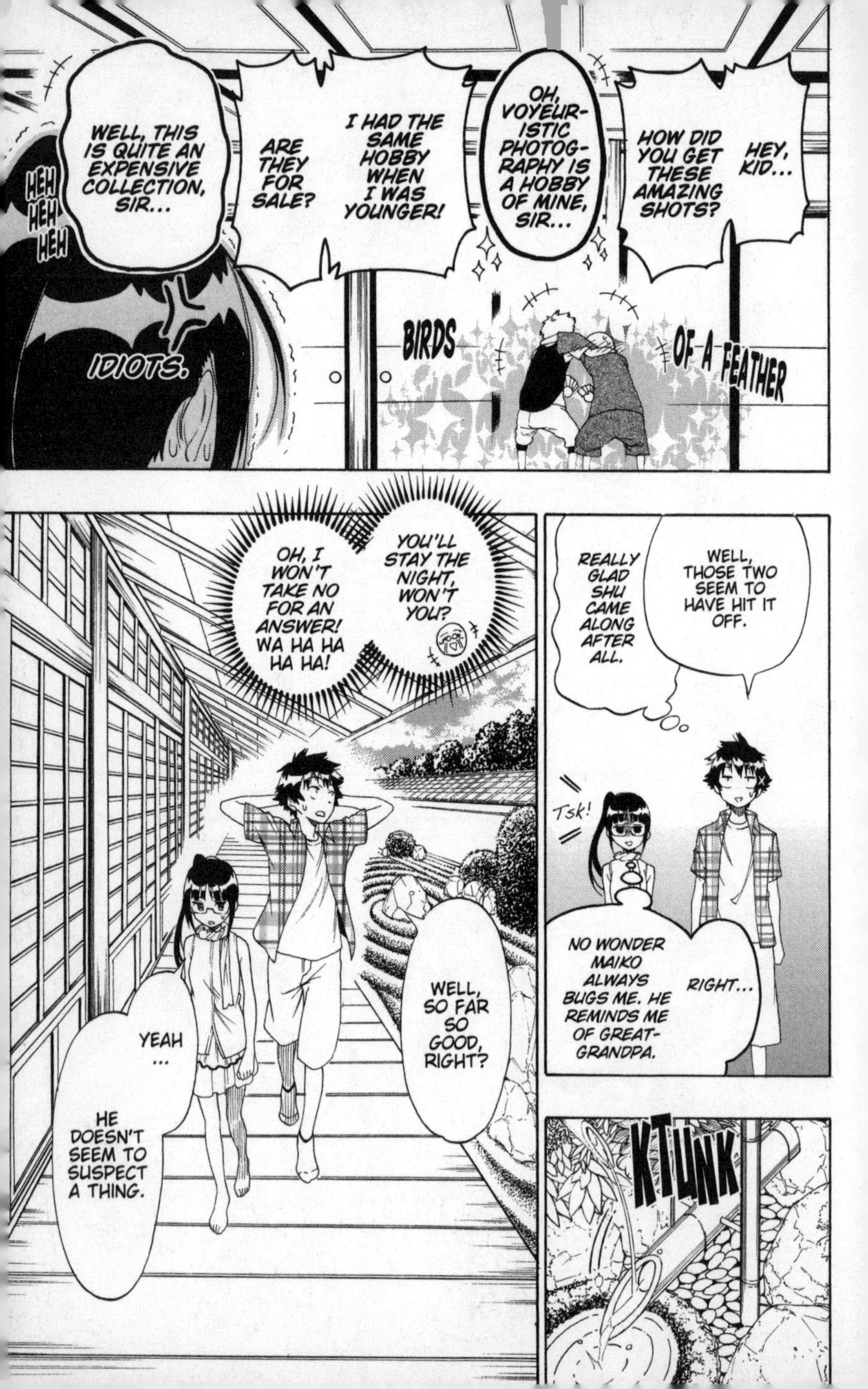
HEY, KID...
HOW DID YOU GET THESE AMAZING SHOTS?
OH, VOYEURISTIC PHOTOGRAPHY IS A HOBBY OF MINE, SIR...
I HAD THE SAME HOBBY WHEN I WAS YOUNGER!
ARE THEY FOR SALE?
WELL, THIS IS QUITE AN EXPENSIVE COLLECTION, SIR...
HEH HEH HEH
BIRDS OF A FEATHER
IDIOTS.
WELL, THOSE TWO SEEM TO HAVE HIT IT OFF.
REALLY GLAD SHU CAME ALONG AFTER ALL.
Tsk!
RIGHT...
NO WONDER MAIKO ALWAYS BUGS ME. HE REMINDS ME OF GREAT-GRANDPA.
KTUNK
YOU'LL STAY THE NIGHT, WON'T YOU?
OH, I WON'T TAKE NO FOR AN ANSWER! WA HA HA HA HA!
WELL, SO FAR SO GOOD, RIGHT?
YEAH...
HE DOESN'T SEEM TO SUSPECT A THING.

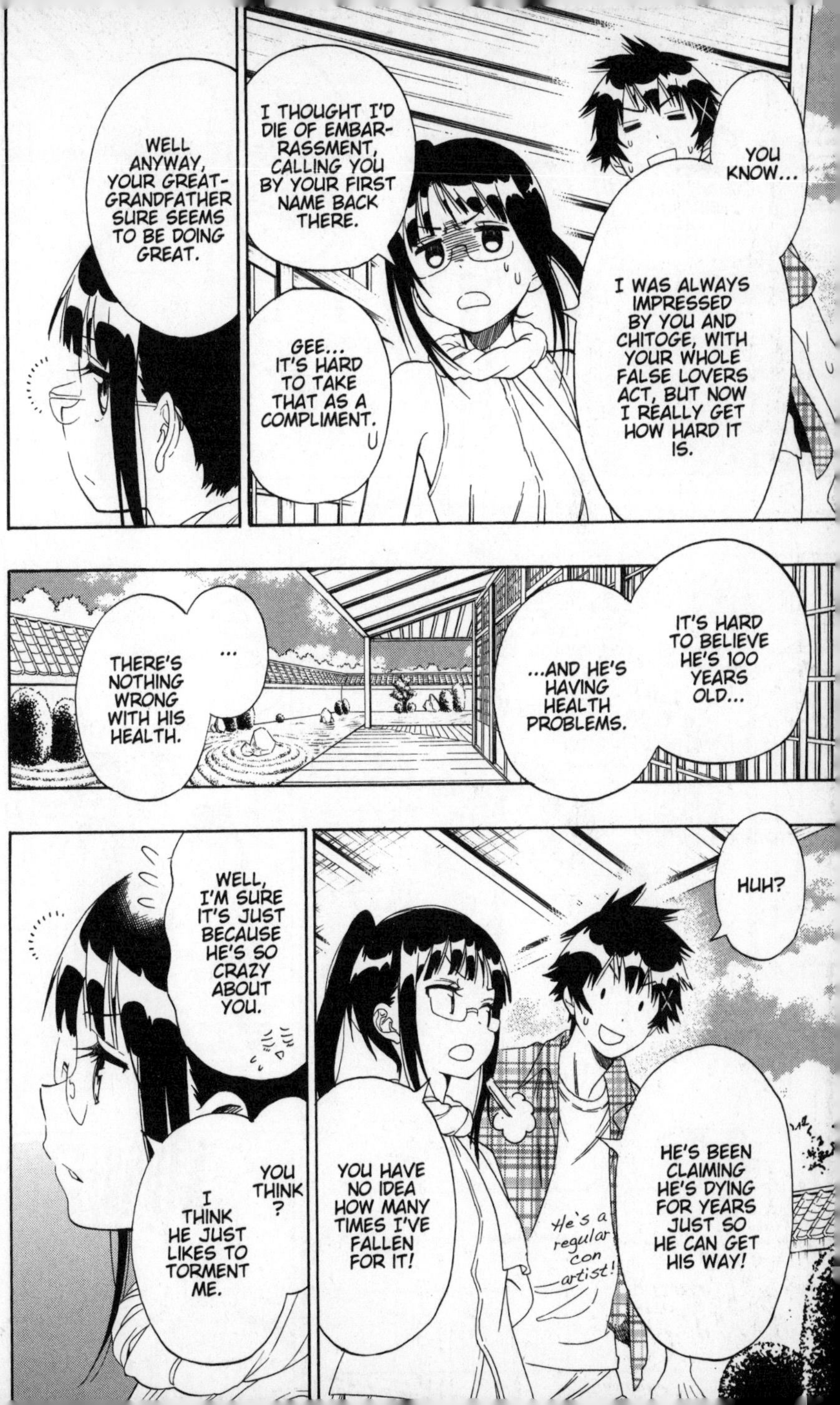
YOU KNOW...
I WAS ALWAYS IMPRESSED BY YOU AND CHITOGE, WITH YOUR WHOLE FALSE LOVERS ACT, BUT NOW I REALLY GET HOW HARD IT IS.
I THOUGHT I'D DIE OF EMBARRASSMENT, CALLING YOU BY YOUR FIRST NAME BACK THERE.
GEE... IT'S HARD TO TAKE THAT AS A COMPLIMENT.
WELL ANYWAY, YOUR GREAT-GRANDFATHER SURE SEEMS TO BE DOING GREAT.
IT'S HARD TO BELIEVE HE'S 100 YEARS OLD...
...AND HE'S HAVING HEALTH PROBLEMS.
...
THERE'S NOTHING WRONG WITH HIS HEALTH.
HUH?
HE'S BEEN CLAIMING HE'S DYING FOR YEARS JUST SO HE CAN GET HIS WAY!
He's a regular con artist!
YOU HAVE NO IDEA HOW MANY TIMES I'VE FALLEN FOR IT!
WELL, I'M SURE IT'S JUST BECAUSE HE'S SO CRAZY ABOUT YOU.
YOU THINK?
I THINK HE JUST LIKES TO TORMENT ME.

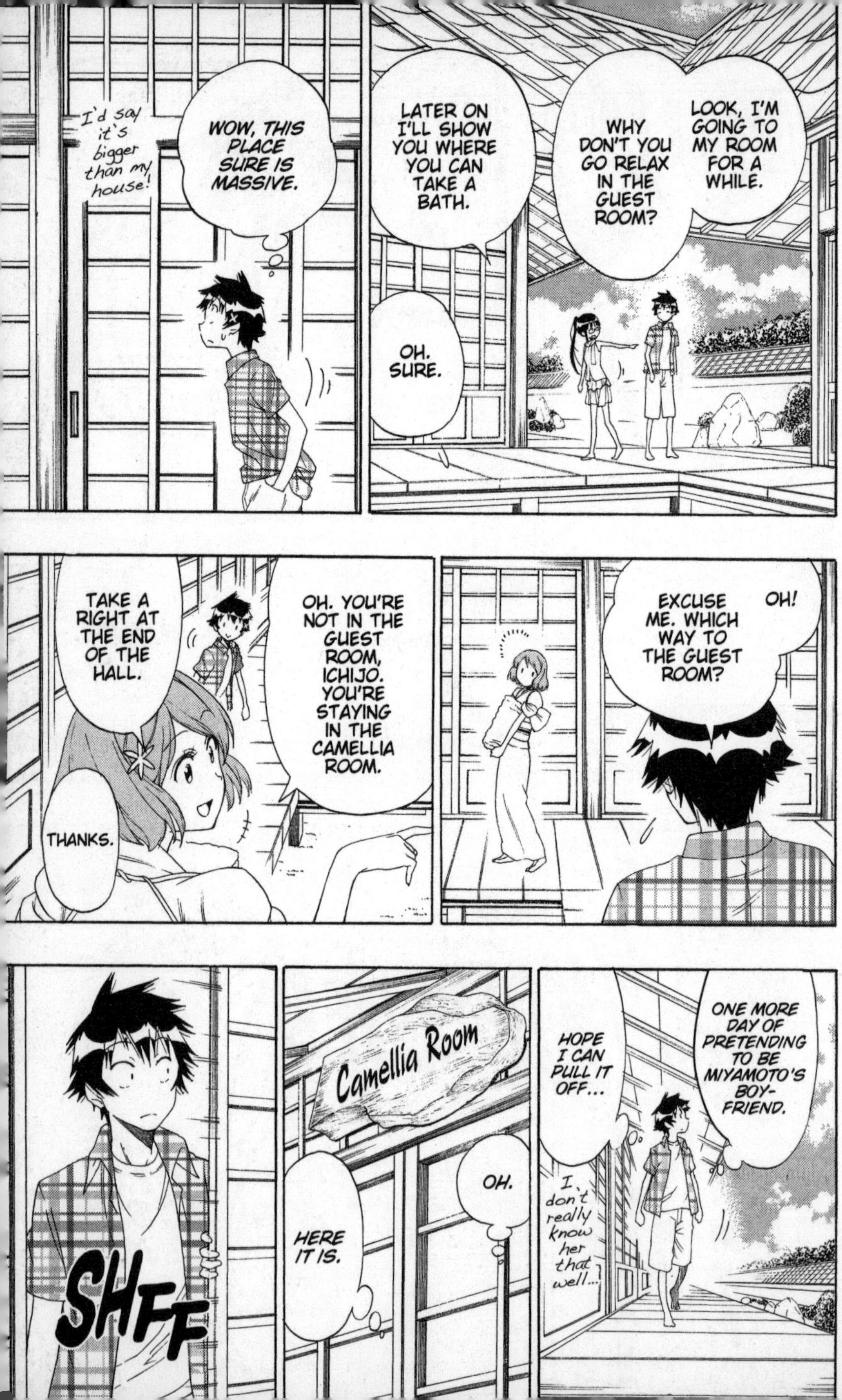
LOOK, I'M GOING TO MY ROOM FOR A WHILE.
WHY DON'T YOU GO RELAX IN THE GUEST ROOM?
LATER ON I'LL SHOW YOU WHERE YOU CAN TAKE A BATH.
OH. SURE.
WOW, THIS PLACE SURE IS MASSIVE.
I'd say it's bigger than my house!
OH!
EXCUSE ME. WHICH WAY TO THE GUEST ROOM?
OH. YOU'RE NOT IN THE GUEST ROOM, ICHIJO. YOU'RE STAYING IN THE CAMELLIA ROOM.
TAKE A RIGHT AT THE END OF THE HALL.
THANKS.
ONE MORE DAY OF PRETENDING TO BE MIYAMOTO'S BOY-FRIEND.
HOPE I CAN PULL IT OFF...
I don't really know her that well...
Camellia Room
OH.
HERE IT IS.
SHFF

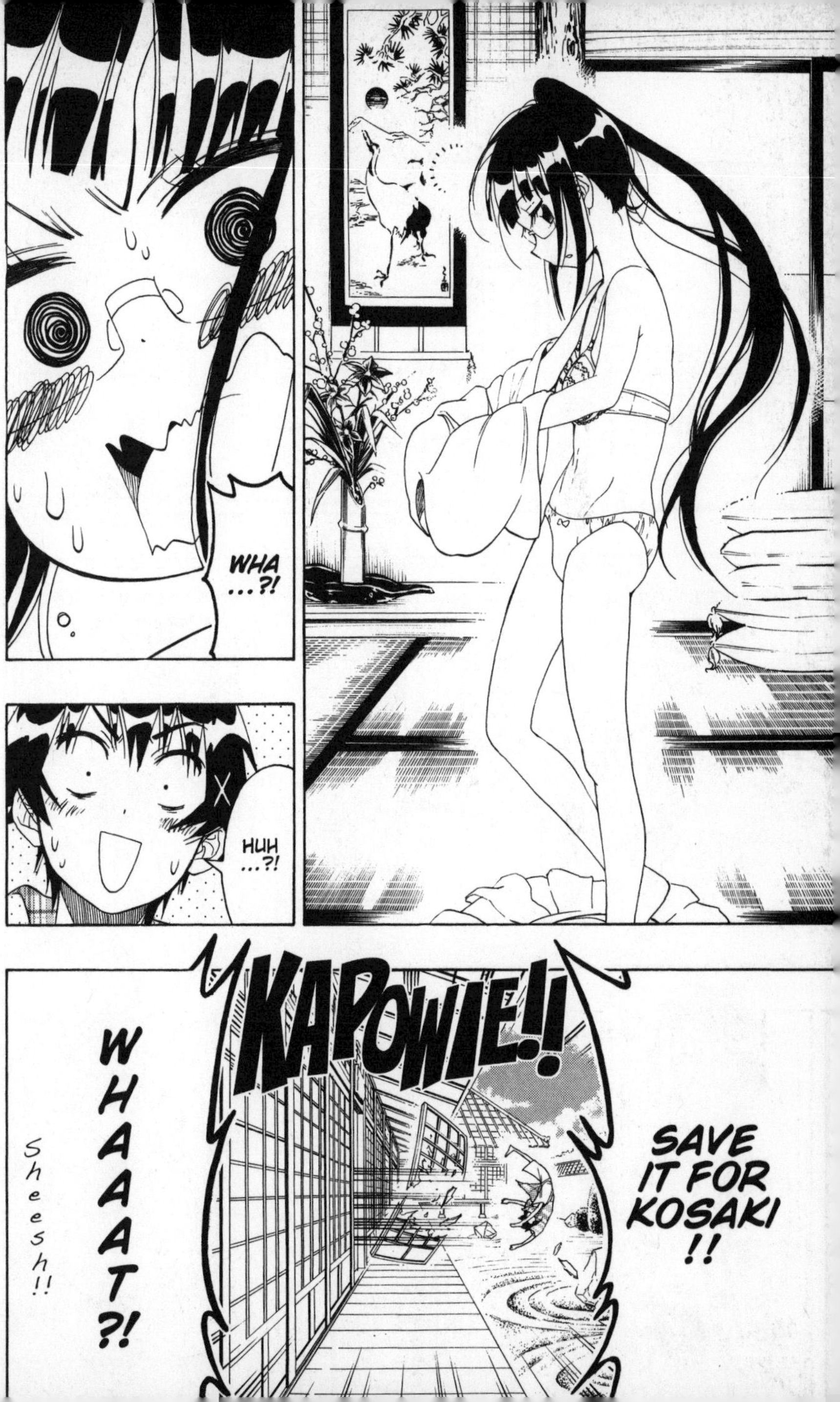
WHA ...?!
HUH ...?!
KAPOWIE!!
SAVE IT FOR KOSAKI !!
WHAAAAT?!
Sheesh!!

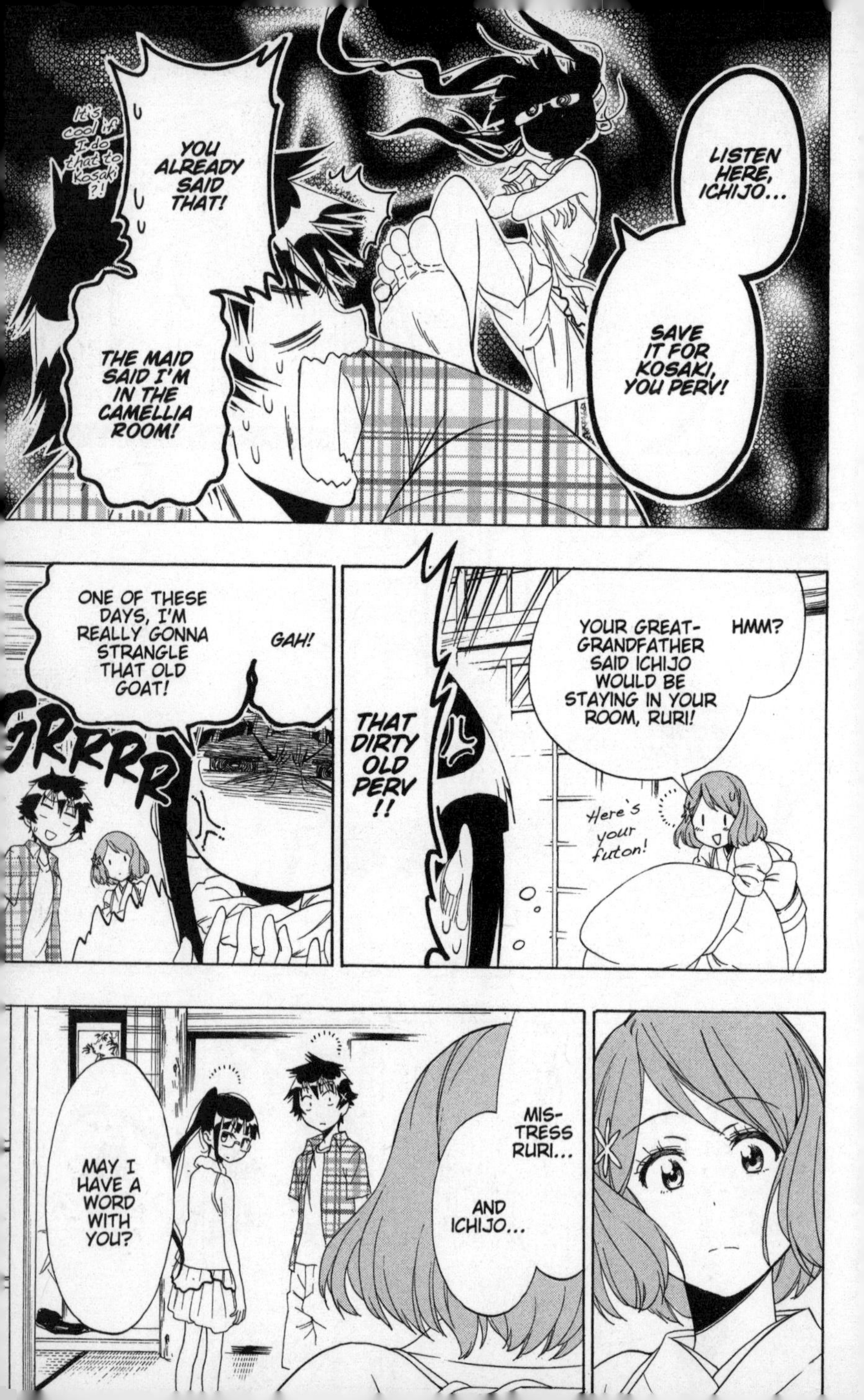
LISTEN HERE, ICHIJO...
SAVE IT FOR KOSAKI, YOU PERV!
YOU ALREADY SAID THAT!
THE MAID SAID I'M IN THE CAMELLIA ROOM!
It's cool if I do that to Kosaki?!
HMM?
YOUR GREAT-GRANDFATHER SAID ICHIJO WOULD BE STAYING IN YOUR ROOM, RURI!
Here's your futon!
THAT DIRTY OLD PERV!!
GAH!
ONE OF THESE DAYS, I'M REALLY GONNA STRANGLE THAT OLD GOAT!
GRRRR
MIS-TRESS RURI...
AND ICHIJO...
MAY I HAVE A WORD WITH YOU?

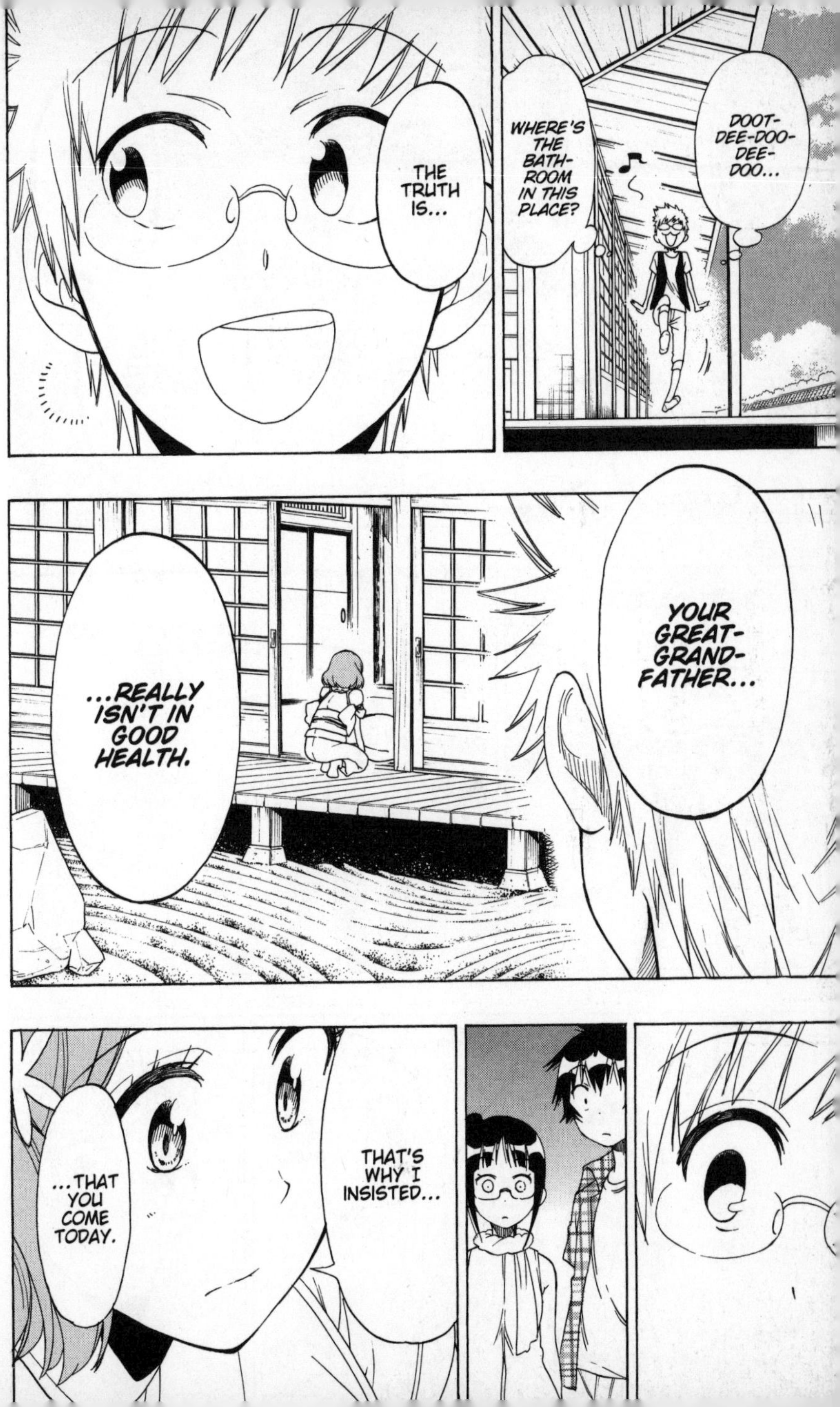
DOOT-DEE-DOO-DEE-DOO...
WHERE'S THE BATHROOM IN THIS PLACE?
THE TRUTH IS...
YOUR GREAT-GRANDFATHER...
...REALLY ISN'T IN GOOD HEALTH.
THAT'S WHY I INSISTED...
...THAT YOU COME TODAY.

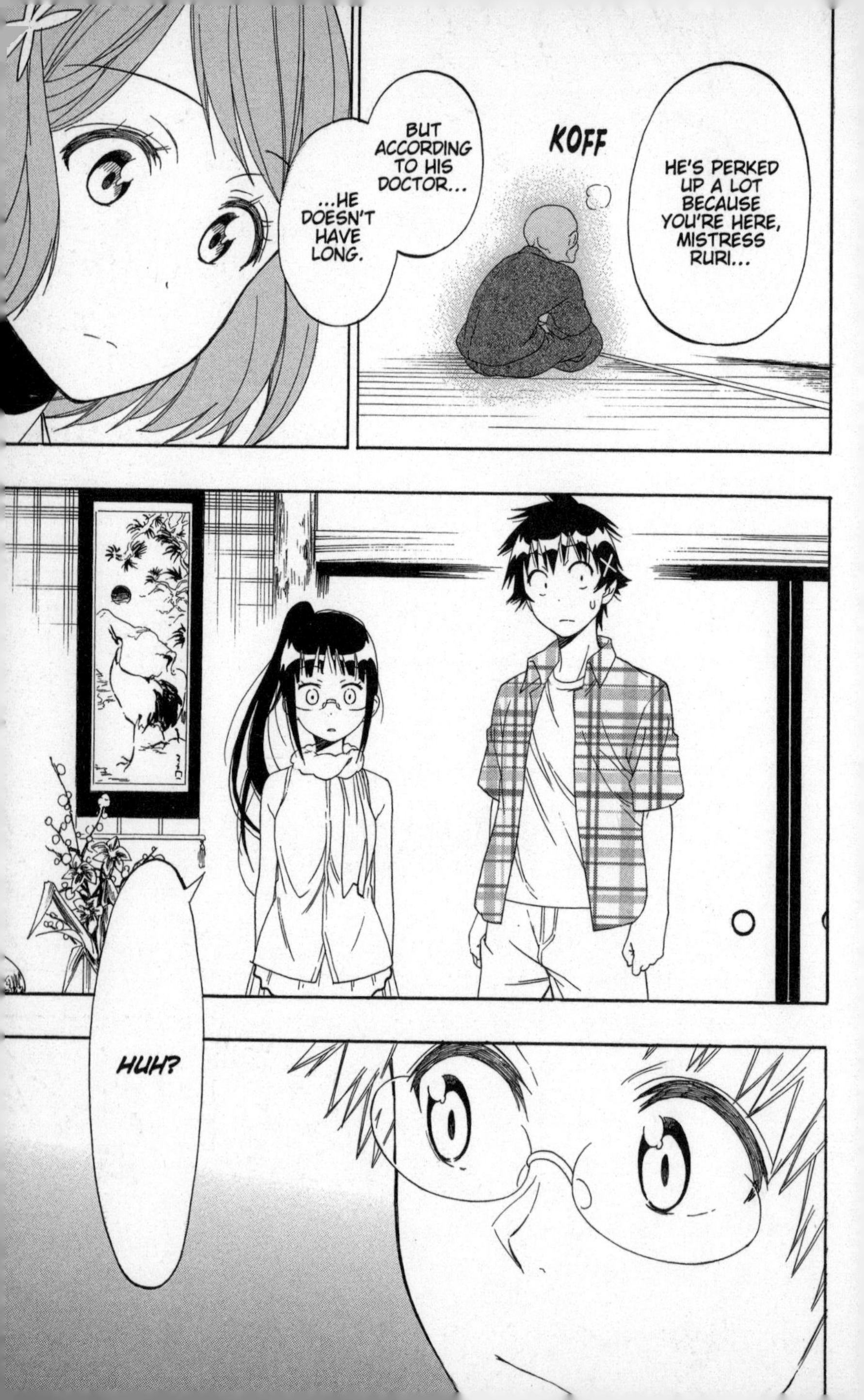
HE'S PERKED UP A LOT BECAUSE YOU'RE HERE, MISTRESS RURI...
KOFF
BUT ACCORDING TO HIS DOCTOR...
...HE DOESN'T HAVE LONG.
HUH?

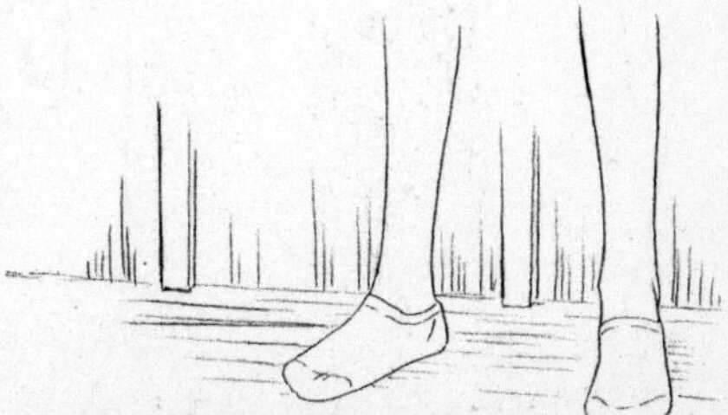

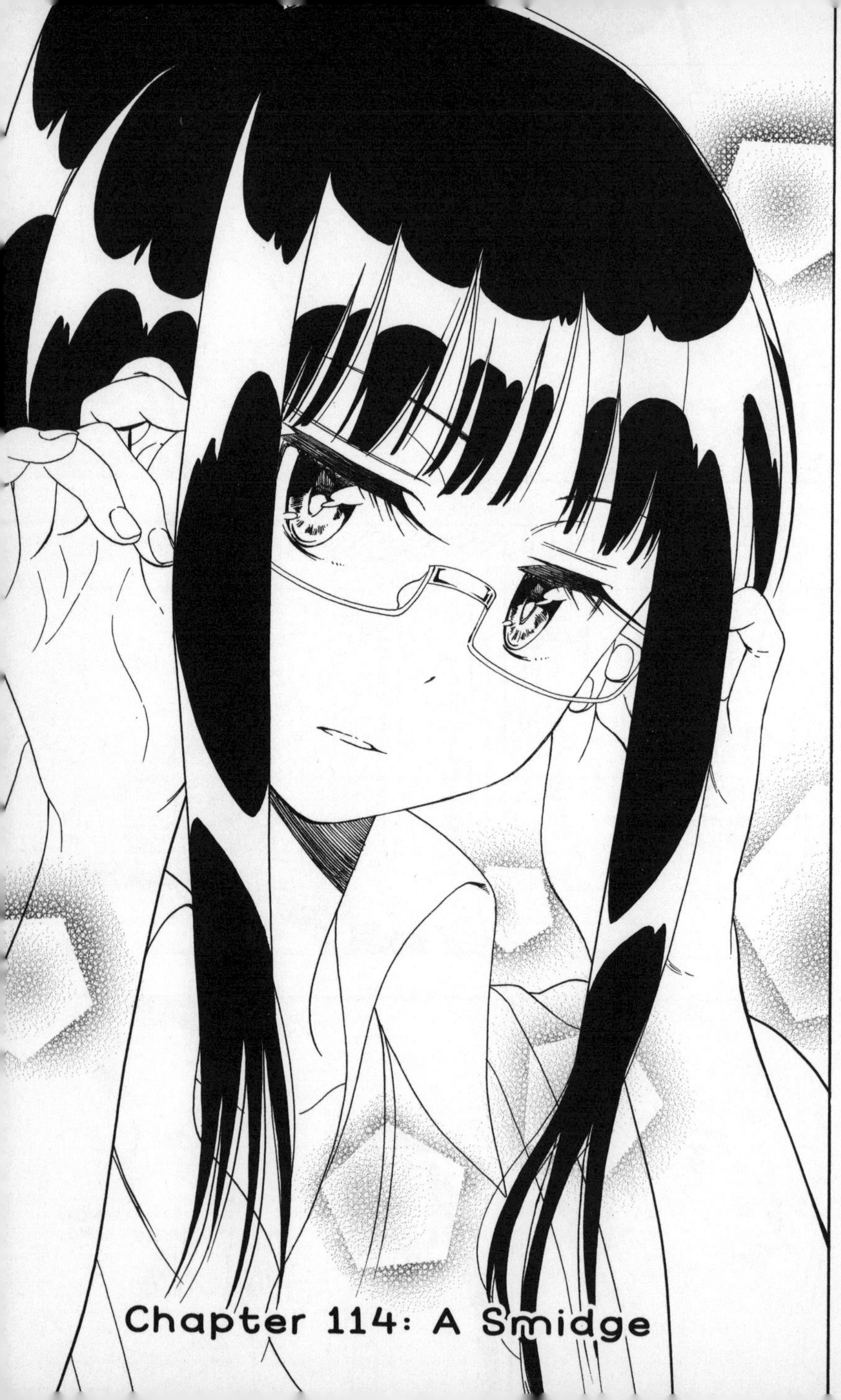

Chapter 114: A Smidge

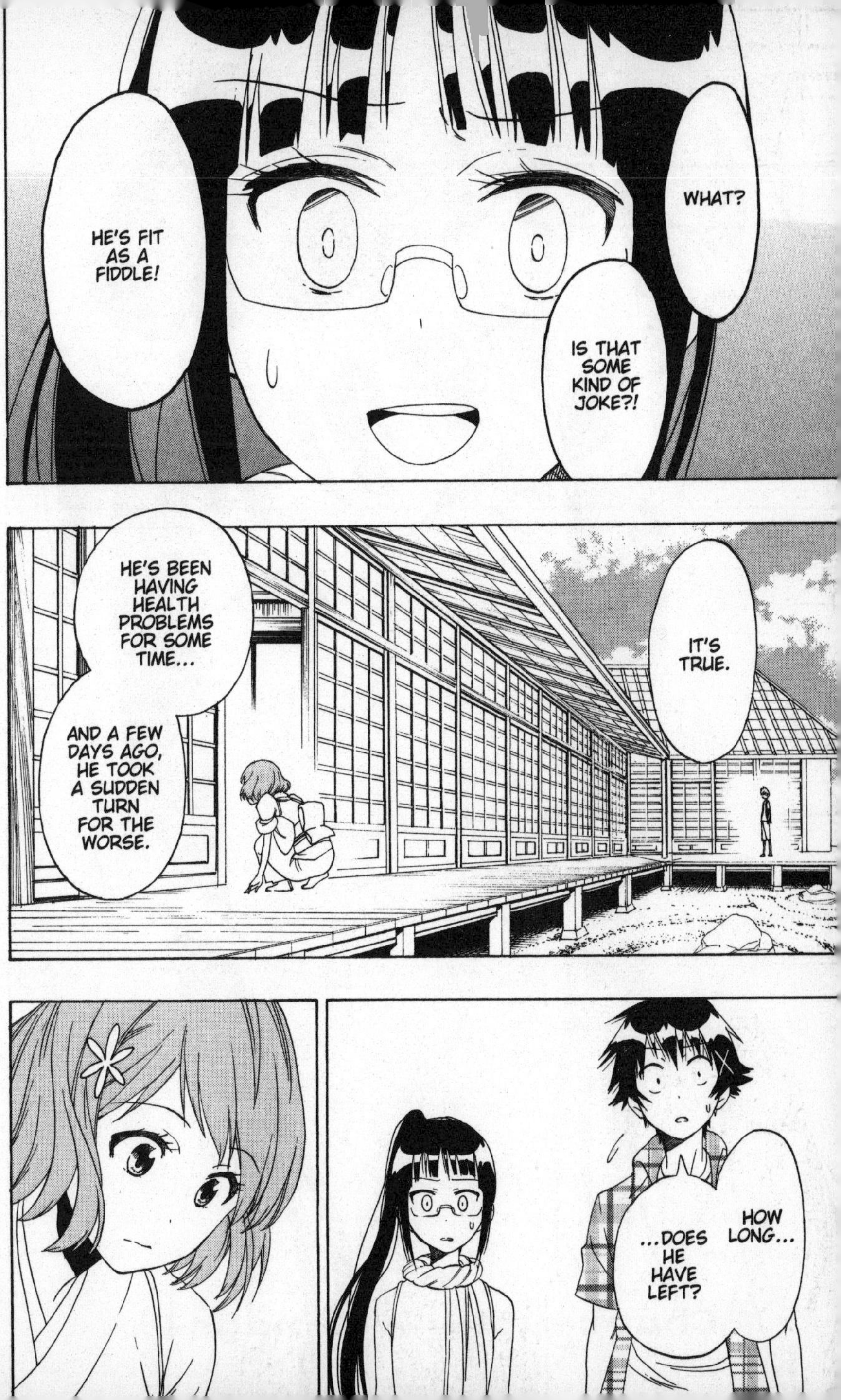
WHAT?
IS THAT SOME KIND OF JOKE?!
HE'S FIT AS A FIDDLE!
IT'S TRUE.
HE'S BEEN HAVING HEALTH PROBLEMS FOR SOME TIME...
AND A FEW DAYS AGO, HE TOOK A SUDDEN TURN FOR THE WORSE.
HOW LONG...
...DOES HE HAVE LEFT?

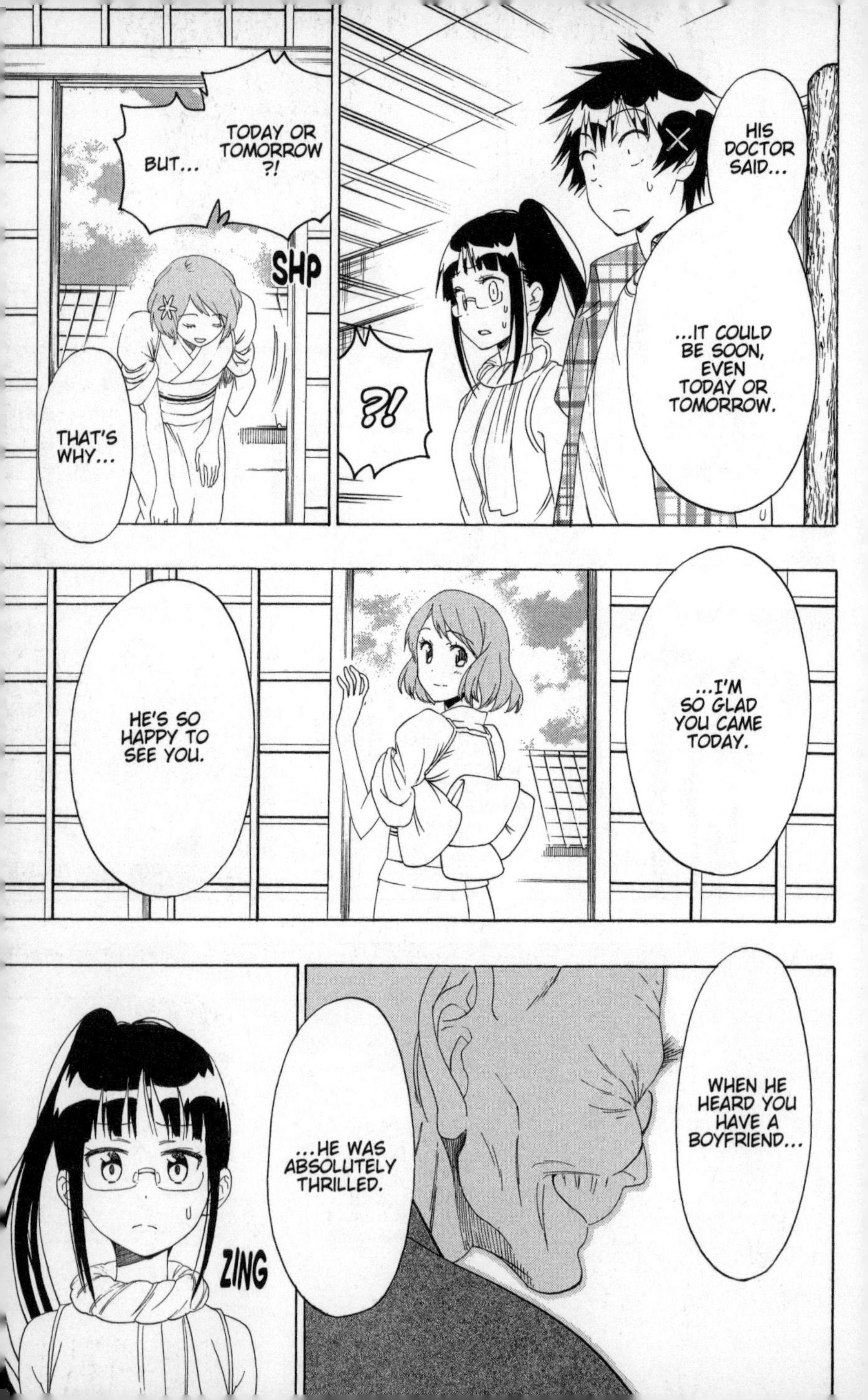
HIS DOCTOR SAID...
...IT COULD BE SOON, EVEN TODAY OR TOMORROW.
?!
TODAY OR TOMORROW ?!
BUT...
SHP
THAT'S WHY...
...I'M SO GLAD YOU CAME TODAY.
HE'S SO HAPPY TO SEE YOU.
WHEN HE HEARD YOU HAVE A BOYFRIEND...
...HE WAS ABSOLUTELY THRILLED.
ZING

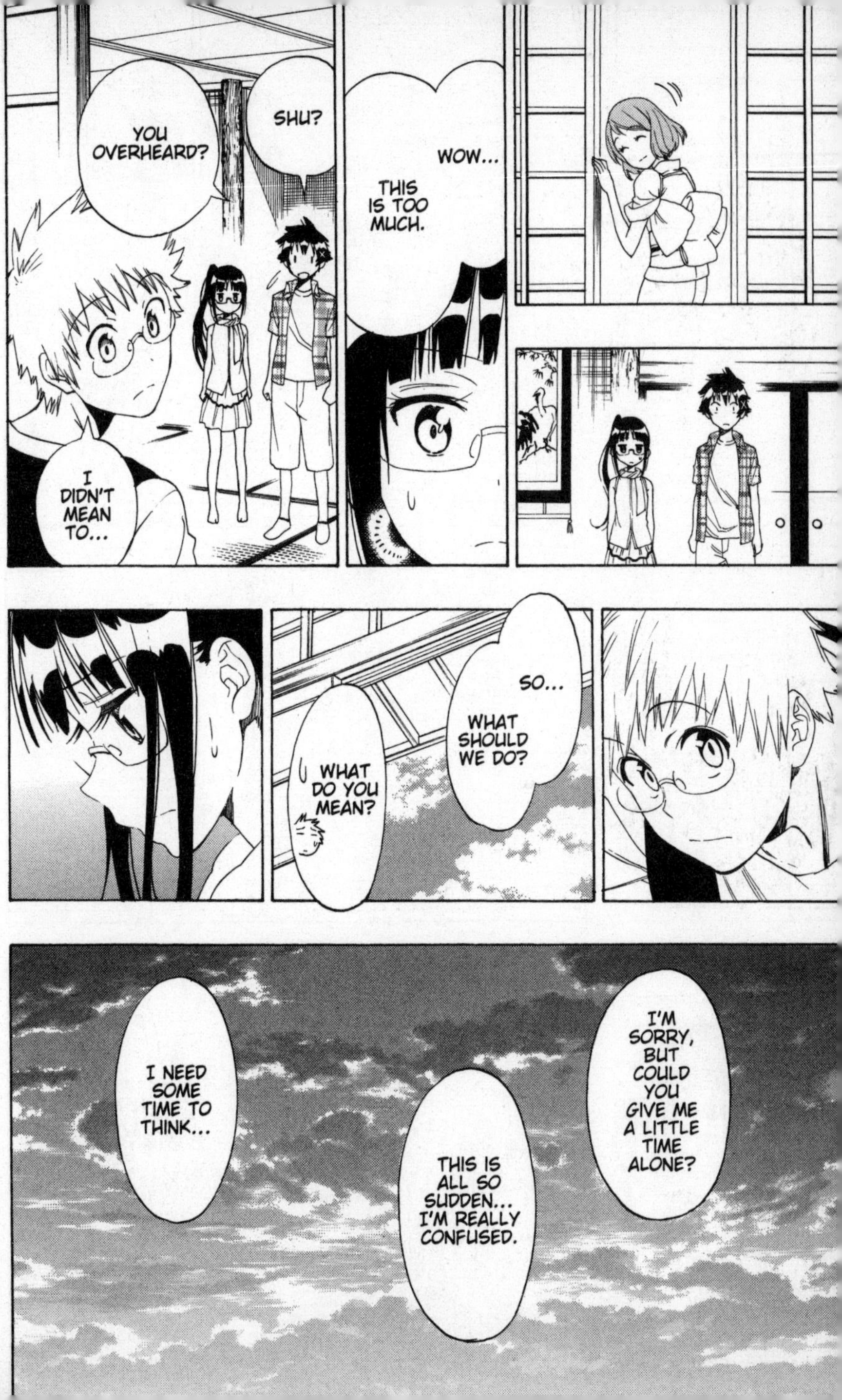
WOW... THIS IS TOO MUCH.
SHU?
YOU OVERHEARD?
I DIDN'T MEAN TO...
SO... WHAT SHOULD WE DO?
WHAT DO YOU MEAN?
I'M SORRY, BUT COULD YOU GIVE ME A LITTLE TIME ALONE?
THIS IS ALL SO SUDDEN... I'M REALLY CONFUSED.
I NEED SOME TIME TO THINK...

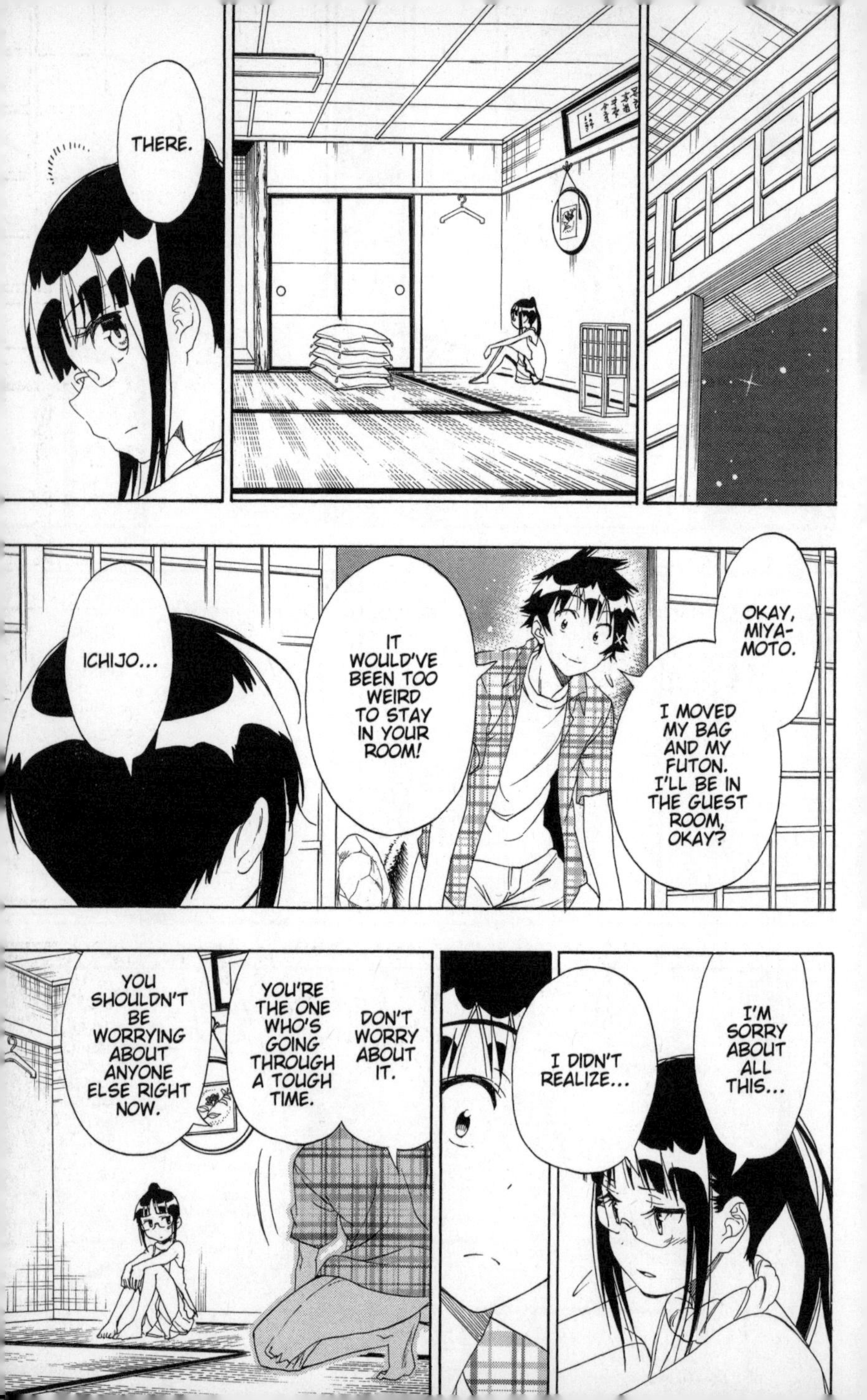
THERE.
OKAY, MIYA-MOTO.
I MOVED MY BAG AND MY FUTON. I'LL BE IN THE GUEST ROOM, OKAY?
IT WOULD'VE BEEN TOO WEIRD TO STAY IN YOUR ROOM!
ICHIJO...
I'M SORRY ABOUT ALL THIS...
I DIDN'T REALIZE...
DON'T WORRY ABOUT IT.
YOU'RE THE ONE WHO'S GOING THROUGH A TOUGH TIME.
YOU SHOULDN'T BE WORRYING ABOUT ANYONE ELSE RIGHT NOW.

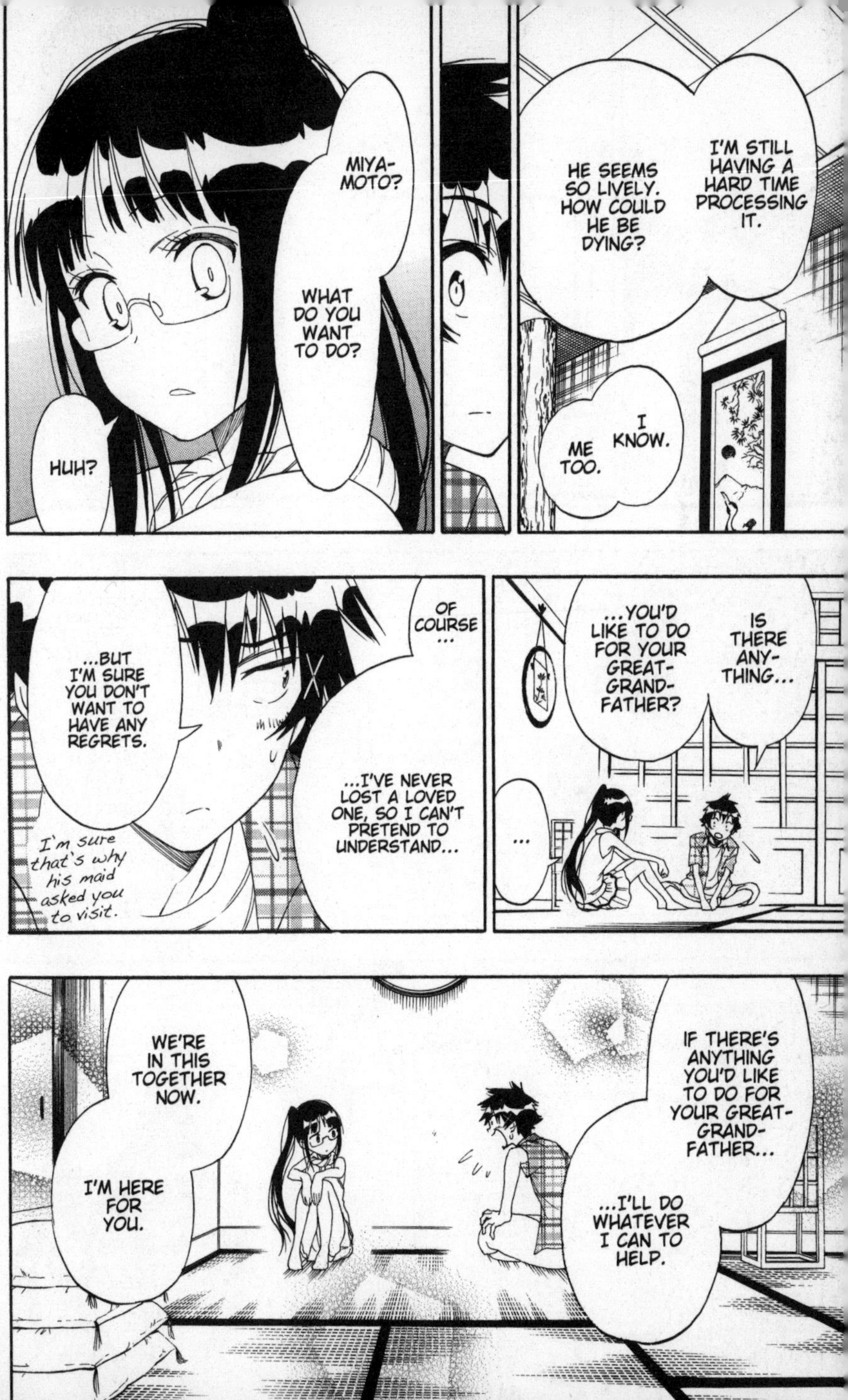
I'M STILL HAVING A HARD TIME PROCESSING IT.
HE SEEMS SO LIVELY. HOW COULD HE BE DYING?
I KNOW.
ME TOO.
MIYA-MOTO?
WHAT DO YOU WANT TO DO?
HUH?
IS THERE ANY-THING...
...YOU'D LIKE TO DO FOR YOUR GREAT-GRAND-FATHER?
...
OF COURSE...
...I'VE NEVER LOST A LOVED ONE, SO I CAN'T PRETEND TO UNDERSTAND...
...BUT I'M SURE YOU DON'T WANT TO HAVE ANY REGRETS.
I'm sure that's why his maid asked you to visit.
IF THERE'S ANYTHING YOU'D LIKE TO DO FOR YOUR GREAT-GRAND-FATHER...
...I'LL DO WHATEVER I CAN TO HELP.
WE'RE IN THIS TOGETHER NOW.
I'M HERE FOR YOU.

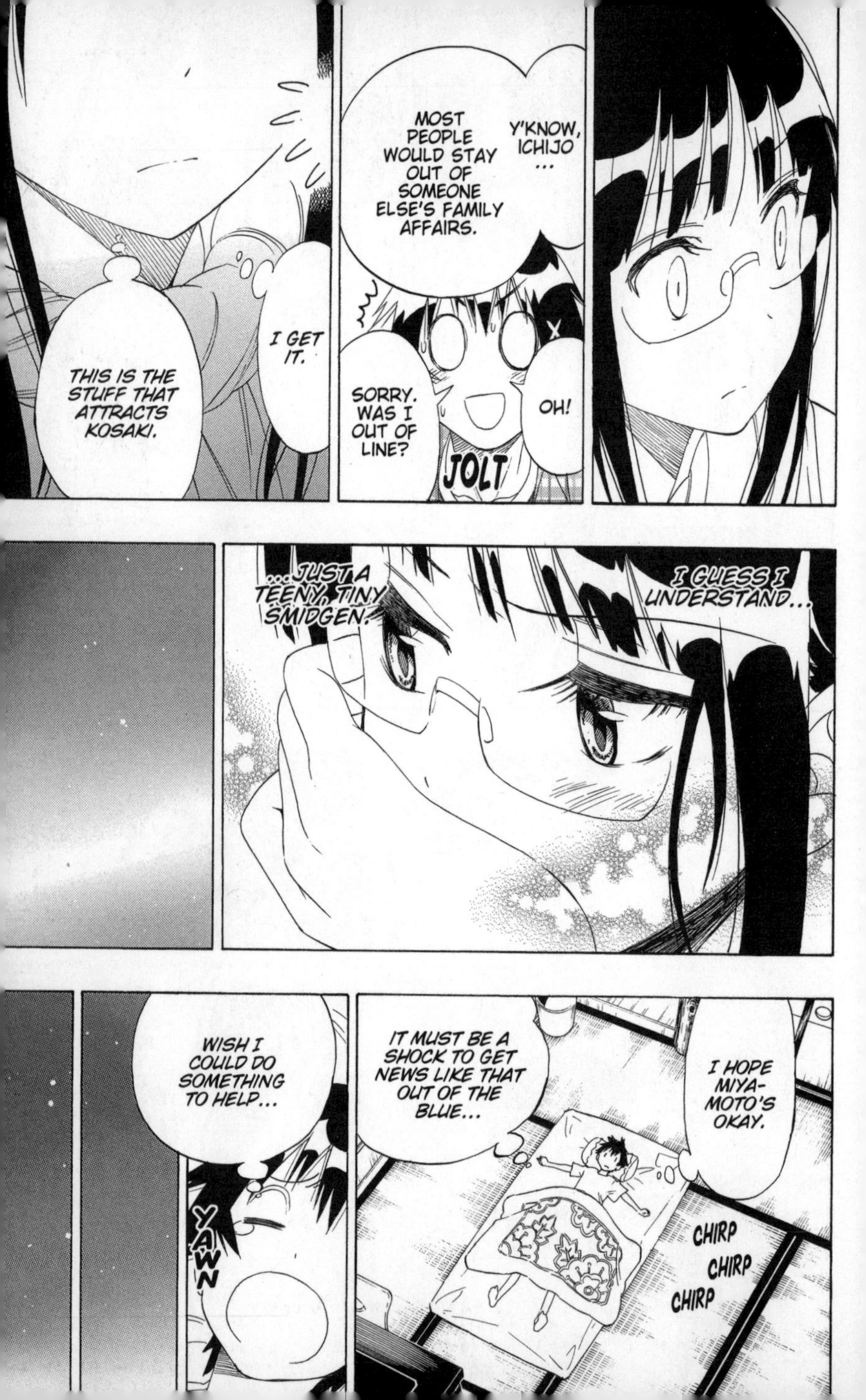
Y'KNOW, ICHIJO ...
MOST PEOPLE WOULD STAY OUT OF SOMEONE ELSE'S FAMILY AFFAIRS.
OH!
JOLT
SORRY. WAS I OUT OF LINE?
I GET IT.
THIS IS THE STUFF THAT ATTRACTS KOSAKI.
I GUESS I UNDERSTAND...
...JUST A TEENY, TINY SMIDGEN.
I HOPE MIYAMOTO'S OKAY.
IT MUST BE A SHOCK TO GET NEWS LIKE THAT OUT OF THE BLUE...
CHIRP
CHIRP
CHIRP
WISH I COULD DO SOMETHING TO HELP...
YAWN

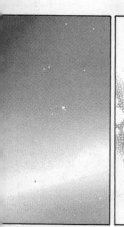

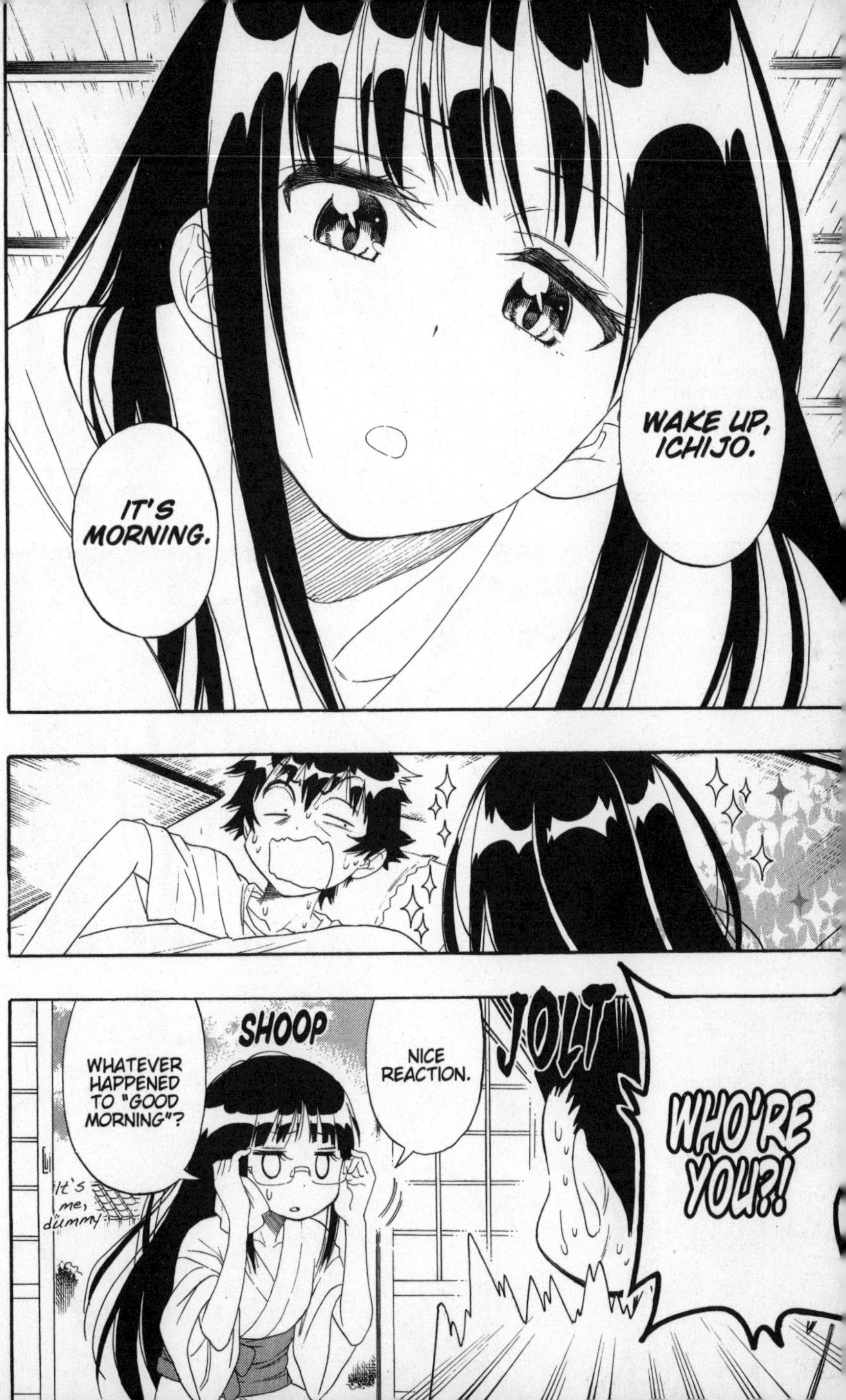
WAKE UP, ICHIJO.
IT'S MORNING.
JOLT
WHO'RE YOU?!
NICE REACTION.
SHOOP
WHATEVER HAPPENED TO "GOOD MORNING"?
It's me, dummy.

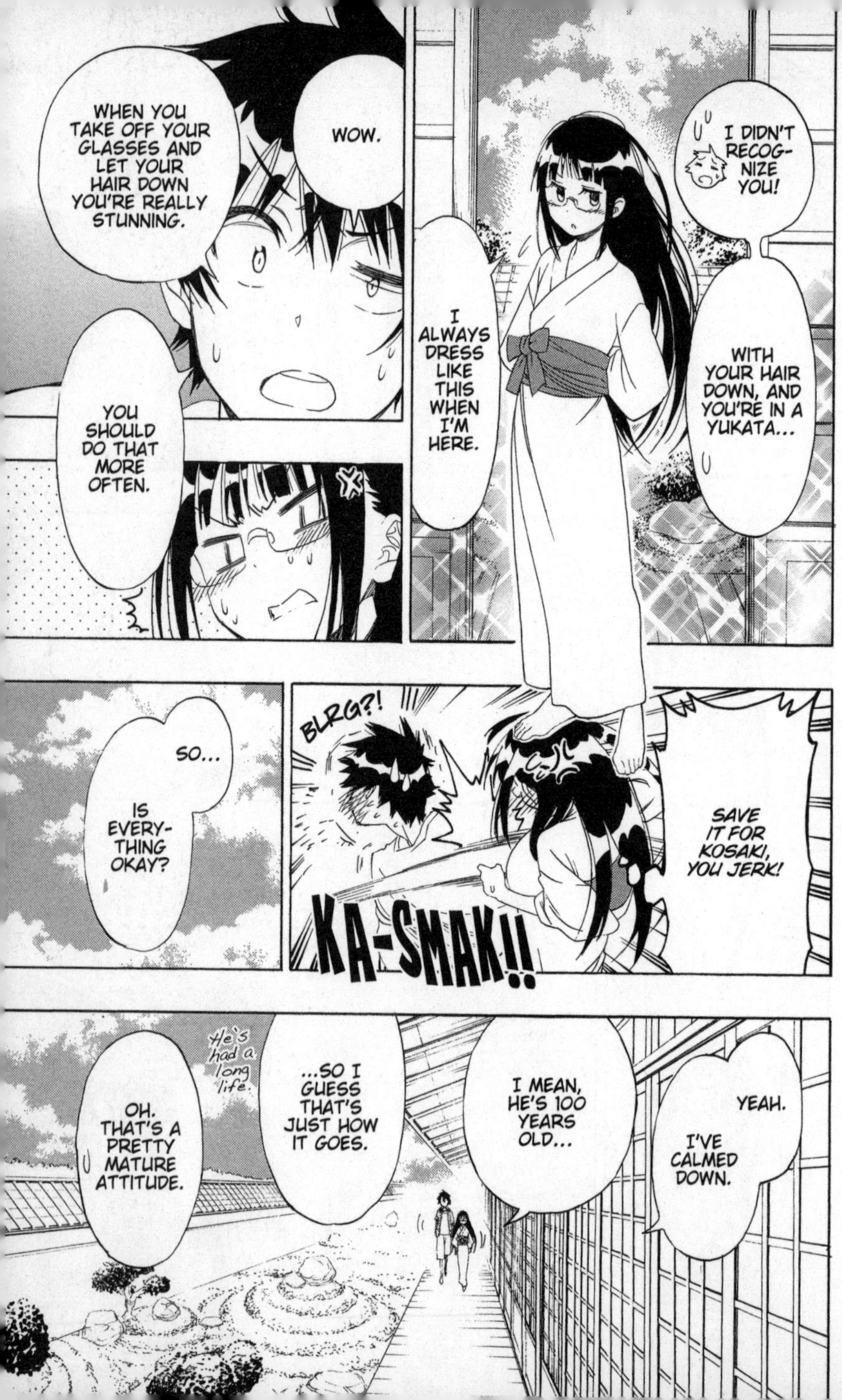
I DIDN'T RECOGNIZE YOU!
WITH YOUR HAIR DOWN, AND YOU'RE IN A YUKATA...
I ALWAYS DRESS LIKE THIS WHEN I'M HERE.
WOW.
WHEN YOU TAKE OFF YOUR GLASSES AND LET YOUR HAIR DOWN YOU'RE REALLY STUNNING.
YOU SHOULD DO THAT MORE OFTEN.
SAVE IT FOR KOSAKI, YOU JERK!
BLRG?!
KA-SMAK!!
SO...
IS EVERYTHING OKAY?
YEAH.
I'VE CALMED DOWN.
I MEAN, HE'S 100 YEARS OLD...
...SO I GUESS THAT'S JUST HOW IT GOES.
He's had a long life.
OH. THAT'S A PRETTY MATURE ATTITUDE.

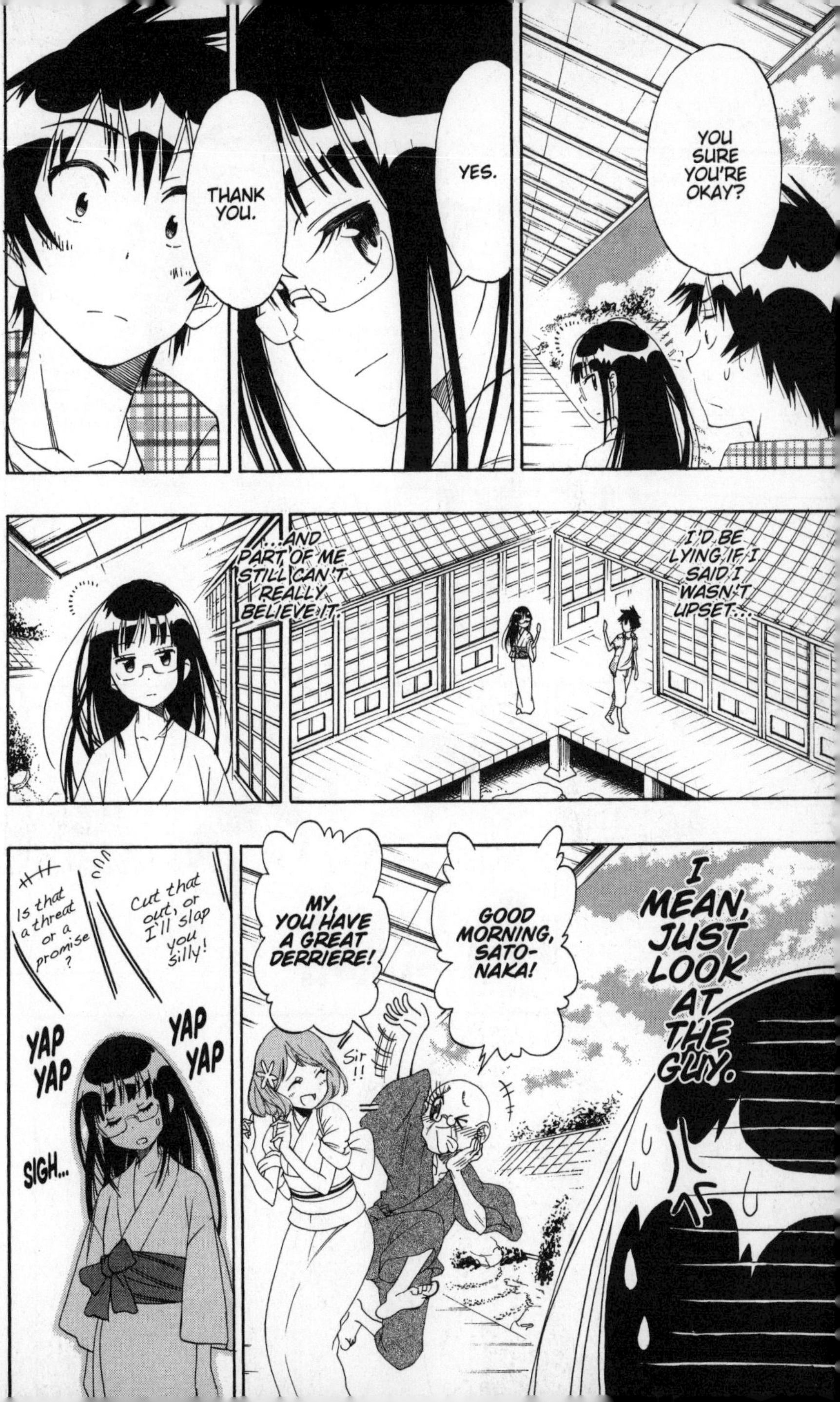
YOU SURE YOU'RE OKAY?
YES.
THANK YOU.
I'D BE LYING IF I SAID I WASN'T UPSET...
...AND PART OF ME STILL CAN'T REALLY BELIEVE IT.
I MEAN, JUST LOOK AT THE GUY.
GOOD MORNING, SATO-NAKA!
MY, YOU HAVE A GREAT DERRIERE!
Sir!!
Cut that out, or I'll slap you silly!
Is that a threat or a promise?
YAP YAP
YAP YAP
SIGH...

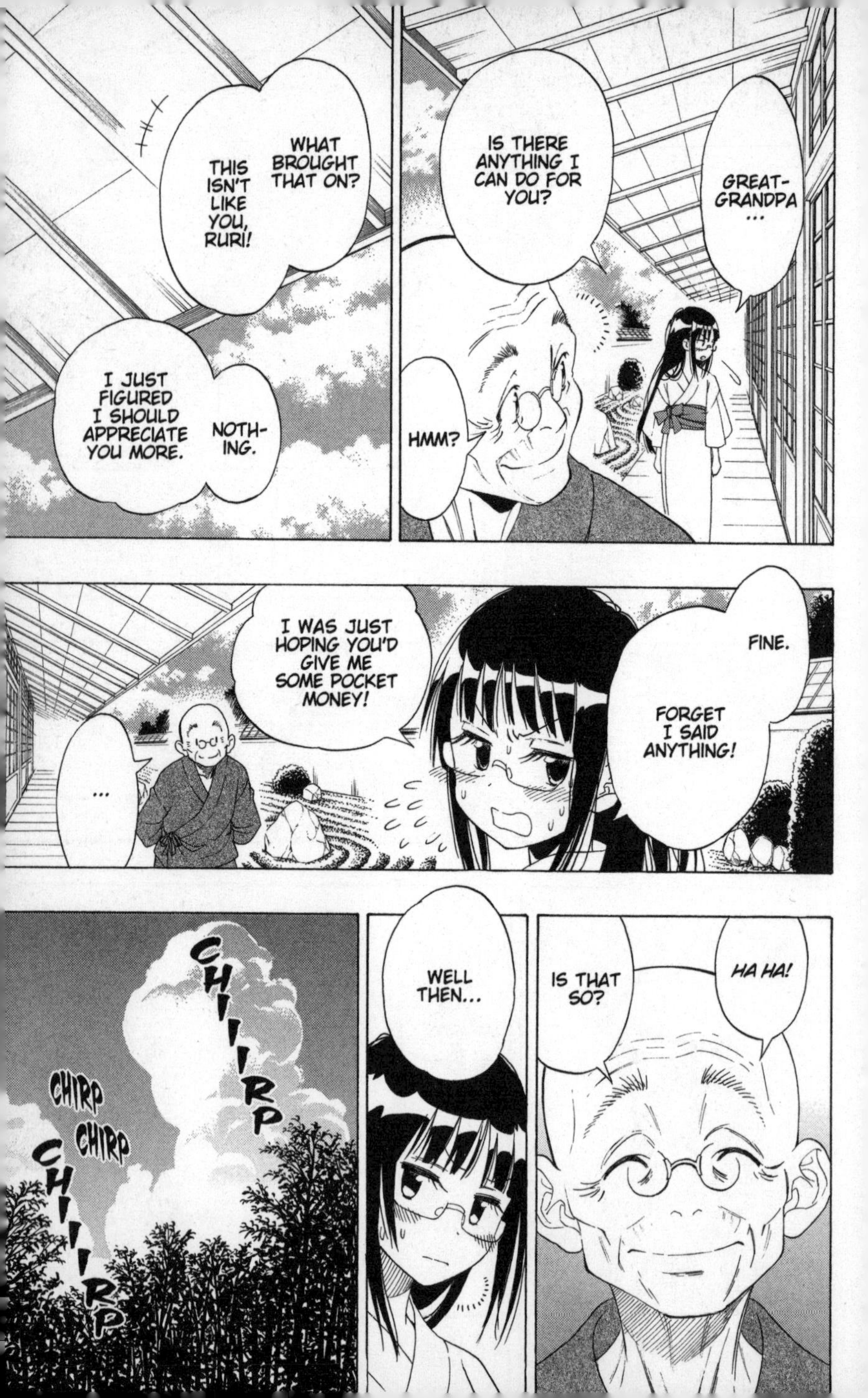
GREAT-GRANDPA...
IS THERE ANYTHING I CAN DO FOR YOU?
HMM?
WHAT BROUGHT THAT ON?
THIS ISN'T LIKE YOU, RURI!
NOTH-ING.
I JUST FIGURED I SHOULD APPRECIATE YOU MORE.
FINE.
FORGET I SAID ANYTHING!
I WAS JUST HOPING YOU'D GIVE ME SOME POCKET MONEY!
...
HA HA!
IS THAT SO?
WELL THEN...
CHIIIIRP
CHIRP CHIRP
CHIIIIRP

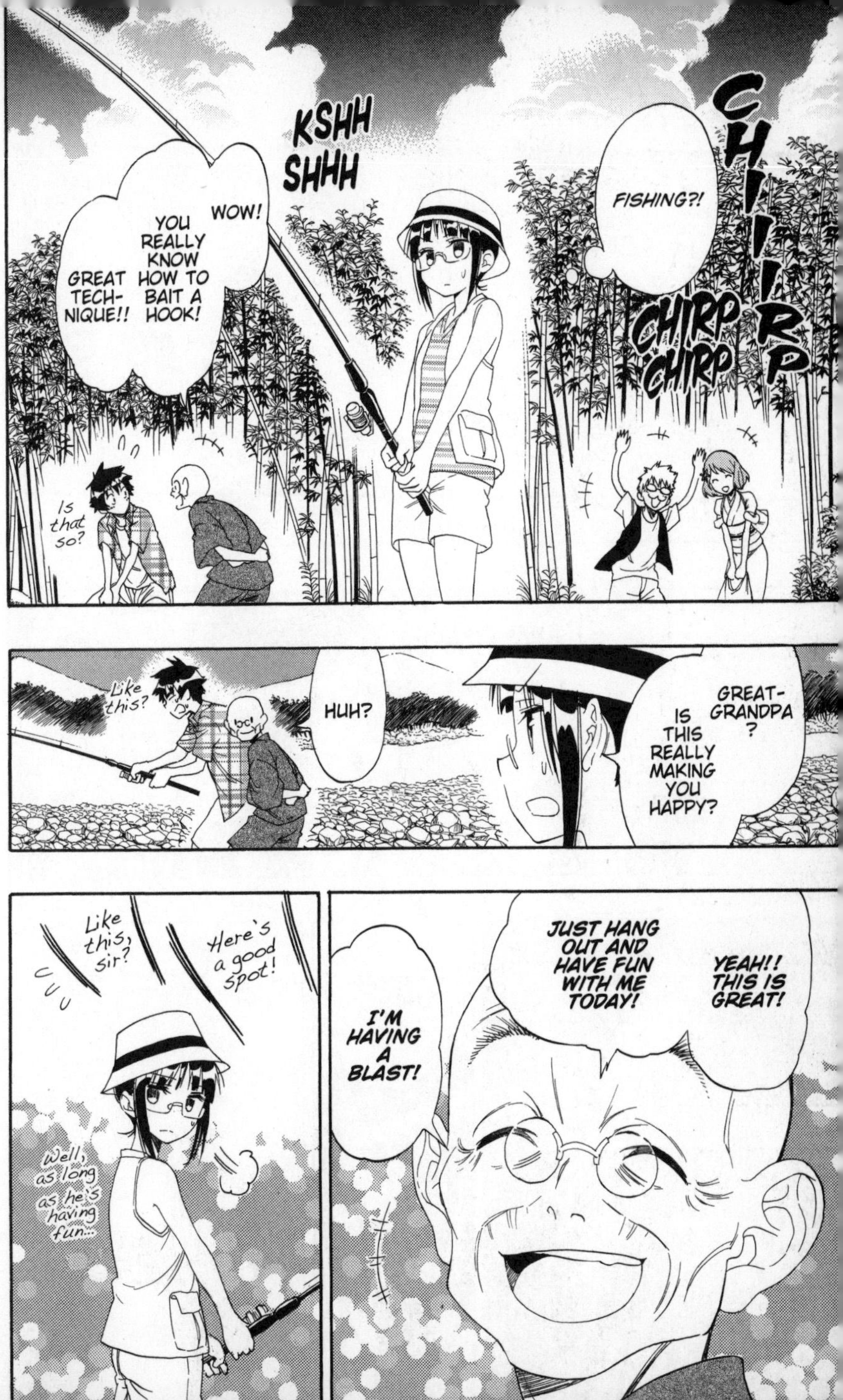
CHIRP
CHIRP CHIRP
FISHING?!
KSHH SHHH
WOW! YOU REALLY KNOW HOW TO BAIT A HOOK! GREAT TECH-NIQUE!!
Is that so?
GREAT-GRANDPA? IS THIS REALLY MAKING YOU HAPPY?
HUH?
Like this?
YEAH!! THIS IS GREAT!
JUST HANG OUT AND HAVE FUN WITH ME TODAY!
I'M HAVING A BLAST!
Here's a good spot!
Like this, sir?
Well, as long as he's having fun...

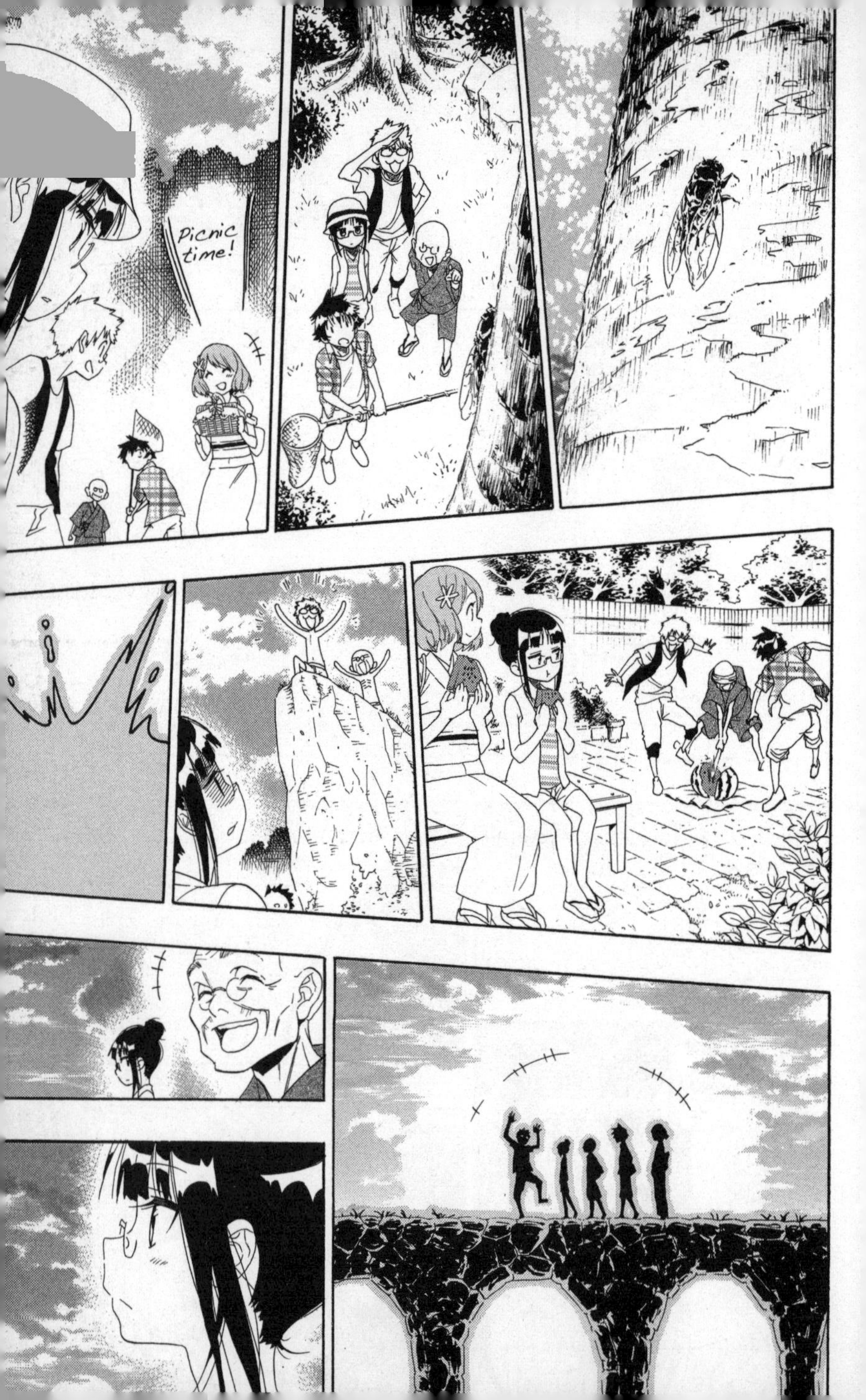
Picnic time!

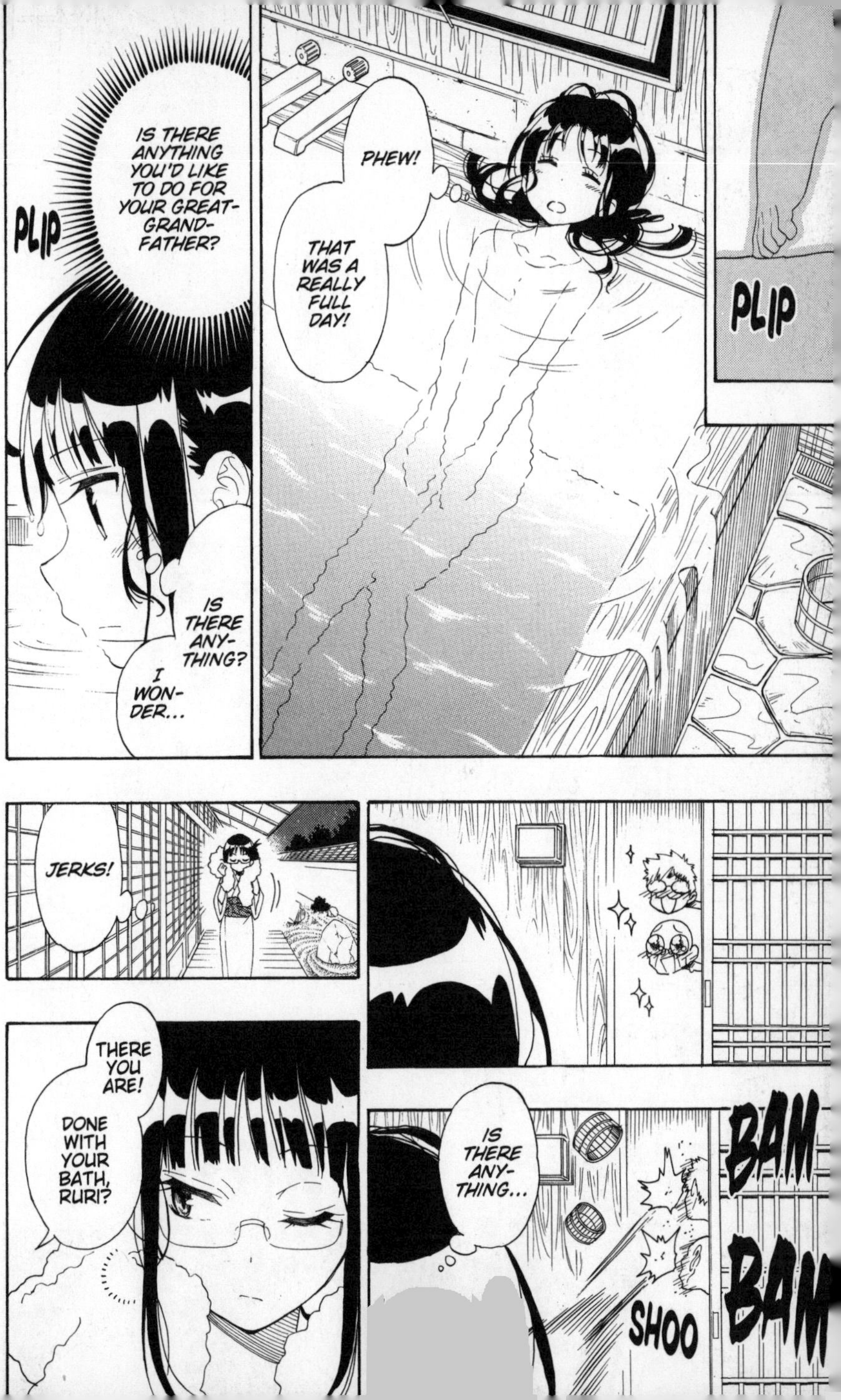
PLIP
PHEW!
THAT WAS A REALLY FULL DAY!
IS THERE ANYTHING YOU'D LIKE TO DO FOR YOUR GREAT-GRAND-FATHER?
PLIP
IS THERE ANYTHING?
I WONDER...
JERKS!
BAM
BAM
SHOO
IS THERE ANYTHING...
THERE YOU ARE!
DONE WITH YOUR BATH, RURI?

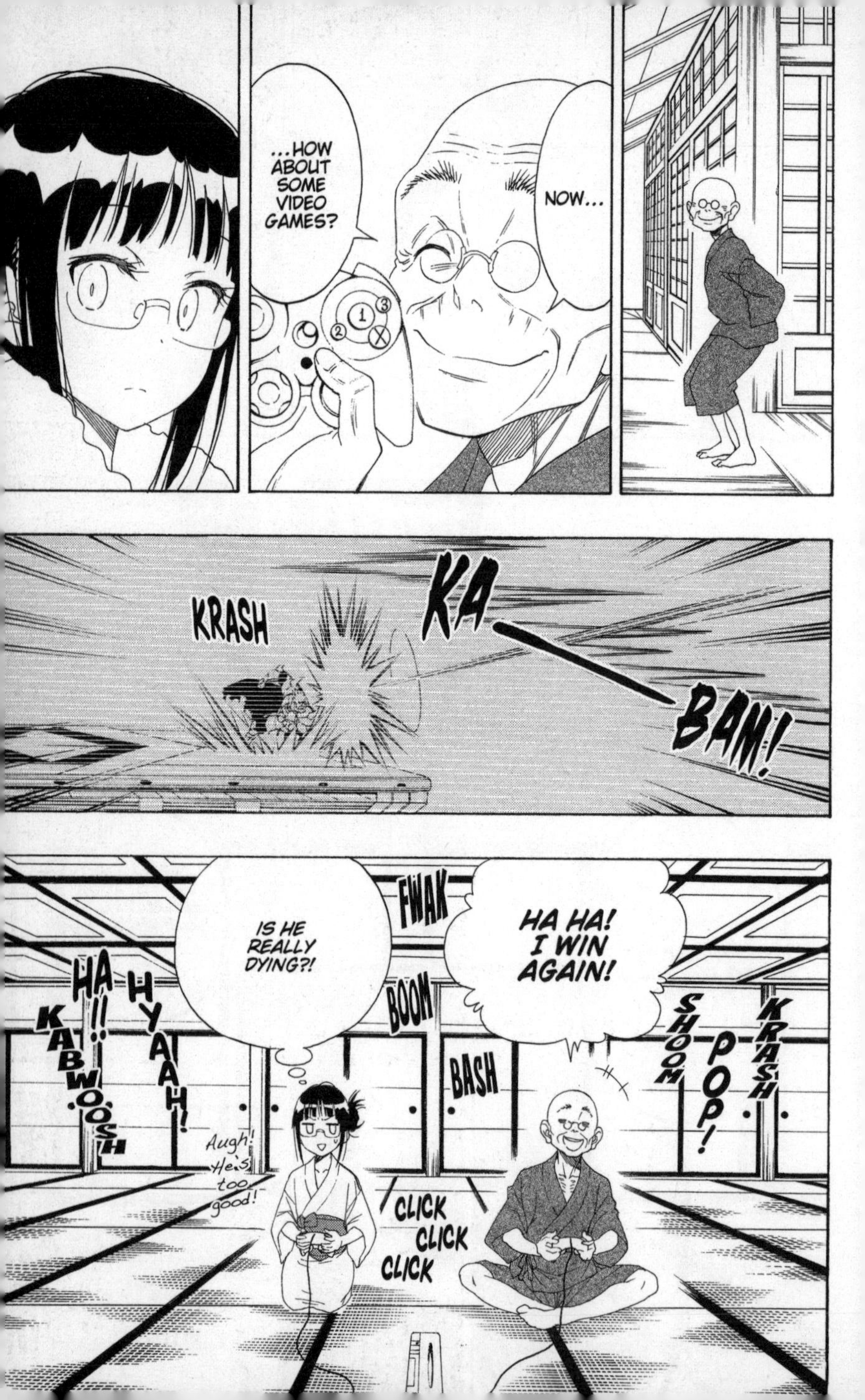
NOW...
...HOW ABOUT SOME VIDEO GAMES?
KA—BAM!
KRASH
KRASH
POP!
SHOOM
HA HA! I WIN AGAIN!
FWAK
BOOM
BASH
IS HE REALLY DYING?!
HYAAAH!
HA!!
KABWOOOSH
Augh! He's too good!
CLICK CLICK CLICK

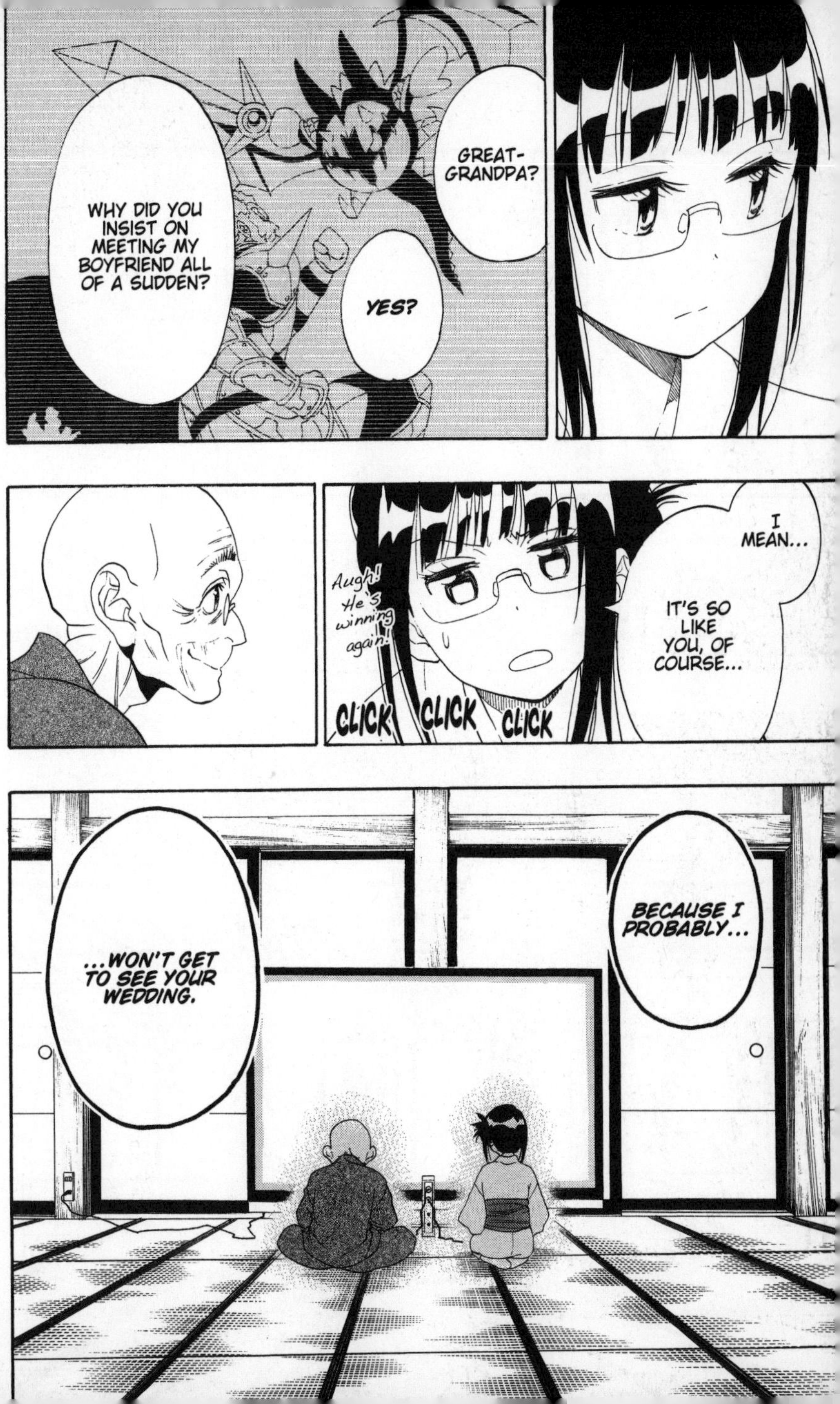
GREAT-GRANDPA?
WHY DID YOU INSIST ON MEETING MY BOYFRIEND ALL OF A SUDDEN?
YES?
I MEAN...
IT'S SO LIKE YOU, OF COURSE...
Augh! He's winning again.
CLICK CLICK CLICK
BECAUSE I PROBABLY...
...WON'T GET TO SEE YOUR WEDDING.

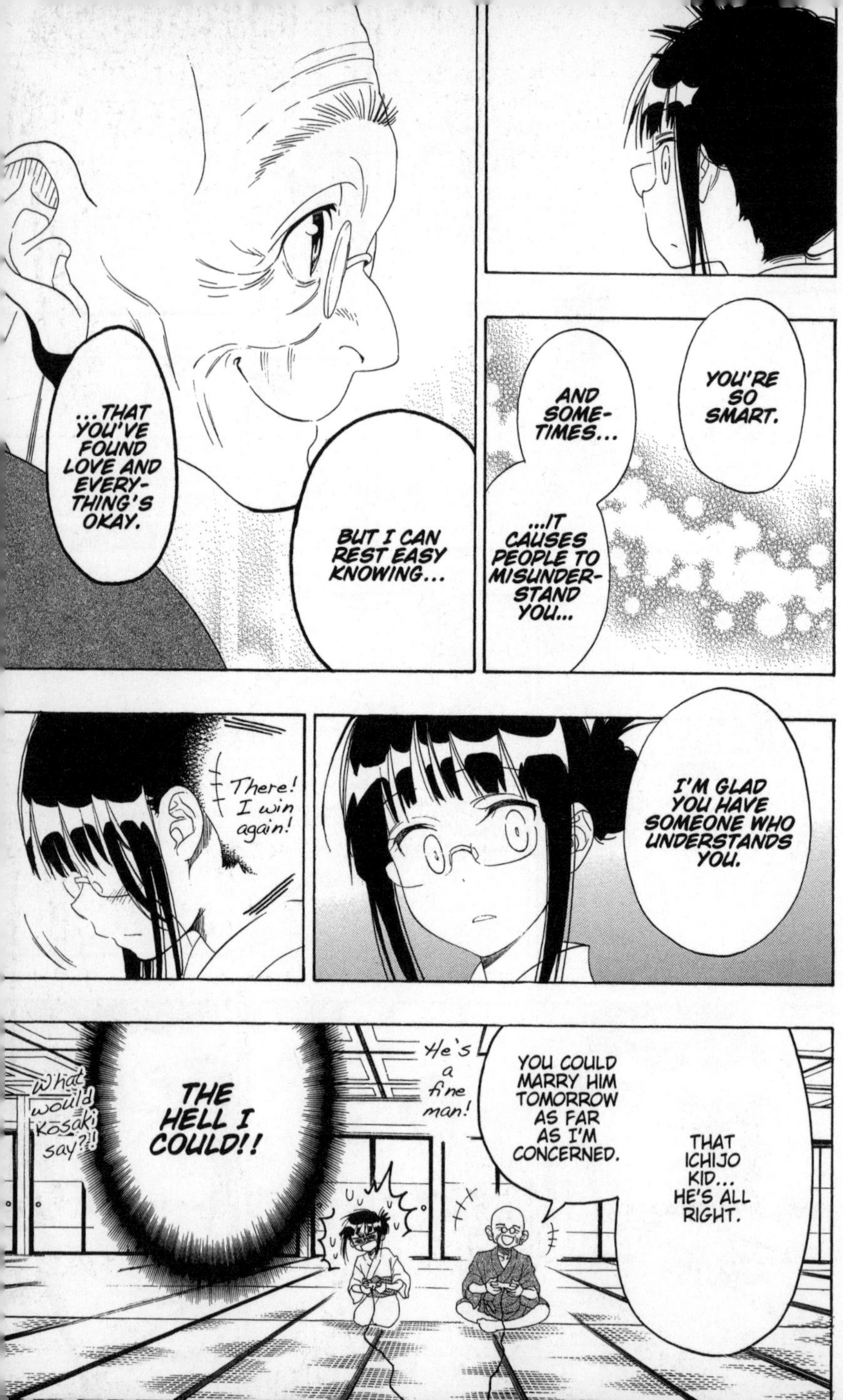
YOU'RE SO SMART.
AND SOME-TIMES...
...IT CAUSES PEOPLE TO MISUNDER-STAND YOU...
BUT I CAN REST EASY KNOWING...
...THAT YOU'VE FOUND LOVE AND EVERY-THING'S OKAY.
I'M GLAD YOU HAVE SOMEONE WHO UNDERSTANDS YOU.
There! I win again!
THAT ICHIJO KID... HE'S ALL RIGHT.
YOU COULD MARRY HIM TOMORROW AS FAR AS I'M CONCERNED.
He's a fine man!
THE HELL I COULD!!
What would Kosaki say?!

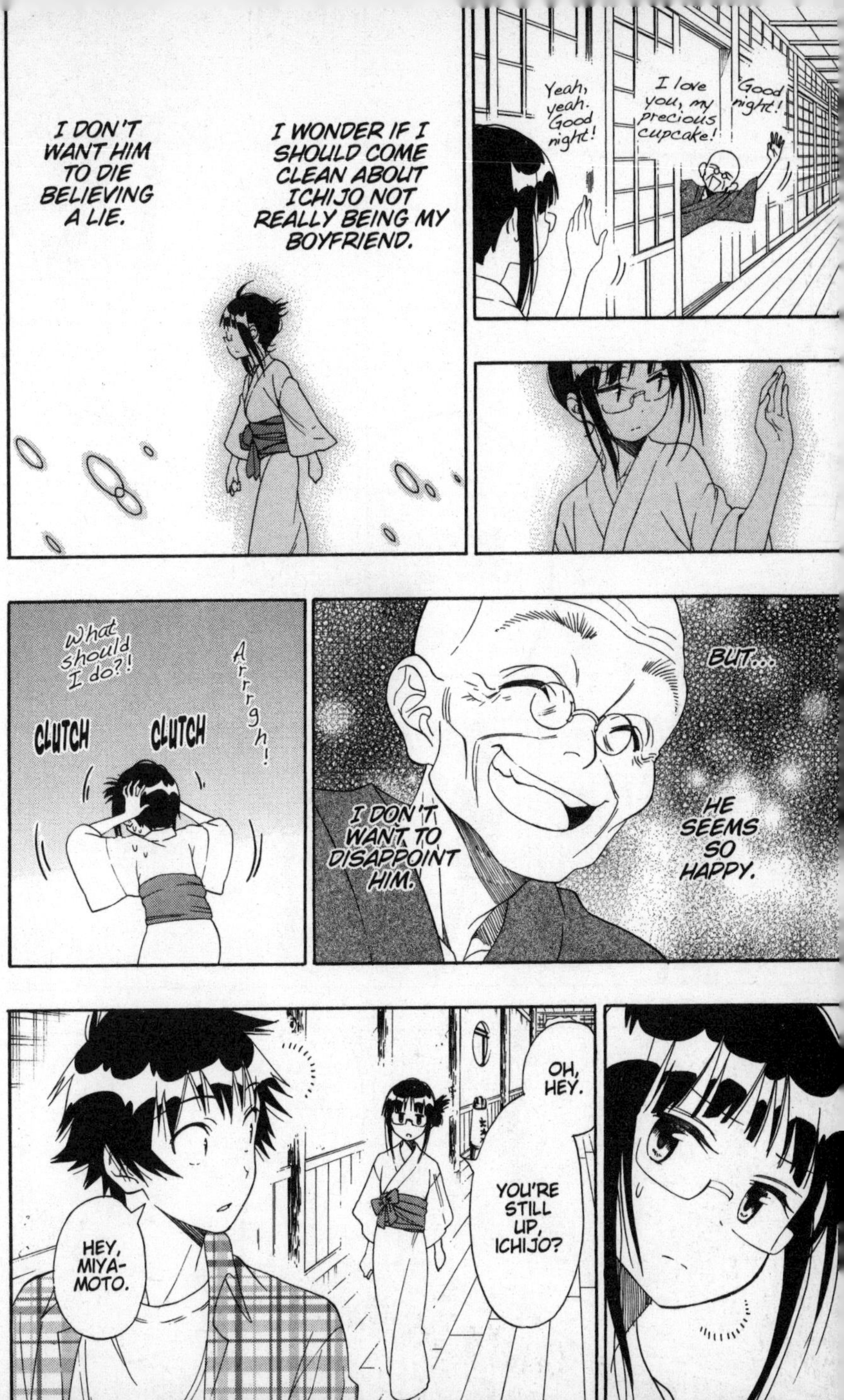
Good night!
I love you, my precious cupcake!
Yeah, yeah. Good night!
I WONDER IF I SHOULD COME CLEAN ABOUT ICHIJO NOT REALLY BEING MY BOYFRIEND.
I DON'T WANT HIM TO DIE BELIEVING A LIE.
BUT...
HE SEEMS SO HAPPY.
I DON'T WANT TO DISAPPOINT HIM.
Arrrgh!
What should I do?!
CLUTCH
CLUTCH
OH, HEY.
YOU'RE STILL UP, ICHIJO?
HEY, MIYA-MOTO.

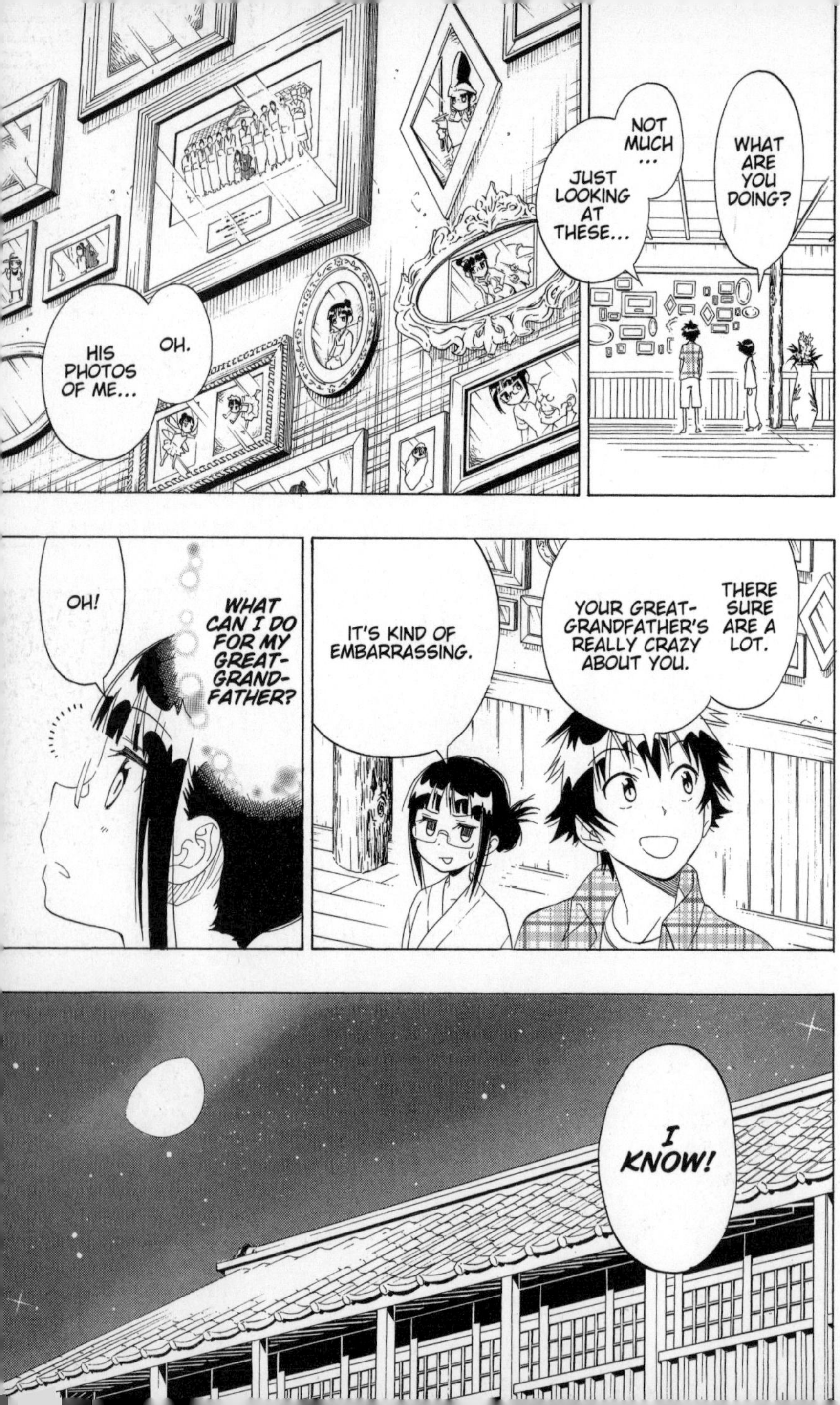
WHAT ARE YOU DOING?
NOT MUCH... JUST LOOKING AT THESE...
OH.
HIS PHOTOS OF ME...
THERE SURE ARE A LOT.
YOUR GREAT-GRANDFATHER'S REALLY CRAZY ABOUT YOU.
IT'S KIND OF EMBARRASSING.
WHAT CAN I DO FOR MY GREAT-GRANDFATHER?
OH!
I KNOW!

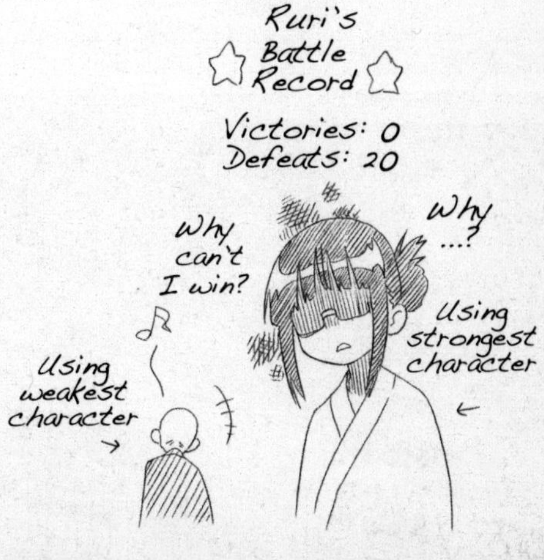
☆ Ruri's Battle Record ☆
Victories: 0
Defeats: 20
Why ...?
Using strongest character
Why can't I win?
Using weakest character

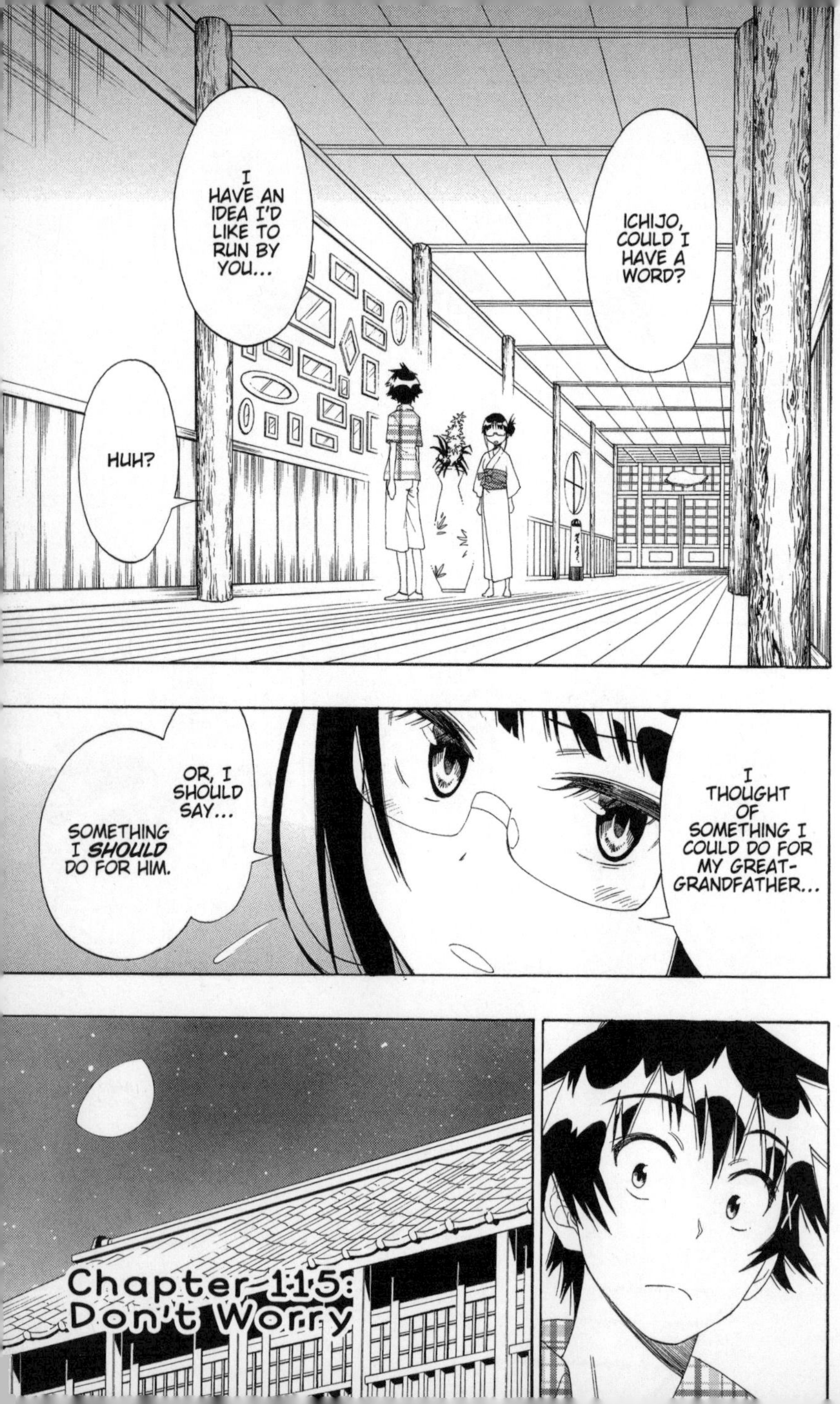
ICHIJO, COULD I HAVE A WORD?
I HAVE AN IDEA I'D LIKE TO RUN BY YOU...
HUH?
I THOUGHT OF SOMETHING I COULD DO FOR MY GREAT-GRANDFATHER...
OR, I SHOULD SAY...
SOMETHING I *SHOULD* DO FOR HIM.
Chapter 115: Don't Worry

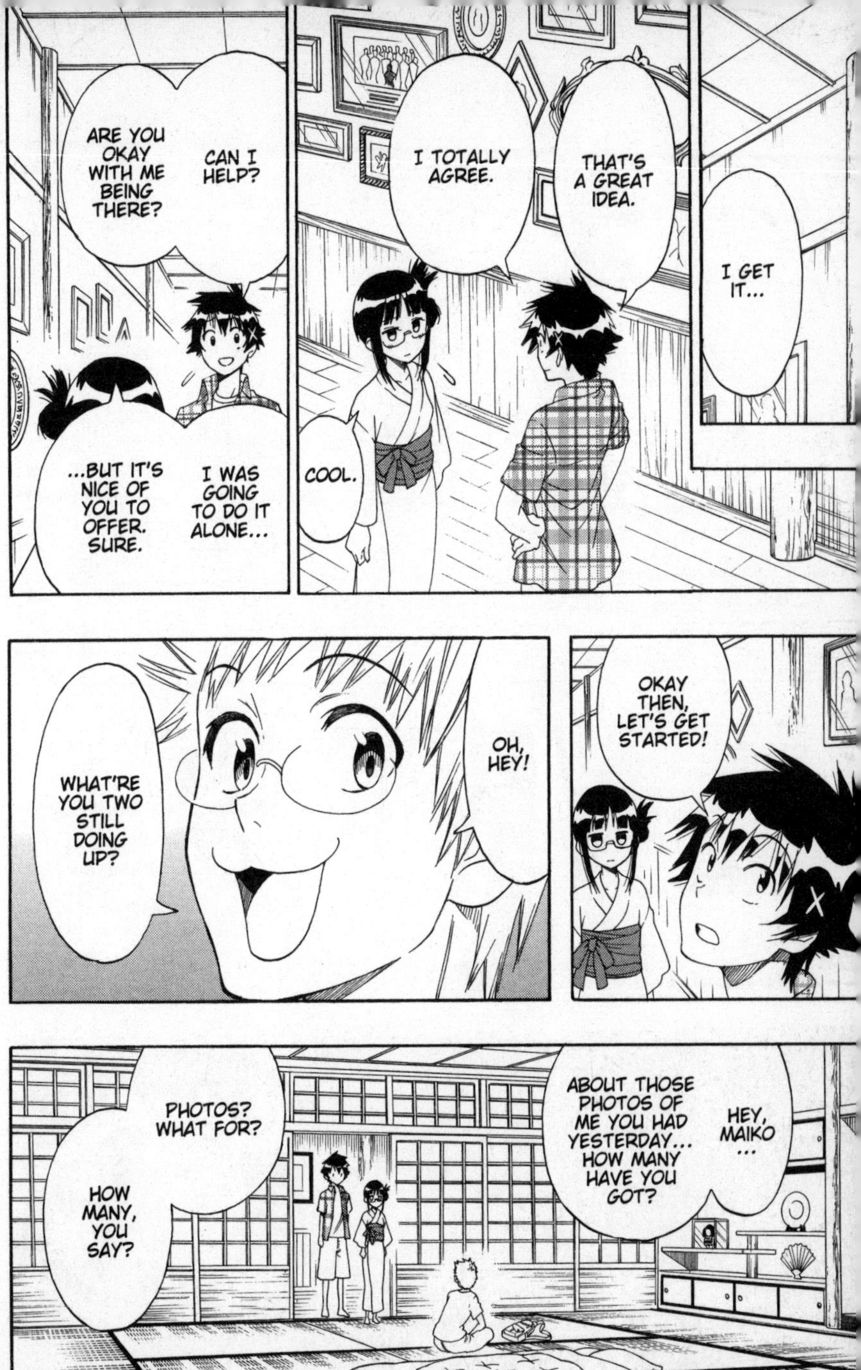
I GET IT...
THAT'S A GREAT IDEA.
I TOTALLY AGREE.
COOL.
CAN I HELP?
ARE YOU OKAY WITH ME BEING THERE?
I WAS GOING TO DO IT ALONE...
...BUT IT'S NICE OF YOU TO OFFER. SURE.
OKAY THEN, LET'S GET STARTED!
OH, HEY!
WHAT'RE YOU TWO STILL DOING UP?
HEY, MAIKO...
ABOUT THOSE PHOTOS OF ME YOU HAD YESTERDAY... HOW MANY HAVE YOU GOT?
PHOTOS? WHAT FOR?
HOW MANY, YOU SAY?

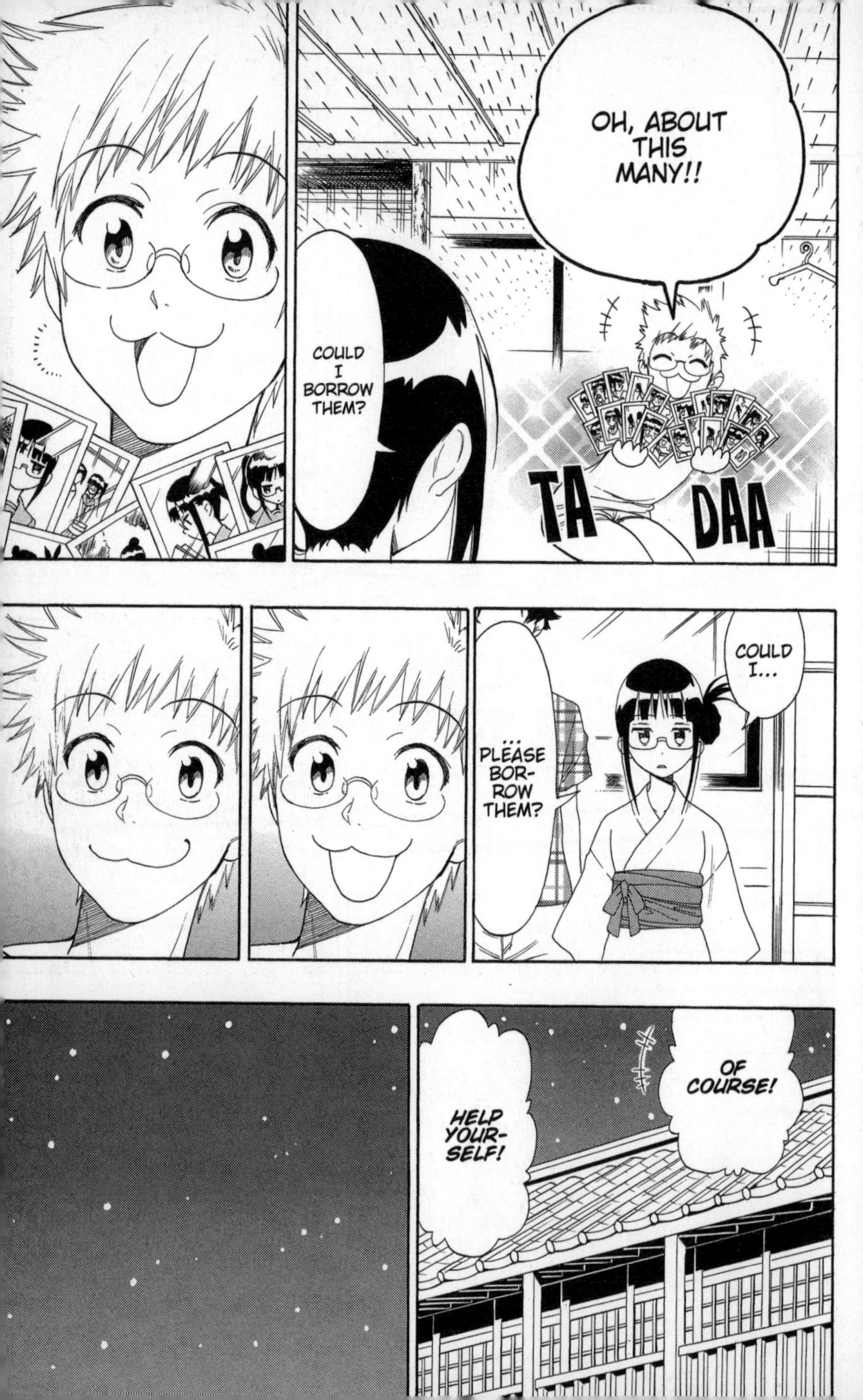
OH, ABOUT THIS MANY!!
TA DAA
COULD I BORROW THEM?
COULD I...
...PLEASE BORROW THEM?
OF COURSE!
HELP YOURSELF!

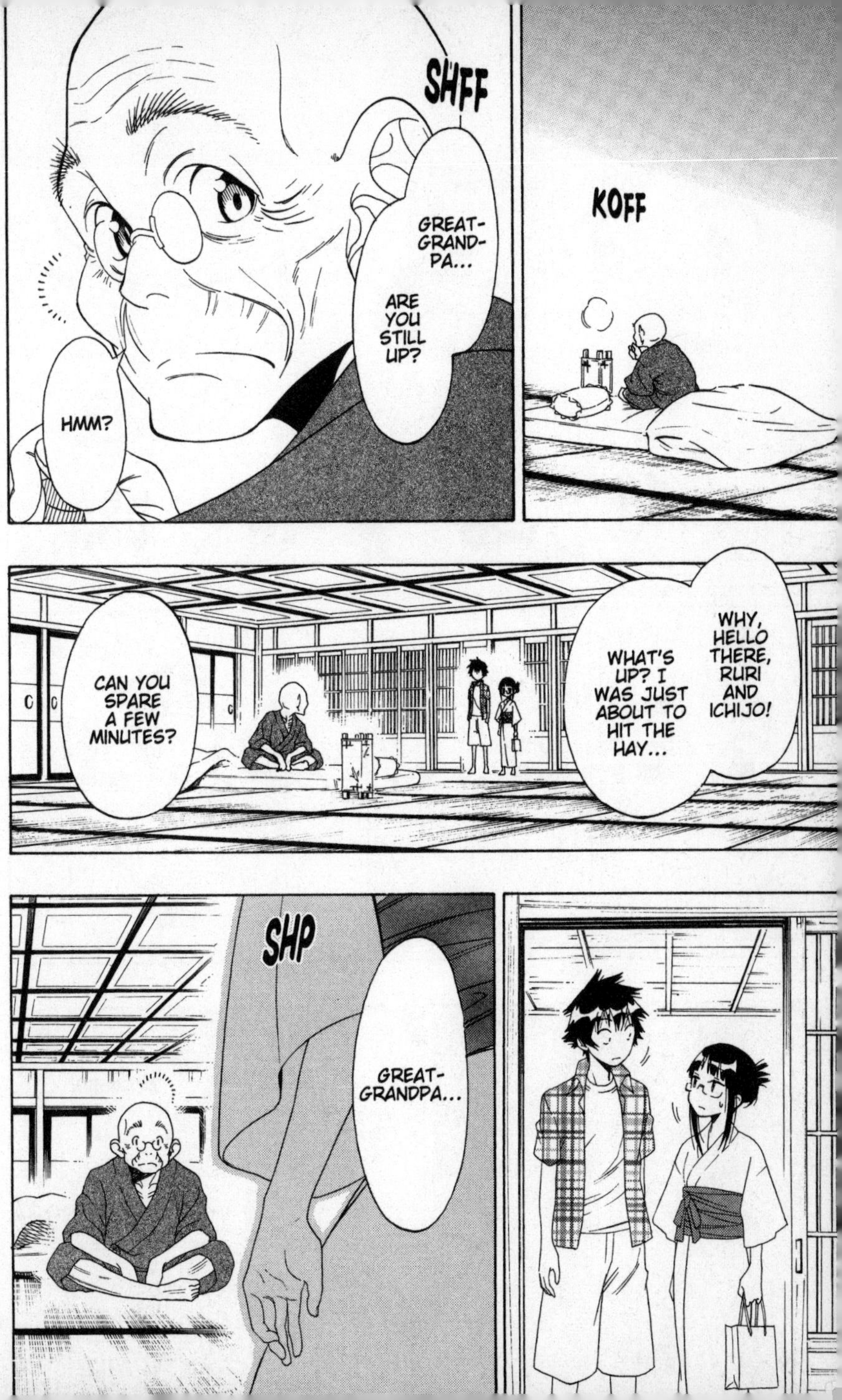
KOFF
SHFF
GREAT-GRANDPA...
ARE YOU STILL UP?
HMM?
WHY, HELLO THERE, RURI AND ICHIJO!
WHAT'S UP? I WAS JUST ABOUT TO HIT THE HAY...
CAN YOU SPARE A FEW MINUTES?
SHP
GREAT-GRANDPA...

I'M SORRY.

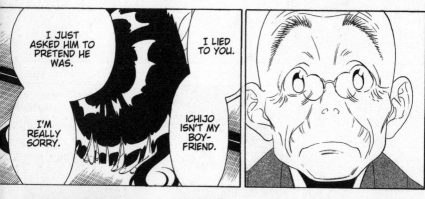

I JUST ASKED HIM TO PRETEND HE WAS.

I LIED TO YOU.

I'M REALLY SORRY.

ICHIJO ISN'T MY BOY-FRIEND.

I'M VERY SORRY.

WE BOTH LIED TO YOU.

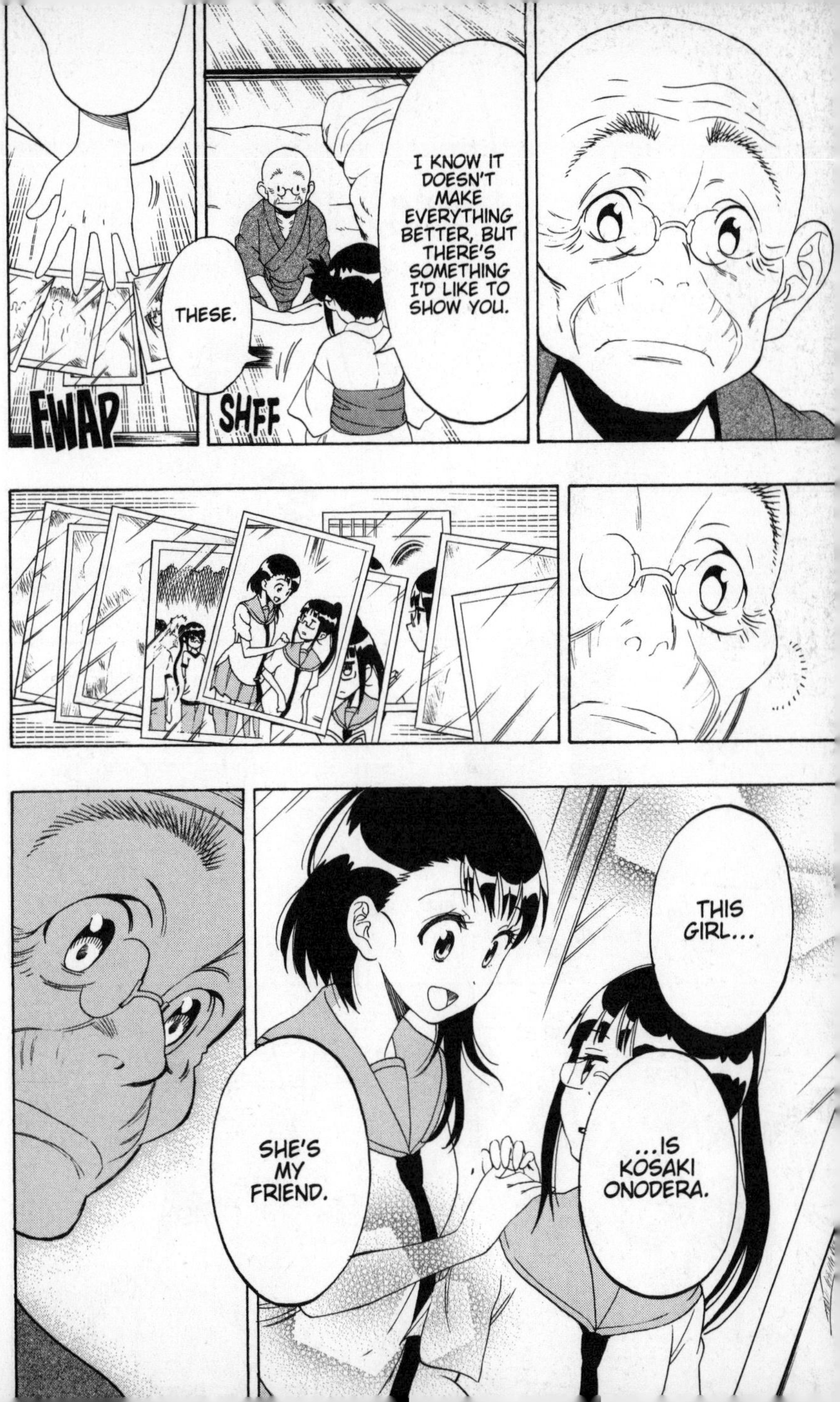
I KNOW IT DOESN'T MAKE EVERYTHING BETTER, BUT THERE'S SOMETHING I'D LIKE TO SHOW YOU.
THESE.
SHFF
FWAP
THIS GIRL...
...IS KOSAKI ONODERA.
SHE'S MY FRIEND.

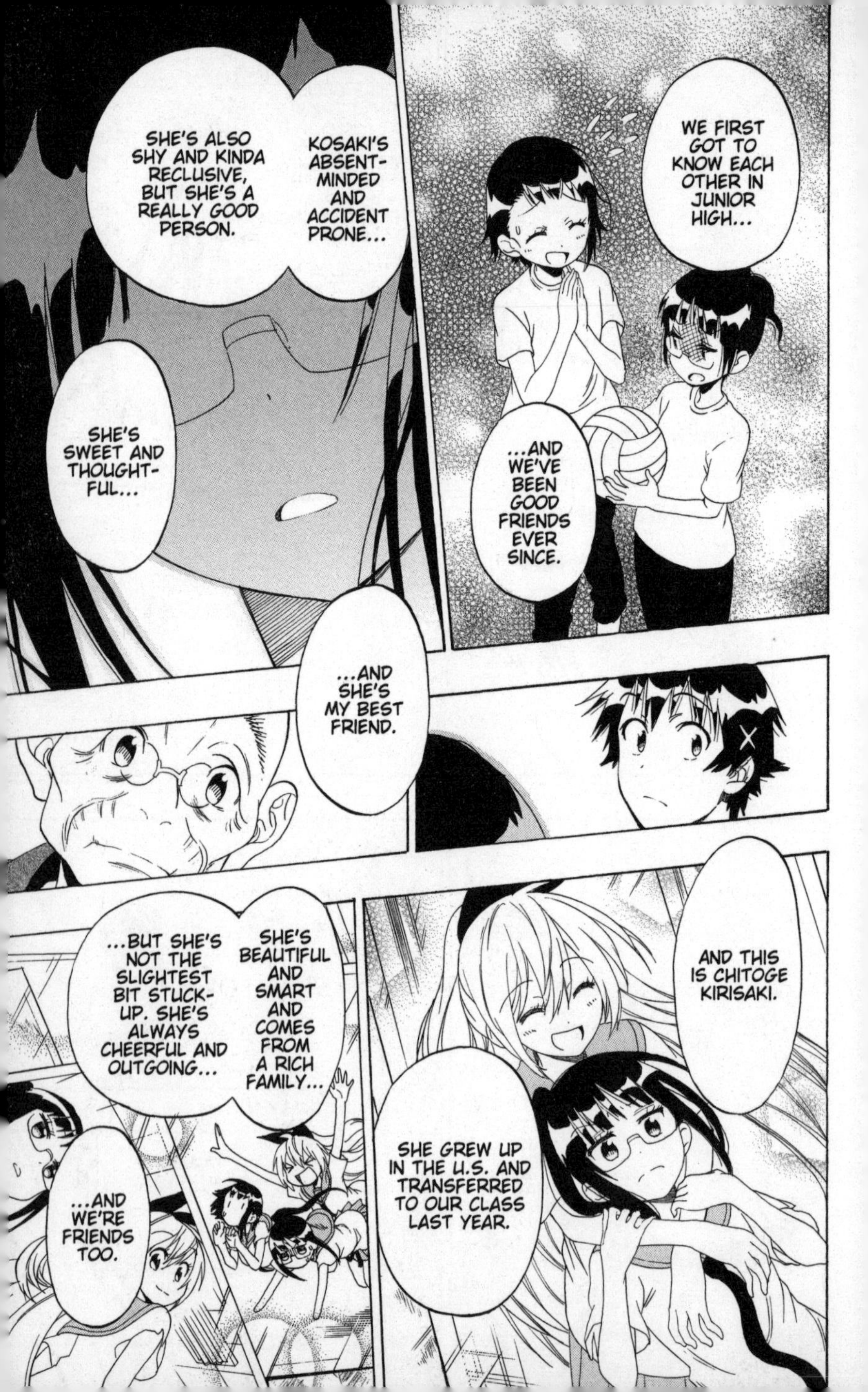
WE FIRST GOT TO KNOW EACH OTHER IN JUNIOR HIGH...
...AND WE'VE BEEN GOOD FRIENDS EVER SINCE.
KOSAKI'S ABSENT-MINDED AND ACCIDENT PRONE...
SHE'S ALSO SHY AND KINDA RECLUSIVE, BUT SHE'S A REALLY GOOD PERSON.
SHE'S SWEET AND THOUGHTFUL...
...AND SHE'S MY BEST FRIEND.
AND THIS IS CHITOGE KIRISAKI.
SHE GREW UP IN THE U.S. AND TRANSFERRED TO OUR CLASS LAST YEAR.
SHE'S BEAUTIFUL AND SMART AND COMES FROM A RICH FAMILY...
...BUT SHE'S NOT THE SLIGHTEST BIT STUCK-UP. SHE'S ALWAYS CHEERFUL AND OUTGOING...
...AND WE'RE FRIENDS TOO.

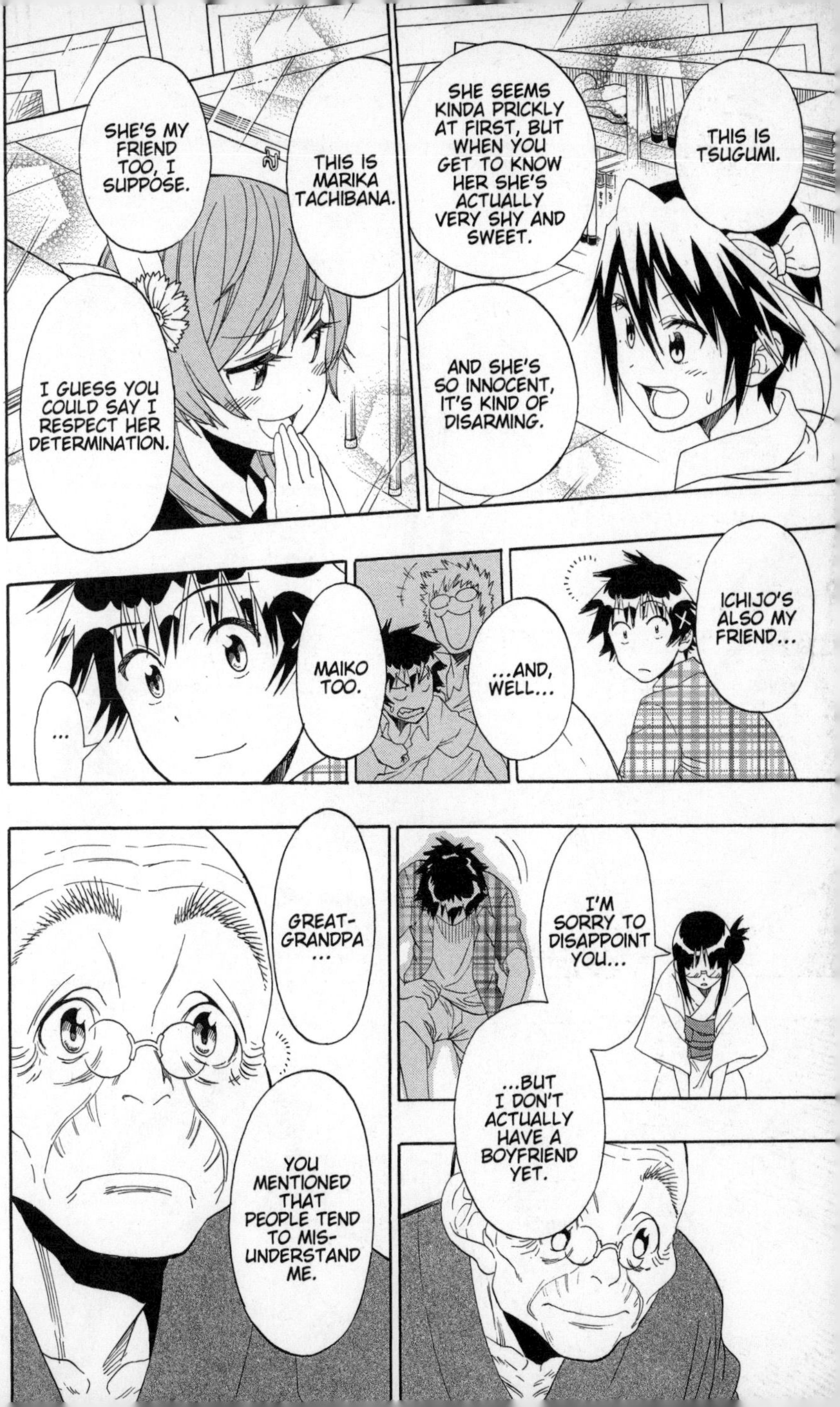
THIS IS TSUGUMI.
SHE SEEMS KINDA PRICKLY AT FIRST, BUT WHEN YOU GET TO KNOW HER SHE'S ACTUALLY VERY SHY AND SWEET.
AND SHE'S SO INNOCENT, IT'S KIND OF DISARMING.
THIS IS MARIKA TACHIBANA.
SHE'S MY FRIEND TOO, I SUPPOSE.
I GUESS YOU COULD SAY I RESPECT HER DETERMINATION.
ICHIJO'S ALSO MY FRIEND...
...AND, WELL...
MAIKO TOO.
...
I'M SORRY TO DISAPPOINT YOU...
...BUT I DON'T ACTUALLY HAVE A BOYFRIEND YET.
GREAT-GRANDPA...
YOU MENTIONED THAT PEOPLE TEND TO MIS-UNDERSTAND ME.

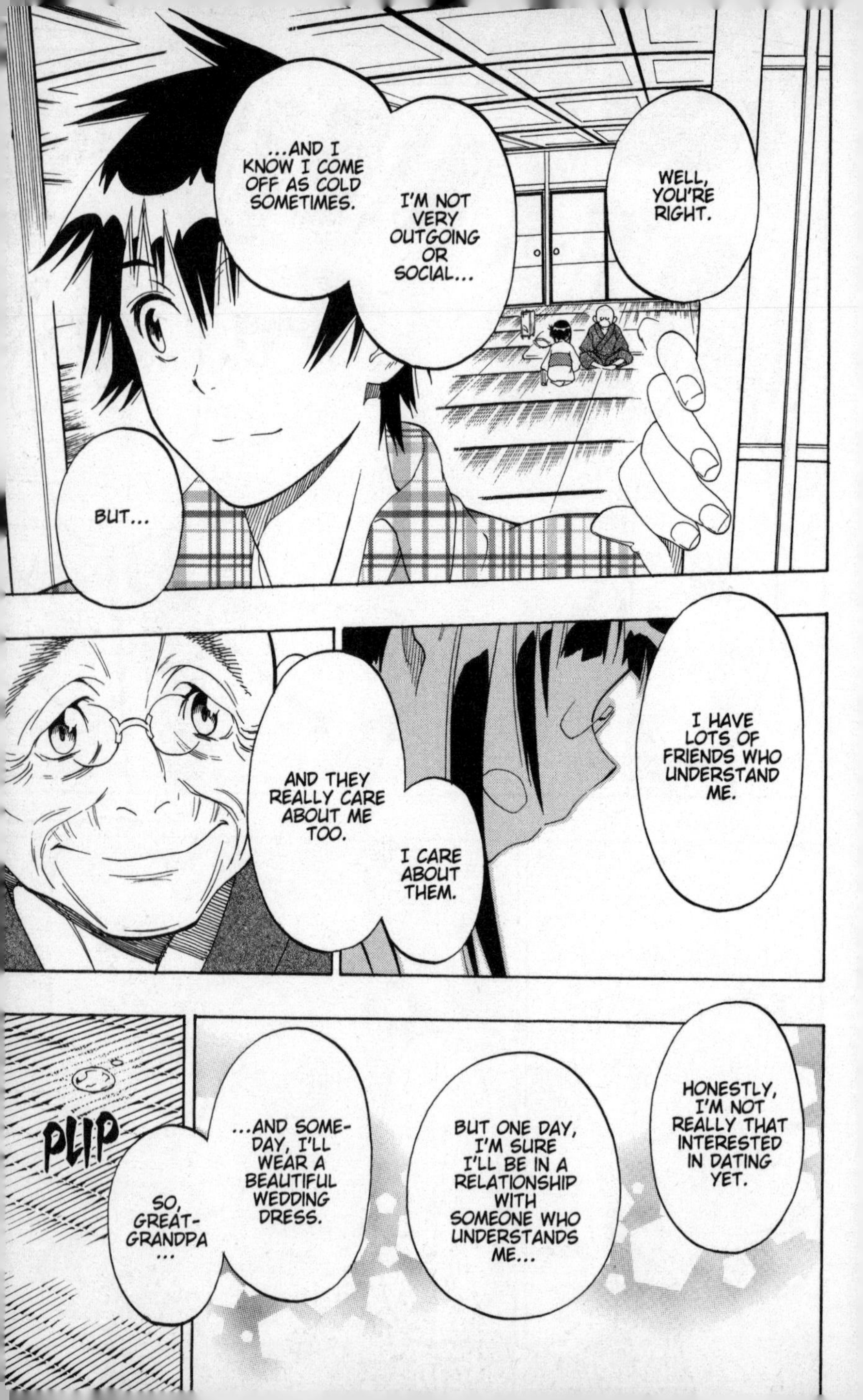
WELL, YOU'RE RIGHT.
I'M NOT VERY OUTGOING OR SOCIAL...
...AND I KNOW I COME OFF AS COLD SOMETIMES.
BUT...
I HAVE LOTS OF FRIENDS WHO UNDERSTAND ME.
I CARE ABOUT THEM.
AND THEY REALLY CARE ABOUT ME TOO.
HONESTLY, I'M NOT REALLY THAT INTERESTED IN DATING YET.
BUT ONE DAY, I'M SURE I'LL BE IN A RELATIONSHIP WITH SOMEONE WHO UNDERSTANDS ME...
...AND SOME-DAY, I'LL WEAR A BEAUTIFUL WEDDING DRESS.
SO, GREAT-GRANDPA...
PLIP

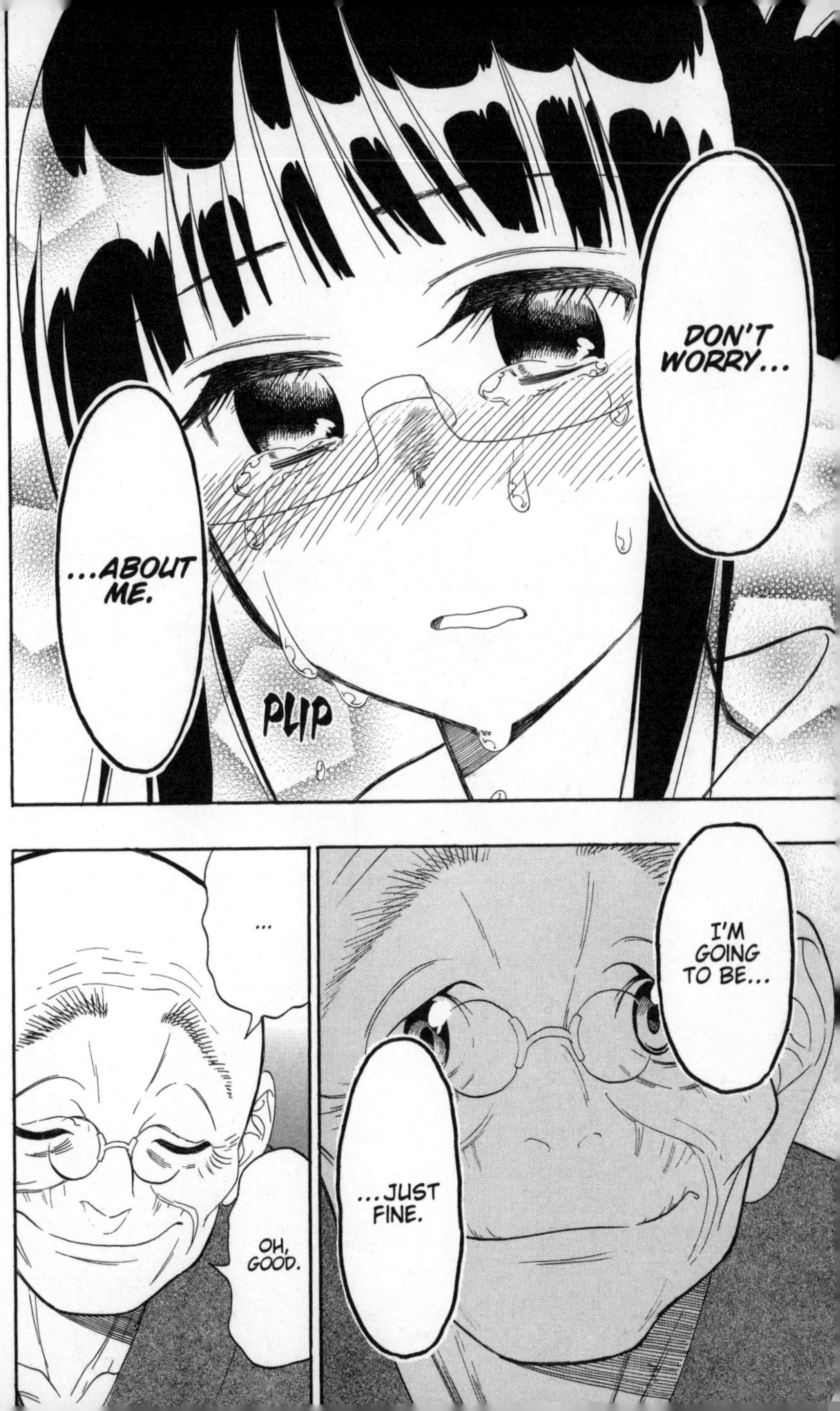
DON'T WORRY...
...ABOUT ME.
PLIP
I'M GOING TO BE...
...JUST FINE.
...
OH, GOOD.

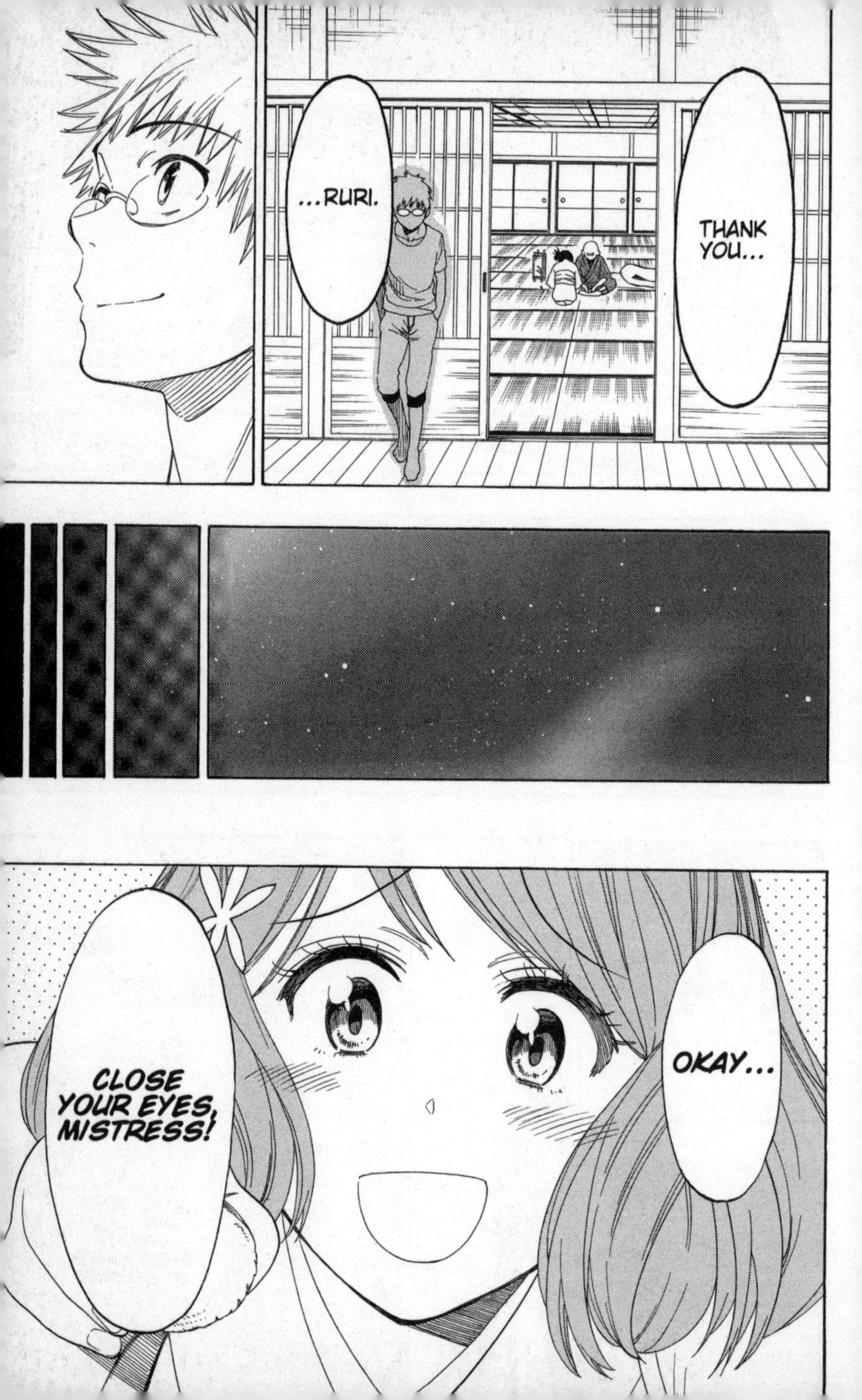
THANK YOU...
...RURI.
CLOSE YOUR EYES, MISTRESS!
OKAY...

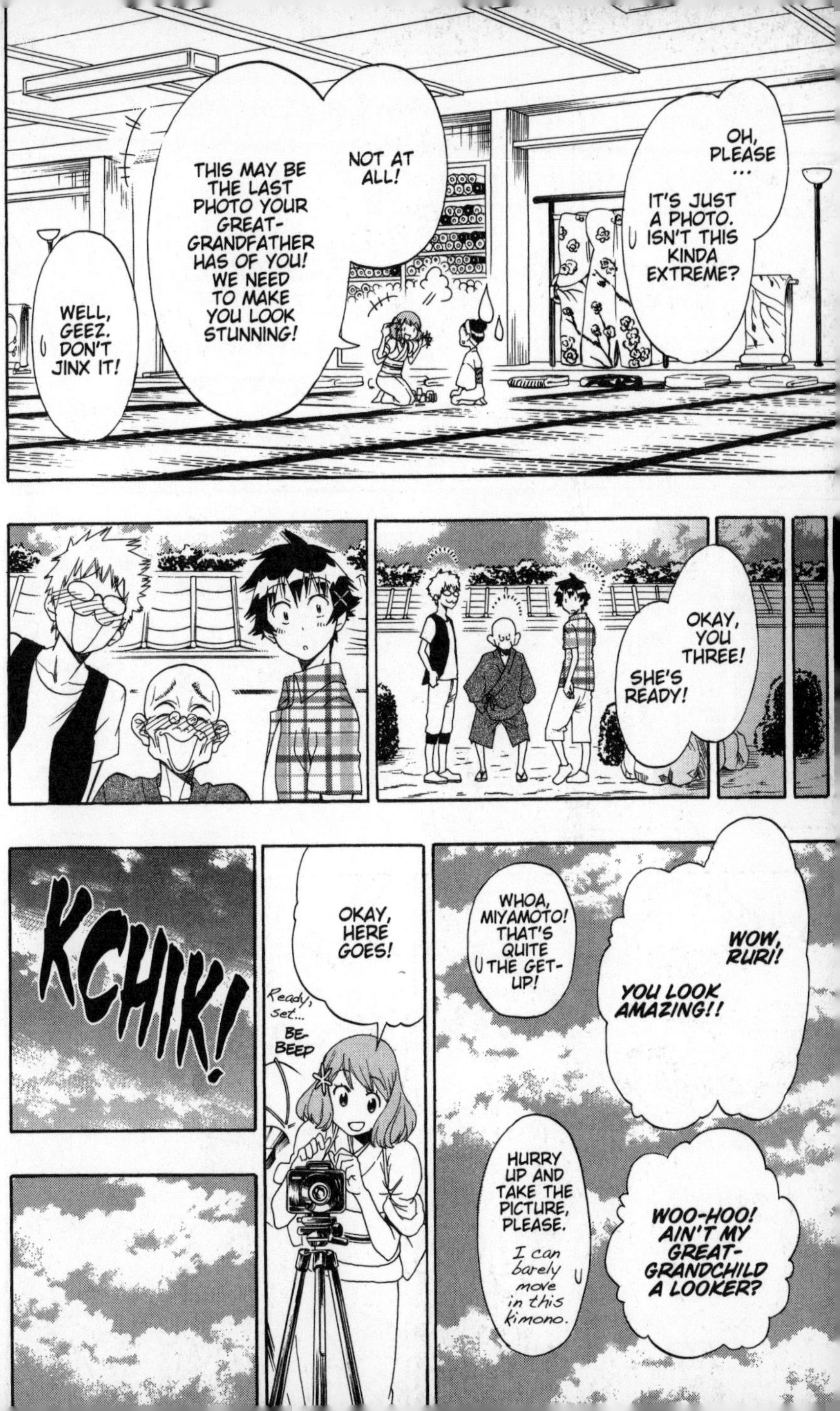
OH, PLEASE...
IT'S JUST A PHOTO. ISN'T THIS KINDA EXTREME?
NOT AT ALL!
THIS MAY BE THE LAST PHOTO YOUR GREAT-GRANDFATHER HAS OF YOU! WE NEED TO MAKE YOU LOOK STUNNING!
WELL, GEEZ. DON'T JINX IT!
OKAY, YOU THREE!
SHE'S READY!
WOW, RURI!
YOU LOOK AMAZING!!
WHOA, MIYAMOTO! THAT'S QUITE THE GET-UP!
WOO-HOO! AIN'T MY GREAT-GRANDCHILD A LOOKER?
HURRY UP AND TAKE THE PICTURE, PLEASE.
I can barely move in this kimono.
OKAY, HERE GOES!
Ready, set...
BE-BEEP
KCHIK!

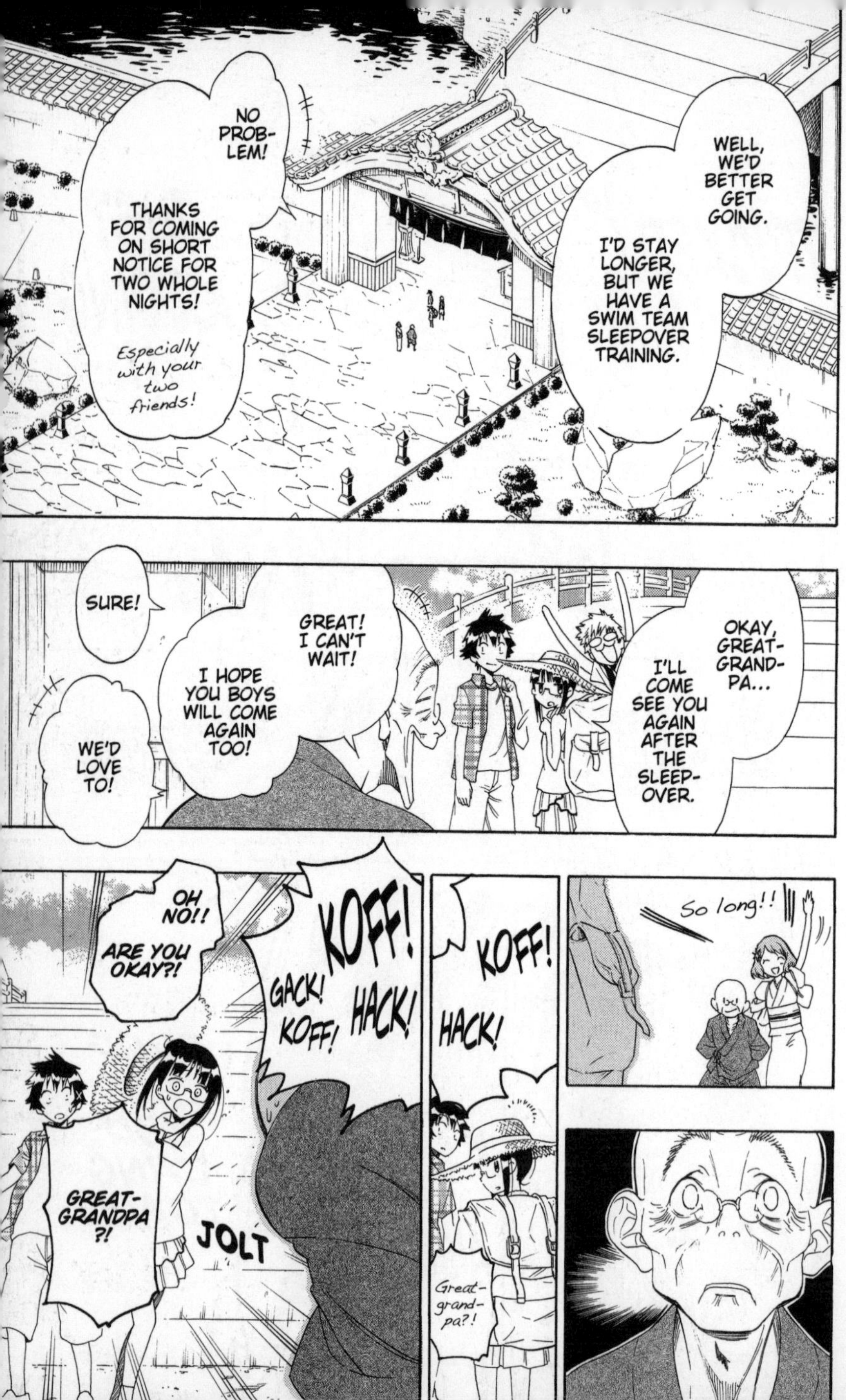
WELL, WE'D BETTER GET GOING.
I'D STAY LONGER, BUT WE HAVE A SWIM TEAM SLEEPOVER TRAINING.
NO PROB-LEM!
THANKS FOR COMING ON SHORT NOTICE FOR TWO WHOLE NIGHTS!
Especially with your two friends!
OKAY, GREAT-GRAND-PA...
I'LL COME SEE YOU AGAIN AFTER THE SLEEP-OVER.
GREAT! I CAN'T WAIT!
I HOPE YOU BOYS WILL COME AGAIN TOO!
SURE!
WE'D LOVE TO!
So long!!
KOFF!
HACK!
Great-grand-pa?!
KOFF!
HACK!
GACK! KOFF!
OH NO!! ARE YOU OKAY?!
JOLT
GREAT-GRANDPA?!

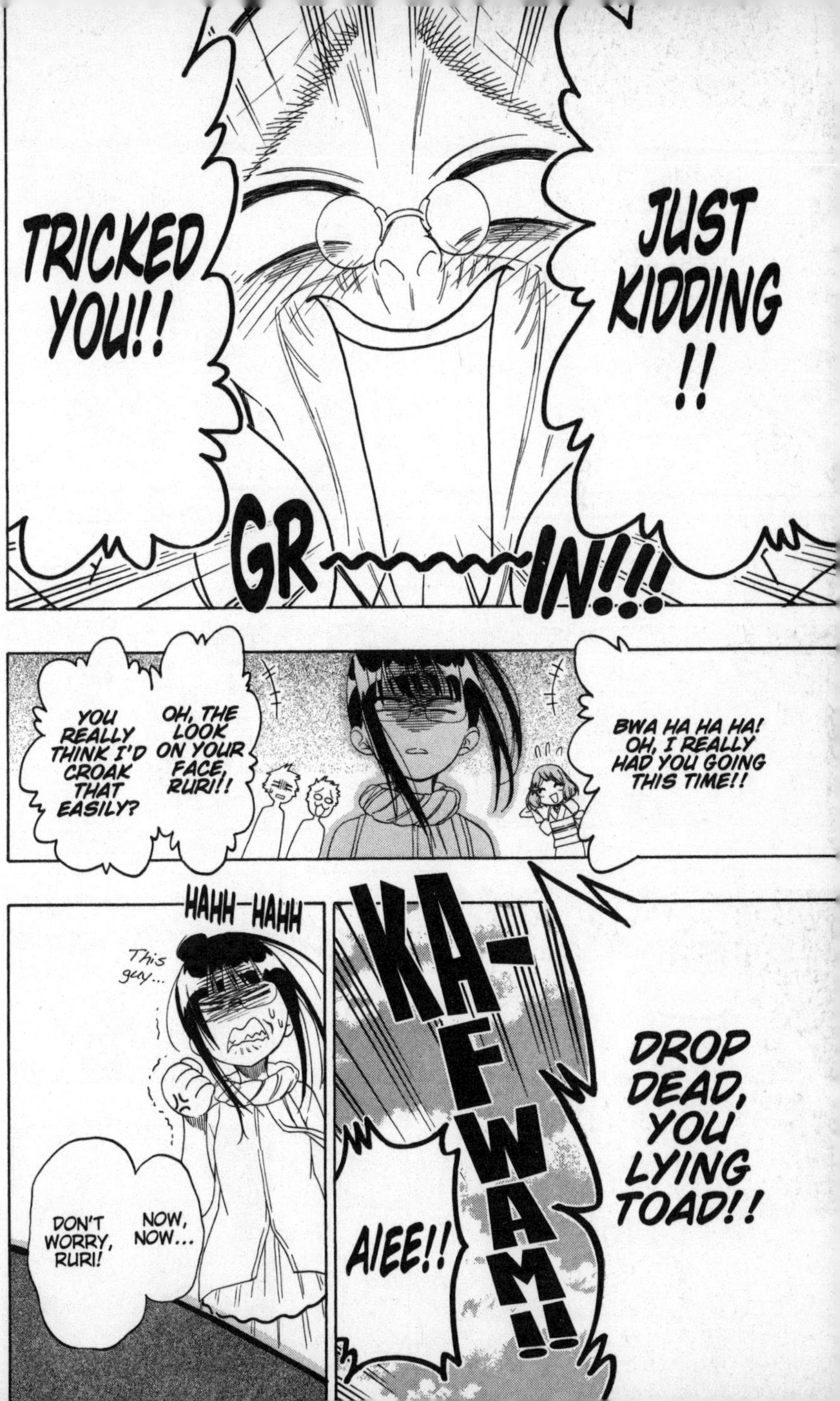
JUST KIDDING!!
TRICKED YOU!!
GR~~~~IN!!!
BWA HA HA HA! OH, I REALLY HAD YOU GOING THIS TIME!!
OH, THE LOOK ON YOUR FACE, RURI!!
YOU REALLY THINK I'D CROAK THAT EASILY?
DROP DEAD, YOU LYING TOAD!!
KA-FWAM!!
AIEE!!
HAHH HAHH
This guy...
NOW, NOW...
DON'T WORRY, RURI!

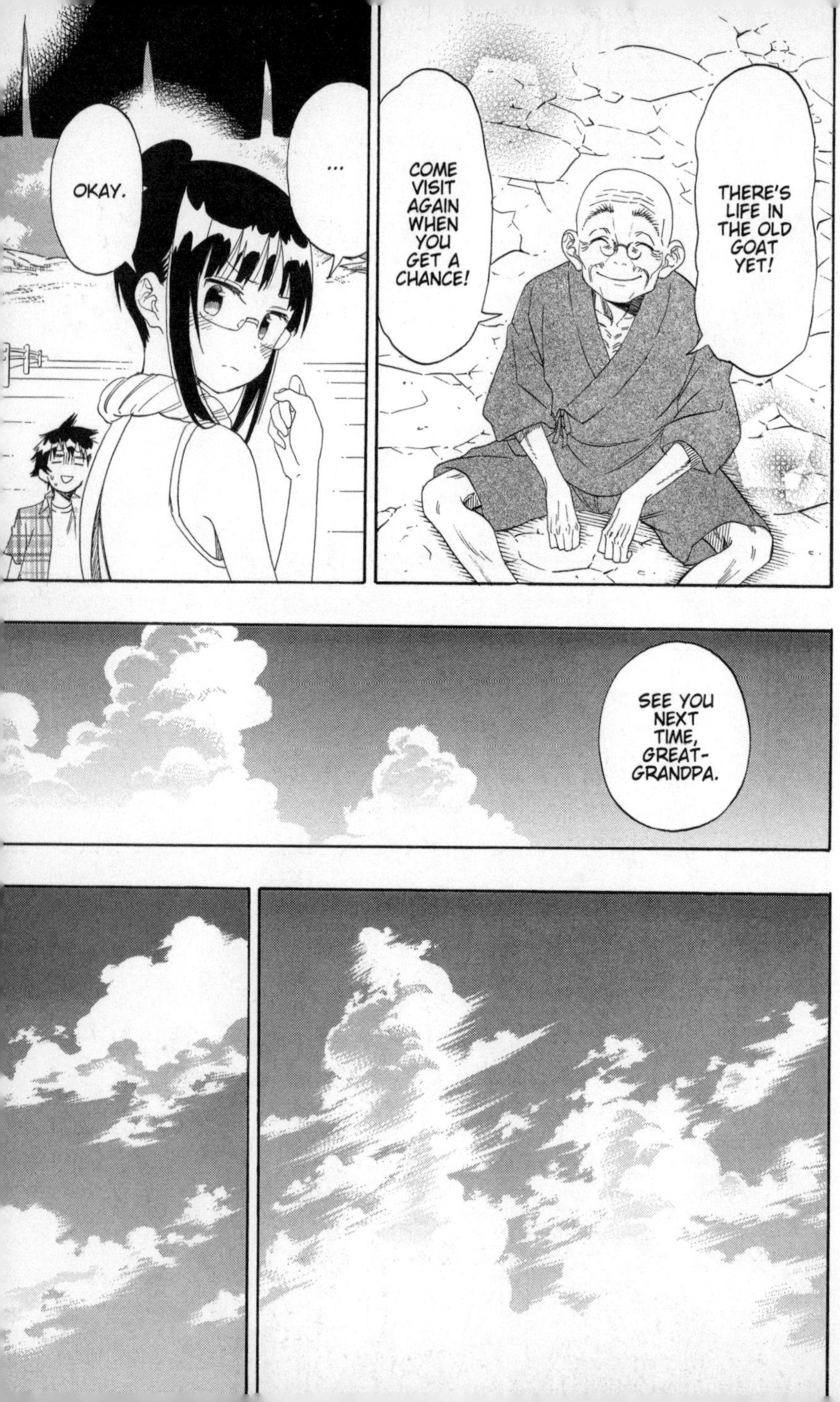
THERE'S LIFE IN THE OLD GOAT YET!
COME VISIT AGAIN WHEN YOU GET A CHANCE!
...
OKAY.
SEE YOU NEXT TIME, GREAT-GRANDPA.

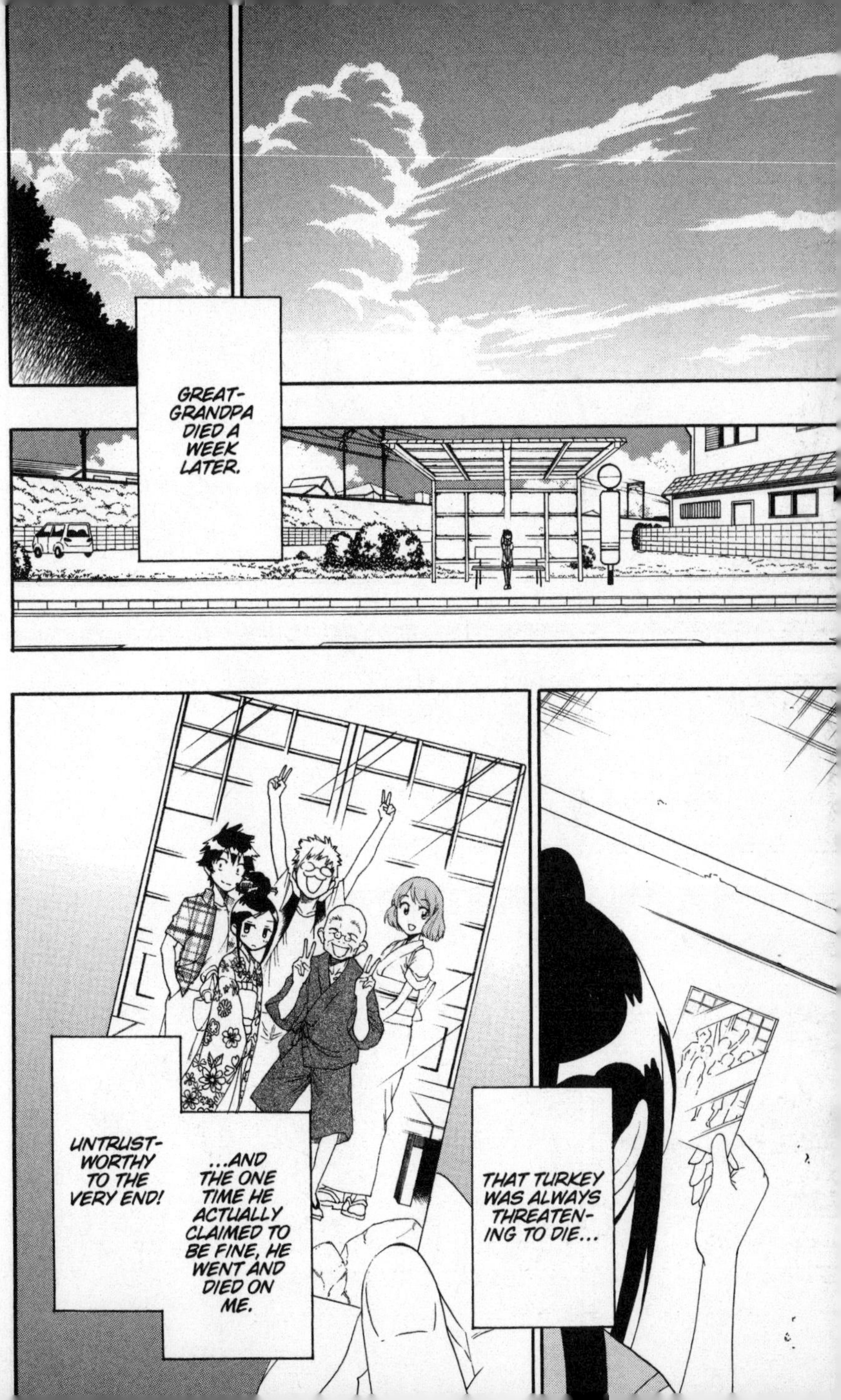
GREAT-GRANDPA DIED A WEEK LATER.
THAT TURKEY WAS ALWAYS THREATENING TO DIE...
...AND THE ONE TIME HE ACTUALLY CLAIMED TO BE FINE, HE WENT AND DIED ON ME.
UNTRUSTWORTHY TO THE VERY END!

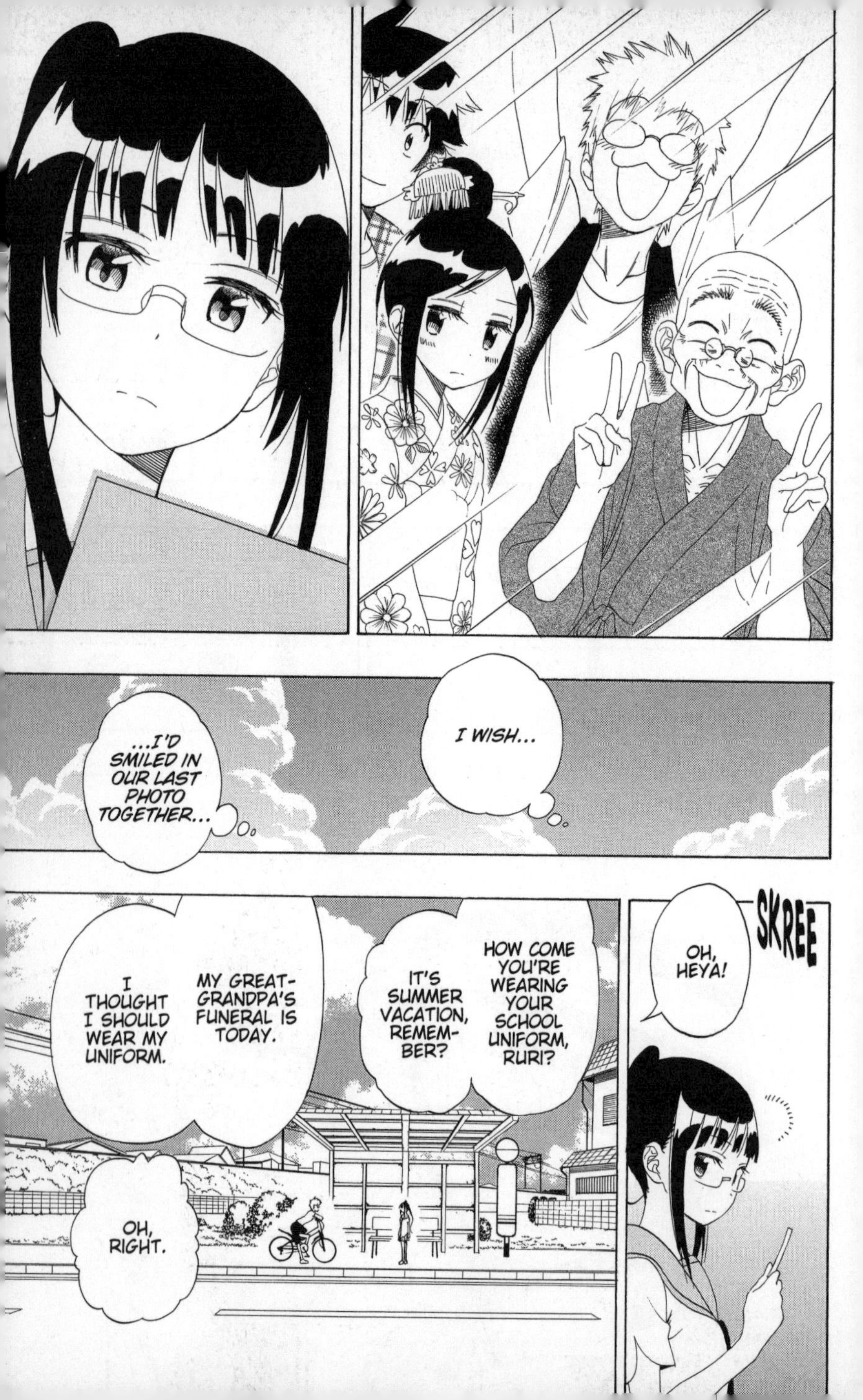
I WISH...
...I'D SMILED IN OUR LAST PHOTO TOGETHER...
SKREE
OH, HEYA!
HOW COME YOU'RE WEARING YOUR SCHOOL UNIFORM, RURI?
IT'S SUMMER VACATION, REMEMBER?
MY GREAT-GRANDPA'S FUNERAL IS TODAY.
I THOUGHT I SHOULD WEAR MY UNIFORM.
OH, RIGHT.

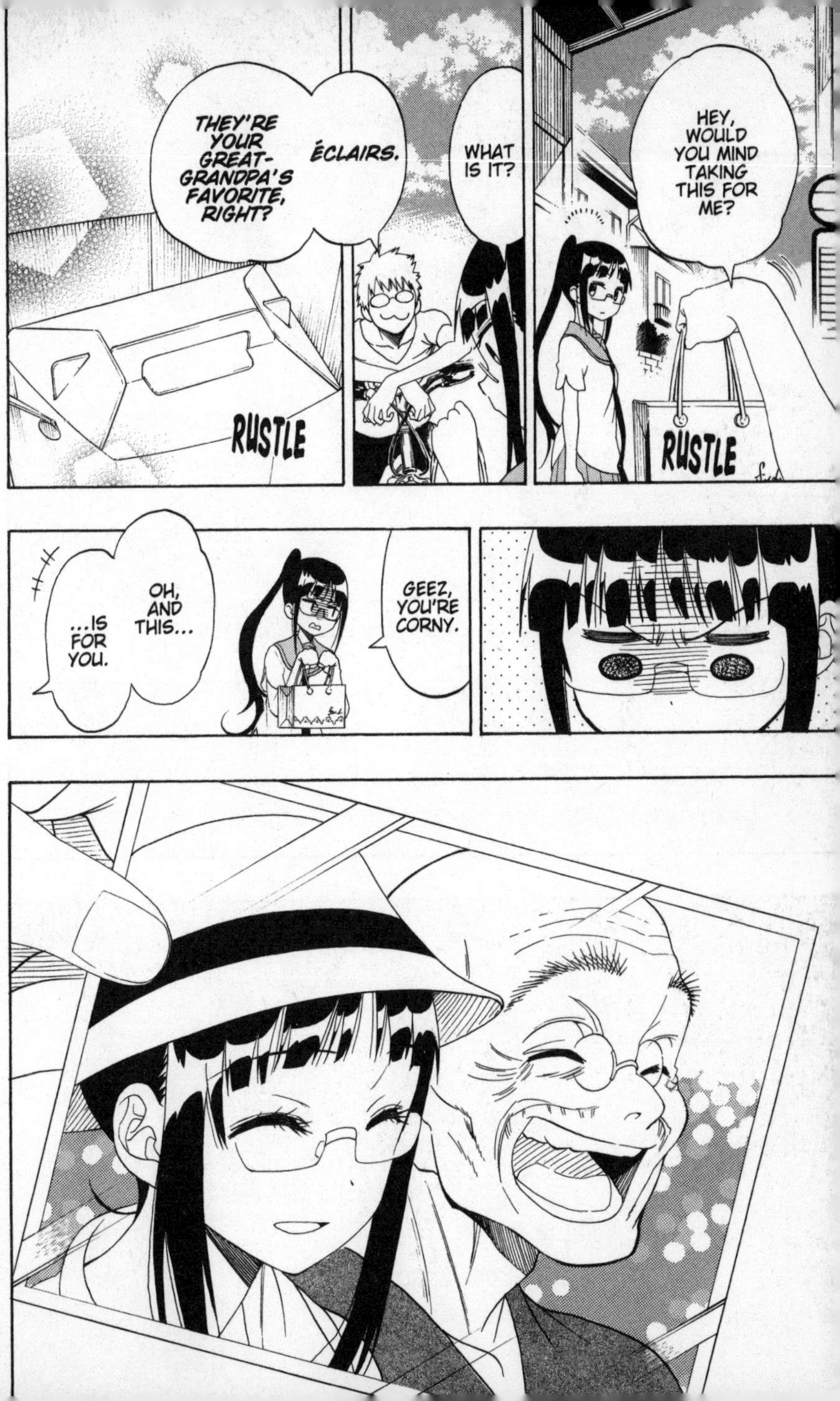
HEY, WOULD YOU MIND TAKING THIS FOR ME?
RUSTLE
WHAT IS IT?
ÉCLAIRS.
THEY'RE YOUR GREAT-GRANDPA'S FAVORITE, RIGHT?
RUSTLE
GEEZ, YOU'RE CORNY.
OH, AND THIS...
...IS FOR YOU.

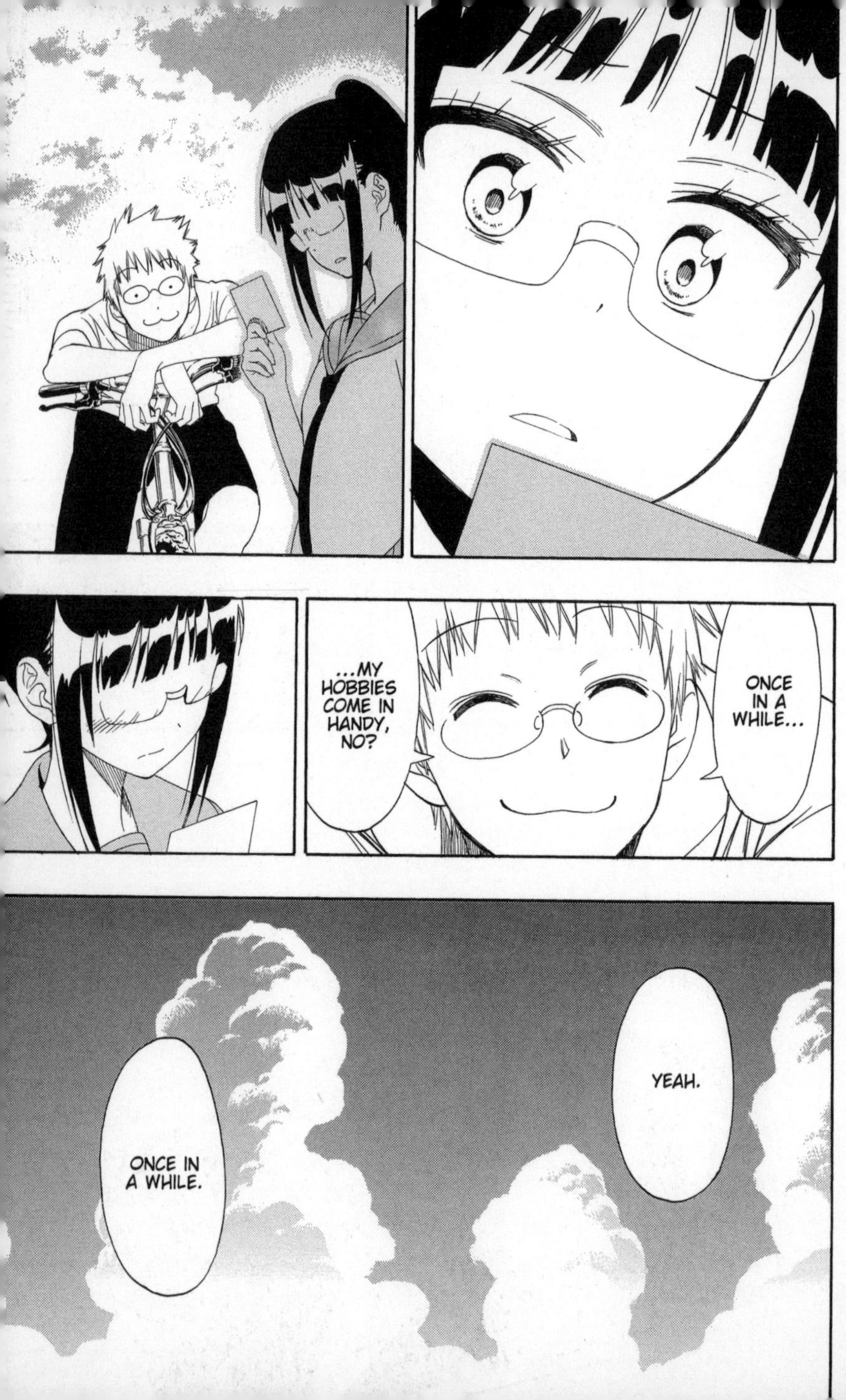
ONCE IN A WHILE...
...MY HOBBIES COME IN HANDY, NO?
YEAH.
ONCE IN A WHILE.

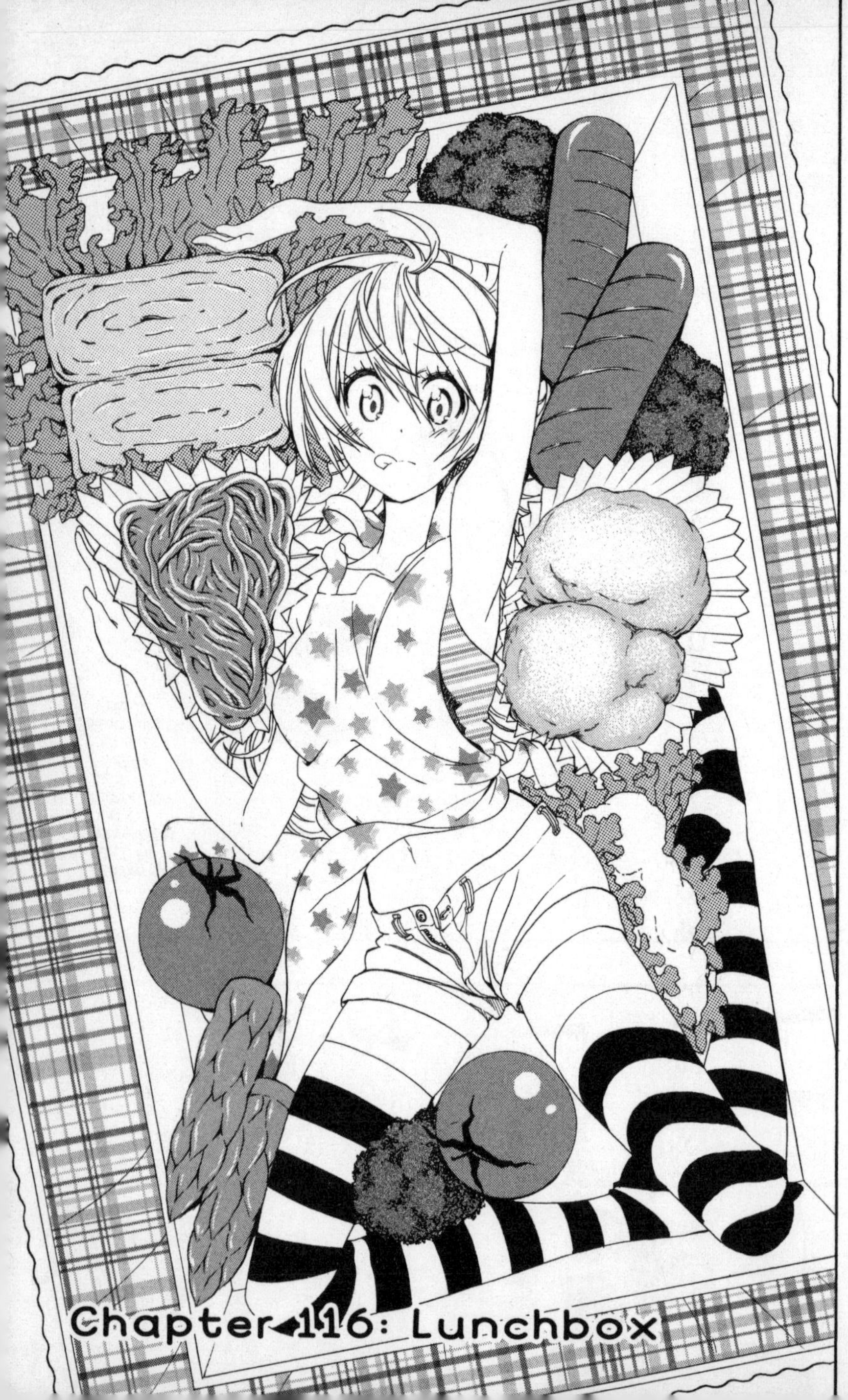

Chapter 116: Lunchbox

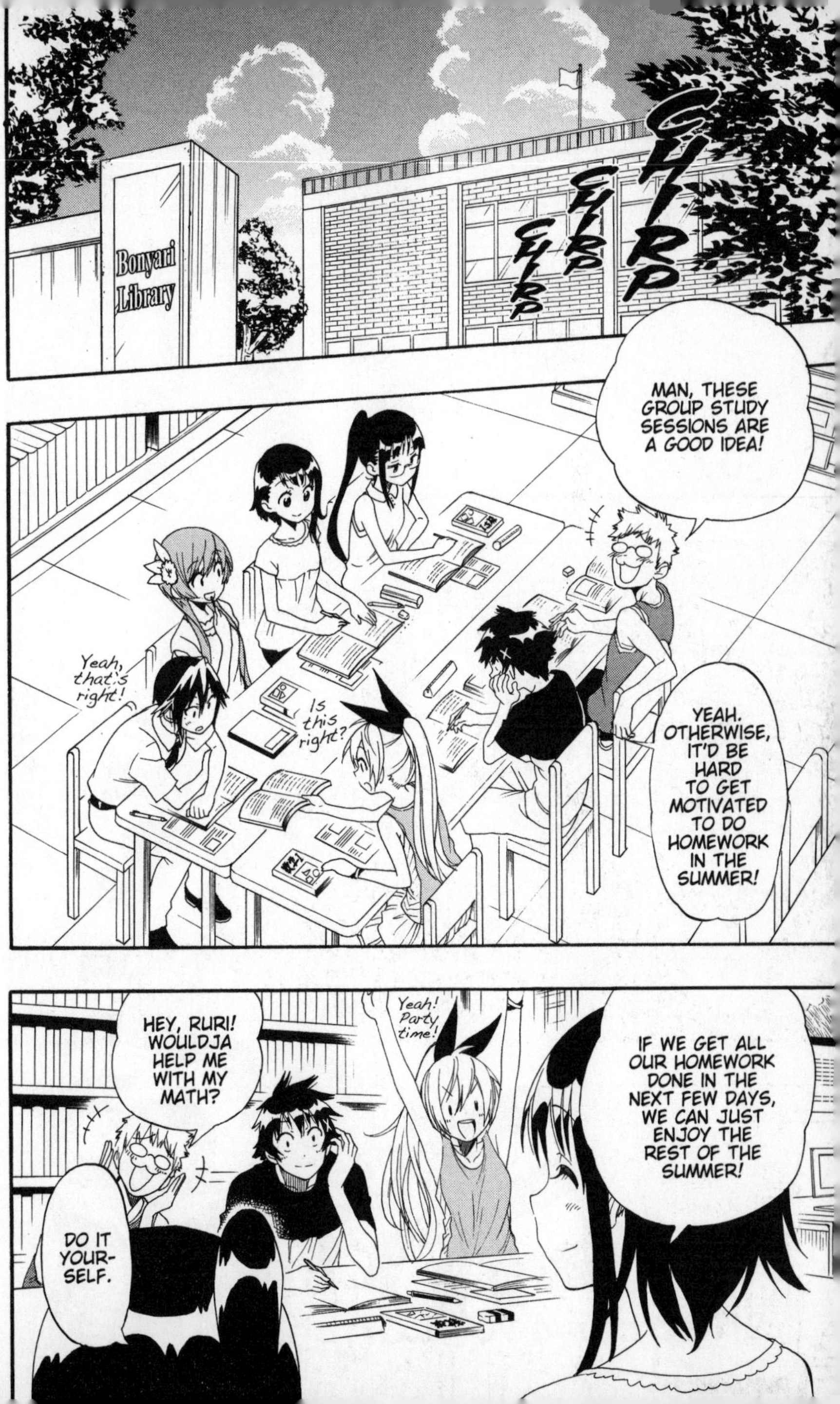
CHIRP
CHIRP
CHIRP
Bonyari Library
MAN, THESE GROUP STUDY SESSIONS ARE A GOOD IDEA!
YEAH. OTHERWISE, IT'D BE HARD TO GET MOTIVATED TO DO HOMEWORK IN THE SUMMER!
Is this right?
Yeah, that's right!
IF WE GET ALL OUR HOMEWORK DONE IN THE NEXT FEW DAYS, WE CAN JUST ENJOY THE REST OF THE SUMMER!
Yeah! Party time!
HEY, RURI! WOULDJA HELP ME WITH MY MATH?
DO IT YOURSELF.

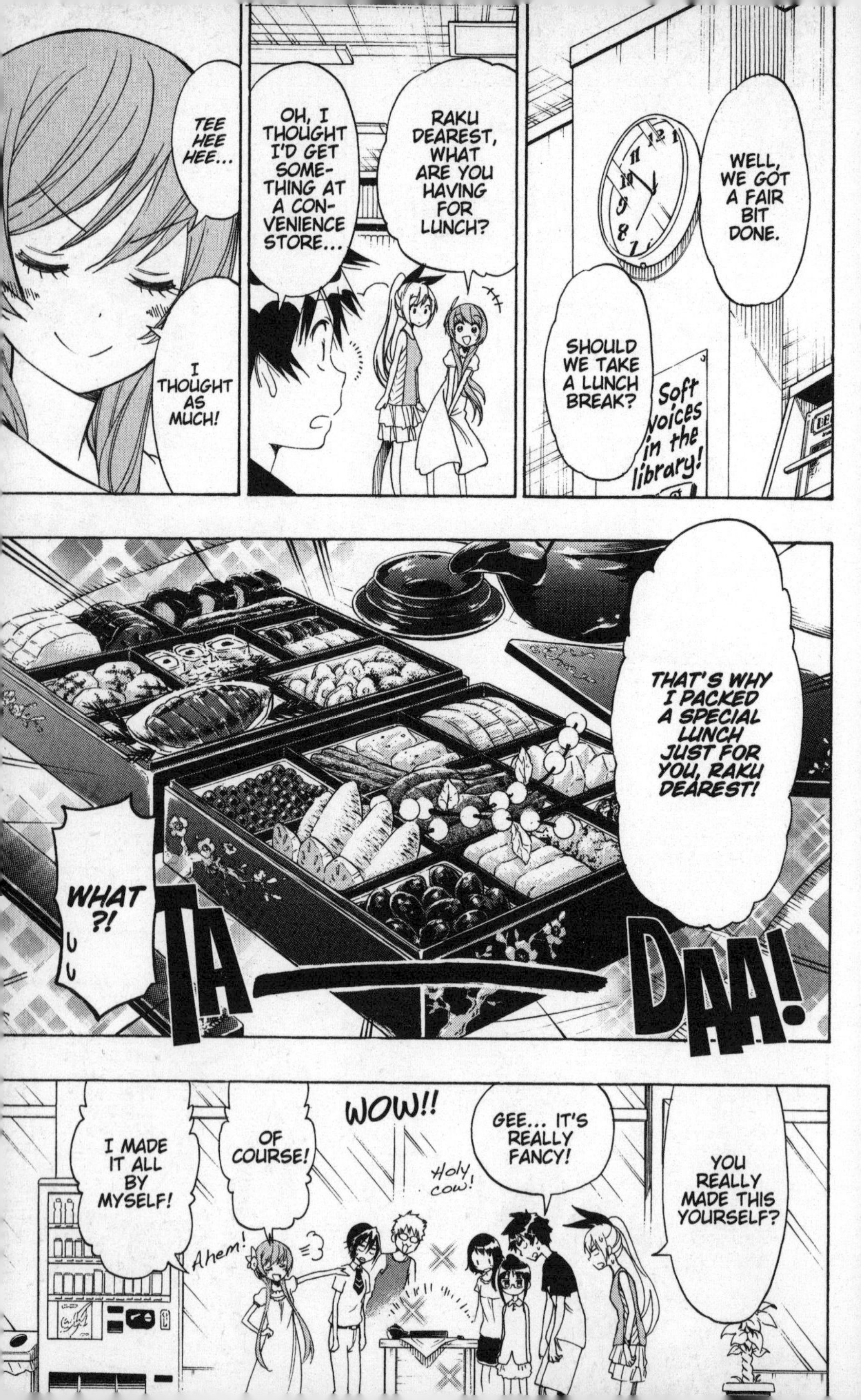
WELL, WE GOT A FAIR BIT DONE.
SHOULD WE TAKE A LUNCH BREAK?
Soft voices in the library!
RAKU DEAREST, WHAT ARE YOU HAVING FOR LUNCH?
OH, I THOUGHT I'D GET SOME-THING AT A CON-VENIENCE STORE...
TEE HEE HEE...
I THOUGHT AS MUCH!
THAT'S WHY I PACKED A SPECIAL LUNCH JUST FOR YOU, RAKU DEAREST!
TA DAA!
WHAT?!
YOU REALLY MADE THIS YOURSELF?
GEE... IT'S REALLY FANCY!
Holy cow!
WOW!!
OF COURSE!
I MADE IT ALL BY MYSELF!
Ahem!

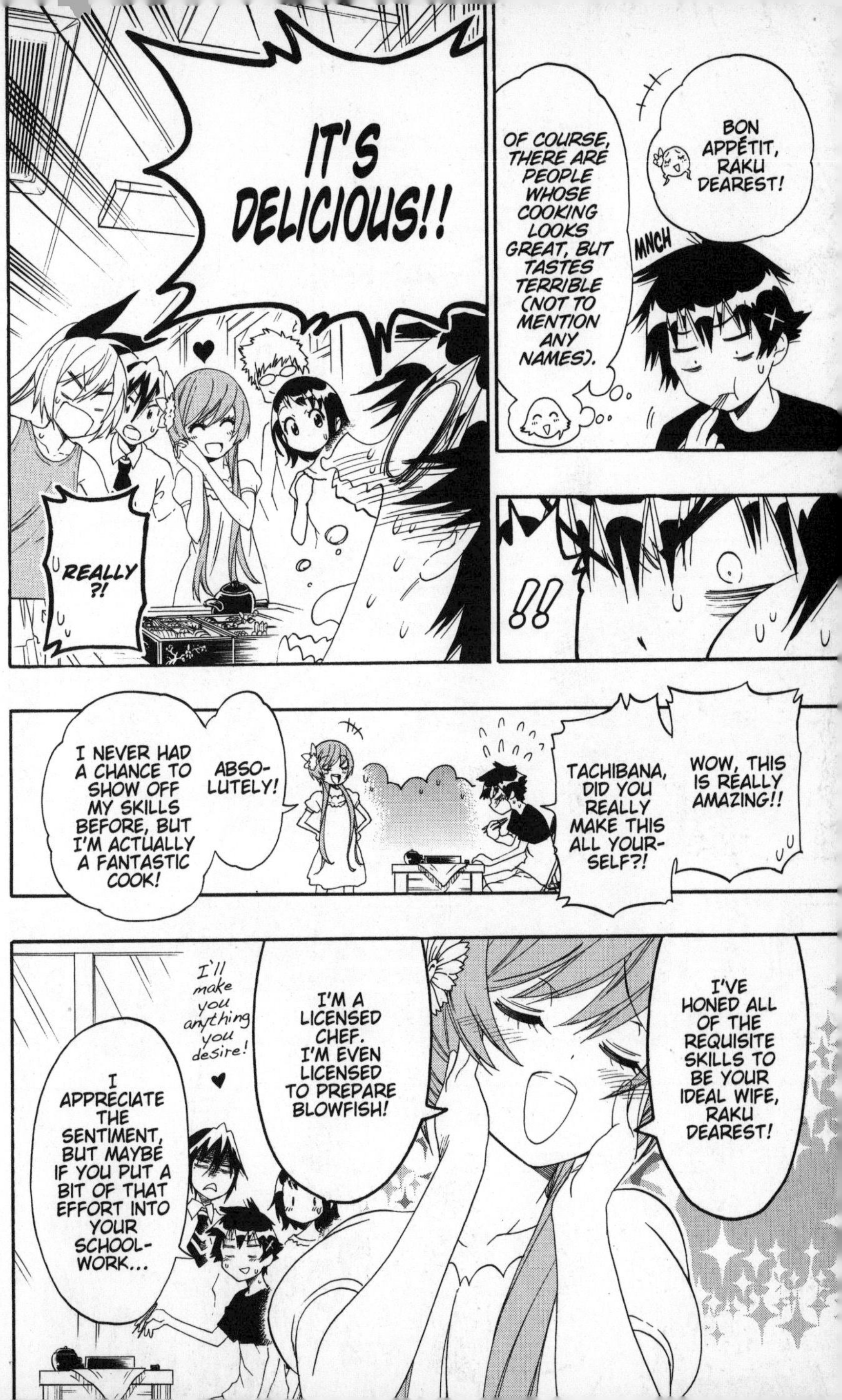
BON APPÉTIT, RAKU DEAREST!
MNCH
OF COURSE, THERE ARE PEOPLE WHOSE COOKING LOOKS GREAT, BUT TASTES TERRIBLE (NOT TO MENTION ANY NAMES).
!!
IT'S DELICIOUS!!
REALLY?!
WOW, THIS IS REALLY AMAZING!!
TACHIBANA, DID YOU REALLY MAKE THIS ALL YOURSELF?!
ABSO-LUTELY!
I NEVER HAD A CHANCE TO SHOW OFF MY SKILLS BEFORE, BUT I'M ACTUALLY A FANTASTIC COOK!
I'VE HONED ALL OF THE REQUISITE SKILLS TO BE YOUR IDEAL WIFE, RAKU DEAREST!
I'M A LICENSED CHEF. I'M EVEN LICENSED TO PREPARE BLOWFISH!
I'll make you anything you desire!
I APPRECIATE THE SENTIMENT, BUT MAYBE IF YOU PUT A BIT OF THAT EFFORT INTO YOUR SCHOOL-WORK...

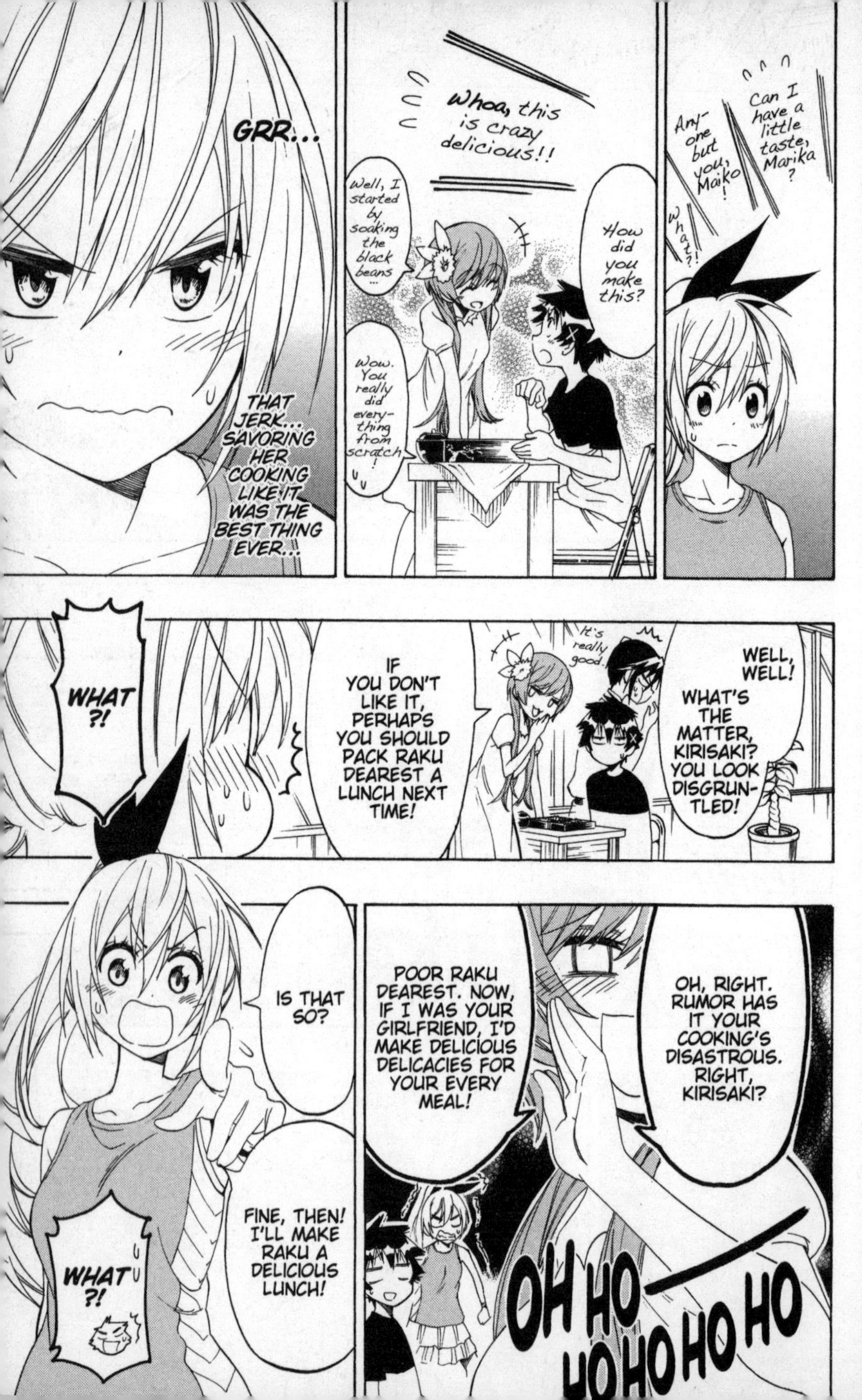
Can I have a little taste, Marika?
Any-one but you, Maiko!
What?!
Whoa, this is crazy delicious!!
How did you make this?
Well, I started by soaking the black beans...
Wow. You really did every-thing from scratch!
GRR...
THAT JERK... SAVORING HER COOKING LIKE IT WAS THE BEST THING EVER...
WELL, WELL! WHAT'S THE MATTER, KIRISAKI? YOU LOOK DISGRUN-TLED!
It's really good.
IF YOU DON'T LIKE IT, PERHAPS YOU SHOULD PACK RAKU DEAREST A LUNCH NEXT TIME!
WHAT ?!
OH, RIGHT. RUMOR HAS IT YOUR COOKING'S DISASTROUS. RIGHT, KIRISAKI?
POOR RAKU DEAREST. NOW, IF I WAS YOUR GIRLFRIEND, I'D MAKE DELICIOUS DELICACIES FOR YOUR EVERY MEAL!
OH HO— HO HO HO HO HO
IS THAT SO?
FINE, THEN! I'LL MAKE RAKU A DELICIOUS LUNCH!
WHAT ?!

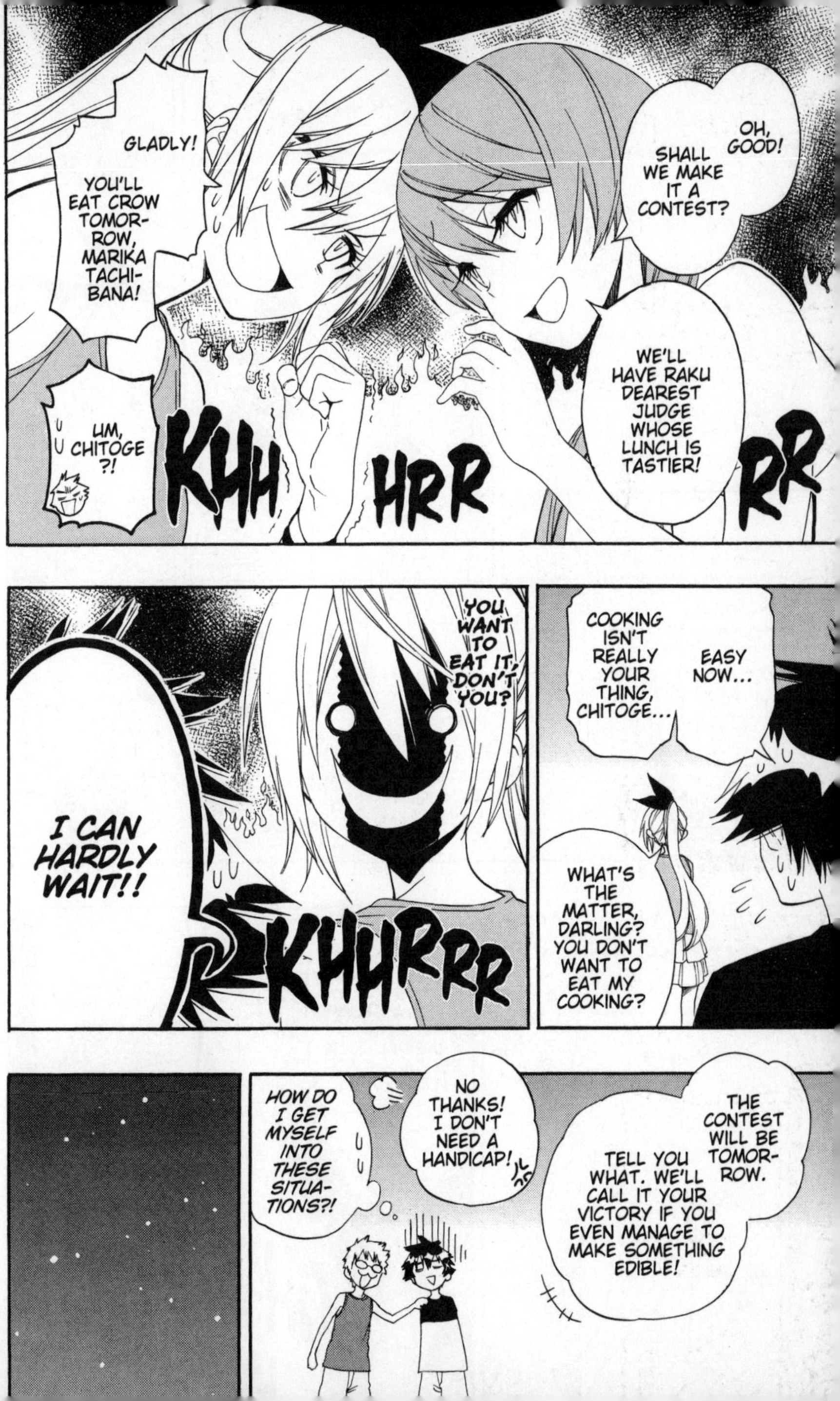
OH, GOOD! SHALL WE MAKE IT A CONTEST?
WE'LL HAVE RAKU DEAREST JUDGE WHOSE LUNCH IS TASTIER!
GLADLY! YOU'LL EAT CROW TOMORROW, MARIKA TACHIBANA!
UM, CHITOGE?!
KUH HRR RR
EASY NOW... COOKING ISN'T REALLY YOUR THING, CHITOGE...
WHAT'S THE MATTER, DARLING? YOU DON'T WANT TO EAT MY COOKING?
YOU WANT TO EAT IT, DON'T YOU?
I CAN HARDLY WAIT!!
KHURRR
THE CONTEST WILL BE TOMORROW. TELL YOU WHAT. WE'LL CALL IT YOUR VICTORY IF YOU EVEN MANAGE TO MAKE SOMETHING EDIBLE!
NO THANKS! I DON'T NEED A HANDICAP!
HOW DO I GET MYSELF INTO THESE SITUATIONS?!

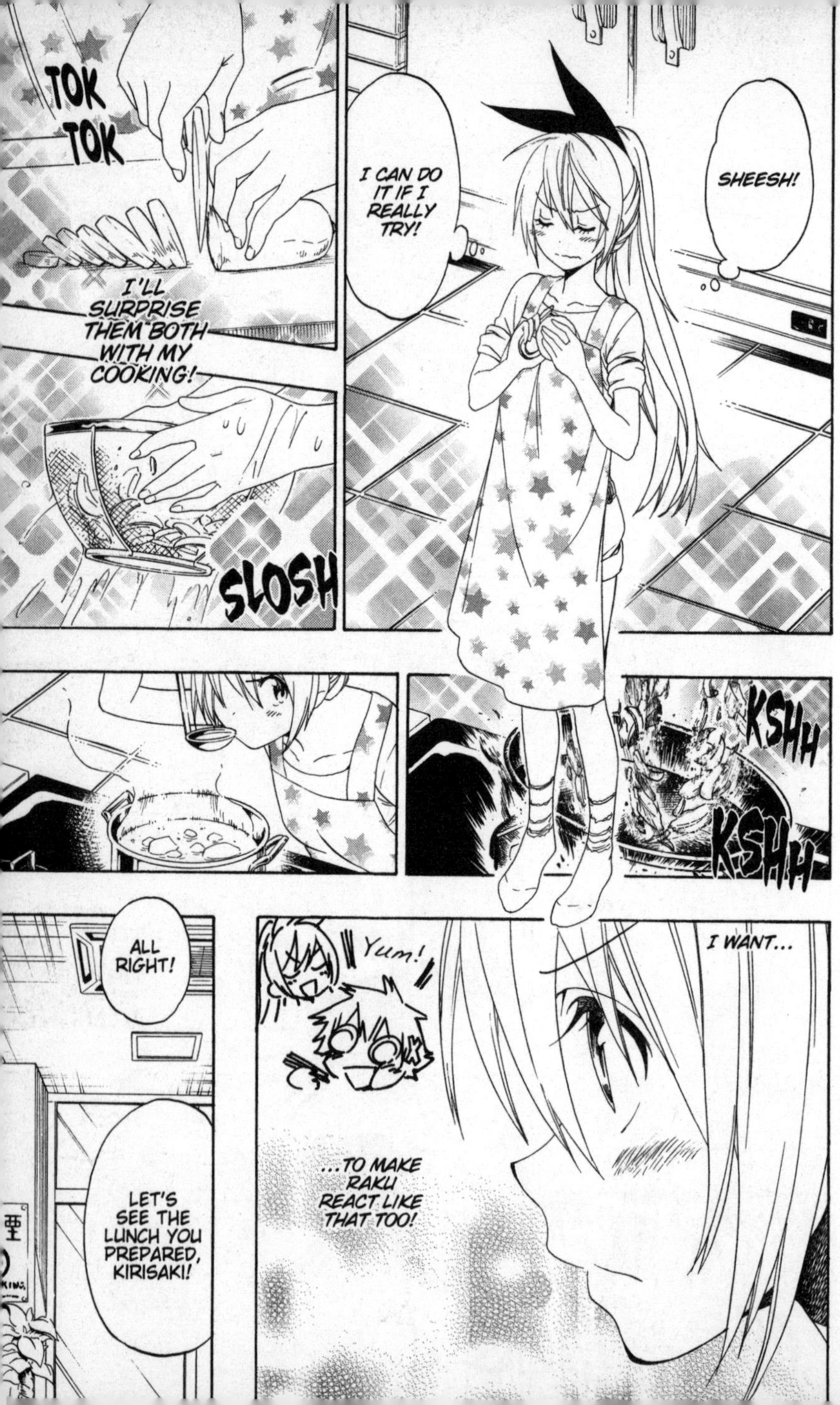
SHEESH!
I CAN DO IT IF I REALLY TRY!
TOK TOK
I'LL SURPRISE THEM BOTH WITH MY COOKING!
SLOSH
KSHH
KSHH
I WANT...
Yum!
...TO MAKE RAKU REACT LIKE THAT TOO!
ALL RIGHT!
LET'S SEE THE LUNCH YOU PREPARED, KIRISAKI!

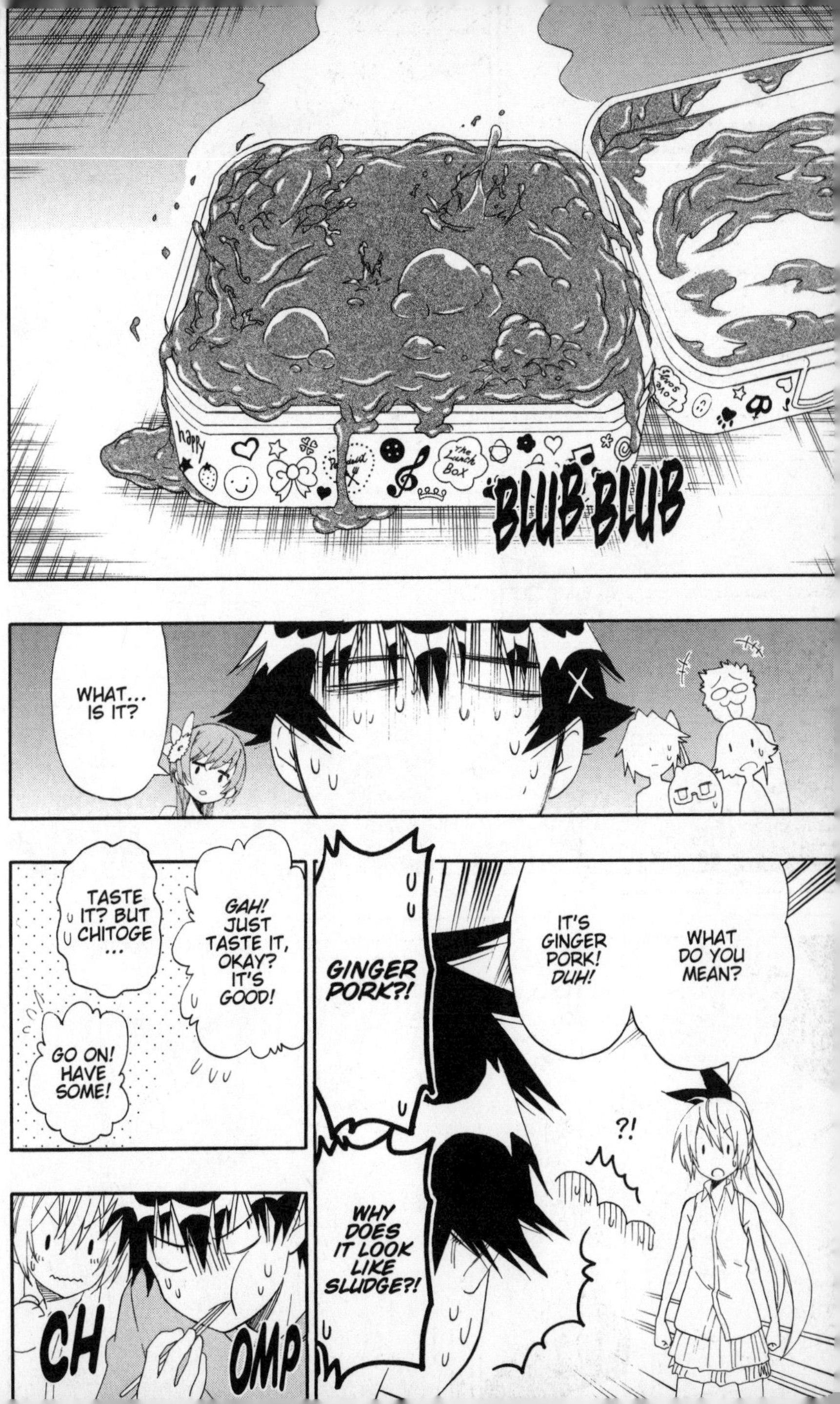
happy
The Lunch Box
BLUB BLUB
WHAT... IS IT?
WHAT DO YOU MEAN?
IT'S GINGER PORK! DUH!
GINGER PORK?!
?!
WHY DOES IT LOOK LIKE SLUDGE?!
GAH! JUST TASTE IT, OKAY? IT'S GOOD!
TASTE IT? BUT CHITOGE...
GO ON! HAVE SOME!
CH OMP

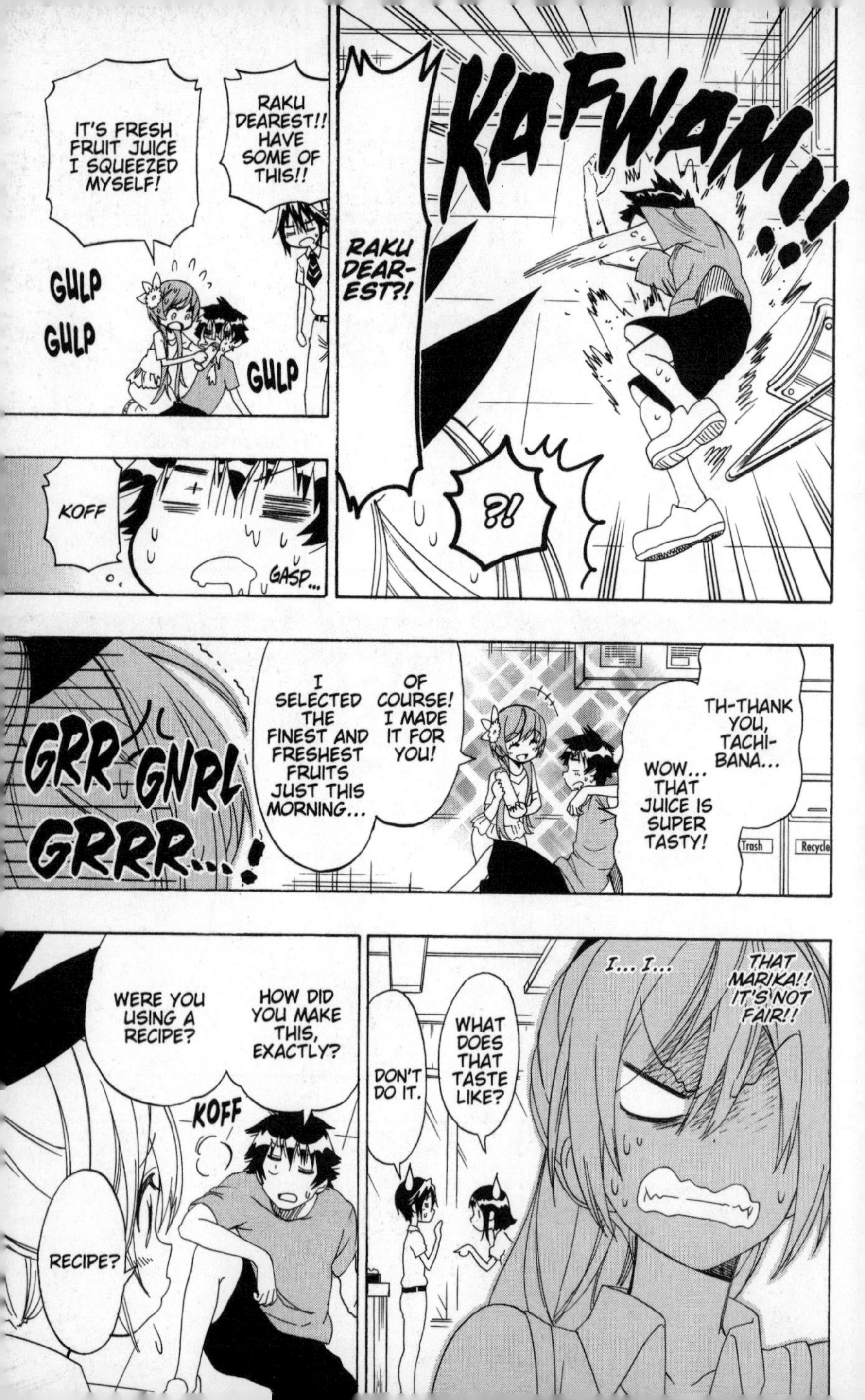
KA FWAM!!
RAKU DEAR-EST?!
?!
RAKU DEAREST!! HAVE SOME OF THIS!!
IT'S FRESH FRUIT JUICE I SQUEEZED MYSELF!
GULP
GULP
GULP
KOFF
GASP...
TH-THANK YOU, TACHI-BANA...
WOW... THAT JUICE IS SUPER TASTY!
Trash
Recycle
OF COURSE! I MADE IT FOR YOU!
I SELECTED THE FINEST AND FRESHEST FRUITS JUST THIS MORNING...
GRR GNRL GRRR...!
THAT MARIKA!! IT'S NOT FAIR!!
I... I...
WHAT DOES THAT TASTE LIKE?
DON'T DO IT.
HOW DID YOU MAKE THIS, EXACTLY?
WERE YOU USING A RECIPE?
KOFF
RECIPE?

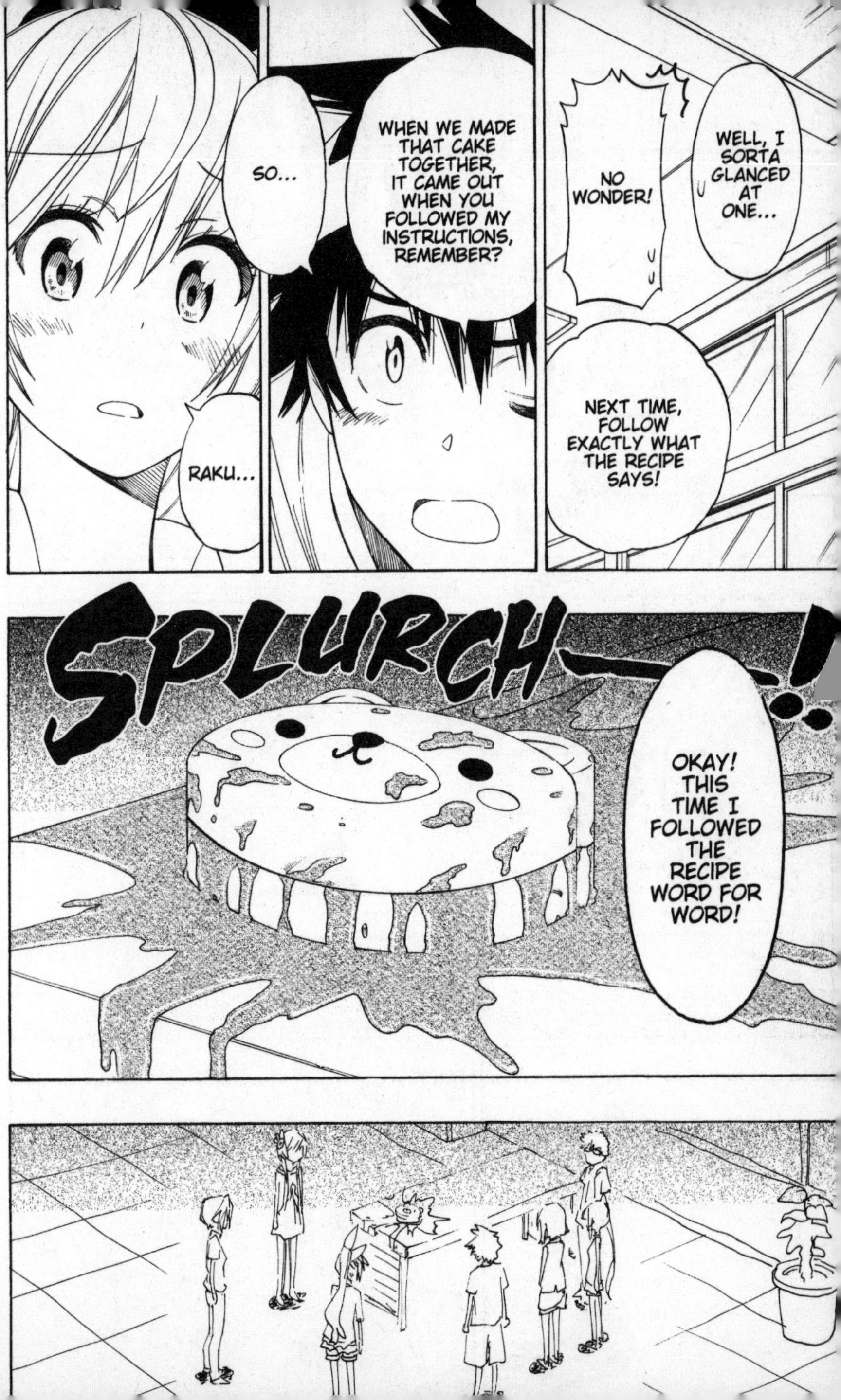
WELL, I SORTA GLANCED AT ONE...
NO WONDER!
NEXT TIME, FOLLOW EXACTLY WHAT THE RECIPE SAYS!
WHEN WE MADE THAT CAKE TOGETHER, IT CAME OUT WHEN YOU FOLLOWED MY INSTRUCTIONS, REMEMBER?
SO...
RAKU...
SPLURCH—!!
OKAY! THIS TIME I FOLLOWED THE RECIPE WORD FOR WORD!

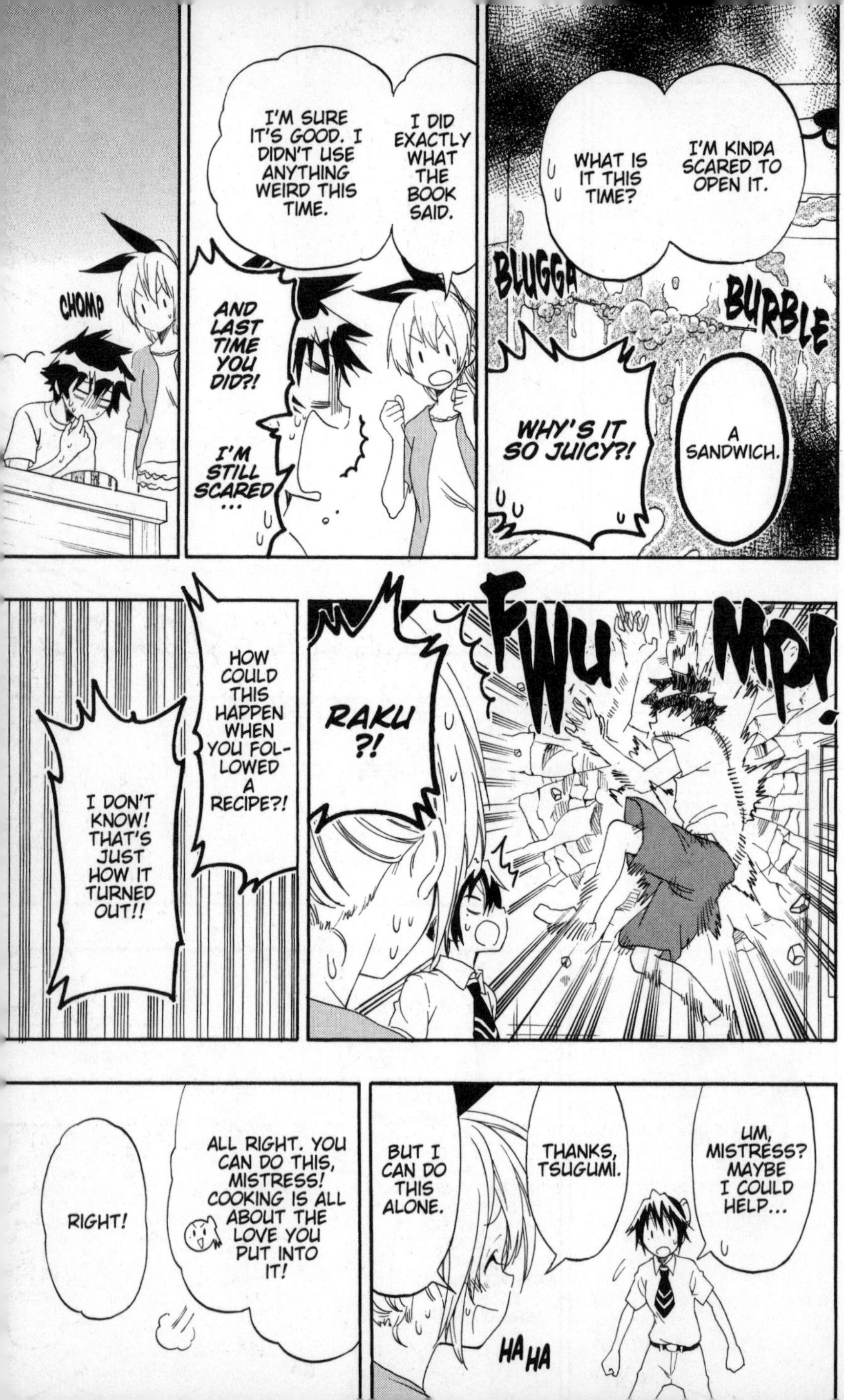
I'M KINDA SCARED TO OPEN IT.
WHAT IS IT THIS TIME?
BLUGGA
BURBLE
A SANDWICH.
WHY'S IT SO JUICY?!
I DID EXACTLY WHAT THE BOOK SAID.
I'M SURE IT'S GOOD. I DIDN'T USE ANYTHING WEIRD THIS TIME.
AND LAST TIME YOU DID?!
I'M STILL SCARED...
CHOMP
FWUMP!
RAKU?!
HOW COULD THIS HAPPEN WHEN YOU FOL-LOWED A RECIPE?!
I DON'T KNOW! THAT'S JUST HOW IT TURNED OUT!!
UM, MISTRESS? MAYBE I COULD HELP...
THANKS, TSUGUMI.
BUT I CAN DO THIS ALONE.
HA HA
ALL RIGHT. YOU CAN DO THIS, MISTRESS! COOKING IS ALL ABOUT THE LOVE YOU PUT INTO IT!
RIGHT!

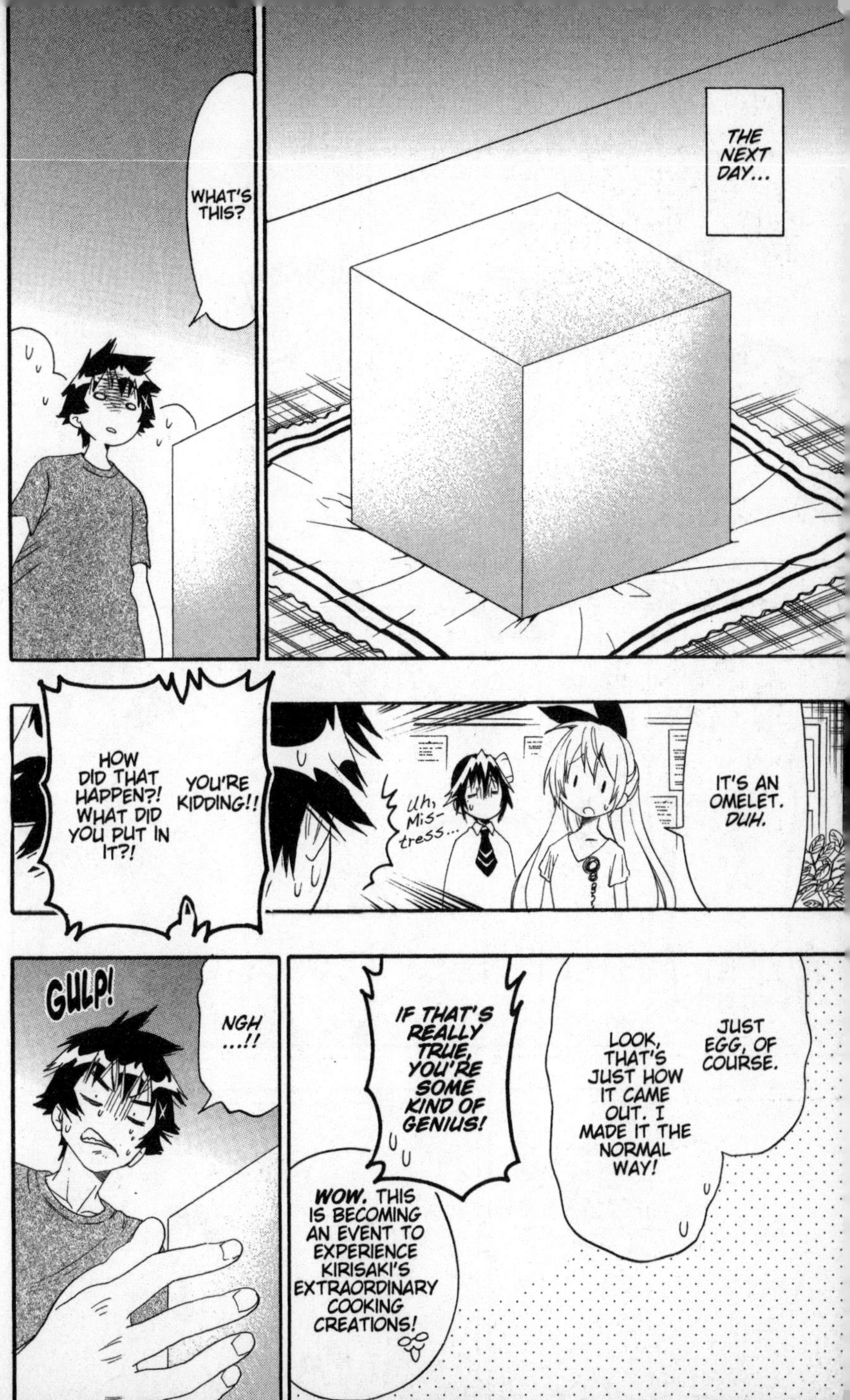
THE NEXT DAY...
WHAT'S THIS?
IT'S AN OMELET. DUH.
Uh, Mistress...
YOU'RE KIDDING!!
HOW DID THAT HAPPEN?! WHAT DID YOU PUT IN IT?!
JUST EGG, OF COURSE.
LOOK, THAT'S JUST HOW IT CAME OUT. I MADE IT THE NORMAL WAY!
IF THAT'S REALLY TRUE, YOU'RE SOME KIND OF GENIUS!
WOW. THIS IS BECOMING AN EVENT TO EXPERIENCE KIRISAKI'S EXTRAORDINARY COOKING CREATIONS!
NGH ...!!
GULP!

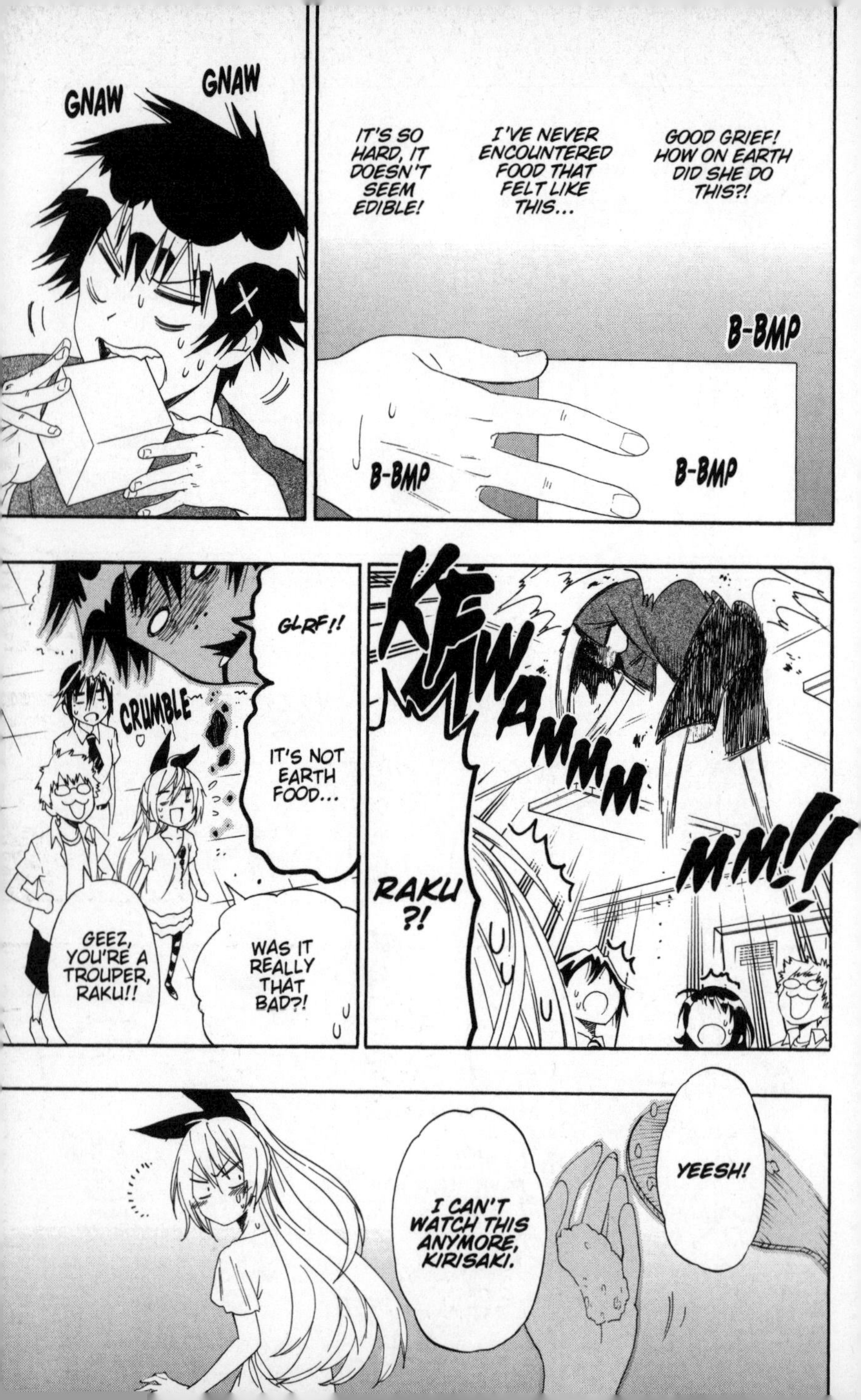
GOOD GRIEF! HOW ON EARTH DID SHE DO THIS?!
I'VE NEVER ENCOUNTERED FOOD THAT FELT LIKE THIS...
IT'S SO HARD, IT DOESN'T SEEM EDIBLE!
B-BMP
B-BMP
B-BMP
GNAW
GNAW
KFWAMMMMMM!!
RAKU?!
GLRF!!
CRUMBLE
IT'S NOT EARTH FOOD...
WAS IT REALLY THAT BAD?!
GEEZ, YOU'RE A TROUPER, RAKU!!
YEESH!
I CAN'T WATCH THIS ANYMORE, KIRISAKI.

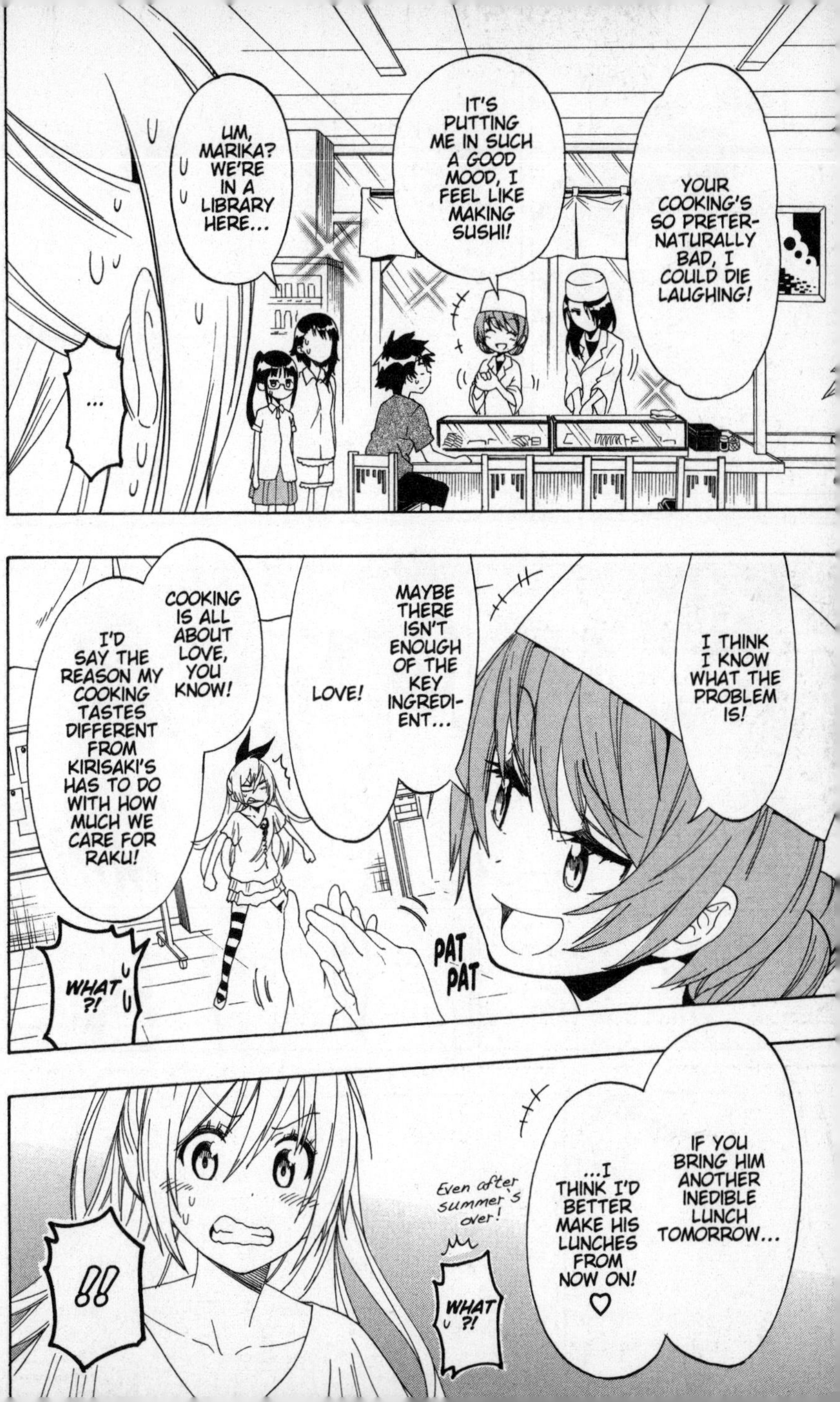
YOUR COOKING'S SO PRETER-NATURALLY BAD, I COULD DIE LAUGHING!
IT'S PUTTING ME IN SUCH A GOOD MOOD, I FEEL LIKE MAKING SUSHI!
UM, MARIKA? WE'RE IN A LIBRARY HERE...
...
I THINK I KNOW WHAT THE PROBLEM IS!
MAYBE THERE ISN'T ENOUGH OF THE KEY INGREDI-ENT...
LOVE!
COOKING IS ALL ABOUT LOVE, YOU KNOW!
I'D SAY THE REASON MY COOKING TASTES DIFFERENT FROM KIRISAKI'S HAS TO DO WITH HOW MUCH WE CARE FOR RAKU!
PAT PAT
WHAT?!
IF YOU BRING HIM ANOTHER INEDIBLE LUNCH TOMORROW...
...I THINK I'D BETTER MAKE HIS LUNCHES FROM NOW ON! ♡
Even after summer's over!
WHAT?!
!!

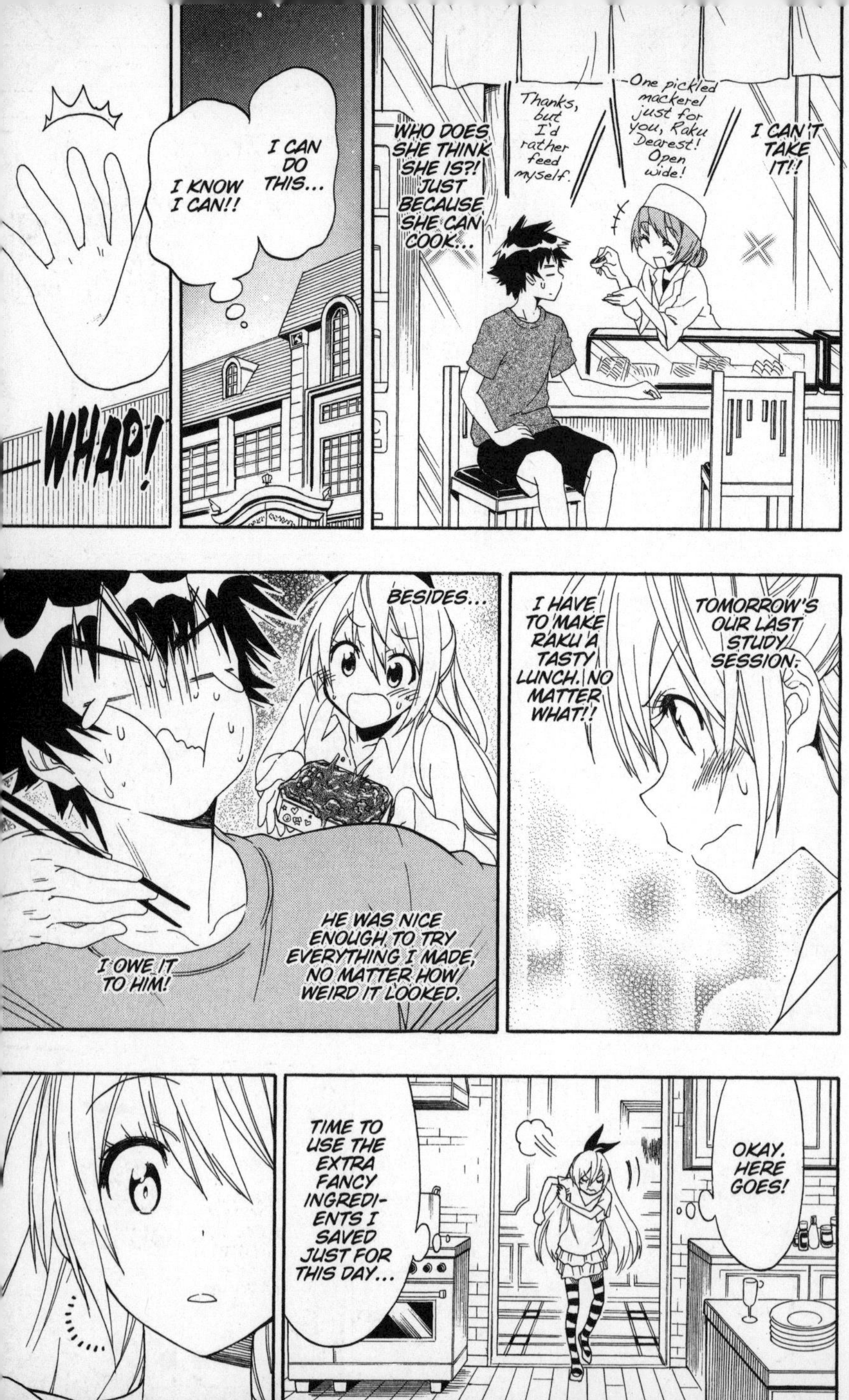
I CAN'T TAKE IT!!
One pickled mackerel just for you, Raku Dearest! Open wide!
Thanks, but I'd rather feed myself.
WHO DOES SHE THINK SHE IS?! JUST BECAUSE SHE CAN COOK...
I CAN DO THIS...
I KNOW I CAN!!
WHAP!
TOMORROW'S OUR LAST STUDY SESSION.
I HAVE TO MAKE RAKU A TASTY LUNCH. NO MATTER WHAT!!
BESIDES...
HE WAS NICE ENOUGH TO TRY EVERYTHING I MADE, NO MATTER HOW WEIRD IT LOOKED.
I OWE IT TO HIM!
OKAY. HERE GOES!
TIME TO USE THE EXTRA FANCY INGREDIENTS I SAVED JUST FOR THIS DAY...

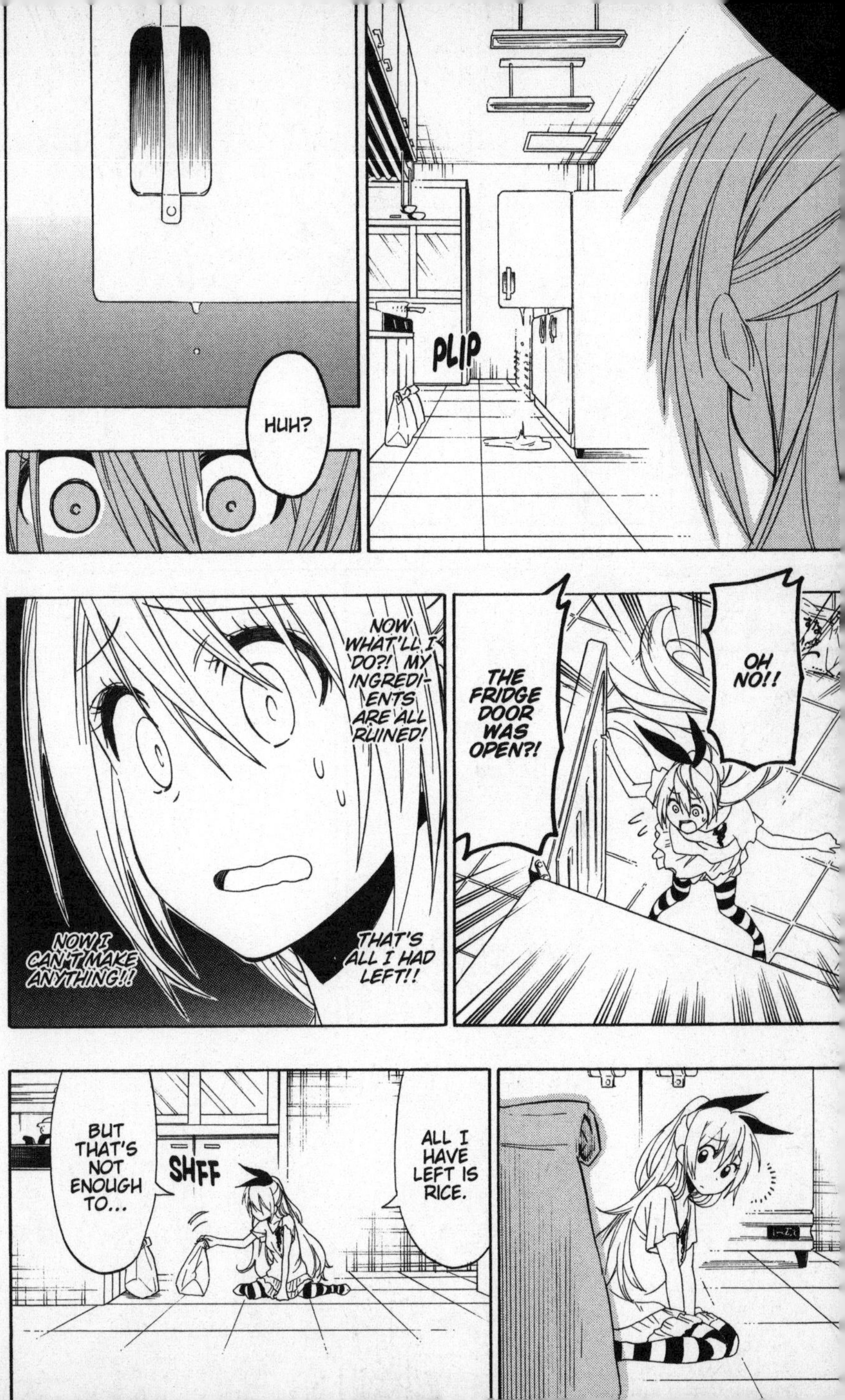
PLIP
HUH?
OH NO!!
THE FRIDGE DOOR WAS OPEN?!
NOW WHAT'LL I DO?! MY INGREDI-ENTS ARE ALL RUINED!
THAT'S ALL I HAD LEFT!!
NOW I CAN'T MAKE ANYTHING!!
ALL I HAVE LEFT IS RICE.
SHFF
BUT THAT'S NOT ENOUGH TO...

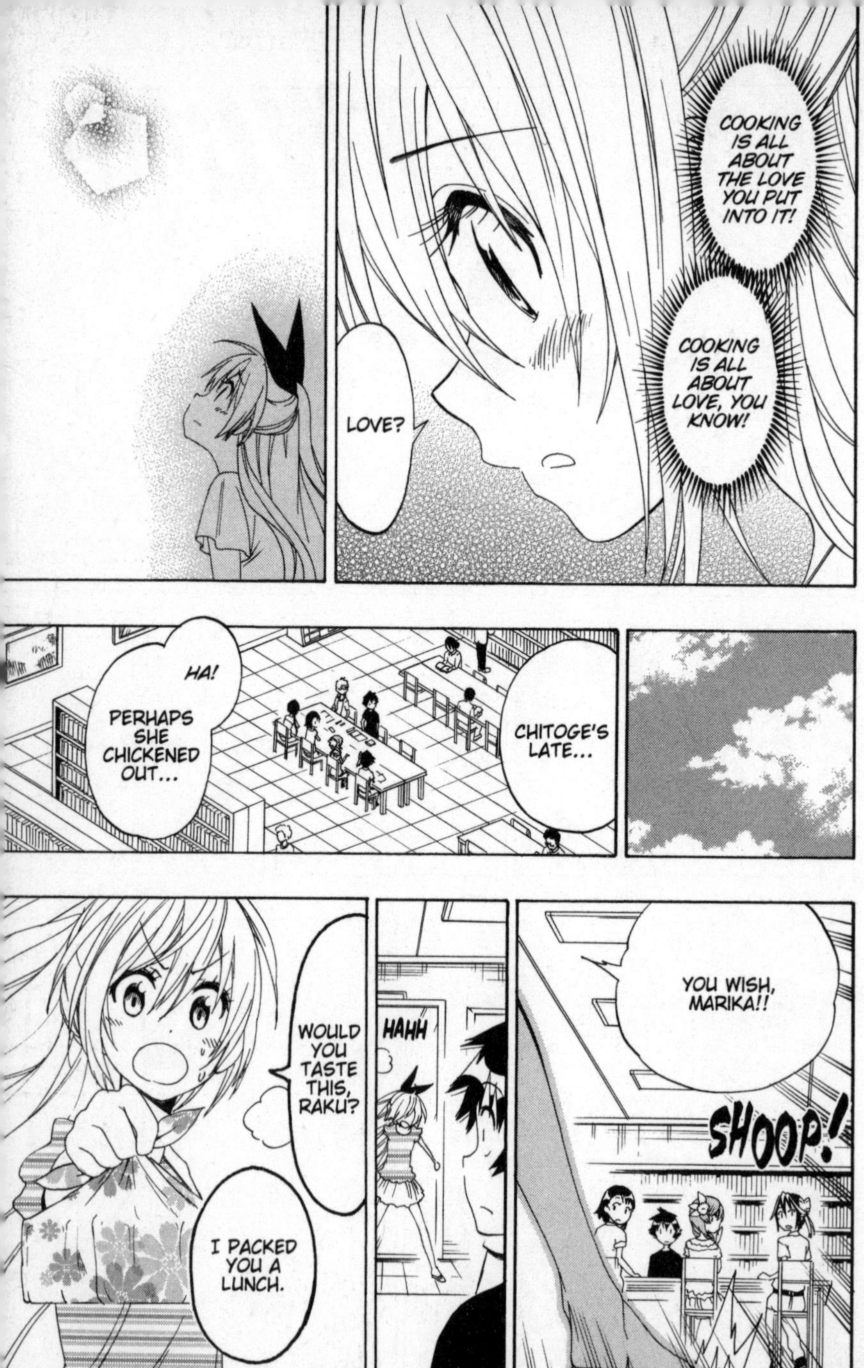
COOKING IS ALL ABOUT THE LOVE YOU PUT INTO IT!
COOKING IS ALL ABOUT LOVE, YOU KNOW!
LOVE?
CHITOGE'S LATE...
HA! PERHAPS SHE CHICKENED OUT...
YOU WISH, MARIKA!!
SHOOP!
HAHH
WOULD YOU TASTE THIS, RAKU?
I PACKED YOU A LUNCH.

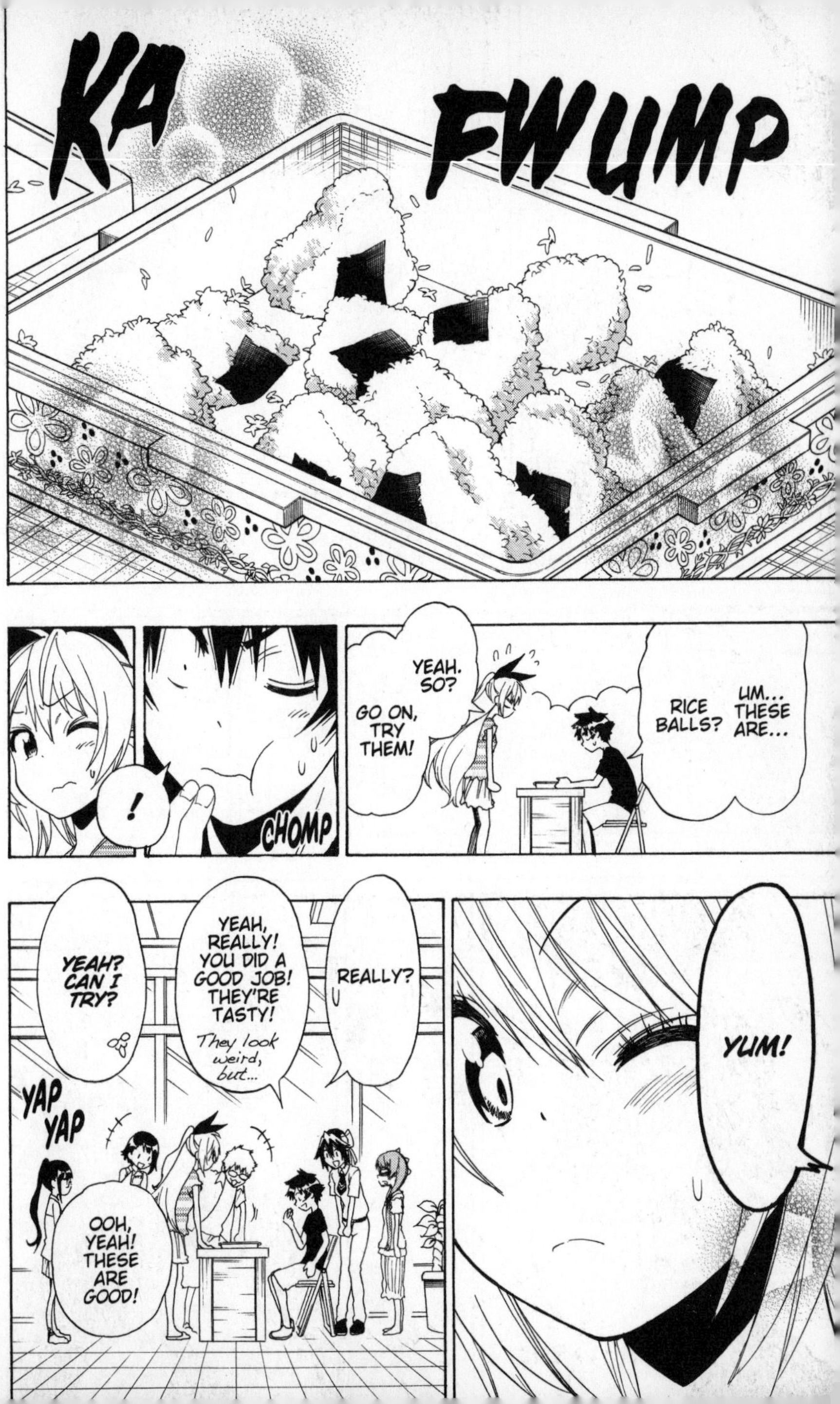
KA FWUMP
UM... THESE ARE...
RICE BALLS?
YEAH. SO?
GO ON, TRY THEM!
CHOMP
!
YUM!
REALLY?
YEAH, REALLY! YOU DID A GOOD JOB! THEY'RE TASTY!
They look weird, but...
YEAH? CAN I TRY?
YAP YAP
OOH, YEAH! THESE ARE GOOD!

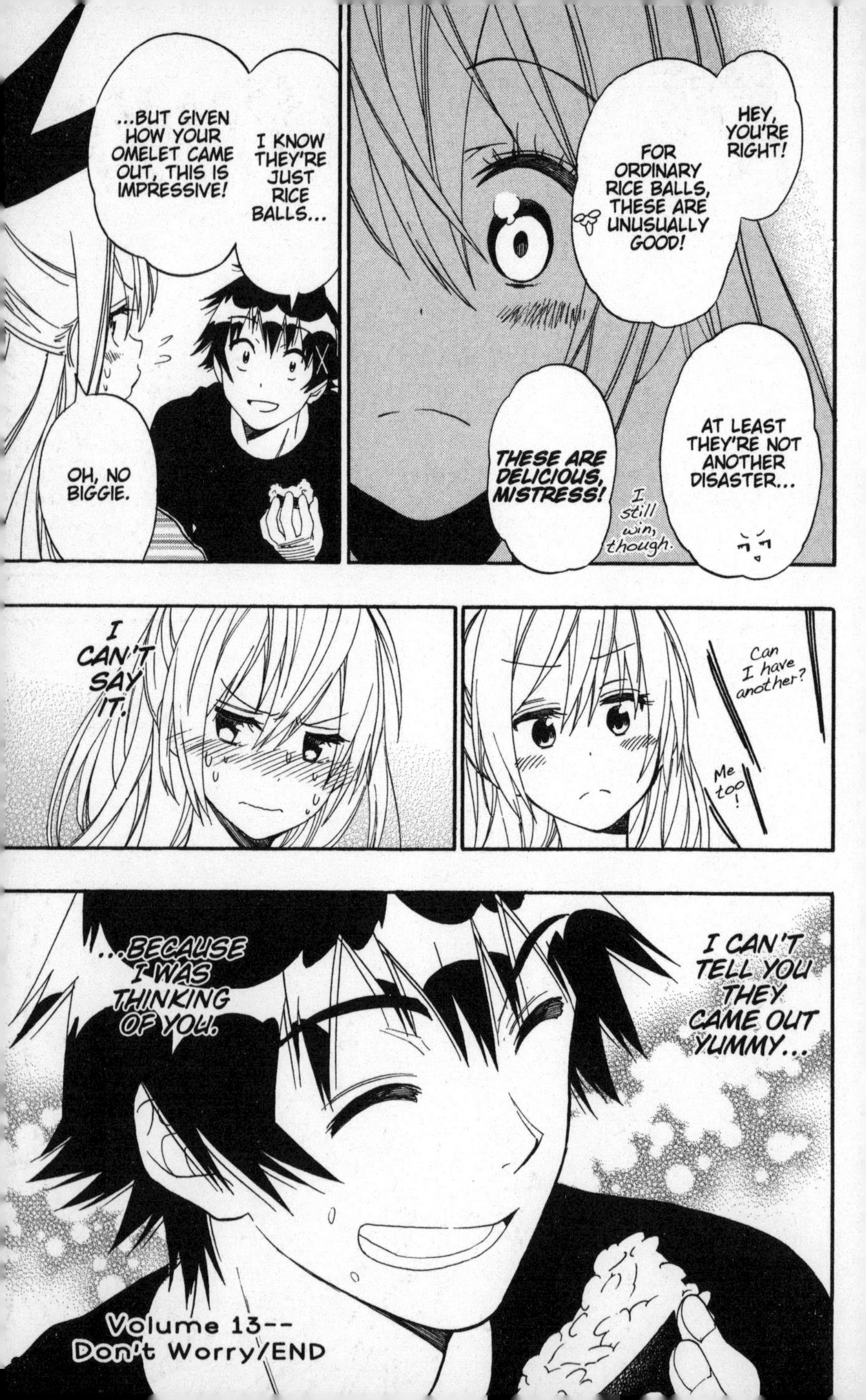
HEY, YOU'RE RIGHT!
FOR ORDINARY RICE BALLS, THESE ARE UNUSUALLY GOOD!
AT LEAST THEY'RE NOT ANOTHER DISASTER...
THESE ARE DELICIOUS, MISTRESS!
I still win, though.
I KNOW THEY'RE JUST RICE BALLS...
...BUT GIVEN HOW YOUR OMELET CAME OUT, THIS IS IMPRESSIVE!
OH, NO BIGGIE.
Can I have another?
Me too!
I CAN'T SAY IT.
I CAN'T TELL YOU THEY CAME OUT YUMMY...
...BECAUSE I WAS THINKING OF YOU.
Volume 13-- Don't Worry/END

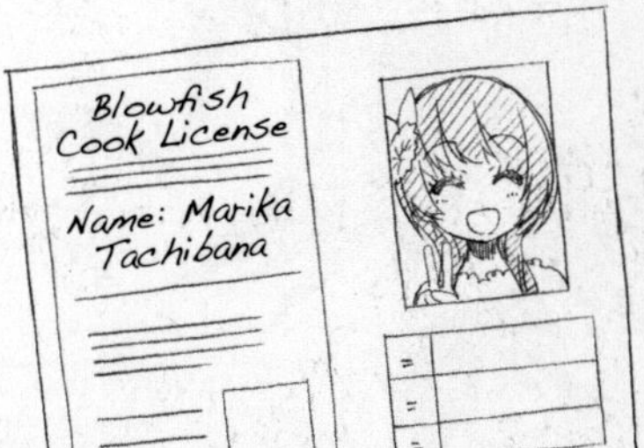
Blowfish Cook License
Name: Marika Tachibana

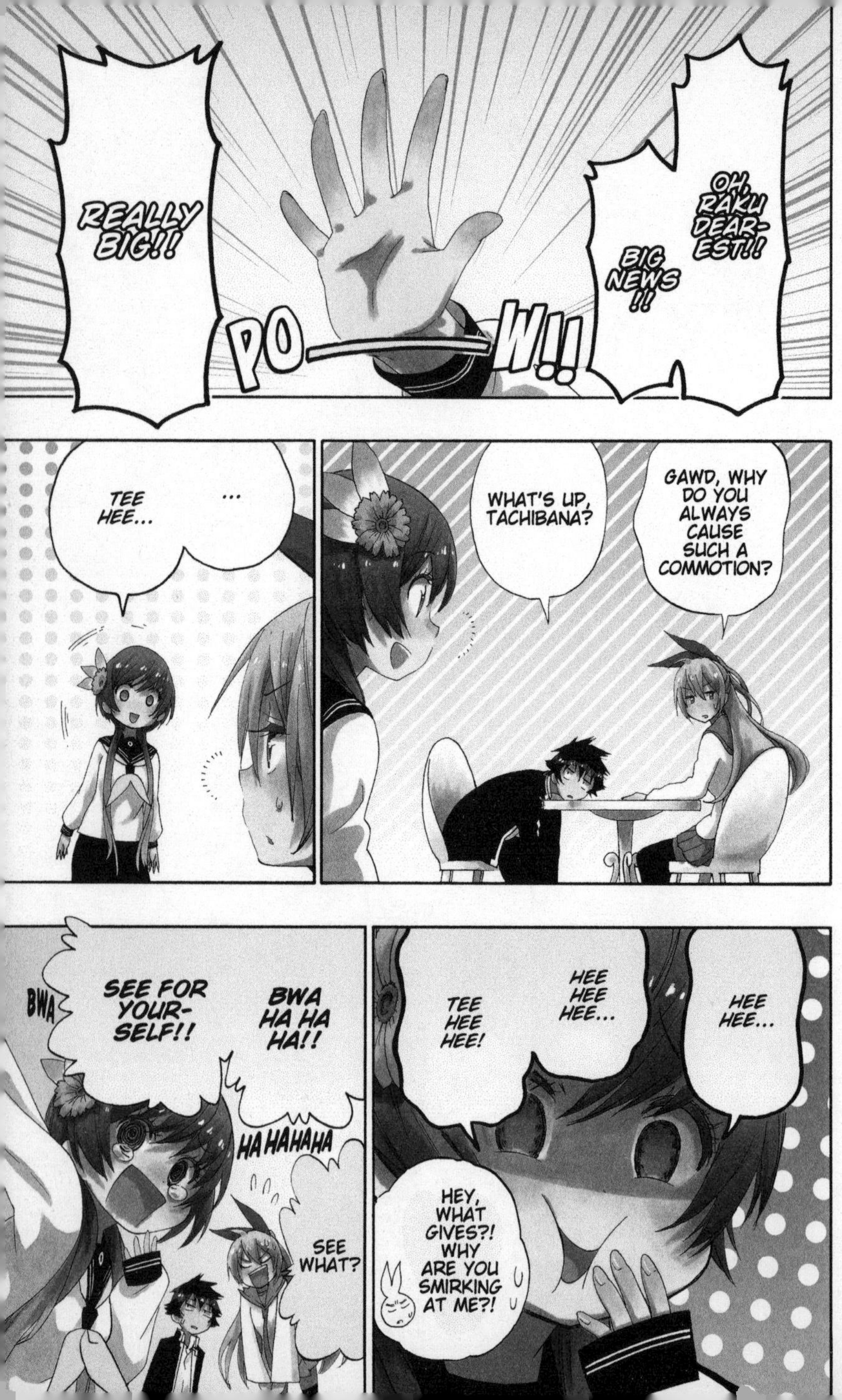
OH, RAKU DEAREST!!
BIG NEWS!!
PO—W!!
REALLY BIG!!
GAWD, WHY DO YOU ALWAYS CAUSE SUCH A COMMOTION?
WHAT'S UP, TACHIBANA?
...
TEE HEE...
HEE HEE...
HEE HEE HEE...
TEE HEE HEE!
HEY, WHAT GIVES?! WHY ARE YOU SMIRKING AT ME?!
BWA HA HA HA!!
SEE FOR YOURSELF!!
BWA
HA HAHAHA
SEE WHAT?

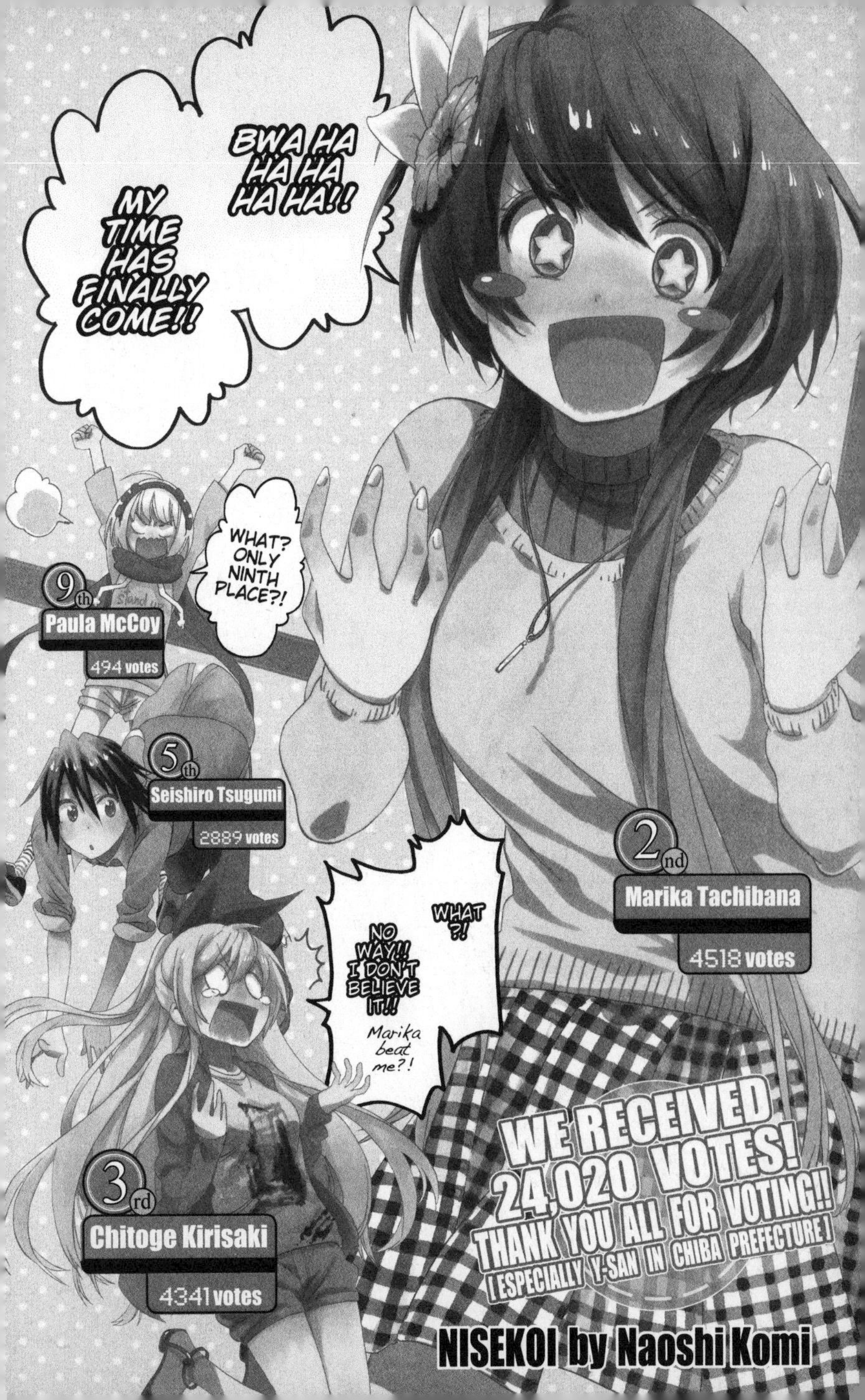
BWA HA HA HA HA HA!!
MY TIME HAS FINALLY COME!!
2nd
Marika Tachibana
4518 votes
WHAT? ONLY NINTH PLACE?!
9th
Paula McCoy
494 votes
5th
Seishiro Tsugumi
2889 votes
WHAT?!
NO WAY!! I DON'T BELIEVE IT!!
Marika beat me?!
3rd
Chitoge Kirisaki
4341 votes
WE RECEIVED 24,020 VOTES!
THANK YOU ALL FOR VOTING!!
[ESPECIALLY Y-SAN IN CHIBA PREFECTURE]
NISEKOI by Naoshi Komi

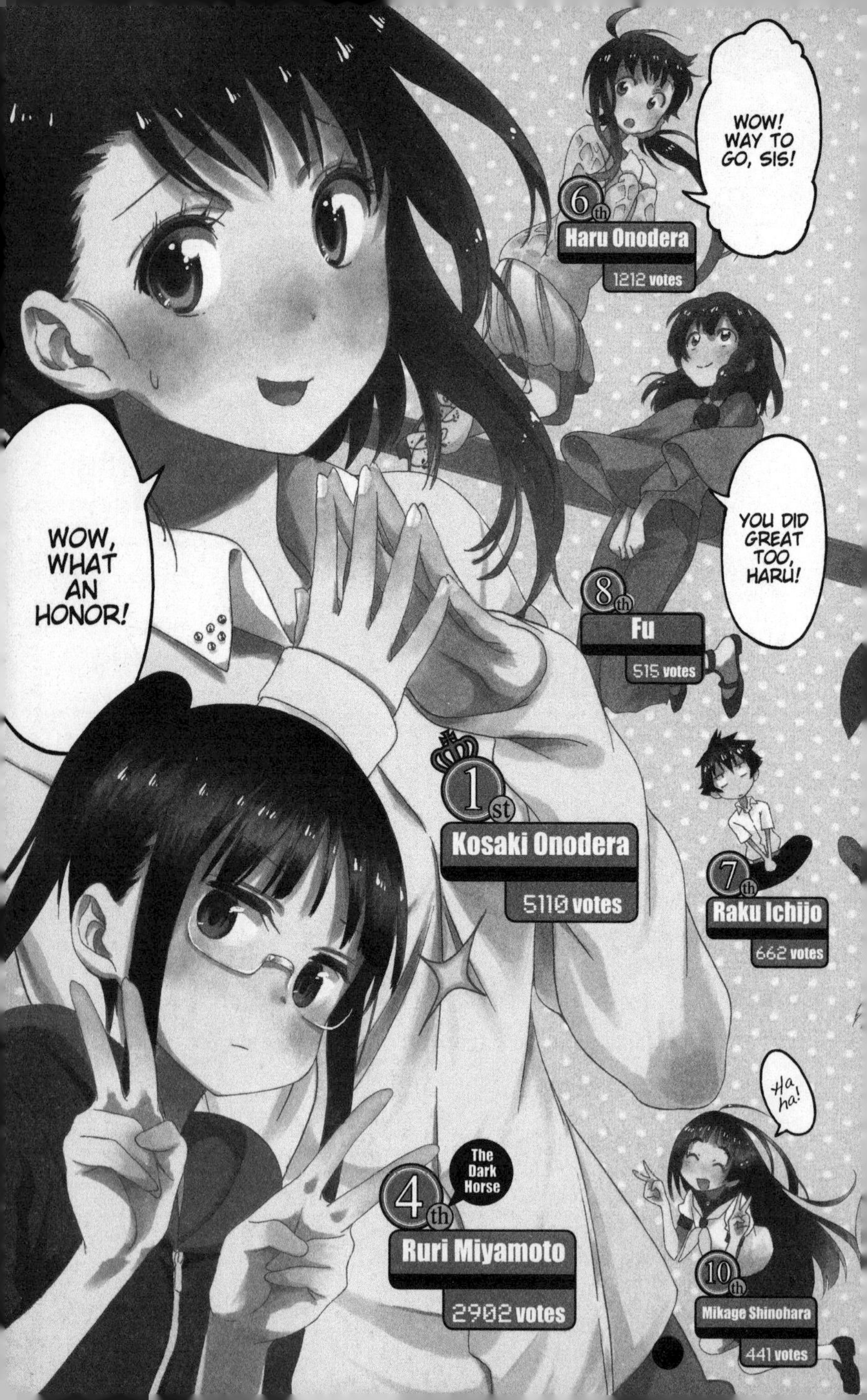
WOW! WAY TO GO, SIS!
6th
Haru Onodera
1212 votes
YOU DID GREAT TOO, HARU!
8th
Fu
515 votes
WOW, WHAT AN HONOR!
1st
Kosaki Onodera
5110 votes
7th
Raku Ichijo
662 votes
Ha ha!
10th
Mikage Shinohara
441 votes
The Dark Horse
4th
Ruri Miyamoto
2902 votes

2nd Poll Character Popularity Vote Results and Reactions!!

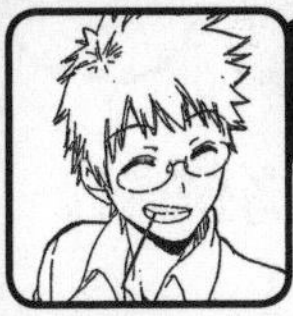

11th place
Shu Maiko

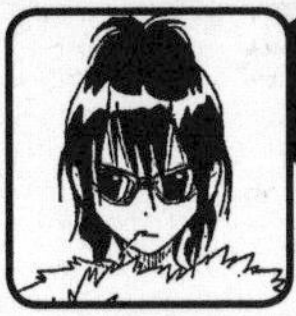

12th place
Hana Kirisaki

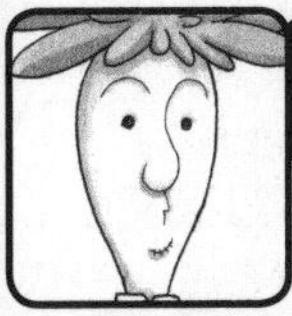

13th place
Naoshi Komi

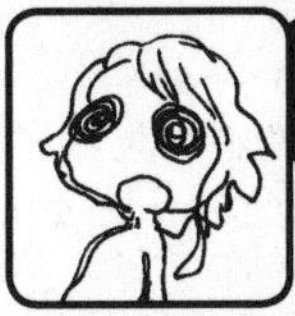

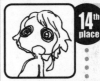

14th place
Scribble Onodera

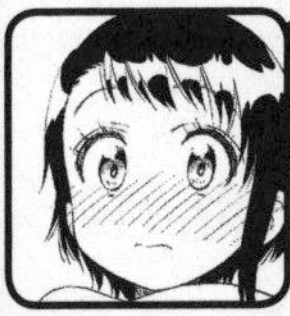

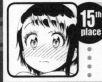

15th place
Junior High Onodera

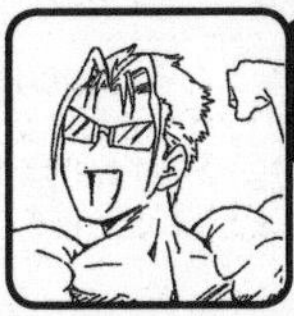

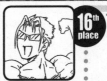

16th place
Claude

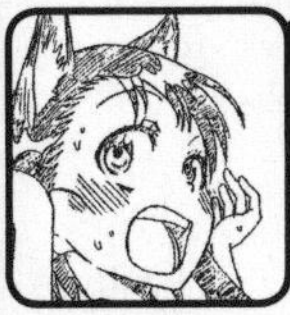

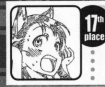

17th place
Kittydera

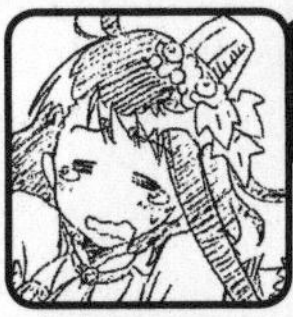

18th place
Magical Confectioner Kosaki

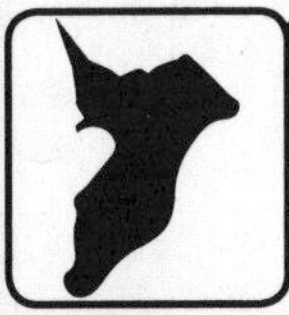

19th place
Y of Chiba

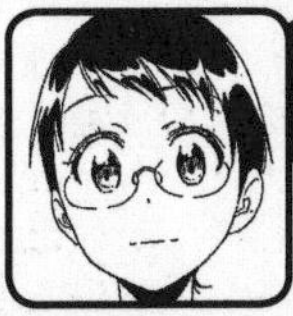

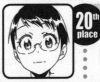

20th place
Ms. Kyoko

21st place
Elraine Figarette (Double Arts)

22nd place
Migisuke

23rd place
Kana Asumi (voice actress for Marika)

24th place
Mimiko Kiki

25th place
MikoDera

26th place
Rurin (from bonus comic in vols. 8 & 9)

26th place
AngelDera

26th place
SukuMizuDera

29th place	29th place	31st place	31st place
Onodera's mother	Cyclops Gengar Suzaku	Bridedera	Honda
33rd place	**33rd place**	**33rd place**	**33rd place**
Raku Ichijo (in Junior High)	Yamada	Ruri Miyamoto's glasses	Juliedera

37th place

The Suzumiya Strawbery Daifuku, Marika in Miko Robes, Junior High Haru, Toru Suzuya, Tsugumi's Special Nikujaga (Chapter 54), Bloody Mary, the Gorilla Doll, Gorizawa, KashiDera, Raku Ichijo (as a child)

Other Curveballs: Takao Gashuin, Ruri's Glasses in the bottom right of the cover page of Chapter 58, the Whiskey Bonbons, Onodera's failed chocolate creations, Raku's Candied Sweet Potatoes

In the first *Nisekoi* Popularity Poll, Onodera came in first, and Chitoge came in second. This time, Onodera's overwhelming popularity was really unmatchable. It's notable that for some reason, readers voted for a lot of very specific versions of Onodera. Between 10th and 20th place, half of the votes seem like they should also count for Onodera, making the actual tally hard to establish. We expected Chitoge to come in second again, but a surprise phenomenon skewed the results...Y of Chiba! Marika only managed to reach 4th place last time, despite amassing 1,500 votes, but she received an all-star level assist. I bet Y never anticipated actually making the rankings! F of Chiba, who voted for Onodera, and K of Kumamoto, who voted for Ruri, also demonstrated love on par with Y of Chiba. All three of them sent in handwritten votes. However, to avoid further escalation that could lead to carpal tunnel syndrome, we decided not to publish the number of votes. We simply wish to express our deep appreciation and respect for the passion of the three postcard musketeers, F, K, and Y, as well as for all of the wonderful *Nisekoi* fans who sent even one postcard. Artist Naoshi Komi commented, "I'm very grateful to everyone who voted. It's wonderful to have people support the characters I've created. Please continue to support *Nisekoi*!"

Bonus Comic!! Magical Confectioner Kosaki!!

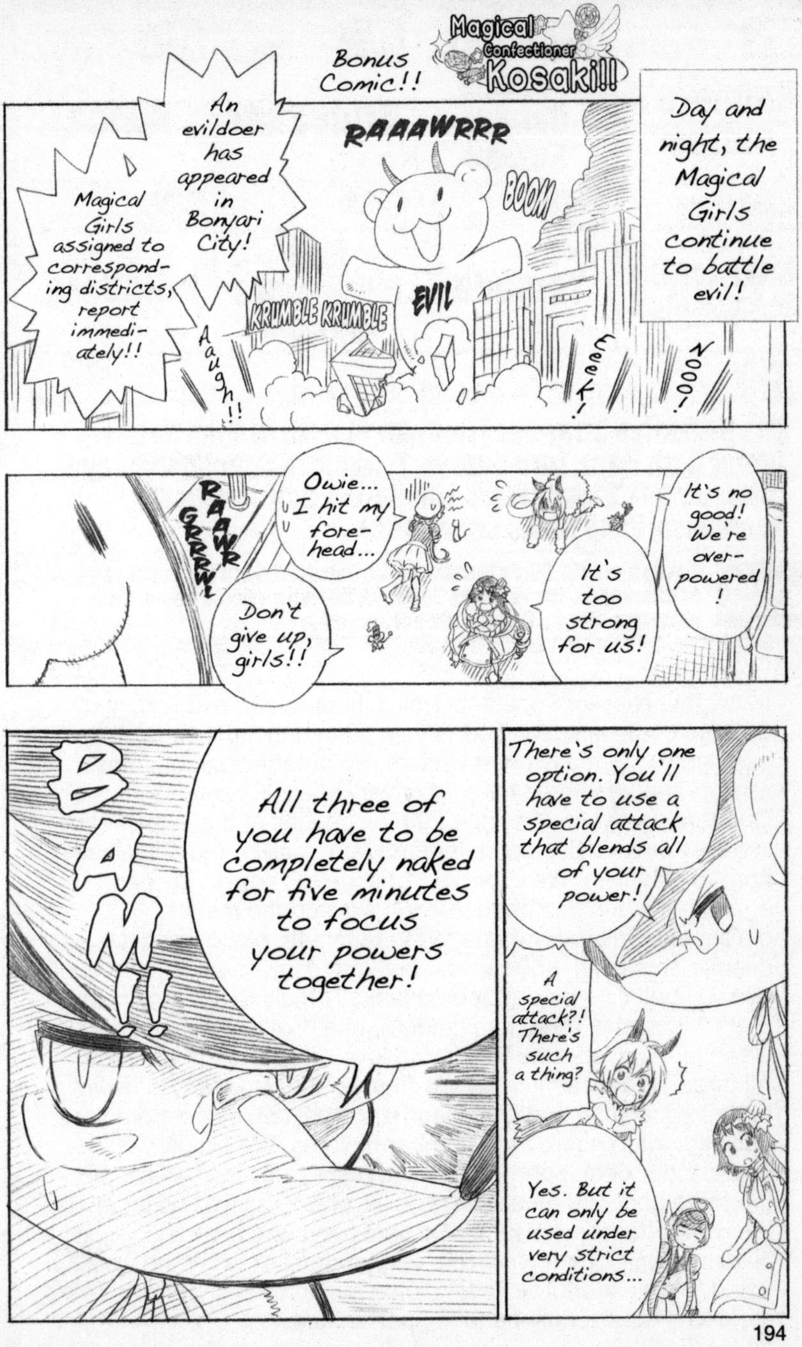

Day and night, the Magical Girls continue to battle evil!
RAAAWRRR
An evildoer has appeared in Bonyari City!
BOOM
Magical Girls assigned to corresponding districts, report immediately!!
EVIL
KRUMBLE KRUMBLE
Nooo!
Eeeek!
Aaugh!!
It's no good! We're overpowered!
It's too strong for us!
Owie... I hit my forehead...
RAAAWR GRRRWL
Don't give up, girls!!
There's only one option. You'll have to use a special attack that blends all of your power!
A special attack?! There's such a thing?
Yes. But it can only be used under very strict conditions...
BAM!!
All three of you have to be completely naked for five minutes to focus your powers together!

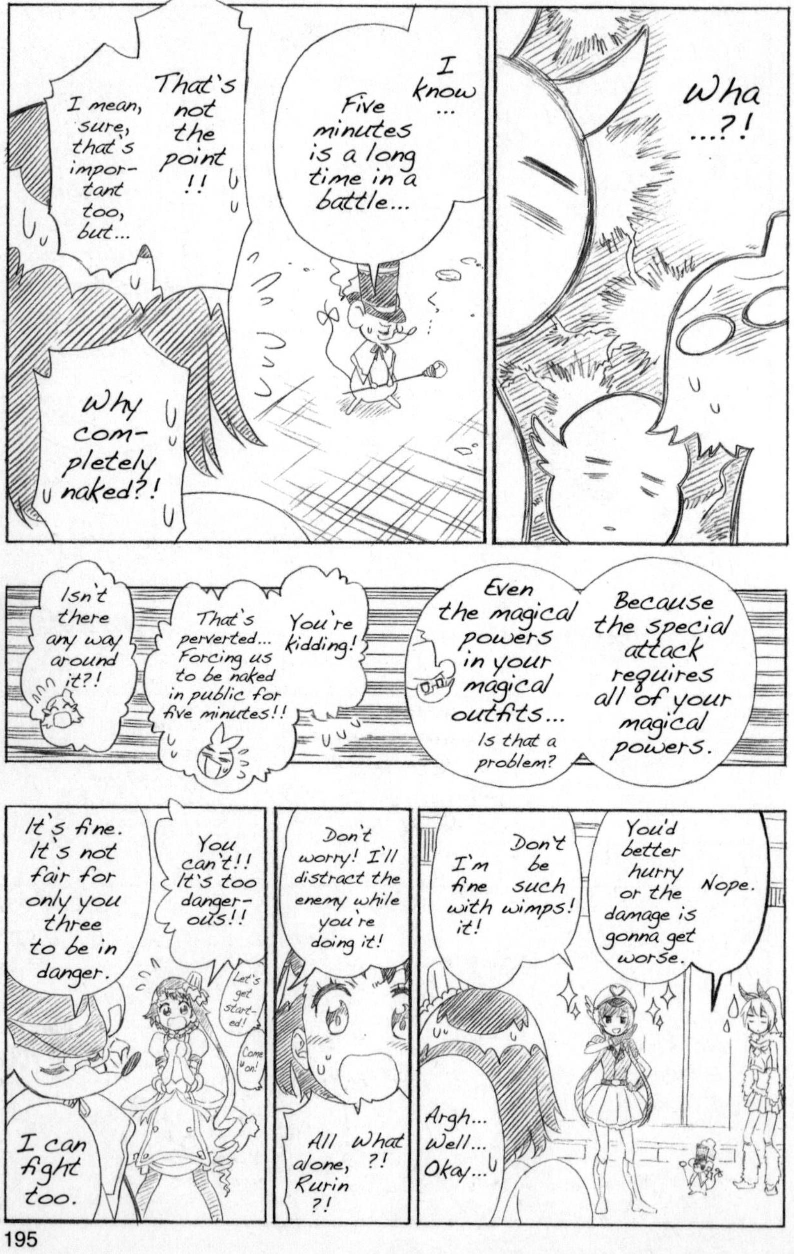
Wha ...?!
I know ...
Five minutes is a long time in a battle...
That's not the point!!
I mean, sure, that's important too, but...
Why completely naked?!
Because the special attack requires all of your magical powers.
Even the magical powers in your magical outfits...
Is that a problem?
You're kidding!
That's perverted... Forcing us to be naked in public for five minutes!!
Isn't there any way around it?!
Nope.
You'd better hurry or the damage is gonna get worse.
Don't be such wimps!
I'm fine with it!
Argh... Well... Okay...
Don't worry! I'll distract the enemy while you're doing it!
What?!
All alone, Rurin?!
You can't!! It's too danger-ous!!
Let's get start-ed!
Come on!
It's fine. It's not fair for only you three to be in danger.
I can fight too.

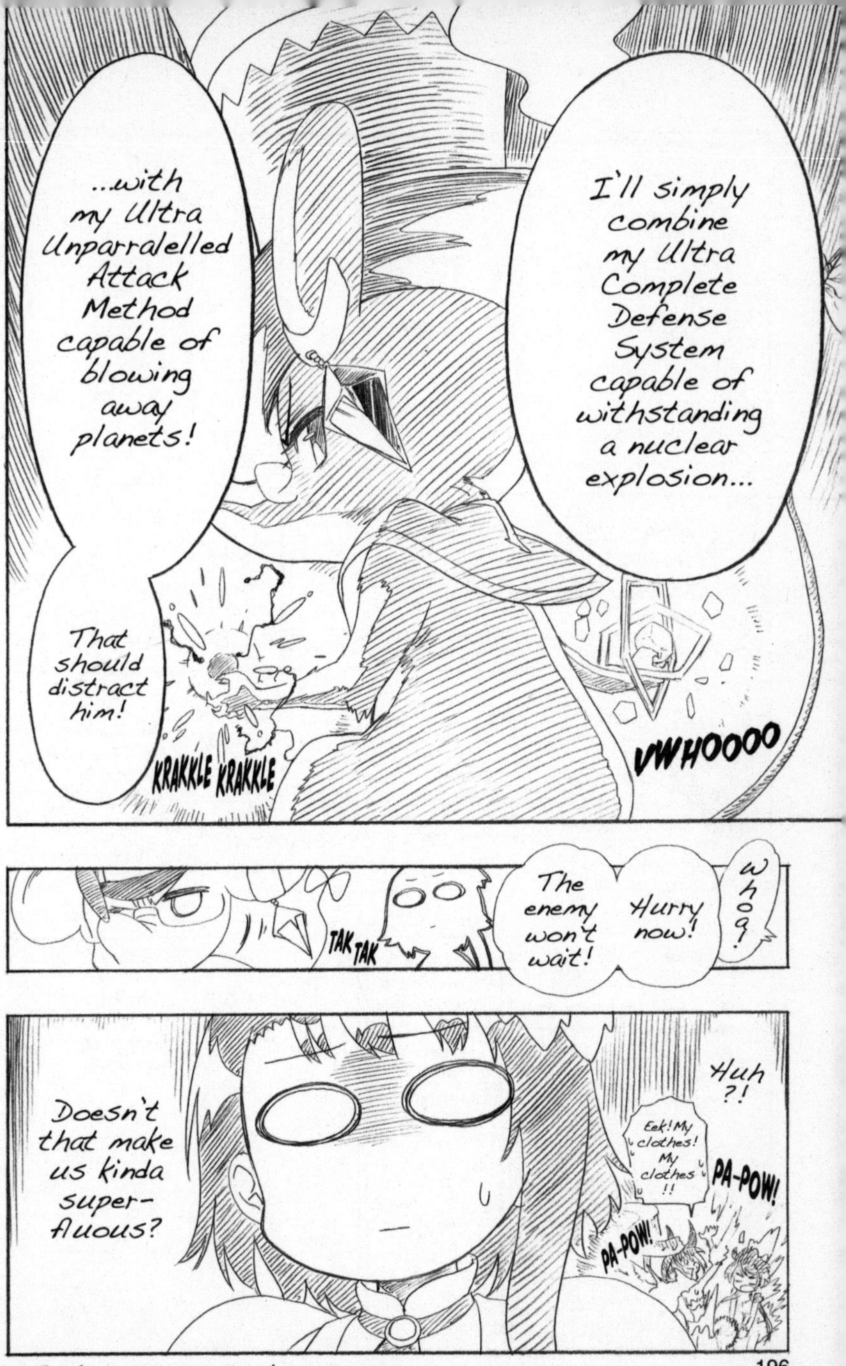
I'll simply combine my Ultra Complete Defense System capable of withstanding a nuclear explosion...
...with my Ultra Unparralelled Attack Method capable of blowing away planets!
VWHOOOO
That should distract him!
KRAKKLE KRAKKLE
Whoa!
Hurry now!
The enemy won't wait!
TAK TAK
Huh?!
Eek! My clothes! My clothes!!
PA-POW!
PA-POW!
Doesn't that make us kinda super-fluous?

To be continued? Hard to say...

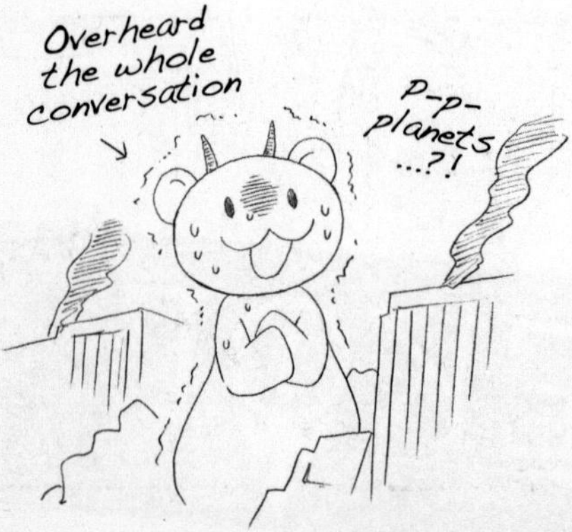
Overheard the whole conversation
P-p-planets ...?!

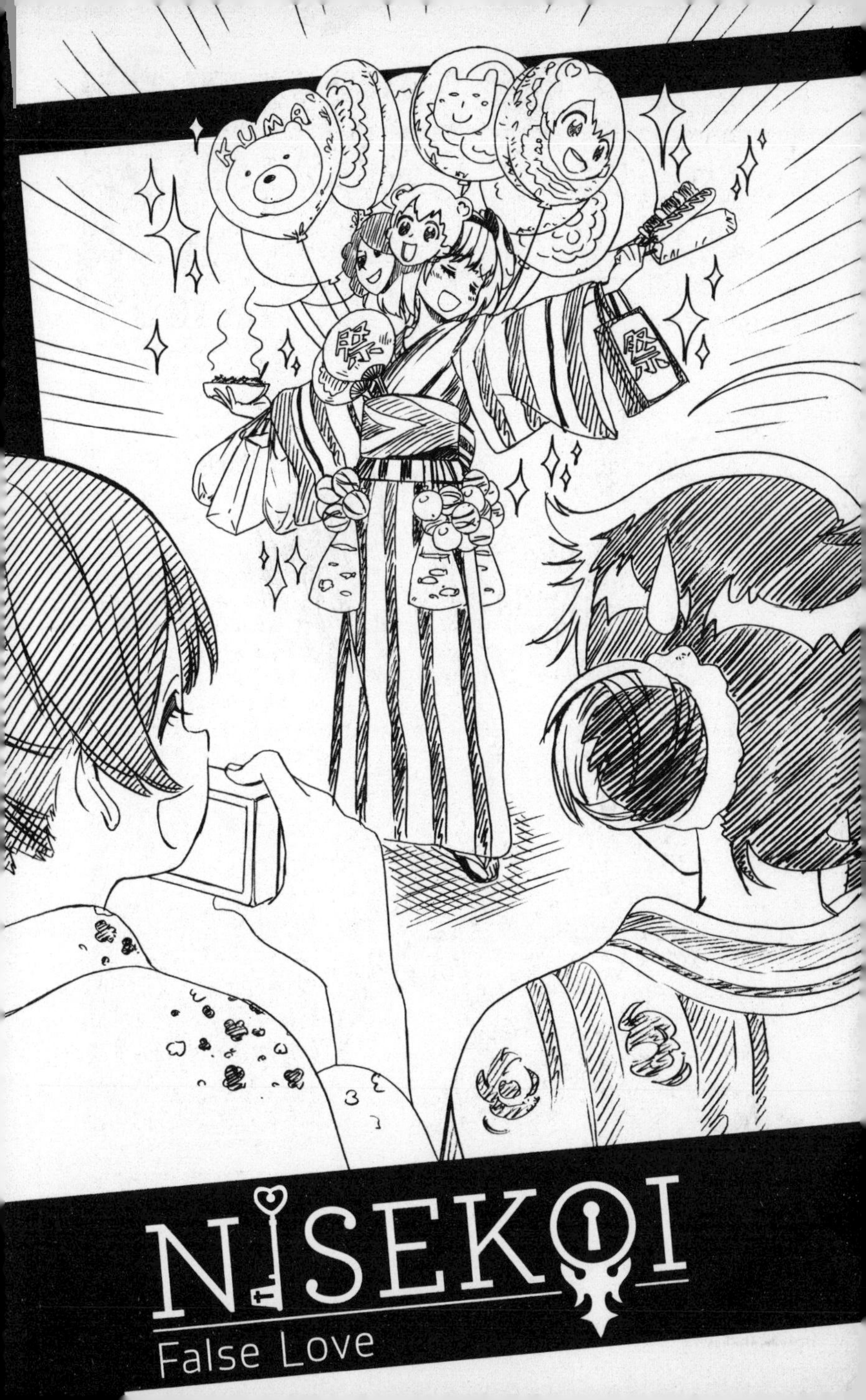
KUMA
祭
祭

NISEKOI
False Love

BAKUMAN。

STORY BY TSUGUMI OHBA
ART BY TAKESHI OBATA

From the creators of *Death Note*

The mystery behind manga making REVEALED!

Average student Moritaka Mashiro enjoys drawing for fun. When his classmate and aspiring writer Akito Takagi discovers his talent, he begs to team up. But what exactly does it take to make it in the manga-publishing world?

Bakuman。 Vol. 1
ISBN: 978-1-4215-3513-5
$9.99 US / $12.99 CAN *

You're Reading the WRONG WAY!

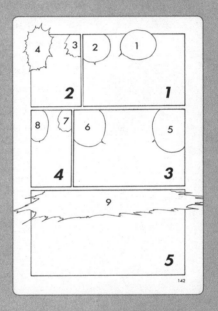

NISEKOI reads from right to left, starting in the upper-right corner. Japanese is read from right to left, meaning that action, sound effects, and word-balloon order are completely reversed from English order.

NISEKOI:
False Love
VOLUME 13
SHONEN JUMP Manga Edition

Story and Art by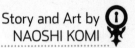
NAOSHI KOMI

Translation ✒ Camellia Nieh
Touch-Up Art & Lettering ✒ Stephen Dutro
Design ✒ Fawn Lau
Shonen Jump Series Editor ✒ John Bae
Graphic Novel Editor ✒ Amy Yu

Printed in the U.S.A.

Published by VIZ Media, LLC
P.O. Box 77010
San Francisco, CA 94107

10 9 8 7 6 5 4 3 2 1
First printing, January 2016

www.shonenjump.com   www.viz.com

...voted to my Japanese-style cell

...e transition to a smartphone.

...obstinate and continue championing

Japanese phones...but the smartphone is really nice.

Naoshi Komi

NAOSHI KOMI was born in Kochi Prefecture, Japan, on March 28, 1986. His first serialized work in *Weekly Shonen Jump* was the series *Double Arts*. His current series, *Nisekoi*, is serialized in *Weekly Shonen Jump*.

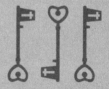